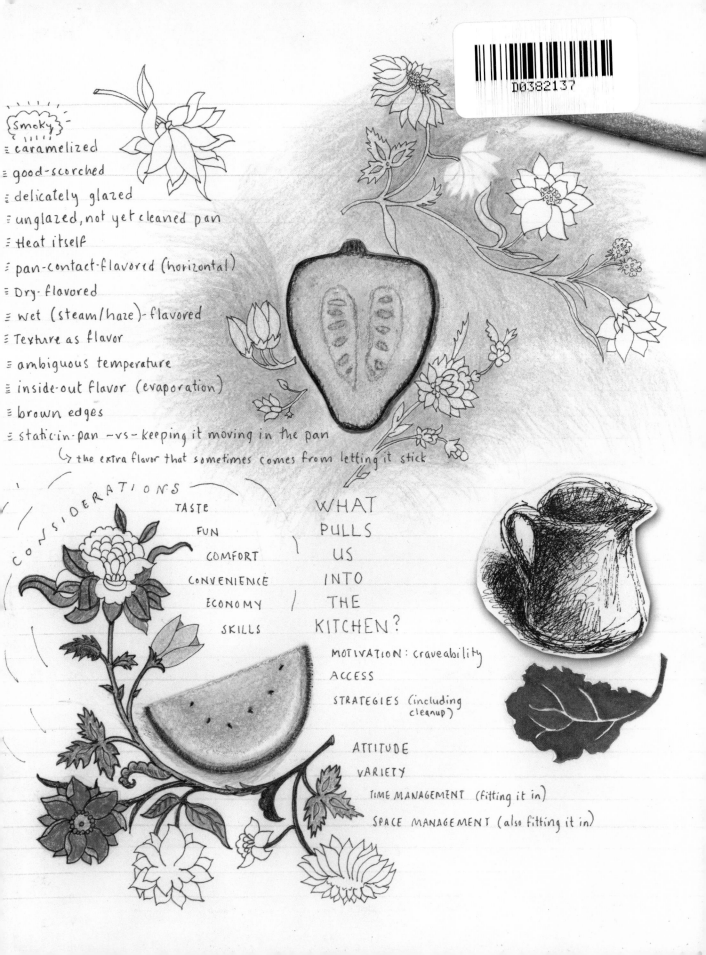

= smoky
≡ caramelized
≡ good-scorched
≡ delicately glazed
≡ unglazed, not yet cleaned pan
≡ Heat itself
≡ pan-contact-flavored (horizontal)
≡ Dry-flavored
≡ wet (steam/haze)-flavored
≡ Texture as flavor
≡ ambiguous temperature
≡ inside-out flavor (evaporation)
≡ brown edges
≡ static-in-pan —vs— keeping it moving in the pan
    ↳ the extra flavor that sometimes comes from letting it stick

CONSIDERATIONS

TASTE
FUN
COMFORT
CONVENIENCE
ECONOMY
SKILLS

WHAT
PULLS
US
INTO
THE
KITCHEN?

MOTIVATION: craveability
ACCESS
STRATEGIES (including cleanup)

ATTITUDE
VARIETY
TIME MANAGEMENT (fitting it in)
SPACE MANAGEMENT (also fitting it in)

Bento.

Mandala
Plates

A Platter of Roasted Vegetables

Layered Plates

MASHED PARSNIPS
GRILLED RADICCHIO WEDGES
SEARED SWEET PEPPERS w GREEN RICE
GREEN APPLE SALADITA

COZY RED LENTIL MASH (caramelized onion)
ROASTED RED PEPPERS and/or TOMATOES
PITA TOASTS
COUSCOUS - QUINOA PILAF /ORANGE SECTIONS
POMEGRANATE SEEDS
GARLICKY CHARD

MASHED CAULIFLOWER
OLIVE OIL-BREAD CRUMB FRIED EGGS
ARTISAN TOASTS
GRATED CARROT SALAD (parsley + lemon)

The Heart of the Plate

The HEART of the PLATE

VEGETARIAN RECIPES FOR A NEW GENERATION

RECIPES, PHOTOGRAPHS, AND ILLUSTRATIONS BY

Mollie Katzen

A RUX MARTIN BOOK

HOUGHTON MIFFLIN HARCOURT

BOSTON   NEW YORK   2013

For information about permission to reproduce selections from this book, write to Permissions, Houghton Mifflin Harcourt Publishing Company, 215 Park Avenue South, New York, New York 10003.

www.hmhbooks.com

Library of Congress Cataloging-in-Publication Data
Katzen, Mollie, date.
The heart of the plate : vegetarian recipes for a new generation / Mollie Katzen ; photographs and illustrations by Mollie Katzen.
pages cm
Includes index.
ISBN 978-0-547-57159-1
1. Vegetarian cooking. 2. International cooking.
3. Cooking (Natural foods) I. Title.
TX837.K25925 2013
641.5'636—dc23
2013010180

Book design by Nancy Austin

Printed in the United States of America

DOW 10 9 8 7 6 5 4 3 2 1

The following recipes have appeared in slightly different form in previous books.

Cumin-Scented Black Bean Burgers (page 292) and Mushroom Popover Pie (page 275) adapted from *Get Cooking: 150 Simple Recipes to Get You Started in the Kitchen* (William Morrow Cookbooks, 2009), used by permission from HarperCollins.

Savory Ricotta "Muffins" (page 278), Mushroom Bread Pudding (page 280), Fried Green Tomato "Burgers" (page 310), Fully Loaded Buttermilk Corn Cakes (page 316), Wild Rice Pancakes with Mushrooms and Goat Cheese (page 318), Beet, Orange, and Ginger Marmalade (page 374), Caramelized Onion and Lemon Marmalade (page 375), Avocado-Grapefruit-Mango Saladita (page 378), and Bittersweet Mocha Bundt Cake (page 420) adapted from *Mollie Katzen's Sunlight Café* (Hyperion, 2002), used by permission of Hyperion.

Strawberry-Avocado Saladita (page 382) and Crispy Sage Leaves (page 394) adapted from *The Vegetable Dishes I Can't Live Without* (Hyperion, 2007), used by permission of Hyperion.

Yellow Coconut Rice with Chilies, Ginger, and Lime (page 196), Bulgur and Spaghetti (page 222), Soba Noodles with Butternut Squash, Miso, Smoked Tofu, Pumpkin Seeds, and Basil (page 266), Muhammara (page 359), and Chipotle Cream (page 371) adapted from *Mollie Katzen's Vegetable Heaven: Over 200 Recipes for Uncommon Soups, Tasty Bites, Side Dishes, and Too Many Desserts* (Hyperion, 1997), used by permission of Hyperion.

This book is dedicated to Minnie Heller and Betty Katzen,
whom I miss every day—and to Sam Black and Eve Shames.
You are my heroes.

CONTENTS

Introduction

Several decades ago, the recipe journals I had been keeping since my teens morphed into what eventually became the Moosewood Cookbook, *reflecting my generation's search for creative alternatives to the traditional meat-and-potatoes American dinner plate. The cuisine, if it can be called that, grew out of a fascination with plant-based dishes from various cultures and an enthusiastic appreciation for a sense of kitchen craft reminiscent of our grandmothers.*

What made *Moosewood* noteworthy at the time, I think, in addition to the food itself, was the idea that vegetarian dishes could comprise an entire dinner (or even a lifestyle), relegating meat to occasional status or possibly allowing us to abandon it altogether. In addition to presenting meatless possibilities, the *Moosewood Cookbook*, with its emphasis on cooking from scratch, was considered doubly novel in an era when quick and convenient were the rage, and vegetables were largely sourced from freezers and cans.

Since the 1970s, I've both expanded my repertoire and simplified my approach. My early recipes were packed with rich ingredients like butter, cheese, sour cream, eggs—in large part to appease those who might be worried that the lack of meat would leave everyone hungry. My confidence for lightening things up, acquired over a period of many years, was born out of a trust that people did not need bulk or richness to feel satisfied. Over time, my assurance also came from a better understanding of how to make food taste wonderful through seasoning, selective and various uses of heat, timing, attention to detail, and a stronger sense of aesthetic economy. A bonus of this approach is that, quite without conscious design, almost half of the dishes in this book are vegan.

Now when I cook, I want as much space on the plate as possible for my beloved garden vegetables. For the most part, that is my

A bonus of this approach is that, quite without conscious design,
almost half of the dishes in this book are vegan.

definition of my cuisine: a beautiful plate of food, simply cooked, maximally flavored, and embracing as many plant components as will harmoniously fit. My food is sharper, livelier, spicier, lighter, and more relaxed than it used to be.

These days, a favorite dinner feature at my house is a variety of vegetarian burgers: black bean burgers seasoned generously with cumin, for example, or patties made of sweet potatoes, chickpeas, quinoa, and spice, possibly topped with a dab of red pepper pesto or a spoonful of colorful slaw. Though you could never detect it, the burgers might well have come from the freezer, since most of them can be made in advance. Supper chez me might also be a pancake made from wild rice, mushrooms, and goat cheese, or it could just as easily be a celestial zucchini-ricotta cake.

A meal is equally likely to arrive at my table via the oven. In place of a heavy, cheesy casserole that my younger self might have prepared, I'm more likely to serve a puffy, crusty, and custardy popover full of mushrooms, or little quiche "muffins" filled with cauliflower, chopped tomatoes, and touches of feta cheese, or a hot, crisp pizza covered with abundant (and adjustable) vegetables. Vegetables are also the main event in an asparagus tart that takes about 15 minutes, thanks to a "cheat" ingredient: store-bought puff pastry.

Reversing the ratio of vegetables (and sometimes fruit) to carbohydrates (aka "starch") is one of my favorite techniques for delivering more garden items to the plate in delicious ways. This "great food flip" will have you gracing a modest serving of soba noodles with butternut squash; surrounding a simple risotto with a fig-, balsamic-, and lemon-laced stir-fry of leeks, escarole, and radicchio; and amping up a batch of black rice with beluga lentils and sautéed minced mushrooms that blend in visually while providing layers of contrasting taste. Finely chopped broccoli merges with millet in one recipe and dives headfirst into mashed potatoes in another; the former becomes a little pilaf that can be stuffed into a grilled portobello, and the latter transforms into main-course patties encrusted with walnuts and sautéed until golden. The next meal might be basmati rice cloaked in a savory blueberry sauce and spooned into a boat of roasted acorn squash.

Lasagna, of course, is generally pillowed with cheese, and the usual ways to veg it up tend to marinara-ize the sauce with zucchini or mushrooms or tuck spinach between the layers. My new approach, seasonal lasagna stacks, omits the tomato sauce and allows generous combinations of vegetables to house minimal noodles, with very light touches of cheese as a subtle presence. Vegan versions of these same lasagnas present the same ingredients in broth, with crumbled tofu replacing the cheese. The results are enthusiastically received every time.

The plant-food road to deliciousness allows you to be an artist as well as a cook, showcasing the beauty of the ingredients as you mix things up in creative yet taste-logical ways. Prepare for your kitchen spirit to be freed up as you embrace color contrasts in bean and rice combinations, pairing orange rice with black beans, yellow rice with red beans, and red rice with fresh green beans—all simple, all in this book. The bright gold of a sweet potato–pear soup begs to be punched up with a dab of a thick cranberry-orange vinaigrette, and a puddle of mango exults in deep magenta roasted beets and a crown of baby arugula. Bright green mashed peas can be topped with a tangle of fresh mint strips and served with Crayola-yellow crispy polenta triangles for dipping. The peas are part of an entire chapter devoted to the ultimate savory comfort food: mashed vegetables (why stop at mashed potatoes?), also featuring curried mashed carrots with cashews.

Creative cooking means allowing yourself to step out of the corral of definitions.

Try setting aside assumptions about what breakfast, lunch, and dinner should be, and feel free to serve eggs fried in olive oil with a thin coating of fine, fresh bread crumbs for an elegant little dinner—plain or as a topping for smoky braised Brussels sprouts, fully deserving of a respectable red wine. Similarly a creamy Tuscan white bean soup can be dinner as well as lunch, especially when accompanied by a grilled bread and kale salad studded with red onions, walnuts, and sweet figs. A group of little dishes—your choice how many (piquillo peppers stuffed with goat cheese over salad; bulgur-walnut kibbeh balls on a circle of Greek yogurt; a slice of grilled Haloumi cheese piled on watermelon and doused with lime juice; small eggplant halves, slapped down in a hot pan and glazed with a sauce made from ginger, plum jam, and chilies) can also be dinner, and you have here more than 200 modular recipes to mix and match at your convenience.

Standard versions of mac and cheese can be heavy and uninteresting—even when they don't come from a box. I have upgraded the dish, taking it in several contrasting directions, combining it with chili for a

For the most part, that is my definition of my cuisine:
a beautiful plate of food, simply cooked, maximally
flavored, and embracing as many plant
components as will harmoniously fit.

Prepare for your kitchen spirit to be freed up
as you embrace color contrasts.

deeply satisfying American hybrid, or with lemon, caramelized onions, and blue cheese in a French-style rendition. And as for the signature quiche of my hippie days, I'm now more likely to make a fluffy, versatile, veg-centric frittata, which is essentially an easy quiche without the crust.

Main-event stews—simmered vegetable-legume combinations of various ethnic influences—are customized with a small, easy accessory to add intrigue. Peruvian stew, with potatoes, beans, tomatoes, and chilies, is accompanied by freshly cooked tiny quinoa-laced corn cakes; a simple lentil stew is taken to the next level with a topping of crunchy fried sage leaves and a hat of tender cottage cheese dumplings. A sunny root-vegetable stew surprises with the subtle presence of pears, entrancing even further with its side-kick of little buttermilk-rosemary-walnut biscuits. Curried yellow split pea soup can be busied up with green peas and a big spoonful of basmati rice pilaf with nuts and raisins. A crown of ethereally thin and crispy fried onion rings lifts a red lentil or eggplant mash into the realm of craveable, using only the most basic pantry ingredients you already have on hand.

Multiple levels of flavor can come from innumerable sources. Almonds are ground

and blended with garlic, olive oil, and sherry vinegar into a glorious faux aioli that you can use as you would mayonnaise—or cover with a blanket of grapes and serve as a first-course dip for crunchy cucumbers. Tofu and a thin omelet can be made over into noodle-impersonating toppings, and soaked chickpeas can be fried in olive oil, adding protein in light and playful ways.

Small bits of fruit and vegetables (blueberries with fresh, sweet corn; apples with olive oil and parsley; pink grapefruit with jicama, cilantro, and pumpkin seeds) are combined in beautiful little "saladitas," a cross between a salad and a salsa, to make cheerful toppings or freestanding appetizers, keeping things refreshing and compelling. "Optional Enhancements" at the end of each recipe allow you to take all of these in your own direction, varying the template each time you cook and keeping your cooking continuously new.

Once you try these recipes as written, fly away with them, if you wish, and make them your own. This is now your book, and soon these will become your recipes. I hope and trust the food you prepare will reward you and the people around you with all the inspiration, delight, and nourishment you deserve.

Select Pantry Notes

Throughout the book, I've kept the supplies and equipment straightforward, so most people in most places can cook most of the dishes with a basic setup. However, a few of my frequently used, choice ingredients (principally oils, vinegars, and sweeteners) may be less than familiar to some. Following those, I've listed the simple tools that I find essential and that I want to be sure you're working with to maximize your good times in the kitchen.

INGREDIENTS

Workhorse Oils for Cooking

Olive oil is my baseline oil. You will notice that I designate "extra-virgin" in the uncooked uses and just indicate "olive oil" when I cook with it. This is to let you know that if you prefer to go to a lesser grade (often called "pure" in the United States) for cooking purposes, saving the more expensive stuff for salads and for finishing, that will work just fine. In my own home cooking, I use extra-virgin for everything; it's the only kind of olive oil I buy.

When I want a more neutral flavor or I want to cook at a higher temperature than olive oil will withstand, I use grapeseed oil, and sometimes peanut oil or coconut oil (which is solid at room temperature and usually comes in jars). These go well with Asian-themed dishes and are high-temperature sturdy and reliable. For very high-temperature frying, I like to use high-oleic (aka high-temperature) safflower oil.

STORAGE: Buy olive oil that is packed in dark bottles, to protect it from light. Assuming you'll be using it often, store it in a cool cupboard away from stove and sun, covered tightly. (You can also keep it in the refrigerator, but you will need to let it warm up a bit to soften before using.) Store the other workhorse oils in the refrigerator for maximum freshness—or at a cool, dark room temperature, if you use them often.

Creative cooking also means allowing yourself to step out
of the corral of definitions.

Flavor Oils for Finishing

High-quality extra-virgin olive oil and roasted nut and seed oils are shiny, extravagant condiments that will give your dish both a finished look and an extra layer of complex, exquisite flavor. They are delicate, and with the exception of the more robust toasted sesame oil (called Chinese sesame oil in this book) and roasted peanut oil, both of which you can cook with, they should be used as condiments only and not exposed to direct heat. These oils are a bit pricey, but they will last a long time, as a little bit goes far.

Truffle oil is in its own category. It is not seasoned with actual truffles but rather with a synthetic compound that mimics truffle flavor. Some chefs love it and others disapprove. I happen to like a touch of it here and there; you can be your own judge.

STORAGE: **Keep all of these oils tightly covered and refrigerated.**

Vinegars

I have an entire cupboard devoted to vinegar, and it is always full. At any given time, there may be several white wine varieties (including sherry and champagne), several made from various kinds of red wine, apple cider vinegar, seasoned (with salt and sugar) rice vinegar, and supermarket-grade balsamic vinegar, a product that is not the true Italian delicacy, but rather an Americanized imitation, and a pretty tasty one at that. Sometimes I will also use authentic, rich Italian balsamic from Modena—which comes packed in small bottles, with bona fide markers and stamps to prove its pedigree—as a finish. You can vary the vinegars you use in basic vinaigrettes and come up with your own signature flavor profile. You can also splash vinegar in or on any dish where you might normally add a squirt of fresh lemon juice for a pleasant acidic edge to punch up flatter, more staid, flavors, adding dimension and a sense of layering. It makes a difference to use these high-quality ingredients, and I find it well worth the extra cost. They will keep indefinitely, and I predict that you will use them sparingly and often.

Sweeteners

Agave nectar, a plant derivative, is my go-to sweetener for recipes that need a touch of sweetness. Increasingly available in mainstream supermarkets, it is relatively inexpensive, keeps indefinitely, and contributes a concentrated, neutral sweetness that blends easily and well with other flavors. Similar to honey or maple syrup, agave falls somewhere between the two in thickness but has less of a flavor presence than either. Sometimes, when I want more flavor, I use pure maple syrup or a light-colored honey. (The taste intensity of honey is indicated by its hue.) Agave, honey, and maple syrup have similar degrees of sweetness, so from that angle, they are interchangeable. Granulated and brown sugars are about a third less sweet. I use these in most baked goods, and if I want a drier effect in a savory dish.

Pomegranate molasses (deeply reduced pure pomegranate juice) is one of my favorite flavor boosters. Even though it falls in the sweetener category, it is actually quite tart, and it lends layers of complexity and mystery to everything it touches. It's even good straight from the bottle as a finishing touch. A wonderful discovery awaits you here, if you haven't already stumbled upon it. Look for pomegranate molasses in Middle Eastern–themed supermarkets, specialty shops, or on the Internet.

TOOLS

If you are armed with good tools that you keep in good condition, and if your kitchen is clear-counter ready, you will want to cook more because you will love it more.

The Knife

This is the most important tool. There is no one right chef's knife for everyone, but there is a right one for you. You just need to find it. How will you know? It will feel good in

There is no one right chef's knife for everyone,
but there is a right one for you.

your hand—the right grip, weight, shape, spirit. It should have a straight blade (serrated is for bread and sectioning citrus, and that's about it) and be so sharp that when you strike a sitting apple, it will grab immediately. When you slice further, you will get crisply defined slices, not shreds and not mush. You might even hear a sound effect, akin to a "whoosh." That will feel as fantastic as the thing you just sliced looks, and when this happens, you will know that this is *your knife*. Keep it sharp by conditioning it on a steel, ideally before each use. I also have mine professionally sharpened annually.

I have a cleaver, too, which I use for attacking the heavier items, most notably winter squash. I also have a couple of strong paring knives (it's just as important to keep these razor sharp as the larger blades) that I use constantly for smaller things such as fruit and vegetable snacks.

Cutting Boards

I recommend that you keep one exclusively for onions, garlic, and shallots. Have another for anything and everything else. Both wood and synthetic are fine; it's up to you.

Food Processor

I admit to an unabashed dependency on my food processor, both the larger edition and the mini-bowl attachment for smaller batches. The regular steel blade is the heavy

lifter, but I also use the grating attachment fairly often. I hope you have one; in addition to a sharp knife, it will make short work of many of these recipes.

Immersion Blender

This works so well that I don't think I've used my stand blender in years. Immersion blenders are inexpensive, easy to store, and supereffective. They also minimize work and cleanup, since you end up using far fewer pots and bowls. They also clean easily—just be sure you power it off (and unplug, if that applies) before cleaning, for safety. Immersion blenders have razor-sharp blades and can be dangerous if used carelessly.

Large (10- to 12-inch) Skillet

This is by far the hardest-working of all my pots and pans. In fact, I leave it out on the stove almost all the time, since I use it so much. Even if this pan seems large for some dishes, I use it anyway to give enhanced horizontal opportunity to whatever I'm cooking. Contact with the surface of the hot pan is valuable seasoning, and maximum space makes this possible.

Tongs

One-handed, spring-loaded, to be exact. These are my go-to grabbers bar none; they might as well be extensions of my hands.

Scissors

I snip a lot—everything from artichokes to fresh herbs to winter squash seeds to pizza dough. My scissors aren't fancy or special, just strong, clean, and sharp. (Also bright red–handled, so I can find them easily if I leave them where they don't belong.)

Sturdy Peeler

A good, strong vegetable peeler, whether Y-shaped or straight across, is good for so much more than removing the peel from vegetables. I use mine for stripping hard cheese, thick-zesting citrus, fashioning vegetable "ribbons" for delicate salads, and shaving chocolate for dessert toppings.

Mandoline

I love my inexpensive little blade board on which I can swiftly render an onion or fennel bulb into a flurry of diaphanous wings. Once you experience the lightness (in every sense) of wafer-thin slices of a radish or beet or carrot, you will look for every excuse to do it over and over. (See Crudité "Chips,"

page 77.) Just be careful to pay complete attention when strumming on this utensil—it is very sharp, and the process goes fast, so keep your eye on your vulnerable hand.

Rasp and Zester

For finely grated citrus zest, use a rasp. For long strands, a few strokes of an old-fashioned zester will provide.

Other Important Items

Soup pot
Medium saucepan with a lid
Spoons of all kinds (but mostly wooden ones of all sizes)
Liquid measuring cups with spouts
Spatulas (rubber ones and small, sturdy metal ones)
Whisks
Colanders of various sizes
Kitchen towels (a large supply, clean and plush)
Oven thermometer
Heat diffuser
Toaster oven

Vegetarian and Vegan Menus

A vegetarian dinner can be as straightforward as a favorite soup, or a mac and cheese, or a risotto, or a "supper from the oven," served with a green salad dressed with your favorite vinaigrette. It can also be a stew and a matching accessory, preceded by a small salad appetizer. Permission is granted to enjoy a plate of eggs or an omelet in tandem with a cooked vegetable, some toast, and a glass of wine. There will certainly be nights when this is all you have time for, and it's also all you need.

At other times, you can have fun assembling modular arrangements of say, roasted vegetables on top of mashed vegetables, topped with a saladita (a cross between a small salad and a salsa). Or you may decide to pair a cooked grain with a marinated vegetable salad, playing with complementary temperatures and textures. A sampling of smaller dishes on a larger plate can add up to a compelling meal, and to this end, I've come up with recipes that do just fine when made in advance and reheated. Flexibility (both the food's and your own) opens doors to new combinations that can expand the scope of your home-food culture. Throughout the book, I've suggested matchmaking among the dishes, hoping that you personalize combinations according to your taste and the preferences of those for whom you cook.

The following 35 menus reflect how I might cluster recipes at my table. You can follow them exactly or consider them templates. Feel free to swap in your own creations and traditional dishes (desserts included), and enjoy a fresh context for some old family favorites.

VEGETARIAN MENUS

I.

Creamy Tuscan-Style White Bean Soup (page 26)
Linguine with Roasted Red Pepper Pesto (page 358)
Kale Caesar (page 68)
Buttermilk-Yogurt-Maple Sherbet (page 415)

2.

Grilled Haloumi Cheese (page 406) on watermelon slices
Mushroom Popover Pie (page 275)
Mashed Broccoli (page 177)
Fruit-Studded Madeleine Cake (page 422)

3.

Mashed Parsnips (page 176) or Mashed Celery Root (page 174),
topped with Browned Potatoes and Onion (page 391)
Maple-Mustard Glaze (page 370)
Cheese-Crusted Roasted Cauliflower (page 335)
Radicchio Salad with Oranges and Pistachios (page 78)

4.

Caramelized Onion Frittata with Artichoke Hearts, Zucchini,
and Goat Cheese (page 284)
Grilled Bread and Kale Salad with Red Onions, Walnuts, and Figs (page 71)
Brown Sugar–Roasted Rhubarb with Cinnamon-Toast Crumbs (page 416)

5.

Brussels Sprout Gratin with Potatoes and Spinach (page 286)
Apple-Parsley Saladita (page 386)
Brûléed Persimmon Pudding (page 418)

6.

Golden Mango–Nectarine Gazpacho (page 55)
Asparagus Puff Pastry Tart (page 282)
Summer Corn and Barley Salad (page 120)
Bittersweet Mocha Bundt Cake (page 420)

7.

Mac, Chili, and Cheese (page 238)
Fried Green Tomato "Burgers" (page 310)
Green salad with avocado, jicama, and Jalapeño-Cilantro-Lime Vinaigrette (page 367)
Grapefruit-Lime Curd (page 414), in a crust or with cookies

8.

Romesco Sauce (page 359), puddled on the plate
Cubes of roasted butternut squash on the sauce
Sautéed assorted mushrooms, scattered
Flash-Fried Kale with Garlic, Almonds, and Cheese (page 346)
A spoonful of fresh ricotta and a fried egg
Cranapple Walnut Cake (page 426)

9.

Tortilla Soup (page 46)
Salad Greens with Goat Cheese–Stuffed Piquillo Peppers (page 85)
Chili Pepitas (page 401)
Mushroom Gravy for Everyone (page 365), puddled on the plate
Chard- or Collard-Wrapped Polenta-Chile Tamale Packages (page 338) on the sauce

10.

Crispy-Coated Eggplant Parmesan "Burgers" (page 308)
Roasted Garlic–Mashed Cauliflower (page 172)
Green Beans and Beets with Pickled Red Onions (page 96)
Couscous with Dates, Pistachios, Pine Nuts, and Parsley (page 217)

11.

Lablabi (Tunisian Chickpea Soup) (page 30)
Bulgur-Walnut Kibbeh Balls (page 312) on a bed of yogurt, topped
with pomegranate seeds
Crunchy Cucumbers and Red Onion with Fresh Cheese (page 73)
Pear Tart with Olive Oil–Cornmeal–Pine Nut Crust (page 428)

12.

Very Simple Lentil Stew (page 146)
Cottage Cheese Dumplings (page 147)
Quinoa-Couscous Pilaf with Carrot, Roasted Almond Oil, and
Pickled Red Onions (page 220)
Green salad with Sherry-Honey-Tarragon-Mustard Vinaigrette (page 367)
Pecan Shortbread Cookies (page 435)

13.

Soft Polenta (page 184) topped with a poached egg
Mixed Mushroom Ragout (page 348)
Shaved Fennel with Apple, Blue Cheese Crumbs, Walnuts, and
Radicchio (see Variation 4, page 75)

14.

Ruby Gazpacho (page 56)
Mini Cauliflower Quiches (page 276)
Green Rice (page 194)
Chocolate Cream Pie (page 424)

15.

Nectarine-Thyme Saladita (page 386)
Fresh Corn Soup (page 32)
Toast duet: one slice topped with Avocado "Mayo" (page 373), the other with
ricotta, store-bought or Homemade (page 413)

16.

Spinach-Basmati Soup with Yogurt (page 45)
SALAD TRIO:
Cauliflower Salad with Salsa Verde (page 103)
Grated Carrot Salad (page 62)
Celery-Almond-Date Saladita (page 376)
Olive Oil Toasts (see page 409)

17.

Cumin-Scented Black Bean Burgers (page 292)
Chili-Cilantro Mayonnaise (page 373)
Strawberry-Avocado Saladita (page 382) or Jicama–Pink Grapefruit Saladita (page 381)
Your own favorite slaw (see page 66)
Warmed corn tortillas

18.

Wild Rice Pancakes with Mushrooms and Goat Cheese (page 318)
Avocado "Mayo" (page 373) or guacamole
Fire-Roasted Bell Pepper Saladita (page 380) or salsa
Chili-Sesame Green Beans (page 345)

19.

Fully Loaded Buttermilk Corn Cakes (page 316)
Chipotle Cream (page 371)
Avocado-Grapefruit-Mango Saladita (page 378)
Green salad with Jalapeño-Cilantro-Lime Vinaigrette (page 367)
Chili Pepitas (page 401)

20.

Spring Farro (page 224)
Asparagus Salad with Roasted Red Peppers and Chickpeas (page 94)
Homemade Ricotta (page 413) with artisan honey and fresh fruit in season

VEGAN MENUS

I.

Mushroom Wonton Soup (page 38)
Coconut-Mango Rice Noodle Salad (page 126)
Eggplant Slap-Down with Ginger-Plum Sauce (page 342)

2.

Yellow Split Pea Dal (page 28), with spinach added
Spiced Basmati Pilaf with Nuts and Raisins, made without butter (page 192)
Onion Pakoras (page 139) dipped in Pomegranate-Lime Glaze (page 369)
Pomegranate-Mint Saladita (page 386)

3.

Curried Mashed Carrots and Cashews, made without honey (page 170)
Forbidden Rice with Beluga Lentils and Mushrooms (page 214)
Mashed White Beans (page 183), left whole
Pan-Grilled Mushroom Slices (page 349)
Sliced cherry tomatoes

10.

Sweet Potato–Pear Soup, made with oil (page 33), dabbed with
Thick Cranberry-Orange Vinaigrette (page 368)
Stir-Fried Noodles with Asparagus, Mushrooms, Tofu, and Cashews (page 263)

11.

Fresh Corn Gazpacho (page 50) or your own favorite hot or cold tomato soup
Grilled Ratatouille Salad (page 104)
Bulgur and Spaghetti (page 222)
Almond Faux Aioli (page 356), spooned onto the Bulgur and Spaghetti

12.

Hot-Sweet-Sour Soup with Tofu and Pineapple (page 42)
Roasted Eggplant Salad with Coconut-Lime Vinaigrette (page 106)
Tofu "Noodles" (Coconut Version, page 399)
Green Rice (page 194), stuffed into seared sweet pepper halves

13.

Wild Rice Chili-Mango Soup, made without honey (page 40)
Cajun-Style Tofu Burgers (page 302)
Toasted baguette
Caramelized Onion and Lemon Marmalade, made without honey (page 375)
Crudité "Chips" (see page 77) or your own favorite slaw (see page 66)

14.

Golden Lentils with Soft, Sweet Onions, made without butter (page 182)
Simple Buckwheat Pilaf, made without butter (page 230)
Twice-Cooked Italian-Style Broccoli (page 325)
Toasted walnuts
Crispy Fried Lemons (page 389)
Hazelnut–Wilted Frisée Salad with Sliced Pear (page 84)

15.

Mashed potatoes made with olive oil, salt, and pepper
Seitan Medallions in Good Gravy (page 306)
Green beans with roasted almond oil and toasted almonds
Spiced Carrots in Thick Cranberry-Orange Vinaigrette (page 102)
Crisp, Ethereal Onion Rings (page 387)

SOUPS

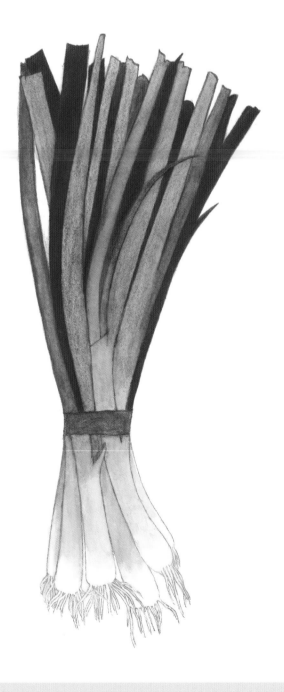

HOT SOUPS

COLD SOUPS

❊ ❊ ❊

Any day that you make a soup instantly becomes Soup Day, and things change for the better. Whatever time you put into it will be returned to you in the form of a quality moment with the first sip, and that moment will extend, as everything around you slows down.

I love the inherent spirit of vegetable meeting liquid when everything simmers together. You can relax about what you're preparing, knowing that the collaboration between broth and bits will soften moods as well as ingredients. Even though I probably have a hundred soup recipes in my repertoire by now, I never get tired of making them—and more importantly, I still feel excited and fresh about creating new ones.

Soup days can be weekend afternoons or weekday evenings when you are home anyway, doing other things. Most soups are good the next day—and the next—season after season, so even if putting one together takes an evening, you will have something to come home to tomorrow. In addition to their inherent mood-soothing properties, soups are the great temperature neutralizer: Hot ones make you feel held on cold days; cold ones can restore your sanity in the summer. There are also in-between ones that will soothe you at any temperature (yours, the room's, or theirs). Soup is never out of season and never out of place.

Many of these soups extend as far as you wish to take them into highly embellished one-bowl meals (Creamy Tuscan-Style White Bean Soup, Yellow Split Pea Dal, and Lablabi are the champions), and almost all of them can be the focus of a meal, especially when paired with matching salads or Meaningful Touches (page 352).

STOCK ADVICE

Vegetable stock is simply water that has been spiked with flavor. Sometimes this happens as a self-generated by-product of making the soup, and at other times the stock is put together ahead of time. Most of the soups in this section create their own stock as they go, as various aromatics, legumes, and/or vegetables simmer in water, rendering premade stock unnecessary.

A couple of these recipes, though, are based on a premade stock. For these (and for the risottos on pages 203 through 212), you are welcome to use your own favorite store-bought stock—and there are quite a few good ones to choose from in most supermarkets. (When I don't have time to make stock from scratch, I use Kitchen Basics Unsalted Vegetable Stock.)

But you can also make your own signature variety and either use it at once or store it in tightly covered (and clearly labeled) containers for up to a month in the freezer.

I've come full circle from my early days of boiling up any and all vegetable scraps in one perpetually simmering pot as part of my effort to be a good citizen. This short-lived phase of hoped-for better personhood was followed by a much longer period not making or using stock, except for adopting a few choice brands of commercial product for risotto making. Mostly, I stuck to soups that came out great made with water.

Lately, though, I've returned to making stock—small, deliberate batches simmered expressly for specific flavor. The difference is highly tasteable.

You don't need an overwhelming kettleful of random scraps, but rather a modest saucepan mingling a few carefully chosen vegetables. One liberating factor about making stock is that you can chop more or less imprecisely. The vegetable dimensions are not terribly important, because they will either be discarded or pureed at the other end of the recipe. That's what I love about making stock: Everything is flexible and forgiving. And if you happen to feel virtuous in the process, consider that a bonus.

The Basic Pound Stock

MAKES ABOUT 6 CUPS ❦ VEGAN

A pound each of onions, carrots, and potatoes, simmered together with a head of garlic, will deliver a trusty and delicious basic vegetable stock, versatile and sturdy. You can make this as sodium-endowed (or not) as you wish.

1 pound onions (2 medium), cut into chunks (peeling optional)

1 pound carrots (4 medium), peeled and cut into chunks

1 pound russet potatoes (2 medium), peeled and cut into chunks

1 head garlic, halved crosswise (unpeeled is OK)

1 teaspoon salt (more or less, per you)

10 cups water

1. Combine everything in a large pot and bring to a boil, uncovered.

2. Lower the heat to a simmer and simmer for about 30 minutes.

3. If you like the way it tastes at this point, it's ready. If you'd like it more intense, let it go a bit longer—up to an hour. The flavor will be stronger and the volume will be slightly less.

4. Cool until comfortable to handle and then strain it into a second pot. If you want it clear, don't press on the vegetables. If you want it a little thicker and slightly opaque, go ahead and press the vegetables a bit through the strainer.

5. Store in a tightly covered container in the refrigerator for up to 3 days or in the freezer for up to a month.

OPTIONAL ENHANCEMENTS

Throw in a rind of Parmesan (up to 4 ounces) ❋
A few mushrooms—fresh or dried ❋ Any additional vegetables that your instinct suggests

NOODLE SOUP IMPROVISATIONS

Once you have a stock that you love (whether you've simmered it yourself or just opened a box), you are equipped to make up your own noodle soup without a recipe. Simply cook and drain a batch of noodles, place them in a bowl, and ladle in some delicious hot stock. You can decide on the proportions of noodles to broth, and you can also choose whether to keep it simple or clutter it with

vegetables (raw, freshly steamed, or left over) or extra seasonings (a spoonful of aromatic Chinese chili, garlic, or bean paste, a dribble of soy sauce, a handful of minced fresh herbs, a dab of pesto, a punch of Sriracha). Make it a meal in a bowl by adding strips of tofu or a fried or poached egg, and you will have a new, quick weekday supper option upon which you can depend.

Humble Potato-Leek Soup

MAKES 5 OR 6 SERVINGS ❧ VEGAN

I intended to make a cucumber vichyssoise and began with a simple base of potatoes and leeks. I took a taste at the stage that is now this soup, and it was so good I decided to leave it alone. In retrospect, I attribute its simple deliciousness to the smashed potato format—potato pieces so soft that they crumble into the broth at the gentlest urging of a fork. It doesn't get any more accessible and doable than this.

Bonus for vegans: This soup is vegan, but somehow it tastes downright buttery from the leeks lending their mysteriously luxurious effect.

❀ The soup tastes more layered when made with the water left over from preparing Mashed Celery Root (page 174), so keep this in mind the next time you find yourself simmering a celery root.

❀ The best way to clean leeks is to trim and slice them first, then place the slices in a large bowl of cold water in the sink. Swish the leeks around, then lift them into a colander while you change the water. Return the leek slices to the bowl of clean water and repeat until they are clean. (You can see less and less grit being left behind in the bottom of the bowl with each go-round.) Spin the leeks dry in a salad spinner.

❀ Two pots are needed for this, but the cleanup is easy, and it saves time—and maximizes flavor—to cook the potatoes in one pot while you sauté the leeks in the other.

1 pound russet potatoes (peeling optional), cut into 1-inch chunks

4 cups water

Up to 1¼ teaspoons salt

2 tablespoons olive oil

4 (packed) cups (about 2 pounds) cleaned leek rings, short of ¼ inch thick

Black pepper

1. Combine the potato chunks, water, and ½ teaspoon salt in a medium-large saucepan. Bring to a boil, lower the heat to a simmer, and cook, covered, until the potatoes are very soft, about 20 minutes.

2. Meanwhile, place another saucepan (slightly larger) over medium-low heat for 1 minute. Add the olive oil and swirl to coat the pan. Add the leeks and another ½ teaspoon salt and cook, stirring, for a minute or two, then lower the heat and continue to cook, stirring, for 5 to 8 minutes. Cover and cook over low heat for another 5 to 8 minutes, or until the leeks are very soft.

3. Add the potatoes and all their cooking water to the leeks, along with black pepper to taste. Cover the pot, turn off the heat, and let the soup sit for about 15 minutes to develop the flavor. Somewhere in there, taste to adjust the salt.

4. You can now reheat the soup and serve it as is, or puree some of it with an immersion blender to add thickness, and then reheat it. Serve hot.

OPTIONAL ENHANCEMENTS

A touch of cream—stirred in just before serving or drizzled on top ❋ A spot of crème fraîche ❋ Minced cucumber and/or chives ❋ Thin strips of fresh basil ❋ A dab of Salsa Verde (page 357)

Full circle: You can also go ahead and take this to the vichyssoise I originally thought I was making. Chill the soup and then puree it with up to ½ cup heavy cream and a peeled, seeded, deliciously sweet cucumber. Serve cold, with a light topping of fresh chives—in long chive lines (with their pretty purple blossoms, if available) or minced.

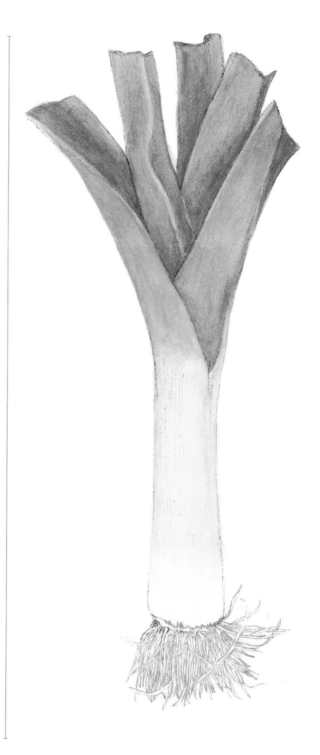

Creamy Tuscan-Style White Bean Soup

MAKES 4 TO 6 SERVINGS ✿ VEGAN

The classic Tuscan white bean treatment extends to a soothing soup format, delicious in its basic form—and it's also a template with huge expansion potential. If you add cooked pasta (see the list of Enhancements) and pair this with a spinach salad and some rustic bread, it will instantly become a dinner that calls out for a big Italian red wine.

✿ You can substitute white pea (navy) beans for the cannellini beans. Soak the beans for a minimum of 4 hours (ideally overnight) in plenty of water to generously cover. This soup should be made with dried, not canned, beans, since the bean-simmering liquid becomes the broth.

✿ Garlic shows up three times here, in various capacities. The overall effect is layered, subtle, and smooth. The roasted garlic flavor in particular intensifies nicely as the soup sits in the refrigerator, if you're not serving the entire batch in one stroke. Roast a head (or make a batch of Roasted Garlic Paste) well ahead of time. In fact, while you're at it, roast 2 or 3 heads (or make extra paste). It's a great ingredient to have on hand.

✿ This soup presents the perfect opportunity to use that special bottle of high-quality extra-virgin olive oil for drizzling on top.

1½ cups (¾ pound) dried cannellini (white kidney) beans, soaked

8 cups water

3–4 large garlic cloves, peeled and halved

1 2-inch sprig fresh rosemary

½ head roasted garlic (or 1½ tablespoons Roasted Garlic Paste; page 173)

2 tablespoons olive oil

1½ cups minced onion (1 medium)

1 medium carrot, diced small

Big pinch of rubbed dried sage

1 teaspoon salt, or more to taste

1 tablespoon minced or crushed garlic

Black pepper

1. Drain and rinse the soaked beans, then transfer them to a soup pot, large saucepan, or Dutch oven along with the water, garlic clove halves, and rosemary. Bring to a boil, lower the heat to a simmer, partially cover, and cook until the beans become very soft, about 1 hour. (You want to err on the side of overdone.) Fish out and discard the rosemary (leave in the garlic). Let the soup cool to room temperature.

2. Squeeze the pulp from the roasted garlic cloves directly into the soup, discarding the skins, or add the Roasted Garlic Paste. Use an immersion blender to puree the mixture to the desired consistency, or puree in batches in a stand blender. Return the soup to the pot, if necessary, and reheat gently.

3. Meanwhile, place a medium skillet over medium heat for about a minute, then add the olive oil and swirl to coat the pan. Add the onion, carrot, sage, and ½ teaspoon salt. Cook, stirring, for about 3 minutes, or until the onion begins to soften. Stir in the minced or crushed garlic plus another ½ teaspoon salt, turn the heat to medium-low, and cook for another 10 minutes or so, until the onion is translucent and the carrot is very soft.

4. Add the cooked vegetables to the bean mixture, stirring well. Cover and cook over very low heat (with a heat diffuser, if you have one, underneath) for another 10 to 15 minutes, allowing the flavors to meld.

5. Adjust the salt, if necessary, and add a generous amount of black pepper to taste. Serve hot with any (or many) of the Enhancements.

OPTIONAL ENHANCEMENTS

A drizzle of high-quality extra-virgin olive oil (or a citrus-spiked olive oil) ✳ A drizzle of rich balsamic vinegar or Balsamic Reduction (page 369) ✳ A drop of truffle oil ✳ Crispy Sage Leaves (page 394) ✳ Thin strips of fresh basil and/or a small spoonful of basil pesto ✳ A touch of grated lemon zest ✳ Finely diced ripe tomato ✳ Olive Oil Toasts (see page 409) ✳ Slow-Roasted Roma Tomatoes (page 393), or mashed, on top ✳ A handful or two of baby spinach leaves (stirred in with the cooked vegetables in step 4) ✳ A dab of sour cream ✳ Minced fresh flat-leaf parsley ✳ Cooked tiny pasta (small rings or tubes, alphabet, ditalini, stellini)—add a spoonful or two to each bowl

Yellow Split Pea Dal

MAKES 6 TO 8 SERVINGS ❧ VEGAN

Good for beginners, this can become your go-to recipe if you want to embrace and perfect just one good curry. It's delicious as written, but is also a great springboard for augmentations and improvisations (the Enhancements, which follow). To turn this into a meal-in-a-bowl, put on a pot of brown basmati rice before you begin and place some rice in each bowl before ladling in the soup.

❋ Note that both ginger and garlic appear twice in the ingredients list—sliced, to simmer with the split peas, and minced, to include in the sauté.

2 cups yellow split peas

2 thick slices fresh ginger, each about 2 inches long

4 large garlic cloves, peeled and halved

10 cups water

2 tablespoons grapeseed, peanut, canola, or coconut oil

2 teaspoons mustard seeds

2 teaspoons cumin seeds

½ teaspoon *each* ground cardamom and ground coriander

1 teaspoon turmeric

2 teaspoons ground cumin

2 cups minced onion (1 large)

1 tablespoon minced or crushed garlic, plus up to 1 teaspoon more, if you love garlic

1 tablespoon minced fresh ginger

Up to 1½ teaspoons salt

¼ cup fresh lemon juice

Black pepper (optional)

Crushed red pepper (optional)

1. Place the split peas, ginger slices, garlic halves, and water in a soup pot, large saucepan, or Dutch oven. Bring to a boil, lower the heat to a simmer, partially cover, and cook until the split peas are very soft, 60 to 70 minutes. If at any time the soup looks like it needs more water, feel free to add some to keep it as thin and souplike as you prefer.

2. Meanwhile, place a medium skillet over medium heat for about a minute, then add the oil and swirl to coat the pan. Add all the spices and cook, stirring, for about a minute, or until they become fragrant and start making popping sounds. Add the onion, minced garlic, minced ginger, and 1 teaspoon salt and stir so the onion becomes evenly coated with the spices. Turn the heat to medium-low and cook, covered, until the onion becomes very soft, 10 minutes or longer, stirring frequently. Stir in the lemon juice toward the end.

3. When everything is very soft in both the pot and the skillet, transfer the onion-spice mixture to the split peas, stir to combine, and simmer over the lowest possible heat for another 5 minutes or so, stirring a few times to let the flavors meld. Fish out and discard the ginger slices (it's OK to leave in the halved garlic), check for salt, add black pepper and crushed red pepper to taste, if desired, and serve.

OPTIONAL ENHANCEMENTS

Minced cilantro (up to ¼ cup or more) mixed in just before serving ✳ A few handfuls baby spinach added in step 3 ✳ Diced cooked potato (stirred in at the end) ✳ Diced cooked carrot (added with the onion) ✳ Minced ripe tomato (stirred in at the end or scattered on top) ✳ Steamed green peas scattered on top ✳ A dab of yogurt, drizzle of buttermilk, or spoonful of Raita (page 371) spooned on top or served on the side ✳ Chopped Indian pickles (many choices at Indian grocery stores) on top or left whole alongside ✳ A touch of your favorite authentic Indian chutney ✳ A touch of heat (chili oil; mustard pickles or other hot Indian pickles; hot sauce; crushed red pepper) ✳ A sprinkling of pomegranate seeds ✳ A drizzle of pomegranate molasses or Pomegranate-Lime Glaze (page 369) ✳ Instead of plain basmati rice, you can get fancy with Spiced Basmati Pilaf with Nuts and Raisins (page 192)

Lablabi (Tunisian Chickpea Soup)

MAKES 5 OR 6 SERVINGS (OR MORE, DEPENDING ON HOW MANY OF THE ENHANCEMENTS YOU INCLUDE) ❧ VEGAN

Chickpeas, with gracious help from cumin, onion, garlic, olive oil, and lemon, transform their cooking water into a perfect soup. I adore this dish, iterations of which are commonly served in Tunisian restaurants, often for breakfast. It seems too simple to be as special as it ends up, which is one of the things I love so much about it.

❊ This soup should be made with dried, not canned, beans, since the cooking liquid becomes the delicious broth, which is untouchable by any store-bought vegetable stock. Soak the chickpeas for a minimum of 4 hours (ideally overnight) in plenty of water to cover generously. Once they're soaked, give the chickpeas plenty of time to cook. Some take longer than others, and you want them soft.

❊ You could puree some of this soup into varying degrees of thickness if you'd like.

❊ With a few (or many) of the Enhancements, Lablabi expands into a beautiful, satisfying meal in a bowl, bordering on a stew.

2 cups (1 pound) dried chickpeas, soaked

8 cups water

3–4 large garlic cloves, peeled and halved

2 tablespoons olive oil

2 cups minced onion (1 large)

2 teaspoons ground cumin

1 tablespoon minced or crushed garlic

1½ teaspoons salt, or more to taste

2 tablespoons fresh lemon juice

Black pepper

1. Drain and rinse the soaked chickpeas, then transfer them to a soup pot, large saucepan, or Dutch oven, along with the water and garlic cloves. Bring to a boil, lower the heat to a simmer, partially cover, and cook until the chickpeas are completely tender, an hour or longer. (You want to err on the soft side.)

2. Meanwhile, place a medium skillet over medium heat for about a minute, then add the olive oil and swirl to coat the pan. Add the onion and cumin, and cook, stirring, for 5 to 8 minutes, until the onion becomes soft. Add the minced garlic and 1 teaspoon of the salt, reduce the heat to low, and continue to cook for another 10 minutes. Cover and cook over the lowest possible heat for 10 minutes longer, then remove from the heat.

3. When the chickpeas are very tender, add the onion-garlic mixture, scraping in as much as you can of whatever adhered to the pan. Collect the remaining parts (this is flavor!) by adding the lemon juice to the skillet and stirring it around, scraping the sides and bottom (deglazing), then pouring all of this into the chickpeas as well. Taste to adjust the salt (you will likely want to add up to another ½ teaspoon) and grind in a generous amount of black pepper to taste. At this point, if you choose, you can puree some of the chickpeas with an immersion blender.

4. Cover and let the soup simmer for another 10 minutes or so before serving.

OPTIONAL ENHANCEMENTS

A few strands of saffron added to the cooking water in step 1 ❋ A spoonful of harissa ❋ Touches of torn fresh flat-leaf parsley, cilantro, or mint ❋ Crushed red pepper ❋ Olive Oil Toasts (see page 409) ❋ A poached or fried egg added to each serving ❋ A drizzle of high-quality extra-virgin olive oil (or a citrus-spiked olive oil) ❋ Cooked diced carrot mixed in ❋ A spoonful of thick yogurt on top ❋ A sprinkling of capers on top ❋ A spoonful or two of cooked brown basmati rice or couscous stirred in ❋ A spoonful of Browned Potatoes and Onion (page 391) ❋ Chopped, pitted olives on top—or a bowl of assorted olives on the side ❋ Crisp, cold radishes on the side—whole or sliced ❋ Chopped or slivered Marcona almonds ❋ Sliced ripe tomatoes on the side

Fresh Corn Soup

MAKES 4 OR 5 SERVINGS ❄ VEGAN (WHEN MADE WITH OIL)

Save this one for the heart of corn season and make it only with the freshest, most recently harvested corn you can get your hands on. It will reward you with a taste memory that will carry forward from year to year. This soup can be served plain, yet it also works beautifully as host to the many Optional Enhancements listed below.

❄ For easiest corn shucking (for cooked dishes), zap the ears for 4 to 6 minutes in a microwave, then wear oven mitts to carefully remove them. Slice off and discard about an inch from the tip, and shake/squeeze the cob from the husks and silk. It will slip right out, miraculously clean.

❄ You have the option of using all butter or all olive oil or some of each.

❄ For enhanced corn flavor, consider adding the shucked cobs to the soup as it simmers.

❄ Be sure to use an immersion blender or a stand blender, not a food processor, to puree the soup. A processor won't get it fine enough.

2 tablespoons unsalted butter, or half olive oil and half butter, or all olive oil

1½ cups minced onion (1 medium)

Up to 1 teaspoon salt

Kernels from 4 freshly shucked ears of corn (about 4 cups), corncobs reserved if desired

4 cups water

1. Melt the butter or heat the olive oil in a soup pot, large saucepan, or Dutch oven over medium heat and swirl to coat the pan.

2. Stir in the onion and ½ teaspoon salt and cook, covered, stirring often, for 8 to 10 minutes, or until the onion becomes very soft. Cover the pot between stirrings to encourage the onion to sweat out its natural juices.

3. Stir in the corn and ¼ teaspoon salt, cover again, and cook for 5 minutes, stirring a few times. (Keep an eye out for any fibrous corn parts or strands of corn silk that you may have missed and pick them out as best you can.)

4. Add the water and increase the heat to medium-high until it reaches a boil. (You can add the corncobs, if using, now.) Turn the heat down to medium-low, cover, and let it cook slowly for another 8 to 10 minutes.

5. Fish out the cobs (if using) and use an immersion blender to puree the mixture to the desired consistency, or puree in batches in a stand blender. Pass it through a strainer with a mesh that is not too fine, pushing assertively with a wooden spoon to force most of the pulp through (ideally you will have very little in the strainer), and it will be velvety on the other side.

6. Return the soup to the pot and reheat gently. Taste for salt (I usually end up adding about ¼ teaspoon more) and serve hot—plain, or with Enhancements.

OPTIONAL ENHANCEMENTS

Lime wedges ❄ Additional fresh corn kernels ❄ A dab of Salsa Verde (page 357) ❄ A dab of Roasted Red Pepper Pesto (page 358) ❄ Sweet Corn and Blueberry Saladita (page 383) on top or on the side ❄ A dot of crème fraîche ❄ Torn cilantro leaves ❄ A spoonful of Pea and Mint Pesto (page 257) ❄ Minced ripe tomato

Sweet Potato–Pear Soup

MAKES 4 OR 5 SERVINGS ❧ VEGAN (WHEN MADE WITH OIL)

People fall in love with this soup. I've witnessed this more than once, so I know it's not a fluke. Fresh pears and sweet potatoes are simmered with touches of cinnamon and white wine and pureed together. This unusual combination is slightly sweet, slightly tart, and deeply soothing. My original version (published in *Still Life with Menu*) included milk or cream, but when I revisited the recipe, the soup was so satisfying without the cream that I stopped right there. I think it's much better without the dairy—still plenty rich tasting and now vegan-friendly as well, if made with oil instead of butter.

❀ Be sure to use the moist, orange variety of sweet potato (not the drier, starchier white type).

❀ Add as much lemon or lime juice as you like, to offset the soup's sweetness.

2 medium orange sweet potatoes (1½ pounds)

4 cups water

1 3-inch cinnamon stick

1½ teaspoons salt

3 large ripe pears (any kind but Bosc, which are too grainy)

1 tablespoon unsalted butter or grapeseed or canola oil

¼ cup dry white wine

2 tablespoons fresh lemon or lime juice, or more to taste

Cayenne or white pepper (optional)

1. Peel the sweet potatoes and cut them into small (about ¾-inch) pieces. Place in a large saucepan with the water, cinnamon stick, and salt. Bring to a boil, cover, and simmer until tender, about 10 minutes. Remove the cover and let simmer an additional 5 minutes over medium heat. Remove and discard the cinnamon stick and let the sweet potatoes rest in their cooking water while you fix the pears.

2. Peel and core the pears and cut them into thin slices (about ¼ inch).

3. Melt the butter or heat the oil in a medium skillet over medium heat, then swirl to coat the pan. Add the pears and cook, stirring often, for about 5 minutes, or until quite soft. Add the wine, cover, and simmer for about 10 minutes longer over the lowest possible heat, until most of the wine is absorbed.

4. Add the pear mixture to the sweet potatoes. Use an immersion blender to puree the soup until smooth, or puree in batches in a stand blender.

5. Return the soup to the pot and reheat over low heat. Add the lemon or lime juice to taste, plus a touch of cayenne or white pepper, if desired, and serve hot.

OPTIONAL ENHANCEMENT

For a boldly colorful—and quite unexpected—topping, add a spoonful of Thick Cranberry-Orange Vinaigrette (page 368) or Beet, Orange, and Ginger Marmalade (page 374) to each serving.

Green Matzoh Ball Soup

MAKES 4 TO 6 SERVINGS (ABOUT 20 MEDIUM MATZOH BALLS)

Broccoli-flecked dumplings double-task as a Passover offering and an ode to Dr. Seuss. What could be bad?

Note to skeptics: Yes, indeed, it works incredibly well to add finely chopped broccoli to a standard matzoh ball mix. The taste is so subtle that you can slip these to people who think they don't like broccoli. They will be surprised, if you choose to disclose. Either way, welcome to an additional serving of vegetables where you least expect it.

❄ It's easiest to use a food processor fitted with the steel blade to mince the broccoli if you cut it into 1-inch pieces first. (It's even easier if you first spray the blade and the inside of the lid with nonstick spray.) This is a good way to get the pieces truly speck-tiny, which is the idea.

❄ The batter needs to be made at least 1 hour (can be up to a day or two) ahead.

❄ Use your favorite boxed stock for the broth or make your own (page 22).

4 large eggs

2 tablespoons grapeseed or canola oil

1 cup finely minced broccoli (trimmed, peeled stalks and florets)

1 cup matzoh meal

1 teaspoon salt

Black pepper (optional)

1½–2 quarts vegetable stock (page 22) or low-sodium store-bought

1. Break the eggs into a medium bowl and beat them with a whisk. When they are smooth, beat in the oil.

2. Add the broccoli, matzoh meal, and salt, and, if you like, some pepper to taste.

3. Cover the bowl with plastic wrap and let the batter firm up in the refrigerator for at least an hour.

4. Put on a large pot of water to boil. When it boils, reduce the heat to a simmer.

5. Meanwhile, form 1-inch balls with the matzoh batter, dampening the palms of your hands slightly so the batter doesn't stick. Gently slide the matzoh balls into the simmering water and let them cook, uncovered, for 40 to 45 minutes; they will almost double in size. If you plan to serve them the same day, leave them in the cooking water until serving time. (They won't overcook.) If you plan to serve them a few days later, drain them, then store in a tightly covered container in the refrigerator. Bring to room temperature before serving.

6. To serve, heat the stock to your desired temperature. Place several matzoh balls in each serving bowl and ladle in the hot stock. Serve pronto.

Roasted Cauliflower and Potatoes in Dark, Delicious Stock

MAKES 4 TO 6 SERVINGS ❈ VEGAN

Two very different cooking methods (high-temperature roasting and simmering over low heat) collaborate to bring you an old-fashioned bowl of deeply flavored, steaming stock filled with tender vegetables. The sum total of your labor adds up to cutting some vegetables, placing them here and there, and being intermittently present to guide them through. You can attend to other things in the meantime.

❈ The stock can be made days or weeks ahead, if you refrigerate or freeze it. All that remains is to roast some cauliflower, potatoes, and onion and put them in there.

❈ If you don't want to make the stock from scratch, you could use your favorite boxed variety.

2 tablespoons olive oil

1 batch Dark, Delicious Stock (page 37)

1 medium head cauliflower (about 2 pounds), trimmed

1 medium potato of any kind (about ½ pound), peeling optional

1 medium onion (about ½ pound), peeled

Salt and black pepper

1. Preheat the oven to 400°F, with a rack in the center position. Line a baking sheet with foil or parchment paper and coat it with the olive oil. (You can use a piece of vegetable to spread it around.) Have the stock in a large pot on the stove.

2. Cut all the vegetables into bite-sized pieces. Spread the pieces in a single layer on the baking sheet.

3. Roast for 30 to 40 minutes, or as long as it takes to get the vegetables fork-tender and golden. (About 15 minutes into the cooking, gently lift the foil or parchment from the corners and/or shake the baking sheet a few times to loosen the vegetables. This helps them cook fairly evenly without burning on the bottom.)

4. Meanwhile, heat the stock.

5. Remove the baking sheet from the oven and sprinkle the vegetables with a scant teaspoon of salt and a fair amount of black pepper. Wait a few minutes for any stuck pieces to come loose from the foil or parchment (a little bit of cooling helps this along), then use tongs to mix the vegetables gently, distributing the seasonings.

6. Transfer the vegetables to the hot stock, adjust the salt and pepper to taste, if needed, and serve.

OPTIONAL ENHANCEMENTS

Up to 2 tablespoons fresh lemon juice sprinkled onto the vegetables as they cool (or into the stock just before serving), and/or lemon wedges for garnish ❈ Up to 1½ teaspoons cumin seeds, roasted along with the vegetables ❈ Green peas (fresh steamed or frozen defrosted) on top ❈ Slow-Roasted Roma Tomatoes (page 393) placed artfully on top or included in the stock ❈ Additional roasted vegetables (your choice, see page 336) ❈ Swirls of sour cream (softened by stirring) across the top ❈ A touch of grated sharp cheddar sprinkled on top

Dark, Delicious Stock

MAKES 6 TO 8 CUPS ❧ VEGAN (WHEN MADE WITHOUT HALF-AND-HALF OR CREAM)

Sweet potato gently pulls the flavor in one direction, while earthy cremini mushrooms nudge it in another. They've somehow worked it out between them, as the result is harmonious—all about depth, rather than a tug-of-war. Well done, vegetables. We have more to learn from our edible plant friends than we might have realized.

❊ Bragg Liquid Aminos, found in natural food stores, is an all-purpose seasoning made from soy protein by Paul C. Bragg, an early health-food store entrepreneur and founder of Bragg Live Foods. Once in a while, I'll add the thin, mysterious elixir to a sauce, soup, or dressing, usually to a nice, umami-ish effect. It will keep forever in your cupboard. Over the decades, I think I've bought it exactly once. Same bottle, still there.

❊ The stock keeps for 3 to 4 days in the refrigerator and for up to a month in the freezer.

1 pound onions (2 medium), peeled and cut into chunks

1 pound sweet potatoes (2 medium), peeled and cut into chunks

½ pound russet potato (1 medium), peeled and cut into chunks

½ pound carrots (2 medium), peeled and cut into chunks

½ pound domestic mushrooms, wiped clean and thickly sliced

½ pound cremini mushrooms, wiped clean and thickly sliced

1 head garlic, peeled and quartered

10 cups water

1 teaspoon salt

Black pepper (optional)

Bragg Liquid Aminos (optional; see notes)

Half-and-half or heavy cream (optional)

1. Combine everything except the Bragg Liquid Aminos and half-and-half or cream, if using, in a very large soup pot. Partially cover and bring to a boil.

2. Lower the heat to medium and boil (not too raucously, but more than a simmer), partially covered, for about 30 minutes. Turn the heat as low as it goes, and simmer, partially covered, for another 30 minutes or so. (The longer it cooks, the more it reduces, so you'll have less, but it will be richer.)

3. Remove from the heat and let sit uncovered for 30 minutes longer. Strain into a second pot, pressing quite firmly on the vegetables, so they donate as much liquid as possible. Add a dash of Bragg Liquid Aminos, if desired, and enjoy plain, or as a basis for other soups.

4. Optional step: You can puree all or some of the pressed vegetables in a food processor, adding some salt, pepper, and if you like, a few tablespoons of half-and-half or cream. Some of this mixture can then be added back in to thicken and extend the stock. It can also be served as a Cozy Mash (see page 167).

Mushroom Wonton Soup

MAKES 6 TO 8 SERVINGS (ABOUT 3 DOZEN WONTONS) ❧ VEGAN

A labor of love. Actually not that much labor and a lot of love—and so worth it. You can use a box or two of your preferred store-bought stock (especially one that features soy and ginger), but I strongly recommend you make a batch of Ginger-Fennel Stock from scratch for an optimal experience. Once the stock is done (and this can happen even weeks ahead, if you have room in your freezer), the only additional step is to make and steam the wontons (also freezeable—see the note). After that, just place the steamed wontons in bowls and ladle in some hot stock and you're there.

❀ Round gyoza wrappers or square wonton wrappers can be found in the freezer section of Asian grocery stores, usually in 1-pound packages of about 50 wrappers each. Defrost the entire pack before taking out the ones you need. You can refreeze the extras, if repackaged airtight in a heavy zip-style plastic bag.

❀ Both the onion and the mushrooms need to be finely minced. Use an extremely sharp knife or a food processor to render them slightly larger than, say, a split pea.

❀ Once steamed, the wontons become beautifully translucent and quite sturdy and can be stored in a single layer on a lightly floured plate or two—uncovered, so they stay dry—for up to 3 days in the refrigerator.

❀ The wontons can also be frozen. Lightly spray a tray or plate with nonstick spray and arrange the wontons (steamed or not) in a single layer—possibly touching, but not overlapping. Freeze for about 15 minutes so they'll stay separate. When

they are firm, transfer them to a heavy zip-style plastic bag or a freezer-worthy container and store in the freezer for up to 3 weeks. No need to defrost before using.

❋ Freestanding wontons make a great dumpling-style appetizer, especially if crisped in hot oil after being steamed.

1 tablespoon grapeseed, canola, or peanut oil

½ cup finely minced onion

1 pound mushrooms, wiped clean, stemmed as necessary, and finely minced

½ teaspoon salt

1 tablespoon dry white wine or fresh lemon juice

½ teaspoon minced or crushed garlic

About 3 dozen 3-inch round gyoza wrappers or 3-inch square wonton wrappers, fully defrosted

Unbleached all-purpose flour, as needed, for storage

Nonstick cooking spray (optional)

1 batch Ginger-Fennel Stock (page 48) or up to 2 quarts (2 boxes) low-sodium store-bought vegetable stock

1. Place a medium skillet over medium heat for about a minute, then add the oil and swirl to coat the pan. Add the onion and cook, stirring, for about a minute. Stir in the mushrooms, salt, wine or lemon juice, and garlic. Turn up the heat to medium-high, and cook, stirring often, for about 10 minutes, or until most of the juices evaporate.

2. When the liquid is pretty much cooked off, remove the mushroom mixture with a slotted spoon, pressing out any remaining liquid, and transfer to a bowl. (Save any leftover mushroom juices for adding to the stock.)

3. Have the gyoza or wonton wrappers ready, along with a small bowl of water and a fork. To fill, lay a wrapper flat on a work surface. Place a heaping teaspoon of the mushroom filling in the center of the wrapper, then apply a little water to the edge with your finger or a pastry brush. Fold over, and crimp tightly but gently with the fork. (It will be a half circle with gyoza wrappers and a triangle if you're using wonton wrappers.) Be careful not to let the fork pierce the wrapper. If in doubt, just press it tightly closed with your fingers or the back of a small spoon.

4. Repeat until you've used all the filling. Store the finished wontons on a lightly floured dinner plate until you're ready to steam them. (If you are making these well ahead of time, keep them stored in a single layer and refrigerate, uncovered. It's important that they stay dry.)

5. To cook, lightly spray a steamer basket with nonstick spray, if you like, and then steam the wontons in batches (as many as will fit snugly in a single layer) for about 3 minutes over simmering water. Meanwhile, heat the stock. Add the wontons to serving bowls, pour hot stock on top, and serve.

Wild Rice Chili-Mango Soup

MAKES 5 OR 6 SERVINGS ✿ VEGAN (WHEN MADE WITHOUT HONEY)

Wild rice partners amazingly well with bright chunks of mango against a chili-laced backdrop. The interplay of sweet mangoes and pepper, bitter-ish wild rice, and sour citrus is what makes this so good.

✺ Red rice (Bhutanese or Wehani) can be substituted for the wild rice. Bhutanese takes about 20 minutes to cook, and Wehani requires about 40. (For more information, see page 198.)

✺ Frozen mango chunks work beautifully for this, and come in 1-pound bags—the exact amount the soup requires. If you have access to fresh mangoes and are willing to roll up your sleeves and extract their pulp, it is fine to do so. You'll likely need to begin with about 3 pounds fresh whole mangoes to end up with the necessary amount for the soup.

✺ If your soup turns out on the sweet side, don't skimp on the lemon or lime wedges at serving time. Make them chubby and squeezable.

✺ This soup benefits from some serious simmering. You can serve it right away or store it in the refrigerator for up to 5 days. It reheats very well, but does thicken during storage, so thin it with a little additional water or vegetable stock if you like. It's also OK to freeze it for up to 3 weeks.

½ cup wild rice

4 cups water

1 teaspoon salt, or more to taste

1–2 tablespoons olive oil or grapeseed oil

1½ cups finely minced onion (1 medium)

1 tablespoon chili powder (plus up to 1 teaspoon each of other chili powders, if desired; see note, page 46)

1 teaspoon dried thyme

1½ tablespoons minced or crushed garlic

1 medium red bell pepper, minced

1 small poblano or Anaheim chili, minced (optional)

1 pound frozen mango chunks, chopped while still frozen into tiny dice, or 3 pounds fresh mangoes, pitted, peeled, and diced

3 cups water or vegetable stock (page 22) or low-sodium store-bought (possibly more)

Up to 2 tablespoons fresh lemon or lime juice (optional)

Light-colored honey (optional)

Black pepper

Crushed red pepper

Lemon or lime wedges (optional)

1. Combine the wild rice, 4 cups water, and ½ teaspoon of the salt in a soup pot, large saucepan, or Dutch oven and bring to a boil. Lower the heat to a very low simmer, cover, and cook until the wild rice is soft, about 45 to 50 minutes. (If some water remains in the bottom of the pot, no worries. Simply include it in the soup.)

2. Meanwhile, place a medium skillet over medium heat for about a minute, then add 1 tablespoon of the oil and swirl to coat the pan. Add the onion, chili powder(s), and thyme and cook, stirring often, for 5 minutes.

3. Stir in ½ teaspoon salt, the garlic, bell pepper, and fresh chili, if using. Turn the heat to medium-low and continue to sauté for another 10 minutes or so, or until the vegetables become very soft. (You may add up to 1 tablespoon more oil, if it seems necessary.)

4. When the rice is very tender and the vegetables are very soft, add the vegetables to the rice, along with the mango and the 3 cups water or stock. (Scrape in all the vegetable bits that might have adhered to the pan, pouring in some of the water or stock and scraping them up with a wooden spoon to get them all included.)

5. Bring the soup to a boil, lower the heat to a simmer, and cook very slowly for about 15 minutes, partially covered, with a heat diffuser, if you have one, underneath to keep the simmer very gentle.

6. Taste to see if you'd like to add some lemon or lime juice, then taste to see if it needs more salt. (Conversely, if the soup seems too tart due to contrarian mangoes, you might want to add a little honey.) Sprinkle in generous amounts of black pepper and crushed red pepper to taste, and serve hot, with lemon or lime wedges on the side, if you like.

OPTIONAL ENHANCEMENT

Add some cooked red or white beans (to make it more of a stew), several tablespoons per serving

Hot-Sweet-Sour Soup with Tofu and Pineapple

MAKES 4 OR 5 SERVINGS ❋ VEGAN

Spicy, and in equal parts sweet and sour, this is about as refreshing as a hot dish can be. It's a good last-minute-ish soup that can be made in less than an hour. After the initial cooking of the aromatic vegetables, garlic, and chili paste, it requires very little simmering.

❋ For the chili paste, I use Lee Kum Kee Chili Black Bean Sauce. You can use any Chinese type: There are many to choose from.

❋ The fresh pineapple needs to be cut ahead of time so it can express its wonderful juices (all of which will become part of the soup). One medium pineapple should yield the 2 cups you'll need for this recipe. Be sure to remove all the skin, so there will be nothing sharp remaining on the fruit. In a pinch, you can just open a can of pineapple chunks (packed in juice, not syrup). No need to drain: Just dump in the entire contents.

❋ Thai basil is ideal, but regular basil works just fine. Since bunches of Thai basil tend to be smaller than those of regular basil, you can increase to 2 bunches if using Thai.

❋ Don't cook the vegetables until soft. Keeping a slight crunch in there makes all the difference.

1 tablespoon grapeseed, canola, or peanut oil

2 cups chopped onion (½-inch pieces; 1 large onion)

2 tablespoons chili paste or black bean chili paste, or more to taste

1 large carrot, sliced or in bite-sized chunks

1 celery stalk, sliced on the diagonal

1 tablespoon minced or crushed garlic

1 teaspoon salt, or more to taste

½ medium red, yellow, or orange bell pepper, cut into 1-inch chunks

About 10 ripe cherry tomatoes, halved or quartered

2 cups chopped fresh pineapple (½-inch pieces)

6 medium domestic mushrooms (very tight and fresh), wiped clean and quartered (stems OK if trimmed)

1 medium bunch fresh basil (Thai or regular)

4 cups water or vegetable stock (page 22) or low-sodium store-bought

½ pound very firm tofu, cut into ¾-inch cubes

2 tablespoons light brown sugar

1 teaspoon soy sauce

1. Place a soup pot, large saucepan, or Dutch oven over medium heat for about a minute, then add the oil and swirl to coat the pan. Add the onion and cook over medium-high heat for 2 to 3 minutes, until the onion is shiny and beginning to soften. Stir in the chili paste, cook for another minute or so, then add the carrot, celery, garlic, and ½ teaspoon of the salt. Stir to combine, turn the heat to medium, and continue to cook for 2 to 3 minutes, until the vegetables are shiny and coated. Turn the heat to low, cover the pan, and let it cook for 5 minutes. The vegetables should be tender but not mushy.

2. Stir in the bell pepper, tomatoes, pineapple, mushrooms, and remaining ½ teaspoon salt. Cover again and cook for another 5 minutes.

3. Meanwhile, pull off 25 to 30 basil leaves from the stems. Tear them in half if they're large.

4. Add the water or stock, basil leaves, and tofu to the vegetables. Bring to a boil, lower the heat to a simmer, then cover and cook for 5 minutes. Stir in the sugar and soy sauce, taste, and adjust the salt and chili paste if needed.

5. Garnish with a few additional fresh basil leaves (torn, if large) in each bowl and serve.

OPTIONAL ENHANCEMENTS

Lemon wedges ❈ Sliced water chestnuts (fresh ones, if you're lucky, but canned are OK) ❈ Very crisp, fresh mung bean sprouts (a handful added to each bowlful upon serving) ❈ Orange sections, removed from their membranes (see page 128), and/or strands of orange zest stirred in right before serving

Tomato-Coconut Soup with Indian Spices

MAKES 5 OR 6 SERVINGS ❋ VEGAN (WHEN MADE WITH BROWN SUGAR OR AGAVE NECTAR)

Coconut and tomato go together so well that I'm surprised they're not combined more often. The soup is subtle and embracing—and not as obviously coconutty as you might think. It's a wonderful vegan take on cream of tomato.

1 tablespoon grapeseed, canola, peanut, or coconut oil

1½ cups minced onion (1 medium)

1½ teaspoons cumin seeds

½ teaspoon *each* ground coriander, turmeric, and ground fennel

¼ teaspoon ground cardamom

⅛ teaspoon ground cloves or ground allspice

1 heaping tablespoon finely minced fresh ginger

2 teaspoons minced or crushed garlic

¾ teaspoon salt, or more to taste

2 cups water

1 28-ounce can plum tomatoes or crushed or diced tomatoes

1 14- to 15-ounce can reduced-fat coconut milk

1 tablespoon brown sugar, light-colored honey, or agave nectar

1–2 tablespoons fresh lemon juice

Black pepper

1. Place a soup pot, large saucepan, or Dutch oven over medium heat for about a minute, then add the oil and swirl to coat the pan. Add the onion and cumin seeds and cook, stirring, for 2 to 3 minutes, until the onion is shiny and beginning to soften and the cumin seeds become fragrant.

2. Stir in the remaining spices, plus the ginger, garlic, and ½ teaspoon of the salt. Turn the heat to medium-low, and cook, stirring frequently, for 5 minutes.

3. Add the water and the remaining ¼ teaspoon salt, scraping up any bits that might have begun to adhere to the bottom of the pan. Bring to a boil, lower the heat to a simmer, cover, and cook for another 5 minutes.

4. If using whole tomatoes, use scissors to break them up. Add the tomatoes and their juice, coconut milk, and sweetener, stirring to blend. Bring it back to a boil, lower the heat to a simmer, cover, and cook for 5 minutes longer. Remove from heat and let the soup cool.

5. If you've used crushed or diced tomatoes and you like the consistency of the soup as is, you can skip this step: Use an immersion blender to puree the mixture to the desired consistency, or puree in batches in a stand blender. Return the soup to the pot, if necessary, and reheat gently.

6. Stir in 1 tablespoon lemon juice as the soup heats. When it reaches the preferred temperature, taste to see if it could use more lemon juice or salt. Season to taste with black pepper and serve.

OPTIONAL ENHANCEMENTS

Fresh mint (minced or cut into thin strips) on top ❋ A touch of heat (chili oil, mustard pickles or other hot Indian pickles, hot sauce, crushed red pepper, etc.) ❋ Lightly toasted unsweetened coconut sprinkled onto each serving ❋ Minced crystallized ginger on top ❋ Lemon zest (grated or in long strands) ❋ A spoonful of yogurt or drizzle of buttermilk

Spinach-Basmati Soup with Yogurt

MAKES 5 OR 6 SERVINGS

Soothing and thick, tart, lightly spiced, and golden-hued, this is the soup to turn to when you need some calm. All will make sense for a moment when you sit down with this bowlful, and you will come away feeling truly well fed. You'll need little else to call this a meal.

❋ You can cook the rice well ahead of time (see page 189). Once it is ready, this dish comes together quickly and can be served as soon as it's assembled. And you can just as easily store it in the refrigerator and reheat (gently) later. It should keep very well for several days and will thicken as it sits. If you like, you can thin the leftovers with water or stock.

2 tablespoons olive oil

2 cups minced onion (1 large)

1 teaspoon ground cumin

½ teaspoon turmeric

¾ teaspoon salt, or more to taste

1 tablespoon minced or crushed garlic

½ pound (or more) fresh spinach, washed, stemmed, and coarsely chopped

3 cups water or vegetable stock (page 22) or low-sodium store-bought

1 cup cooked brown basmati rice

1 cup plain yogurt, at room temperature

Black pepper

1. Place a soup pot or Dutch oven over medium heat for about a minute, then add the olive oil and swirl to coat the pan. Add the onion, cumin, turmeric, and ¼ teaspoon of the salt and cook, stirring, for 5 to 8 minutes, or until the onion becomes soft. Add the garlic and another ¼ teaspoon of the salt, reduce the heat to low, and continue to cook for another 5 minutes or so. Toss in the spinach plus the remaining ¼ teaspoon salt. Stir, then cover and cook over medium-low heat for 5 minutes longer.

2. Add the water or stock, bring to a boil, then lower the heat to a simmer. Cover and cook over the lowest possible heat for 10 minutes.

3. Turn off the heat and stir in the rice and yogurt. Taste to adjust the salt and add black pepper to your liking. It's now ready to serve.

OPTIONAL ENHANCEMENTS

A light scattering of golden raisins ❋ A spoonful of harissa or Fire-Roasted Bell Pepper Saladita (page 380) ❋ Crunchy Chickpea Crumble (page 403), on the side or sprinkled on top ❋ A sprinkling of lightly toasted chopped walnuts or pine nuts ❋ Minced fresh mint

Tortilla Soup

MAKES 5 OR 6 SERVINGS ❧ VEGAN (WHEN MADE WITHOUT CHEESE)

Brick-red broth—spiked just right with chili and spice—provides a setting for playfully dueling textures: tender avocado, chewy-crisp corn tortilla strips, and if you like, melted cheese. If you choose the optional pumpkin seed and fresh corn Enhancements, it becomes even livelier.

This soup is worthy of real tortillas (as are you), so please don't shortcut with chips out of a bag. There is nothing like the texture of freshly pan-crisped tortillas, still warm and slightly chewy. Prepare them at the last minute, as the soup sits, the avocado bathes in fresh lime juice, and your dinner guests sip their margaritas in anticipation. The assembly that follows can be a hands-on, make-your-own activity that everyone will appreciate, especially if you set up all the Enhancements on the table.

❀ Various brands of chili powder differ, so find and adopt your own favorite. Depending upon your palate, you could go beyond this to a hotter and possibly even smoky realm by adding a touch of New Mexico chili powder (ground dried New Mexico chilies) and/or chipotle chili powder (ground dried smoked jalapeños) when you add the regular chili powder.

❀ The canned tomatoes can be the "fire-roasted" kind. (The soup will be smokier and possibly hotter if you use the kind with added chilies.)

2 tablespoons olive oil

1½ cups minced onion (1 medium)

3 medium poblano and/or Anaheim chilies (about ¾ pound), seeded and minced

2 teaspoons chili powder

2 teaspoons ground cumin

Up to 1 teaspoon salt

1 tablespoon minced or crushed garlic

4 quarts vegetable stock (page 22) or low-sodium store-bought

1 28-ounce can diced tomatoes

Black pepper

Up to ¼ cup torn or minced cilantro (OK to include some of the thinner stems)

2 tablespoons fresh lime juice

1 medium ripe avocado

4 fresh corn tortillas

Nonstick cooking spray

1 cup grated Jack cheese (optional)

Crushed red pepper

1. Place a soup pot, large saucepan, or Dutch oven over medium heat for about a minute, then add the oil and swirl to coat the pan. Add the onion and cook, stirring, for 5 minutes. Add the chilies, chili powder, cumin, and ½ teaspoon salt. Sauté for 2 to 3 minutes, then stir in the garlic, cover, and cook for 8 to 10 minutes over medium-low heat, stirring often, until everything is very soft.

2. Add the stock and tomatoes and their juice. Bring to a boil, lower to a simmer, partially cover, and simmer for 10 minutes. Taste to adjust the salt and add some black pepper. At this point, you can leave the soup chunky or puree some or even all of it (an immersion blender does this most easily). Turn off the heat, toss in the cilantro, cover, and let stand while you prepare the avocado and tortillas.

3. Pour the fresh lime juice onto a medium plate with a rim. Peel and pit the avocado and slice it into the lime juice, swishing it around gently to coat.

4. Place a skillet of at least the same circumference as the tortillas over medium heat for about a minute. Spray both sides of each tortilla with nonstick spray and briefly heat each one on both sides until just this side of totally crisp. (The idea is to retain some chewiness.) Quickly remove from the pan and tear or cut with scissors into strips or randomly shaped pieces.

5. To serve, place a little cheese, if using, in each bowl, ladle in some soup, and top with avocado slices and the tortillas. Serve right away, topped with a light sprinkling of crushed red pepper.

OPTIONAL ENHANCEMENTS

A drizzle of sour cream, thinned by whisking slightly, or a dab of crème fraîche or Mexican crema ❋ Additional minced or torn cilantro leaves ❋ Toasted pepitas (pumpkin seeds) or Chili Pepitas (page 401) ❋ A scattering of fresh corn kernels, in season

Ginger-Fennel Stock

MAKES ABOUT 8 CUPS ❋ VEGAN

You can't help but feel peaceful sipping this. Medicinal in the best sense, it will also warm you internally, from all that ginger. A perfect environment for Mushroom Wontons (page 38), this is also a wonderful use for the orphaned top of a fennel bulb you might have recently shaved into a salad.

1–2 fennel tops (stalks and fronds—everything north of the bulb), coarsely chopped

1 medium tart apple, cored and sliced (peel is OK if organic)

1 pound onions (2 medium), peeled and cut into chunks

5–6 scallions, trimmed and cut into big pieces

6 medium (2-inch cap) shiitake mushrooms (about ¼ pound), wiped clean and sliced

6 thick slices fresh ginger, each about 2 inches long

4 large garlic cloves, halved (peeling optional)

1 teaspoon salt

10 cups water

1. Combine everything in a soup pot or Dutch oven and bring to a boil.

2. Lower the heat to a simmer, partially cover, and cook for 45 minutes to an hour. (Longer simmering will yield a more intense flavor, but less volume.)

3. Strain and serve with any or all of the Enhancements listed below or store in tightly covered containers in the refrigerator for 3 or 4 days or in the freezer for a month.

OPTIONAL ENHANCEMENTS

A few drops of soy sauce ❋ Up to 2 tablespoons mirin ❋ A drizzle of Chinese sesame oil ❋ Very thinly sliced scallions

Minty Melon-Lime Soup

MAKES 4 OR 5 SERVINGS ❧ VEGAN

The soup is all about the melon, so hold off on the project until you find a perfect specimen (warm hues on the skin; a telltale fragrance when you sniff the ends). It will be well worth the quest. Serve this on a warm day for any meal—even breakfast (my favorite).

❀ You will thank yourself for zesting the lime before juicing it.

1 large, perfectly ripe honeydew (orange or green), cantaloupe, or another sweet muskmelon, peeled, seeded, and cut into chunks (8 cups)

½ teaspoon lime zest

½ cup fresh lime juice (from about 4 limes), or more to taste

About 20 large fresh mint leaves

⅛ teaspoon salt

About ½ cup fresh blueberries (optional)

1. Place everything except the blueberries in a food processor or blender and puree until smooth. You will probably need to do this in several batches if you are using a stand blender. Alternatively, place everything in a deep bowl and puree with an immersion blender.

2. Refrigerate in a container with a tight-fitting lid until very cold, at least 1 hour.

3. Serve in bowls or in glasses, dotted with the blueberries, if desired.

Fresh Corn Gazpacho

MAKES 4 TO 6 SERVINGS ❋ VEGAN

August supper. Or lunch.

First stop, Pickled Red Onions (page 395). They're quickly assembled, but need at the very least an hour to pull themselves together. So if you don't already have some on hand, do that now.

Since you will be pulping them anyway, this is a great use for very sweet, in-season tomatoes that have gotten too soft for most other dishes. They're usually the last ones left in the bin, and thus easy to come by. If you shop at a farmers' market, you might be able to get them at a reduced price as "seconds." (You'll be doing the farmer a favor by taking them off his/her hands.)

❋ Sample the cucumbers before adding them, to be sure they're truly tasty. (I always buy a few extras, just in case one might be bitter.) This makes all the difference, as does a very good, fruity extra-virgin olive oil, so please use the best available.

❋ You can make this up to a day ahead, short of adding the corn. The corn should be shucked and added at the last possible minute so it will be maximally fresh and sweet.

2 pounds very ripe tomatoes

About 25 fresh basil leaves

2 tablespoons extra-virgin olive oil

1½ teaspoons cumin seeds

1 teaspoon minced or crushed garlic

2 small (6-inch) cucumbers (peeled if the skin is bitter)

1 medium very sweet red or orange bell pepper, halved and seeded

1 batch Pickled Red Onions (page 395)

½ teaspoon salt, or more to taste

1 tablespoon fresh lime juice, or more to taste

1–2 tablespoons finely minced jalapeño pepper (optional)

Black pepper

1–2 teaspoons agave nectar or sugar (optional)

Kernels from 2 freshly shucked ears of corn (about 2 cups)

Corn tortillas or tortilla chips (optional)

1. Wash your hands, roll up your sleeves, and have fun manually squeezing the tomatoes straight out of their skins into a large bowl. Discard the skins. Add the basil leaves.

2. Heat the olive oil in a very small skillet over low heat and toast the cumin seeds for a minute or two, until golden and fragrant. (Stay attentive, as they can burn quickly.)

3. Add the garlic and cook, stirring, for 30 seconds, then immediately remove the pan from the heat and scrape all the contents (including every last drop of the oil) into the tomatoes.

4. Cut 1 of the cucumbers and 1 of the bell pepper halves into chunks. Add these to the tomatoes, along with the pickled onions and all their liquid. Use an immersion blender to puree everything to your desired consistency, or puree in batches in a stand blender. Return the mixture to the bowl, if necessary.

5. Finely mince the remaining cucumber and bell pepper half, and stir these in, along with the ½ teaspoon salt, 1 tablespoon lime juice, the minced jalapeño (if desired), and a generous dose of black pepper. Taste to adjust the seasonings, adding more salt and possibly some sweetener or more lime juice, then cover the bowl tightly and chill. (*The soup can now be stored, covered and refrigerated, for up to 1 day until serving time.*)

6. Stir in the corn right before serving. Serve cold, topped with any number of the Enhancements, and possibly with some warmed corn tortillas or chips alongside.

OPTIONAL ENHANCEMENTS

An extra drizzle of high-quality extra-virgin olive oil ❋ Very sweet orange cherry tomatoes for color contrast, halved or quartered on top ❋ Ripe avocado, diced or sliced, or a dab of Avocado "Mayo" (page 373) ❋ Torn fresh flat-leaf parsley and/or cilantro leaves ❋ A spoonful of Salsa Verde (page 357) ❋ Toasted pepitas (pumpkin seeds) or Chili Pepitas (page 401) ❋ A dab of sour cream or Mexican crema ❋ Crumbled or grated feta or Mexican queso fresco on top

Cucumber-Melon-Peach Gazpacho

MAKES 4 OR 5 SERVINGS ❀ VEGAN (WHEN MADE WITH AGAVE NECTAR)

Dappled like a summer fruit version of a Seurat painting, this refreshing hot-weather special might come out slightly different each time, depending on the colors and flavors of your melon and peach.

Make sure to serve it very cold, for maximum effect. The assembled soup needs to sit in the refrigerator for at least 4 hours (and preferably overnight) to allow the flavors to deepen. So begin this project the day before you want to serve it.

❀ Choose a perfectly ripe but still firm peach that is unabashedly fragrant. If it's a little on the soft side, that's fine. You can also substitute a nectarine, for a firmer texture. Make sure it's ripe and unblemished, with a little give and some aroma.

❀ I always like to buy several cucumbers as an insurance policy against bitterness. Be sure to taste before adding, because a bitter one can wreck everything.

❀ Make the Minty Melon-Lime Soup in advance. Also get the Pickled Onions going well ahead of time, and you'll be well on your way.

❀ After the soup is thoroughly chilled, you can more effectively taste for lime, sweetness, and vinegar. The lime, especially, needs time. It's the interplay among all these sweet-acidic components that gives this dish its sparkle.

1 batch Minty Melon-Lime Soup (page 49)

Heaping ¼ cup Pickled Red Onions (page 395)

1 large ripe peach, peeled, pitted, and cut into tiny dice or small, thin slices (OK if it mushes a little)

1 small (6-inch) cucumber (peeled if the skin is bitter), cut into tiny dice

Up to 2 tablespoons white wine vinegar

Lime zest and/or fresh lime juice (optional)

Agave nectar or light-colored honey (optional)

1. Place the Minty Melon-Lime Soup in a large bowl. Add the pickled onions (it's OK if some pickling liquid is included), plus the peach, cucumber, and 1 tablespoon vinegar.

2. Stir to combine, cover tightly, and refrigerate for at least 4 hours, but preferably overnight.

3. Taste to see if it needs more vinegar or lime zest or juice, if using. Add agave nectar or honey to taste, if desired. Serve cold.

OPTIONAL ENHANCEMENTS

Lime wedges or slices ❀ A very light scattering of finely minced jalapeño ❀ Tiny dice of firm, ripe avocado ❀ Additional melon (a contrasting color, such as cantaloupe or Sharlyn), diced ❀ Thin strips of fresh mint

Golden Mango-Nectarine Gazpacho (Ajo d'Oro)

MAKES 4 TO 6 SERVINGS ❀ VEGAN

I started out trying to create my own version of an *ajo blanco*—white, garlicky gazpacho made from pureed blanched almonds and bread. Many unsatisfactory tests later, I ended up deep-sixing the bread and almonds because I could not love their texture. Keeping the garlic and sherry vinegar, I then wandered off into golden fruit territory and deliciousness ensued.

❀ Choose smooth-surfaced nectarines, heavy for their size and smelling deeply of themselves. They should also give ever so slightly when gently squeezed.

❀ This is a good excuse to purchase a bottle of sherry vinegar, which is wonderfully potent and, when sniffed, leaves no room for doubt about its origin. The cider vinegar lends another acidic presence to push back nicely against the sweetness of the fruit.

❀ A very good olive oil makes all the difference here. This is the time to pull out that special bottle you've been saving or just use the best extra-virgin available.

❀ The soup will keep for about 5 days, tightly covered, in the refrigerator.

1 pound frozen mango chunks, not defrosted (see note, page 100), or 3 pounds fresh mangoes (3 or 4), pitted, peeled, and chopped

2 medium perfectly ripe nectarines, pitted and cut into chunks

1 teaspoon minced or crushed garlic, or more to taste

¾ teaspoon salt, or more to taste

1 tablespoon fresh lime juice

2 tablespoons sherry vinegar

1 tablespoon cider vinegar

¼ cup high quality extra-virgin olive oil

Up to 4 cups cold water

1. Combine the mangoes, nectarines, garlic, ¼ teaspoon of the salt, the lime juice, and the vinegars in a food processor and process until uniformly blended.

2. Keep the machine running while you drizzle in the olive oil. When it's incorporated, transfer the mixture to a large bowl (ideally one with a tight-fitting lid).

3. Stir in cold water until the soup reaches your desired consistency, then adjust the salt, adding the remaining ½ teaspoon or more to taste. You can serve it now (especially if it's still quite cold from the frozen mangoes) or refrigerate it to let the flavors meld.

4. Serve cold, and seriously consider the following list of slightly unusual Enhancements.

OPTIONAL ENHANCEMENTS

A tiny drizzle of roasted almond oil ❀ Almond Oil Toasts (page 409) ❀ Very finely minced cucumber ❀ A touch of chopped or crumbled rosemary (fresh or dried) ❀ Marcona almonds—whole, on the side, or chopped and sprinkled on top ❀ Cooked beets of a contrasting color (pink or magenta)—peeled and sliced, minced, or grated

Ruby Gazpacho

MAKES 4 OR 5 SERVINGS ❦ VEGAN

This vermilion mix of watermelon, strawberries, tomatoes, pickled onions, and ginger will be even brighter if you get it started a good two days ahead, for maximum flavor development. Each component is made separately and deepens on its own before blending with the others. The final combination then benefits greatly from another spell of absorption as it sits in the refrigerator getting better and better. Once you get the hang of this, you will want to make it again.

❀ This recipe looks long and complicated at first glance, but as you read through (and please do), you will see that it is actually very straightforward—mostly about time and bowls and refrigerator space, and just a bit of advance planning.

❀ You will need four bowls with tops. (A stacking Pyrex set will come in very handy; a good, strong plastic wrap will also work.) Finally, you'll need one big bowl for the ultimate combination of all the separate components.

❀ This is a very good opportunity for extremely ripe tomatoes too soft for other uses.

GARNISH

Pickled Red Onions (page 395)

Make these well ahead of time. If possible, use white balsamic vinegar, to keep the color bright.

WATERMELON

4 cups seeded watermelon chunks

1 tablespoon finely minced fresh ginger

2 tablespoons fresh lime juice

Combine in a bowl. Cover and refrigerate for at least 1 hour, but ideally overnight.

TOMATOES

1½ cups mushed (skins OK) very ripe, sweet tomatoes (from about 1 pound tomatoes)

1 tablespoon balsamic vinegar

¼ teaspoon salt

¼ teaspoon agave nectar or sugar

Combine in a bowl. Cover and refrigerate for at least 1 hour, but ideally overnight.

STRAWBERRIES

Generous 1½ cups hulled and chopped strawberries (from 1 pound strawberries)

1 tablespoon balsamic vinegar

Up to 2 teaspoons agave nectar or sugar (depending on strawberry sweetness and your taste)

Combine in a bowl. Cover and refrigerate for at least 1 hour, but ideally overnight.

ASSEMBLY

1. Combine the watermelon, tomato, and strawberry mixtures in a large bowl. Add a generous ¼ cup of the pickled onions (it's OK if some liquid is included).

2. Use an immersion blender to puree all or most of the soup, or puree in batches in a stand blender. Cover again and refrigerate for at least another 4 hours, but ideally overnight.

3. Taste to adjust the lime, vinegar, salt, and/or sweetness. Serve cold, with any of the suggested Enhancements listed below, if desired.

OPTIONAL ENHANCEMENTS

Additional Pickled Red Onions heaped on top ❈ Thin strips of fresh basil ❈ Minced crystallized ginger ❈ A drizzle of very fruity extra-virgin olive oil ❈ Lime wedges ❈ Jicama as swizzle sticks

SALADS

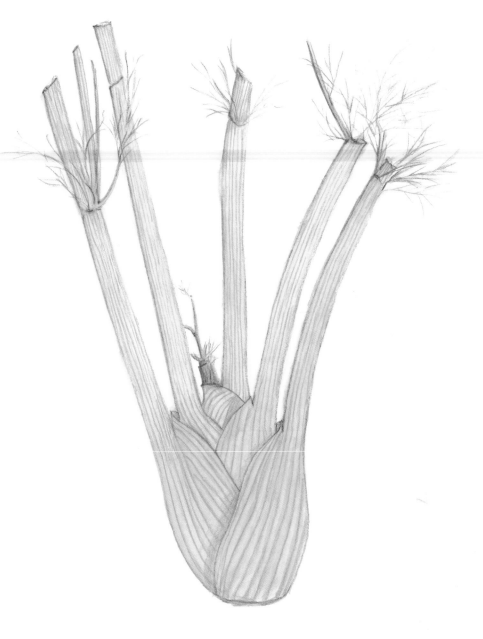

[continues]

RICE AND GRAIN SALADS

PASTA AND NOODLE SALADS

※ ※ ※

Is salad a main course? Side dish? Appetizer? Topping? Palate cleanser? First, second, third course? Snack? Team player on a platter? The answer, of course, is all of the above.

What's the definition of a salad?

Mostly it's served cold, but not always.

Mostly it's a combination of vegetables in dressing, but not always.

Leftover vegetables, grains, noodles, or beans—splashed with some vinaigrette—can be a salad. So can any arrangement of vegetables on a platter or in a bowl, lightly coated with some unifying sauce and served at room temperature as a starter (or finisher).

To me, the difference between a salad and a "vegetable dish" is that a salad is *bright*—both in flavor and in color—and tends to be crunchier (except in the case of eggplant or Brussels sprouts, which should always be tender). So for "salad" purposes, I want to sparkle up the vegetable as much as possible, allowing it to be more colorful, acidic, and edgy, with all participating ingredients clear, distinguishable, and clean-tasting. Minimal cooking, if any (again, except with B. sprouts or eggplant), keeps it spunky, and fresh herbs will shine the light.

These recipes feature various treatments of bread, beans, grains, noodles, and vegetables. Many of them can (and some even should) be made in advance and marinated, then served as much as a day later. It's fun to group several on a platter, with some Olive Oil Toasts (page 409) tying it all together. Add some of the Saladitas or Meaningful Touches on pages 376 to 409, and call this meze (the Greek word for an assortment of small dishes that precede a meal). Pair any of these with a soup or stew that seems a balanced and compelling fit, and you've got dinner. Your creativity can be as engaged by decisions of what to serve with what as with inventing something from scratch, and the meal can be different every time.

Note that additional vinaigrettes can be found on pages 366 to 368, and the ones assigned to specific recipes in this chapter can be used on your own green salad creations.

Grated Carrot Salad

MAKES 4 SERVINGS ❋ VEGAN

Carrots shine here, in their sparsely but perfectly furnished happy place.

❋ Peak-of-summer farmers' market carrots are the way to go, specimens so fresh and newly dug, you can pretty much peel them with a few flicks of a fingernail, and so carrot-fragrant that you could track them down with your eyes closed. That said, you can make this in any season with the best and sweetest carrots you can find.

❋ A good olive oil makes all the difference.

❋ This will keep surprisingly well for several days in a tightly covered container in the refrigerator.

1½ pounds very sweet (and if possible, colorful) carrots, peeled and coarsely grated

2–3 tablespoons extra-virgin olive oil

1–2 tablespoons fresh lemon juice, or more to taste

¼ teaspoon salt (optional)

1. Combine everything in a bowl and toss to thoroughly blend.

2. Serve right away or cover tightly and chill. Serve cold or at cool room temperature.

OPTIONAL ENHANCEMENTS

Finely minced fresh flat-leaf parsley ❋ A spoonful of Greek yogurt on top ❋ A light sprinkling of dried fruit (pick one: cranberries, sliced sour cherries, golden raisins) ❋ Slices of kiwi on top ❋ Minced or grated green apple mixed in, with peels left on for color ❋ Toasted nuts on top

Asian Slaw

MAKES 3 OR 4 SERVINGS ❋ VEGAN

Once you bond with this recipe, make it your own, with (m)any of the suggestions for Enhancements. The levels of ginger, sweet, and tart are negotiable per your palate. The ginger can intensify as the salad sits, so take this into account.

❋ As with most slaws, this comes together quickly, but needs some sitting time. It also keeps (and the flavor continues to deepen) for several days after it's made. However, any green vegetable(s) whose color you want at maximum glory should be added within 15 minutes of serving.

❋ See the note about cutting cabbage on page 64.

2 cups finely shredded purple and/or green cabbage (½ pound)

2 cups coarsely grated carrots (2 medium, about ½ pound)

4 scallions, whites finely minced, greens cut into very thin ovals (whites and greens kept separate)

1 small very sweet bell pepper, very thinly sliced

Up to 2 teaspoons finely minced fresh ginger

½ teaspoon salt

Up to 1 tablespoon agave nectar or sugar

Up to 4 tablespoons fresh lemon or lime juice

¼ pound snow peas

Cilantro leaves, torn or chopped (optional)

Roasted peanut oil or Chinese sesame oil

1. Combine the cabbage, carrots, scallion whites, bell pepper, 1 teaspoon of the ginger, and the salt in a bowl. Stir to blend, then cover and let sit at room temperature for an hour.

2. Whisk 2 teaspoons of the agave or sugar into 2 tablespoons of the lemon or lime juice and pour this into the vegetables, stirring to thoroughly combine. Cover again and let the slaw marinate for at least another hour in the refrigerator. At this point, taste to see if you'd like to increase the ginger, sweetener, or lemon/lime juice.

3. Trim the stem ends from the snow peas and use a very sharp knife to slice the pods into long, very thin strips. Stir these in just before serving, and top the slaw with the cilantro (if using), scallion greens, and a drizzle of oil.

OPTIONAL ENHANCEMENTS

Hijiki seaweed (about 1 ounce), soaked for 30 minutes in cold water—water squeezed out as much as possible (if choosing this option, reduce salt) ❁ A tuft of Egg "Noodles" (page 398) or Tofu "Noodles" (page 399) on top ❁ Thin strips of shiso leaves mixed in with the snow peas ❁ A scattering of lightly toasted peanuts ❁ A dab of Wasabi Mayonnaise (page 372) mixed in or on top ❁ Radishes, thinly sliced or in strips ❁ Orange sections or thinly sliced kumquats ❁ Minced fresh (or canned in juice, drained) pineapple ❁ Sliced lychees (canned, drained)

Peanut Coleslaw

MAKES 4 OR 5 SERVINGS ❧ VEGAN

The ever-popular savory peanut sauce extends its vegetable conquest to the humble cabbage salad with winning results. First, you tenderize the cabbage—ever so slightly—with dashes of salt, sugar, and vinegar. Next comes a velvety coating of softened peanut butter, followed by touches of carrot, cilantro (if you like it), and crushed red pepper for the requisite scattered smacks of heat. A final little blizzard of chopped, toasted peanuts provides a crunchy coating that will have everyone licking their plates and clamoring for a second batch.

❀ Use the least-processed, freshest-tasting peanut butter you can find. The salt measurement in the recipe is based on the creamy, lightly salted variety I use in my own kitchen. If you are making the recipe with unsalted peanut butter, adjust the seasoning accordingly.

❀ Slice the cabbage very thin, either by hand with a super-sharp knife or in a food processor with the thinnest slicing blade. Don't grate the cabbage, or it will get pulpy and the slaw will be more of a mash.

❀ As with all slaws, this packs down dramatically after it's combined. You can then put it into a smaller container, so it will take up less refrigerator space while it sits. The flavors will deepen, yet the cabbage will retain its texture. Hold off on adding the cilantro and chopped peanuts, though, until shortly before serving.

⅓ cup finely minced red onion

5 cups finely shredded green and/or purple cabbage (about 1¼ pounds)

1 teaspoon salt

2 tablespoons sugar

2 tablespoons cider vinegar

2 tablespoons peanut butter (lightly salted is OK)

½ teaspoon minced or crushed garlic

2 tablespoons hot water, or more if needed

1 large carrot, coarsely grated

Crushed red pepper

Cilantro leaves, torn or chopped (optional)

½ cup chopped lightly toasted peanuts

1. Put on a kettle of water to boil. Place the minced onion in a small colander in the sink. When the water boils, pour most of it over the onion and set aside. Reserve a couple of tablespoons of the hot water for step 3.

2. Place 4 cups of the cabbage in a very large bowl and sprinkle with the salt, sugar, and vinegar. Toss to coat (it will seem a bit cumbersome at first) and let it sit while you get other things ready.

3. Measure the peanut butter into a small bowl, then add the garlic and 2 tablespoons of the hot water. Mash with a spoon and then whisk smooth, adding a touch more hot water, as needed, to achieve the consistency of stirred sour cream.

4. Pour the peanut sauce onto the cabbage, add the onion, and toss with tongs or a fork until completely coated. Let it sit for 5 to 10 minutes, until it packs down enough to make room for the additional cup of cabbage and the grated carrot. Mix them in when that space appears.

5. Cover and refrigerate for at least 2 hours and up to overnight, allowing everything to slaw-ify and meld.

6. Shortly before serving, season to taste with the red pepper and stir in the cilantro (if using) and chopped peanuts.

OPTIONAL ENHANCEMENTS

Finely minced sweet bell pepper mixed in or clustered on top ✺ Strips of firm or baked tofu (or Tofu "Noodles," page 399) or Seitan Medallions (page 306), without their gravy and cut into strips, on top ✺ Chopped pineapple, sliced lychees, or orange sections (canned fruit is OK if it's well drained) ✺ Freshly cooked Browned Potatoes and Onion (page 391) on top (hot-on-cold is nice) ✺ Brown rice or noodles underneath

SLAWS BEYOND "COLE"

You might be surprised by the variety of vegetables that can be handily grated—or artfully cut—into a slaw. Add your improvised version to the side of a plate or the top of an open-face sandwich, or serve it as a delightful snack. (I often hand-grate a small slaw before cooking; it's become my favorite nosh while making dinner.)

THINGS THAT ARE NICE ABOUT MAKING A SLAW

- A slaw can (and actually should) be made ahead and refrigerated, as its flavor will develop as it sits (my impromptu dinner-cooking snack notwithstanding). This convenient fact renders last-minute salad flurry unnecessary.

- Because it's made ahead, you can put it together during cooler times of day in hot weather.

- When making a slaw, you don't need to fuss over proportions of dressing to vegetables, when to toss, or how much to add. You can largely wing it, as slaws are flexible and sturdy.

- Slaws can utilize bits and pieces of vegetables left over from other preparations: the other half of the carrot or cabbage, that wedge of red onion, or peeled broccoli stalks, which, it turns out, are perfect slaw material.

- A slaw is also a great place to experiment with esoteric vegetables about which you might be curious: rutabaga, kohlrabi, turnip, oddball radishes (such as daikon), and various colored beets that are possibly new to you.

- Apples mingle beautifully with vegetables in this format, especially organic green apples that you can leave unpeeled.

HERE IS THE GENERAL IDEA

3 pounds combined:

Cabbage	Parsnip
Carrot	Daikon or other radish
Rutabaga	Kohlrabi
Turnip	Broccoli stalk
Beet (any color)	Green apple

Keep the cabbage separate. Peel the vegetables but not the apple and then shove chunks down the feed tube of a food processor fitted with the medium or large grating attachment (or use a hand grater). The cabbage is best shredded with a supersharp knife or in a food processor with the thinest slicing blade. It gets mushy if grated.

TOSS IN

¾ teaspoon salt, or to taste

Up to 2 teaspoons agave nectar, light-colored honey, or sugar

2 tablespoons fresh lemon juice

A drizzle of extra-virgin olive oil (optional)

Now you have a basic slaw, which you can eat as is (today, tomorrow, or the next day). Makes about 6 cups (it packs down), plus the volume of any additions.

BEFORE SERVING, YOU CAN

Make it creamy with a touch of mayonnaise, yogurt, or crème fraîche ❋ Add minced red onion or Pickled Red Onions (page 395) ❋ Spruce it up with chopped pineapple or dried fruit, a speck of celery seed, and/or a sprinkling of toasted, chopped nuts

Kale Caesar

MAKES 2 TO 3 MODEST MAIN-DISH SERVINGS

Pile this high! It could well become a new favorite in your household.

The trick here is to cut the kale into very thin strips with a sharp knife. No rubbing or salting needed—just a fine, careful cutting job, a quick dressing, and you're there.

❋ Look for hyperfresh lacinato kale with smallish, very dark green leaves. Cutting the kale before washing and drying it helps it fit into your salad spinner. You can refrigerate the clean, dry kale (in the salad spinner, if your fridge has room) until shortly before serving.

❋ Make the dressing well in advance. It keeps at least 2 weeks in the refrigerator. You can also make the croutons ahead of time. Store them at room temperature in a cookie tin for a day or two or freeze for a month in a heavy zip-style plastic bag.

❋ Vegetarian Worcestershire sauce is pretty widely available these days. Look for it at Trader Joe's, in natural food stores, or online.

1 large or 2 small bunches very fresh lacinato kale (½ pound total)

Caesar Dressing, as needed (*recipe follows*)

Cheese-Topped Croutons (*recipe follows*) or Olive Oil Toasts (see page 409), in large bite-size pieces

Shredded Parmesan (optional)

Black pepper

1. Hold each kale leaf by the stem and use a sharp knife to release the leaf from the central stalk. Make a pile of the leaves, roll them tightly, and cut crosswise into superthin strips. Transfer to a large bowl of cold water and swish around to clean. Spin very dry, then transfer to a large bowl.

WHAT ABOUT THE STEMS?

For the larger green leaves (kale, collards), position your very sharp knife right up against the stem and slice off the leaf on either side. Discard the stems and chop the rest. That said, if the leaves are young and very small and the stem is barely developed, you can simply trim the very end of the stem (the part that extends below the leaf) and leave the rest.

The stems of baby spinach and feathery herbs (parsley, cilantro) are manageable, but if you don't want them, slice or tear them off. I tend to slice or pull off and discard the obvious big stems before beginning my chopping project, then I comb through with my hands as I go, sorting out and tossing away some or most of the smaller stems as I chop—if I want to. The tiniest final stems can stay. All of this is the judgment call of the cook (aka you), since, I reiterate, it's all edible.

With larger-leafed herbs, such as mint or basil, the big base stems should go, and smaller ones can stay. But if you're in the mood for precision and you have a sharp paring knife, you can go further and remove the skinny "handle" at the base of the leaves.

Arugula and watercress are the most confusing, as their stems are so central and integrated with the leaves. (And they're edible, too.) So I recommend you be loose and casual with these two, and just tear or chop the entire leaf, stem included, except for anything that seems too clunky to eat.

2. Just before serving, toss with all or some of the dressing (I use about 6 tablespoons), mixing very thoroughly until evenly coated. Add the croutons or toasts as you go, plus some Parmesan, if desired.

3. Heap onto plates and serve, passing around the pepper mill.

CAESAR DRESSING

MAKES ABOUT ¾ CUP

1 tablespoon fresh lemon juice

1 tablespoon Worcestershire sauce (see note)

1 tablespoon anchovy paste (optional)

1 teaspoon Dijon or any prepared mustard

¼ teaspoon minced or crushed garlic
(about ½ small clove)

⅛ teaspoon salt (optional if adding the anchovies)

2 tablespoons grated Parmesan

¼ cup extra-virgin olive oil

Up to 3 tablespoons mayonnaise

1. Combine the lemon juice, Worcestershire sauce, anchovy paste (if using), mustard, garlic, salt (if using), and Parmesan in a medium bowl.

2. Whisk until thoroughly combined, then continue whisking as you drizzle in the olive oil. When all the oil is incorporated, stir in the mayonnaise until completely blended.

3. Store in a tightly covered jar in the refrigerator until ready to use.

CHEESE-TOPPED CROUTONS

MAKES 12 CROUTONS (ABOUT 4 PER SERVING)

Use any kind of grating cheese with assertive flavor. This works well with day-old bread, so it's a great way to use up what's left of a baguette.

12 ½-inch slices cut on the diagonal from a baguette

Olive oil

½ cup (packed) grated cheese (about 2 ounces)

1. Preheat the oven or a toaster oven to 350°F, with a rack in the center position. Line a baking sheet with foil.

2. Lightly brush both sides of the bread slices with oil, then arrange them on the prepared sheet. Place the sheet in the oven for about 5 minutes, or until the bread is lightly toasted. (Keep an eye on it, so it doesn't burn.)

3. Remove the sheet from the oven and change the oven setting to broil. Divide the grated cheese evenly among the tops of the toasts, then broil for about 3 minutes, or until the cheese melts and just begins to turn brown. (Again, pay close attention.) Set aside to cool.

Grilled Bread and Kale Salad with Red Onions, Walnuts, and Figs

MAKES 1 MAIN-DISH SERVING IF IT'S ME EATING IT; 2 MAIN-DISH SERVINGS; OR UP TO 4 FIRST-COURSE OR SIDE SERVINGS FOR MOST PEOPLE

Fresh kale is wilted ever so slightly by tender-crisp, hot onions and glazed with reduced vinegar before being graced with freshly made croutons, shaved cheese, and perfect fresh figs. A single pan handles all the parts of this recipe that need heat, and the flavor that accumulates in there is absorbed by the bread as it toasts. The deliciousness builds, step by step, and the results are glorious. (My feelings about this dish are pretty much summed up in the yield estimate.)

❋ The ripeness of the figs is key. Make sure they are very soft when gently squeezed. If you can't find fresh figs, go ahead and use dried ones. Slice them first and then soak them in a little balsamic vinegar or lemon juice to soften them up. (Give this maceration a little extra time.)

❋ Try to get a bunch of lacinato kale with smallish, very deep green leaves, for a more tender result. Also, cutting the kale before washing and drying it ensures it will all fit into your salad spinner and become drier and crisper.

❋ Soak the figs and cut, wash, and dry the kale ahead of time, but plan to assemble the finished salad shortly before serving, as the perfect texture of the freshly grilled bread will not hold. (Store the prepared kale in the refrigerator—in the salad spinner, if your fridge has room.)

❋ Once the ingredients are ready, the final assembly will go quickly. (Open your windows in anticipation of step 8.)

❋ Tongs are a great utensil for stir-frying the kale, grilling the bread, and tossing the salad.

❋ You'll be pleased to know that no pan-washing is needed between steps.

5–6 ripe figs (see note)

1–2 tablespoons fresh lemon or lime juice

1 3-ounce piece Parmesan

1 loaf ciabatta or sourdough baguette (fresh or day-old)

1 large or 2 small bunches lacinato kale (½ pound total)

3 tablespoons olive oil

1 small red onion, cut in half and then into ¼-inch-thick slices

¼ teaspoon salt

2 tablespoons balsamic vinegar

½ cup chopped walnuts, lightly toasted

Black pepper

Lemon or lime wedges

1. Stem the figs and slice them lengthwise into about 5 wedges apiece. Place them in a medium dish and sprinkle with the lemon or lime juice. Toss gently to coat and set aside.

2. Shave strips of Parmesan from the block of cheese, using a sturdy vegetable peeler. Lovely cheese ribbons will ensue. Set aside.

3. Slice the bread into approximately a dozen thin (as in almost see-through) slices. Larger slices from a ciabatta can be halved for easier handling and consumption. Set aside.

[continues]

4. Hold each kale leaf by the stem and use a very sharp knife to release the leaf from the stem (it's OK to leave the narrow part of the stem that blends into the leaf farther up). Make a pile of the leaves, roll them up tightly, and cut crosswise into thin strips. Transfer to a large bowl of cold water and swish around to clean. Spin very dry and transfer to a large bowl. Set aside.

5. Place a large deep skillet over medium heat for about a minute. Add 2 tablespoons of the olive oil and swirl to coat the pan. Turn up the heat to medium-high and add the onion and ⅛ teaspoon of the salt. Cook, stirring and/or shaking the pan a little, for 2 to 3 minutes, until the onion becomes shiny and is still this side of tender.

6. Transfer the hot onion to the kale in the bowl and stir everything around a bit, then return the entire bowlful of kale-plus-onion to the pan. Stir-fry quickly—for just a minute or so—over medium-high heat until the kale turns an even deeper shade of green and wilts slightly.

7. Return it all to the bowl, tossing in the remaining ⅛ teaspoon salt. You can add some of the Parmesan ribbons at this point, if you'd like them to melt in slightly.

8. Remove the pan from the heat, wait a minute or two, then add the vinegar to the pan (stand back—it will sizzle), swirl it around, and pour what's left of it onto the kale. (It will mostly evaporate.)

9. Without bothering to clean the pan, return it to the stove over medium heat. Wait another minute, then add the remaining 1 tablespoon olive oil and swirl to coat the pan. Add the bread slices in a single layer and grill on each side until lightly golden and perfectly crisp.

10. Transfer the toasts to the kale, along with the figs and all their juice. Toss quickly (no need to get things uniform), adding the remaining cheese and walnuts as you go. Serve right away, passing a pepper mill and offering wedges of lemon or lime to be aimed straight at the figs.

OPTIONAL ENHANCEMENTS

Not a fig person? You can swap in a crisp fall apple, sliced thin and doused with lemon juice. ✳ Go in an entirely different direction and substitute slices or chunks of a very sweet, ripe heirloom tomato or a few handfuls of very sweet, ripe cherry tomatoes for the figs.

Crunchy Cucumbers and Red Onion with Fresh Cheese

MAKES 3 OR 4 SERVINGS (MORE, IF ADDING THE MELON)

Summer memories (past and freshly minted) are hereby delivered to you in the form of the world's most refreshing salad. It's all about the perfection of the cukes and the choice of cheese. Serve very cold to your most cherished people (or just to yourself).

✱ Seasoned rice vinegar is already lightly sweetened and salted. I like to add a little extra sweetener (agave nectar or sugar) to this dish, but that is optional, per your taste.

✱ Be sure to taste the cucumbers before they go in, to be sure they are very sweet.

✱ The cheese cubes get equal billing with the cucumber. If the cheese is crumbled, it will become part of the dressing, which is not what this recipe intends.

✱ The ideal refrigerated sitting time for this salad is 4 to 5 hours, but it keeps for up to 5 days, covered and refrigerated. The onion becomes brighter and more colorful as the salad sits.

✱ Strongly consider the melon suggestion in the Enhancements. So good!

¼ cup seasoned rice vinegar

Up to 2 teaspoons agave nectar or sugar (optional)

1 medium red onion, cut into ½-inch dice

4 small (6-inch) cucumbers (peeled if the skin is bitter), cut into ½-inch chunks

1 cup or more diced fresh cheese (Mexican queso fresco, ricotta salata, manouri, or feta)

Salt (optional)

Black pepper

1. Put on a kettle of water to boil.

2. Pour the vinegar into a medium bowl. Add the agave or sugar, if using, and stir until it dissolves.

3. Place the onion in a colander in the sink. When the water boils, pour it over the onion, then refresh the onion briefly in cold water and drain thoroughly. Transfer to the bowl and toss to coat, adding the cucumbers as you go.

4. Cover tightly and refrigerate for at least an hour, or for up to 5 days.

5. Shortly before serving, toss in the cheese gently, so as not to break the pieces. Season to taste with a little salt, if desired, and some pepper. Serve very cold.

OPTIONAL ENHANCEMENTS

Diced cantaloupe or watermelon (the same amount and size as the cucumbers, added when you toss in the cheese) ✱ Add lime juice to taste (a tablespoon or two) and serve with lime wedges ✱ Substitute Grilled Haloumi Cheese (page 406) for the fresh cheese for a chewier, smokier effect ✱ Toss in or on some almonds (blanched and lightly toasted or Marcona) just before serving ✱ Top with thin strips of fresh mint or basil or a sprig or two of rosemary ✱ For an A-plus presentation, spoon the salad into the seeded cavities of perfect, smallish cantaloupe halves

Feathered Fennel Variations

MAKES 4 SERVINGS

I can't think of anything cleaner tasting than crisp fennel shaved paper-thin on a mandoline. Dressed with just a drizzle of excellent olive oil, a sprinkling of fresh lemon juice, and pinches of salt and pepper, it becomes one of the most refreshing salads imaginable. Serve this freestanding as a first or in-between course, as an ethereal topping, or as a side dish.

In addition to being an engaging soloist, fennel loves the company of fruit, nuts, and cheese—and sometimes even a contrasting green to give it color, crunch, heft, pungency, and some sweet, juicy counterpunch. Once you've gotten the hang of shaving fennel, consider building this salad out. The possibilities are many.

SIMPLE SHAVED FENNEL
(The Basic Recipe)

❧ VEGAN

Choose a fennel bulb that is tight and smooth and ranges from white to light green, with no brown areas. Please use your best olive oil. Attention to these details will make all the difference.

2 medium fennel bulbs (1 pound)

2 tablespoons high-quality extra-virgin olive oil

¼ teaspoon salt

Pinch of finely ground black pepper

4 teaspoons fresh lemon juice

1. Remove the stalks and fronds from the fennel bulbs, saving some of the fronds for this salad and reserving the rest for another dish (pages 76 and 124).

2. Slice the bulbs paper thin on a mandoline or in a food processor fitted with a very thin, precise slicing blade. You can also try getting this effect with a very sharp knife. You should end up with about 4 packed cups.

3. Transfer the fennel to a medium bowl, drizzle with the olive oil, and sprinkle with the salt and pepper. Toss to coat, then cover tightly and refrigerate for at least an hour and up to a day. (Not longer, as it will start to fade.)

4. Shortly before serving, drizzle with the lemon juice. Serve cold or at cool room temperature, topped with a few of the most delicate fronds.

VARIATIONS

For each of these combinations, use 1 recipe of Simple Shaved Fennel as the base, and then artfully layer, place, and/or sprinkle the other ingredients around and on. (The contrasting salad greens, especially, can bring a light final touch.)

1.
Sliced grapes
Sliced or chopped almonds, lightly toasted
Shaved Parmesan (sheared from a solid piece of cheese with a sturdy vegetable peeler)
Chopped arugula

2.
Orange sections (blood oranges are especially nice), removed from membranes (see page 128)
Sliced olives
Sliced, pitted dried plums (aka prunes)
Thin strips of romaine hearts
Pickled Red Onions (page 395)

3.
Pink grapefruit sections, removed from membranes (see page 378)
Pomegranate seeds
Torn or chopped watercress

4.
Apple (unpeeled, cut into matchsticks), drizzled with a little extra lemon juice
Crumbled blue cheese
Chopped walnuts, lightly toasted
Thin strips of radicchio or minced Belgian endive

FIVE LITTLE SALADS

I am a big fan of little salads. The smaller, simpler scale takes the pressure off and allows you to light-heartedly toss a few ingredients together without it becoming a formal project.

1. MINIATURE TOSSED SALAD

Celery leaves combined with fresh flat-leaf parsley—slightly chopped or left whole—are wonderful tiny salad material. Dots of raisins and capers, plus a few drops each of olive oil and fresh lemon juice, make it a welcome punctuation to a dish or a meal.

2. FROND TUFT

An airy tumble of fennel fronds can be served as its own little dish or as a touch for another dish.

3. HERB TANGLE

A handful of very fresh green herbs jumbled together—on their own, or bound together by some crisp strips of lettuce and a splash of vinaigrette—qualifies as a small salad. An herb tangle can be served before or after a main dish or soup, as well as on top, as a final decorative touch. Choose herbs that match the flavors of whatever you're serving. Make sure the leaves are clean and dry, and tear (don't cut) them, so they'll stay green.

Candidates include cilantro, basil, thyme, mint, scallions or chives, and chervil. You can also add cress, microgreens, and tiny sprouts, available in higher-end produce departments.

Tiny amounts of olive oil, salt, and pepper are always welcome, but this is also very nice served plain in small amounts.

4. SHORTCUT MARINATED VEGETABLES

Drizzle leftover plain cooked vegetables with any vinaigrette (pages 366 to 368) up to several hours before serving, so the vegetables can marinate their way into a second act. Serve cold or at room temperature as a lunch main or first course for dinner.

5. WATERCRESS WITH EDIBLE BLOSSOMS

Surprisingly, many edible flowers are a peppery match for the spunky flavor of watercress. Take it to the edge with small strips of radish, add a tiny bit of vinaigrette, and sweeten the impact with a few slices of fresh fig, apple, or pear.

CRUDITÉ "CHIPS"

Crudités (raw vegetables taste so much better when called this) can be a real treat when served as a snack with a dip or as an appetizer. When serving vegetables raw, the cut is everything, so pay attention to how you prepare them and make sure they are appropriately thin and appetizing, so your guests won't be facing down intimidating chunks. To that effect, I often use a mandoline for shaving vegetables into wafers, then I store them in a bowl of water in the refrigerator for an hour or two. This allows them to crisp to the point of chipness, allowing for the most refreshing crunch when the vegetables are drained, patted dry, and served cold. I especially love doing this with root vegetables: beets (some of which sport target-like concentric circles of pigment on the inside), small turnips, carrots, and radishes. It's important that all your vegetables be newbies, freshly procured from a farmers' market or produce vendor that sells vegetables very recently harvested.

Radicchio Salad with Oranges and Pistachios

MAKES 4 SERVINGS

It was 1983 and I was on my first trip to Italy when I ordered a dinner salad at a Venetian restaurant, expecting the *insalata* to be, if not all, then mostly *verde*. Imagine my surprise, then, when the leaves turned out to be white-striped and deep magenta. I proceeded to take my introductory radicchio bite. Compellingly bitter, impeccably crisp and juicy—and fully enhanced by a generous coating of olive oil—it won my heart on the spot.

Here, romaine and arugula join forces with the radicchio, and an orange-laced yogurt dressing coats the leaves, allowing the pistachios to adhere at random. If you choose to put a bed of couscous or extra yogurt underneath each serving (see Optional Enhancements), you will be rewarded with a foundation that both absorbs the delicious juices and boosts the volume of the dish, herding it into light main-dish terrain.

These days, I grow radicchio in my garden. Once, before I had a chance to harvest it, one of the plants bolted into a frenzy of stunning blue flowers. I decorated the table with them before serving the salad.

❀ You can wash and spin the salad leaves and keep them cold and very dry, prepare the vinaigrette, and remove the orange sections from their membranes well ahead of time. Dress and finish the salad immediately before serving.

½ pound very fresh radicchio (any type), torn or chopped into bite-sized pieces

Handful of arugula, torn if the leaves are large

About 6 crisp romaine leaves, torn into bite-sized pieces

Yogurty Orange Vinaigrette (*recipe follows*)

2 oranges, sectioned, sections removed from membranes (see note, page 128)

½ cup lightly toasted pistachios

1. Wash the radicchio, arugula, and romaine, then spin them completely dry and transfer to a large bowl.

2. Add about 6 tablespoons of the vinaigrette, tossing as you go to thoroughly coat all the leaves. Add the orange sections toward the end, mixing them in gently so they don't break.

3. Sprinkle in the pistachios with the final toss and serve pronto.

YOGURTY ORANGE VINAIGRETTE

MAKES ABOUT ¾ CUP

This tangy dressing will keep very well for 2 weeks in a tightly covered container in the refrigerator. Shake well or stir from the bottom before using.

❀ If you plan to add the optional orange zest, grate the orange before juicing it.

1 heaping tablespoon finely minced shallot

Up to ½ teaspoon grated orange zest (optional)

1 teaspoon agave nectar or light-colored honey

3 tablespoons fresh orange juice

1 tablespoon cider vinegar

¼ heaping teaspoon salt

¼ cup extra-virgin olive oil

¼ cup plain Greek yogurt

1. Combine the shallot, orange zest (if using), agave or honey, orange juice, vinegar, and salt in a small bowl or jar with a lid and whisk to thoroughly blend. Keep whisking as you drizzle in the olive oil, keeping up the action until it is completely incorporated.

2. Whisk in the yogurt and mix until uniform. Cover and refrigerate until ready to use.

Olive Oil–Buttermilk Sherbet and Strawberries on Green Salad

MAKES 4 MODEST OR 5 MAIN-DISH SERVINGS

We think of sherbets as desserts, but when made with minimal sweetening, a sherbet can be a surprising (and wholly refreshing) topping for a salad. This one is made with olive oil and buttermilk, which churn into a delightful frozen texture in any ice cream machine.

Once the sherbet is made, the rest of this dish is straightforward. You dress some very fresh salad greens in vinaigrette and arrange them on a plate with a scoop of sherbet in the center and strawberries scattered over the top. It's a surprising, heat-busting lunch that will provide you with yet another reason to look forward to summer.

❋ If you can find some Little Gems lettuce, it is the nicest kind for this salad. Short of that, just use the freshest, crispest, most perfect leaf lettuce you can find.

❋ You can make both the sherbet and the vinaigrette up to a week ahead of assembling the salad. Assemble the finished dish immediately before serving.

❋ You will end up with a full quart of sherbet, far more than you'll need for one go-round of this salad. I have complete confidence that there will be encores, and the sherbet will keep for a month in your freezer. It may get a little icy, but just let it warm up for a while at room temperature (or in the refrigerator, if the weather is very hot) and it will smooth out.

Raspberry Vinaigrette (*recipe follows*)

1 pound very fresh salad greens, washed, thoroughly dried, chilled, and torn into bite-sized pieces

Olive Oil–Buttermilk Sherbet (*recipe follows*)

About 12 large, perfectly ripe strawberries (about ¾ pound), wiped clean, hulled, and thickly sliced

Light-colored honey (optional)

Black pepper

1. Put 1 to 2 tablespoons of the vinaigrette in a large salad bowl. Add half the salad greens and begin mixing by lifting them from the bottom (tongs work great). Continue adding the salad greens and tossing, drizzling in additional small amounts of the dressing until all the leaves are lightly coated. Divide the dressed greens among four or five salad plates.

2. Push the greens on each plate into a circle, creating wreaths of the leaves with round spaces in the center. Add a scoop of the sherbet to each center spot.

3. Arrange the strawberry slices on both the greens and the sherbet in any fashion that suits you. Drizzle with a little honey, if you like, and serve right away. Pass a pepper mill and enjoy.

RASPBERRY VINAIGRETTE

MAKES A GENEROUS ½ CUP ❧ VEGAN

1 tablespoon finely minced shallot

3 tablespoons raspberry vinegar

2 teaspoons agave nectar or sugar

Heaping ¼ teaspoon salt

6 tablespoons extra-virgin olive oil

1. Combine the shallot, vinegar, agave or sugar, and salt in a small bowl or a jar with a lid, and whisk until thoroughly combined.

2. Continue whisking as you drizzle in the olive oil. When it is incorporated, the dressing is ready to serve, or to be refrigerated until ready to use.

3. Immediately before using, shake well or stir from the bottom.

OLIVE OIL–BUTTERMILK SHERBET

MAKES A GENEROUS QUART

Read the manufacturer's instructions ahead of time, to see if the container of the ice cream machine needs to be frozen before you begin, and plan accordingly.

1 quart buttermilk

3 tablespoons extra-virgin olive oil

3 tablespoons agave nectar or light-colored honey, or more to taste

1. Whisk all the ingredients together until completely blended, then taste to adjust the agave or honey if necessary.

2. Pour the mixture into an ice cream machine and process according to the manufacturer's directions. Transfer to a container with a lid, leaving some room for the sherbet to expand as it freezes further, and freeze until ready to use.

3. Allow the sherbet to soften a bit before scooping out and serving.

Wilted Spinach Salad with Crispy Smoked Tofu, Grilled Onion, Croutons, and Tomatoes

MAKES 3 OR 4 MODEST MAIN-DISH SERVINGS ❦ VEGAN

I prefer to wilt spinach for salad, rather than serving it completely raw, as the leaves become softer and more responsive to the other ingredients. You don't actually cook the spinach for this, but rather heat the other ingredients and transfer them from the hot pan to the leaves. The spinach then wilts slightly on contact. For additional tenderness, you can pan-swish the spinach to tame it further. However you do it, this salad should be served immediately after assembly, allowing each element (especially the croutons) to remain articulate.

Sautéing the firm smoked tofu in hot oil makes it into respectable vegetarian bacon.

❧ There are many varieties of baked, seasoned tofu, of which smoked is one of the more common flavors. Some skew toward sweet, others to savory. Experiment until you find one you like. If you can't find smoked tofu, use firm, plain tofu and faux-smoke it yourself by sprinkling some smoked paprika or chipotle powder (½ teaspoon or more, to taste) into the hot oil before adding the tofu. And if you wish, you can take it all the way to Tofu "Bacon" (page 400).

❧ Even if the spinach comes "prewashed," I always wash it (again) myself and spin it dry. This makes it both cleaner and crisper. Discard any unappealing stems and comb through to delete any unfortunate leaves.

❧ Use an airy, lacy baguette, full of holes, for the croutons.

10 ounces spinach

3 tablespoons olive oil

4 ounces smoked tofu (see note), sliced into thin strips

½ medium red onion, cut into ¼-inch slices

Up to ¼ teaspoon salt

About 10 very thin (⅛-inch) slices baguette (fresh or day-old; sourdough or plain)

1 teaspoon champagne vinegar or white wine vinegar

Black pepper

Handful of very sweet cherry tomatoes, halved or quartered

1. Pick over, wash, and thoroughly dry the spinach, then place it in a large bowl. It will look voluminous, but will pack down dramatically when wilted.

2. Place a medium skillet over medium heat for about a minute. Add 2 tablespoons of the olive oil and swirl to coat the pan. When the oil is hot enough to sizzle a crumb of the tofu, toss in the strips, spreading them in a single layer. Keeping the heat at medium or maybe even a little bit higher, toss and cook the tofu for 8 to 10 minutes, or until crisp.

3. Add the onion slices to the tofu, sprinkle with salt, and keep the heat fairly strong. Cook for another 2 to 3 minutes, or until the onion is shiny and just beginning to soften, but remains mostly crunchy. When they are done to your liking, transfer the hot tofu and onion slices directly to the spinach. Pour in any excess oil

from the pan as well. Use tongs to distribute the hot ingredients through the spinach, then return the pan to the stove.

4. Add another tablespoon of the oil to the pan and swirl to coat. Throw in the bread slices, using tongs to distribute them so they lay flat in a single layer. Pan-toast for just a couple of minutes on each side, then add them to the spinach, mixing them in gently.

5. If you prefer the spinach more deeply wilted, return the pan to the turned-off stove and add some of the spinach, swishing it around to slightly cook the leaves further and also to sweep up and include every last drop of flavor in the pan.

6. Return the spinach to the bowl and toss again, this time adding the vinegar and some black pepper. Toss in the tomatoes at the last second and serve right away.

OPTIONAL ENHANCEMENTS

Hard-cooked egg, quartered, chopped, or grated ❋ Toasted pine nuts or chopped toasted almonds ❋ Minced jicama ❋ Chopped sweet red bell pepper ❋ Apple, swapped in for the tomatoes

Hazelnut–Wilted Frisée Salad with Sliced Pear

MAKES 4 SERVINGS ❀ VEGAN

Frisée is a delicate, slender chicory with an insistently spunky texture. It works well with the crunch of a good nut partner (hazelnuts being ideal) and also readily pairs with pears. Hence this easy salad, which is a winter favorite, compatible with a wide range of soups.

❀ Within a day or two of sitting at room temperature, pears can suddenly become overripe. Choose specimens that are smooth and firm, but not hard, and make sure they have no bruises, then let them ripen at room temperature out of direct sunlight. Check them every day (twice a day in hot weather) and use as soon as you can detect an aroma and the flesh near the stem yields a little when gently pressed.

❀ To skin hazelnuts, spread them out on a baking sheet and toast in a 300°F oven for about 10 minutes, shaking the pan once or twice during the process. Transfer them to a bed of cloth or paper towels and, when the nuts are cool enough to comfortably handle, rub them vigorously. Most (but not all) of the skins will detach.

❀ This semiwilted preparation is sturdy, so you can prepare it up to an hour in advance, short of adding the pears.

1 head frisée (about ½ pound)

3 tablespoons olive oil

½ cup coarsely chopped hazelnuts, skinning optional (see note)

¼ teaspoon minced or crushed garlic

¼ scant teaspoon salt

2 teaspoons white wine vinegar

¼ teaspoon sugar (optional)

2 tablespoons fresh lemon juice

1 perfectly ripe pear, any kind

Black pepper

1. Core the frisée, then pull apart the leaves, wash them, and spin until very dry. Chop into bite-sized pieces and transfer to a large bowl.

2. Heat the olive oil in a medium skillet over medium-low heat. When it is warm (not hot), add the nuts, garlic, and salt and stir to get everything coated with everything else. Cook, stirring, until the nuts give off a toasty aroma, 3 to 5 minutes.

3. Transfer the contents of the pan to the frisée, using tongs for easiest distribution, and using them to swish the pan with frisée to mop out more of the flavor and slightly wilt the leaves.

4. Add the vinegar to the pan and stir it around to pick up whatever might still be sticking. Scrape all of this into the salad and sprinkle in the sugar, if using. Toss again to blend as thoroughly as possible.

5. Drizzle the lemon juice onto a plate and slice the pear into the lemon juice, moving the slices around until they're coated. At this point, you can very gently toss the pear slices, along with some pepper, into the salad, or you can prepare individual plates of the salad, top each with pears, and pass the pepper mill. In either case, be sure to include all the lemon juice.

6. Serve as soon as you can after the pears are sliced and added.

OPTIONAL ENHANCEMENTS

Fresh mild cheese (feta, farmer, ricotta salata, Mexican queso fresco) crumbled in with the pears or spooned on top ❀ A drizzle of roasted hazelnut oil is a nice finishing touch

Salad Greens with Goat Cheese–Stuffed Piquillo Peppers

MAKES 4 MODEST MAIN-DISH SERVINGS (3 PEPPERS APIECE)

Scene-stealingly delicious, deep red packages make an impressive first course or lunch main.

And how easy are they? The stuffing is simply goat cheese, mashed straight from the package. The peppers come from a jar. Just fork out a few already-tasty little grill-marked red triangles. All that remains for you to do is push bits of cheese into the opening at the top of each pepper.

❁ Roasted piquillo peppers are available in many grocery and specialty stores. My favorite brand is DeLallo Grilled Piquillo Peppers.

❁ Take the cheese out of the refrigerator ahead of time, so it can become soft enough to easily maneuver.

❁ You can briefly heat the peppers in a hot, oil-slicked skillet just long enough to get the cheese slightly melted. Transfer them directly to the salad, which will wilt and tenderize slightly upon contact. Don't forget the toppings.

12 piquillo peppers (from a 12-ounce jar), thoroughly drained and patted dry

5 ounces soft, fresh goat cheese (herbed, peppered, or plain), at room temperature, mashed slightly

About 1 pound salad greens, cleaned, dried and chilled

Jalapeño-Cilantro-Lime Vinaigrette (page 367)

Up to 1 tablespoon extra-virgin olive oil (optional)

1. Hold open each pepper and use a teaspoon to carefully fill the cavity with approximately 1 heaping teaspoon of the softened goat cheese. You may need to help this along by shaking in the cheese, then softly squeezing it in, so it makes a perfect little packet. Serve right away at room temperature or chill and serve cold.

2. Just before serving, toss the salad greens with the vinaigrette. Drizzle with a little olive oil just before serving, if desired.

OPTIONAL ENHANCEMENTS

Avocado slices, plain or soaked in a little fresh lime juice ❁ Chili Pepitas (page 401) ❁ Dabs of Salsa Verde (page 357) ❁ A drizzle of softened (by stirring) sour cream or Mexican crema

Gazpacho Salad

MAKES 4 MODEST MAIN-DISH SERVINGS ❦ VEGAN (WHEN MADE WITH AGAVE NECTAR)

Traditional Andalusian gazpacho is a puree of salad ingredients and, sometimes, bread. In this interpretation, the vegetables are left chunky and the bread is brushed with olive oil and grilled into large croutons, thirsty for the delicious juices that will invariably collect on the bottoms of the plates. Thereafter, simply pick up the dish and drink what, if anything, remains. It's like a farmers' market cocktail—as intoxicating as any, in its own glorious little way.

❀ The first three steps have you making a quick, customized version of pickled red onions. Get them going at least 15 minutes ahead, as they need time to sit. You can also make the onions up to 2 days in advance. Cover and refrigerate.

❀ Sherry vinegar has a distinctive taste, leaving no ambiguity as to its origin, and makes a big difference. If you don't have any, it's OK to substitute red wine vinegar in this recipe.

❀ Taste the cucumber before it goes in, to be sure it is very sweet.

❀ The bread gets toasted or grilled shortly before you put together the salad. And once the salad is made, it's ready to serve. No chilling is involved.

1½ cups chopped red onion (½-inch pieces; 1 medium)

3 tablespoons sherry vinegar

1 tablespoon agave nectar or light-colored honey

½ teaspoon salt

2 small (6-inch) cucumbers (peeled if the skin is bitter), diced

½ pound perfectly ripe tomatoes, cored and cut into 1-inch chunks

1 medium sweet bell pepper (any color), diced

¼ cup extra-virgin olive oil

½ teaspoon cumin seeds

½ teaspoon minced or crushed garlic

4–6 average slices ciabatta or another artisan bread (about ⅓ pound), fresh or day-old

Black pepper

1. Put on a kettle of water to boil. Place the onion in a colander in the sink.

2. Meanwhile, combine the vinegar, agave or honey, and salt in a medium bowl and whisk to blend.

3. When the water boils, pour it over the onion. Rinse the onion in cold water, shake off the excess (not necessary to dry it), and add them to the vinegar mixture. Stir to coat, cover, and let sit for a minimum of 15 minutes, and ideally up to 1 hour or longer.

4. Combine the cucumbers, tomatoes, and bell pepper in a medium bowl.

5. Heat 1 tablespoon of the olive oil in a small skillet over medium-low heat and add the cumin seeds. Toss for a minute or two, until the seeds become fragrant. (Watch carefully, as they can burn in a matter of seconds.) Remove from the heat and stir in the garlic. Let it sit for about 30 seconds to absorb, then scrape all this mixture into the salad and mix well.

6. Shortly before serving, either toast the bread, brushing the toasted pieces with about 1 tablespoon of the olive oil, or brush the bread slices with the oil first and grill them lightly on both sides in an unoiled skillet over medium heat. (Watch them carefully, so they don't burn.)

7. After the bread is toasted or grilled, cut it into bite-sized pieces and toss them into the salad, along with the onion and all its liquid. Drizzle in the remaining 2 tablespoons olive oil, season to taste with black pepper, and serve right away.

OPTIONAL ENHANCEMENTS

Hard-cooked egg wedges ❋ Crumbled feta or manouri cheese or Grilled Haloumi Cheese (page 406) ❋ A dab of Almond Faux Aioli (page 356) on top ❋ Roasted almonds or Marcona almonds (rosemary-infused are even better) ❋ Roasted almond oil swapped in for some of the olive oil ❋ Olives ❋ Capers

Fattoush

MAKES 3 OR 4 MODEST MAIN-DISH SERVINGS AND IS EASILY MULTIPLIED
❧ VEGAN (WHEN MADE WITH AGAVE NECTAR OR SUGAR)

Pita toasts are broken into pieces and tossed with cucumbers, bell pepper, herbs, greens, and tomatoes in this vegetable-centric version of the well-loved Middle Eastern bread salad. Serve it with Lablabi (page 30) for a terrific soup and salad combo.

The traditional vinaigrette is flavored with sumac, a tart spice made from purple berries. You can find powdered sumac in Middle Eastern grocery stores or online. You can also substitute the more common za'atar spice mix, of which sumac is often the star component.

Purslane is often considered a weed, but it is succulent and nutritious and highly valued in Turkish and Mediterranean cuisines. If you can't find it, use romaine, and this will still taste fine.

❧ Pita chips can substitute for the freshly toasted pita bread. You can also use lavash (floppy flatbread), torn into bite-sized pieces and lightly toasted.

❧ The bulk of this salad needs to be marinated for about 2 hours. You can also make the vinaigrette well ahead.

❧ Taste the cucumbers before adding them to the salad, to be sure they are truly tasty and sweet.

❧ Give yourself a little extra time to remove enough leaves from a bunch of fresh mint to make a packed cup.

2 small (6-inch) cucumbers (peeled if the skin is bitter), diced

1 medium sweet bell pepper (any color), diced

1 pint sweet, small cherry tomatoes, halved if large (about 2 cups)

4 scallions, minced (whites and light greens)

2 large handfuls fresh flat-leaf parsley leaves and thin stems (1 packed cup), coarsely chopped

2 large handfuls fresh mint leaves (1 packed cup), whole or coarsely chopped

Sumac Vinaigrette (*recipe follows*)

Black pepper

1 medium head purslane (about ½ pound), sturdier stems removed, leaves and smaller stems coarsely chopped, or romaine hearts, cored and torn or chopped

2 whole-wheat pita breads (ideally thin-walled ones), lightly toasted and broken into large bite-sized pieces

Salt

1. Combine the cucumbers, bell pepper, tomatoes, scallions, and herbs in a shallow dish and toss with about 6 tablespoons of the dressing and black pepper to taste. Add the purslane (but not the romaine, if using) and toss to coat. Cover and let it sit for at least 30 minutes and up to 2 hours. (Refrigerate if the room is hot.)

2. About 30 minutes before serving, toss in the pita (and romaine, if using) and mix until thoroughly coated.

3. Taste and adjust the amount of vinaigrette if necessary, and add a light sprinkling of salt and pepper, if desired. Serve cold or at cool room temperature.

OPTIONAL ENHANCEMENTS

Put a few spoonfuls of Basic Tahini-Lemon Sauce (page 361) in the bottom of the bowl and build the salad on top, then stir it upward to coat ❋ A light sprinkling of toasted sunflower seeds, chopped almonds, or chopped walnuts ❋ A very light sprinkling of lightly toasted cumin seeds ❋ Crumbled feta or manouri cheese or a topping of Grilled Haloumi Cheese (page 406) ❋ Olives ❋ Other greens and herbs, such as arugula or cilantro, tossed in ❋ Crunchy Chickpea Crumble (page 403) on top or on the side

SUMAC VINAIGRETTE

MAKES ABOUT ¾ CUP ❋ VEGAN
(WHEN MADE WITH AGAVE NECTAR OR SUGAR)

This dwells at the refreshingly tart end of the salad dressing spectrum. Even if you add the full tablespoon of sweetener, it will still be delightfully puckery.

❋ Sumac is a pleasantly sour spice ground from the berries of a wild bush native to the Mediterranean. Look for packages of it in Middle Eastern food shops or in the spice section of well-stocked grocery stores.

❋ By "fresh tomato juice," I mean the juices left in the bottom of the bowl after freshly cut tomatoes have spent some time there. Make some on purpose, or just halve and squeeze a ripe tomato into a bowl. (It's fine—actually charming—if a few tomato seeds are included.)

1 teaspoon minced or crushed garlic

3 tablespoons fresh lemon juice

3 tablespoons fresh tomato juice (see note)

2 teaspoons sumac (see note)

½ teaspoon salt

Up to 1 tablespoon agave nectar, light-colored honey, or sugar

6 tablespoons extra-virgin olive oil

1. Combine the garlic, lemon juice, tomato juice, sumac, salt, and 2 teaspoons of the sweetener in a small bowl or a jar with a lid, and whisk to thoroughly blend.

2. Keep whisking as you drizzle in the olive oil. When the oil is incorporated, taste to see if you'd like to add the remaining 1 teaspoon sweetener.

3. Store tightly covered in the refrigerator. It will keep for a good 2 weeks. Shake and/or stir from the bottom before each use.

Peach Panzanella

MAKES 6 MODEST MAIN-DISH SERVINGS

A traditional panzanella ("little swamp" in a Tuscan dialect) is a bread salad with a lot of tomatoes, some olive oil, possible cucumbers, and other accoutrements. One of the better strategies for reconstituting stale bread, it is normally a pleasantly mushy affair, with yesterday's bread having absorbed today's tomato juices and olive oil.

This panzanella is different. Rather than being swampified, the bread is reincarnated as grilled toast and served on the side as an eager sop for an expanded cucumber salad graced with thick slices of summer peaches and vine-ripened tomatoes. The ingredients are so lovely and compelling that the table pretty much decorates itself. Give everyone a shallow soup bowl or rimmed plate, so individual servings can be customized. This is the best kind of summer party: a craft project and dinner all rolled into one.

About the peaches and tomatoes: They must be at their breathtaking best, because they are utterly exposed. And speaking of the best, remember that bottle of the highest-quality, fruity extra-virgin olive oil you've been saving for a special occasion? That would be now.

Make the cucumber salad at least 4 hours—and up to a day—ahead of time, for maximum flavor.

❀ After serving this, I sometimes have modest amounts of all the components (minus the bread) left over. I combine everything in one container, refrigerate it, and the next day, buzz it with my immersion blender. It comes out like a fabulous cross between a juice and a gazpacho.

1 recipe Crunchy Cucumbers and Red Onion with Fresh Cheese (page 73)

2–3 medium ripe heirloom tomatoes (about 1 pound)

2–3 medium perfectly ripe peaches or nectarines (about 1 pound)

Extra-virgin olive oil

5–6 thick slices ciabatta or another artisan bread (about ½ pound), fresh or day-old

1. At least 4 hours ahead of time, prepare the cucumber salad. You can add the cheese shortly before serving, as indicated, or keep it in a separate bowl to be part of the "assemble your own" experience at the table.

2. Thickly slice the tomatoes and peaches and layer them on a plate or a platter with a rim. Drizzle them with 2 to 3 tablespoons of olive oil and place the platter on the table, along with a cruet of olive oil for drizzling.

3. Arrange any or all of the Optional Enhancements on the table as well.

4. Have a basket or bowl ready and waiting for the bread. You can either toast the bread and brush the toasted pieces with 1 tablespoon olive oil, or brush them with the oil first and then grill them lightly on both sides in an unoiled skillet over medium heat. (Watch them carefully, so they don't burn.) Cut in half diagonally to make triangles, if desired, and bring the warm toasts to the table just as people are sitting down.

5. Pass everything around, letting each guest create his or her own customized bowl or plate. Have fun catching/sopping the dripping juices with the toasts as you all partake.

OPTIONAL ENHANCEMENTS

Drizzle with authentic Italian balsamic vinegar or with Balsamic Reduction (page 369) ✻ Top with fresh basil, cut into thin strips ✻ Garnish with sprigs of fresh rosemary (even nicer if flowering) ✻ Sprinkle on Marcona almonds (rosemary-infused are even better) ✻ Olives ✻ Black pepper

Gingered Asparagus with Soy Caramel

MAKES 6 SERVINGS ❈ VEGAN

Bright green lengths of lightly cooked asparagus luxuriate in ginger- and garlic-infused oil before being drizzled with elusive, dark, sweet Soy Caramel.

Effective marinating requires contact space—as horizontal as possible. To this end, use a shallow bowl or gratin dish that is a good fit for the volume of asparagus.

❈ Choose asparagus that's on the chubbier side for maximally satisfying texture.

❈ And for optimal beauty and tenderness, prepare the asparagus as follows: After you have snapped off and discarded the tough bottoms, shave the lower half (or so) of what remains by laying each piece on a cutting board and scraping lightly with a sturdy vegetable peeler. (If you don't lay them as flat as possible, they'll tend to break, and you want them whole.)

❈ The asparagus needs at least 30 minutes to marinate, and it's also fine to leave it, covered and refrigerated, overnight. Add the Soy Caramel (which can be made well in advance) just before serving.

2 pounds thickish asparagus, trimmed of tough ends, peeled if desired (see note)

3 tablespoons grapeseed or peanut oil

¼ teaspoon salt, or more to taste

1 teaspoon minced or crushed garlic

1½ tablespoons finely minced ginger

Soy Caramel (page 364)

1. Set up a pot or shallow pan of water (or a steamer over a pot of water) and bring the water to a boil. Lower the heat and cook the asparagus in (or steam it over) the simmering water until just tender, 3 to 8 minutes, depending on the thickness. (You want it firm, but not too crunchy.)

2. Drain in a colander, refresh under cold running water, then drain again. Pat the asparagus dry with a kitchen towel, then leave it on the towel for a few minutes to dry further.

3. Combine the oil, salt, garlic, and ginger in a shallow dish of asparagus proportions.

4. Add the asparagus in a single layer (or as single a layer as possible), rolling it around to get it coated. Let it sit to absorb flavor for at least 30 minutes (longer is fine). Cover and refrigerate if it's going to sit for longer and/or if your kitchen is hot and/or you like things cold.

5. Serve at room temperature or cold, laid out on plates, with a generous spoonful of Soy Caramel ladled over the top. The caramel will disappear somewhat into the asparagus, leaving the surface shiny. Pass the rest of the caramel at the table, for people to drizzle on, if they like.

OPTIONAL ENHANCEMENTS

Pickled ginger on top ❈ A shower of scallions—finely minced whites and/or very thin green ovals ❈ A light sprinkling of sesame seeds ❈ Finely minced sweet cucumber scattered on top ❈ A cluster of thin noodles (cooked and lightly oiled) on top, or a bed of them below, are perfect with the Soy Caramel

Asparagus Salad with Roasted Red Peppers and Chickpeas

MAKES 6 SERVINGS ❋ VEGAN (WHEN MADE WITH AGAVE NECTAR)

Nothing fancy here, just a quiet gem of a salad you might well adopt as your trademark dish. With that bunch of fresh asparagus you picked up on your foray through the market and some canned roasted red peppers and chickpeas from your well-stocked cupboard, this salad is just one fast vinaigrette away from your table.

❋ Assuming you are using roasted red peppers from a jar, it's fine to include some of the packing liquid, if you like the way it tastes. Alternatively, you can roast fresh ones (see page 358). A 12-ounce jar of roasted red peppers is approximately equal to 1 large bell pepper.

❋ Peeling the southern third or so of asparagus stalks after you've snapped off the tough bottoms is a bit of work, but rewards you with greater tenderness plus more visual appeal. To peel without breaking, lay each asparagus on a cutting board and sweep it gently, as horizontally as possible, with a sturdy vegetable peeler.

❋ You can roast the asparagus instead of steaming or blanching it. Roasted asparagus has a deeper flavor than steamed or blanched, but is less bright and green. The roasting instructions are on page 336. Roast the trimmed asparagus whole (possibly even on the same baking sheet as the peppers, if you're roasting those too) and cut it into pieces and add it to the salad when it's done.

❋ You can swap in green beans for the asparagus when the season shifts.

❋ This keeps well for up to 4 days and goes very nicely as an accompaniment to other dishes. (I love it as a topping or a bed for scrambled eggs.) It is also good snacking material. The flavor deepens as it sits, at least for the first few days. The green color will fade a bit, though.

1 pound asparagus, trimmed of tough ends, peeled if desired (see note)

1 teaspoon minced or crushed garlic

2 teaspoons agave nectar or light-colored honey

2 tablespoons white or red wine vinegar

Up to 1 teaspoon salt

6 tablespoons extra-virgin olive oil

2 large roasted red bell peppers, peeled, seeded, and cut into strips, or two 12-ounce jars roasted red peppers, drained

2 15-ounce cans chickpeas, rinsed and drained

Black pepper

Up to 2 tablespoons fresh lemon juice (optional)

1. Cook the asparagus in one of the following ways:

a. Roast it (see page 336), then cut it into 1½-inch pieces.

b. Cut the raw, trimmed asparagus into 1½-inch pieces and steam over simmering water or cook in simmering water for 3 to 5 minutes (depending on the thickness), or until bright green and just tender. Transfer to a colander (or if you've steamed it, just remove the steaming basket) and refresh under cold running water until it cools to room temperature. Drain thoroughly, then dry with a kitchen towel.

2. Meanwhile, combine the garlic, agave or honey, vinegar, and ½ teaspoon salt in a large bowl and whisk to thoroughly blend. Keep whisking as you drizzle in the olive oil, keeping up the action until it is completely incorporated.

3. Add the asparagus, roasted peppers, and chickpeas to the vinaigrette, tossing to coat. Taste to adjust the salt and add some black pepper. Splash in lemon juice to taste, if desired, shortly before serving.

OPTIONAL ENHANCEMENTS

Crumbled or cubed mild cheese of your choice ✳ Chopped or torn fresh flat-leaf parsley leaves ✳ Very sweet cherry tomatoes, halved or quartered, if large ✳ Olives ✳ Minced arugula ✳ Lemon or lime wedges ✳ A bed of couscous underneath or a sprinkling of couscous over the top ✳ Add up to 2 cups cooked elbow macaroni, small shells, ditalini, or your own favorite pasta shape ✳ A sprinkling of lightly toasted slivered almonds, added when serving ✳ Hard-cooked egg wedges on the side or coarsely grated hard-cooked eggs sprinkled on top—or a topping of Egg "Noodles" (page 398)

Green Beans and Beets with Pickled Red Onions

MAKES 4 TO 6 SERVINGS ❀ VEGAN

Marinating cooked vegetables in vinaigrette is a basic technique that is straightforward and reliably delicious. But sometimes it's nice to go more quietly into that good place, holding off on the vinegar (or lemon/lime juice) and soaking the vegetables in just the oil—infused, perhaps, with touches of allium and salt. This method gives the vegetables a more subtle flavor and also allows anything green to hold on to its color. In this recipe, freshly cooked green beans and beets rest in a pool of shallot-packed, garlic-graced roasted almond oil and olive oil. Their brighten-up moment comes at serving time, when they're crowned with a sparkling mound of Pickled Red Onions just before being presented.

❀ Although green beans, beets, and onions are available year-round, wait until summer so you can make this with fresh vegetables in the height of their season. Summer beets, especially, are the best. Try to find yellow ones, which are a visual treat juxtaposed with the green beans and the vividly pink onions.

❀ When shopping for green beans, carefully select one at a time. It's worth it to end up with uniform beans that are smooth and firm, and you won't need to sort through and discard the bummer ones once you're home, sometimes ending up with too few usable ones.

❀ Roasted almond oil is a transformative ingredient that I hope you have splurged upon and now keep in your refrigerator at all times.

❋ Prepare the beets at least an hour before serving.

❋ Make sure you have a batch of Pickled Red Onions (page 395) on hand before you begin. They need at least an hour to come together.

1 pound (3–4 medium) beets, preferably yellow

3 tablespoons roasted almond oil

2 tablespoons extra-virgin olive oil

3 tablespoons finely minced shallot

½ teaspoon minced or crushed garlic

½ teaspoon salt

Black pepper

1½ pounds very fresh green beans, trimmed

Pickled Red Onions (page 395)

1. Remove the beet greens (save them to cook separately, if they're nice) and trim the stems to within an inch of the beet. Cook the beets, whole and unpeeled, either in simmering water until fork-tender, about 30 minutes, or by roasting. To roast them, preheat the oven to 400°F, with a rack in the center position. Line a baking sheet with foil. Lay the beets on the foil, add a splash of water (a tablespoon or two), and press together the edges of the foil to form a packet. Roast for about 30 minutes, or until the beets are fork-tender. (Be careful when opening the packet. There will be steam.)

2. Cool, then peel the beets with a sharp paring knife and cut into ¼-inch dice.

3. In a wide, shallow pan (the easiest to work with) put on water to boil.

4. Meanwhile, combine the oils, shallot, garlic, salt, and black pepper to taste in a wide, shallow bowl or a gratin dish and stir briefly to blend. Add the beets.

5. When the water boils, carefully add the green beans and reduce the heat to a simmer. Cook for 5 or so minutes, until perfectly tender but not mushy. The cooking time will depend on the thickness and age of the green beans and how you like them.

6. When the beans are done, drain them in a colander and refresh under cold running water. Drain again, then pat them dry with a kitchen towel.

7. Add the green beans to the beets, rolling them around until thoroughly coated. Let everything sit to absorb flavor for at least 30 minutes. Cover and refrigerate if the salad will sit for longer and/or if your kitchen is hot and/or you like things cold. (*The salad can be made as much as 4 hours ahead.*)

8. Serve cold or at cool room temperature, topped generously with Pickled Red Onions. Be sure to include some of the onion liquid to sparkle things up further.

OPTIONAL ENHANCEMENTS

Toasted almonds—whole, chopped, or slivered ❋
Green peas—lightly steamed, if fresh; defrosted under running water, if frozen

Citrusy Beets

MAKES 4 MODEST MAIN-DISH SERVINGS ❦ VEGAN (WHEN MADE WITH AGAVE NECTAR)

I love both oranges and grapefruit in beet salads and have always had trouble choosing between them. Then, one day, I realized I didn't need to.

Try experimenting with various colors of beets, alone or in combination, and see which of the optional toppings suits your taste.

Serve as a first course or as a small plate entrée for a light lunch or brunch.

❀ Prepare the beets (step 1) at least an hour ahead of time. I like roasting them for maximum flavor. However, you can simmer them in water if you don't feel like turning on the oven. In either case, wait to peel them until after they are cooked and cooled. Prepare the other ingredients while the beets are cooking.

❀ If you are adding Pickled Red Onions, which I highly recommend, put them together at least an hour ahead of time (see page 395).

❀ If you choose to add zest, remove it before juicing the oranges.

❀ This dish keeps well and can be made up to a day ahead if covered tightly and stored in the refrigerator. If you are adding mint leaves or avocado, lay these items on top (minimally mix them in) at the last minute, so they can be at their best.

1 pound (3–4 medium) beets, any color

2 tablespoons cider vinegar

½ teaspoon minced or crushed garlic

¼ heaping teaspoon salt

1 tablespoon agave nectar or light-colored honey

¼ cup extra-virgin olive oil

2 oranges, peeled and sectioned, sections removed from membranes (see page 128)

1 large ruby grapefruit, peeled and sectioned, sections removed from membranes (see page 378), sections halved, if large

1. Remove the beet greens (save them to cook separately, if they're nice) and trim the stems to within an inch of the beet. Cook the beets, whole and unpeeled, either in simmering water until fork-tender, 30 to 40 minutes, or by roasting. To roast them, preheat the oven to 400°F, with a rack in the center position. Line a baking sheet with foil. Lay the beets on the foil, add a splash of water (a tablespoon or two), and press together the edges of the foil to form a packet. Roast for about 30 minutes, or until the beets are fork-tender. (Be careful to avoid the steam when opening the packet.)

2. Cool the beets completely, then peel them with a sharp paring knife and cut into bite-sized chunks or elegant half-circles (your call).

3. Combine the vinegar, garlic, salt, and agave or honey in a medium bowl and whisk until the sweetener is dissolved. Drizzle in the olive oil, continuing to whisk until it is incorporated.

4. Add the beets to the dressing and stir gently until coated. Let sit at room temperature for at least an hour before adding the fruit. (Cover and refrigerate if it's going to sit for longer—up to a day is fine—and/or if your kitchen is hot and you like things cold.)

5. Add the orange and grapefruit sections and stir gently until coated. Serve cold or at cool room temperature, plain or topped with any or all of the Optional Enhancements.

OPTIONAL ENHANCEMENTS

Pickled Red Onions (page 395) ❋ Long strands of orange zest (cut with a zester or a sharp knife) ❋ Thin strips of fresh mint ❋ Avocado ❋ Fresh raspberries, blackberries, blueberries, or sliced strawberries as garnish

Roasted Beets Surrounded by Mango

MAKES 4 MODEST MAIN-DISH SERVINGS ❀ VEGAN

Deep magenta beets are coated with bright mango vinaigrette and then arranged in a frothy circle of mango gold. If there were a flag of the plant-food world, it would look something like this plate. Serve on its own as a light lunch or as a salad course before or after a meal of heavier fare. It will both refresh and enchant.

❀ The beets need to be roasted well ahead of time. Store them tightly wrapped in their roasting foil and peel shortly before assembling this salad. Boiled beets will work fine, but roasted ones will deliver more depth. You can make the vinaigrette while the beets are in the oven.

❀ Frozen mango works perfectly for this and conveniently comes in chunks packed in 1-pound bags. If you use fresh mangoes, don't worry about smushing them while pitting and peeling, since you'll be pulping them anyway. Leftover mango pulp, if any, can be blended into a smoothie.

❀ If you were lucky enough to purchase beets with fresh, intact greens, save the leaves to flash cook later for a quick dinner vegetable fix. Clean thoroughly, then braise in a little water and finish with olive oil and touches of garlic, salt, and pepper.

1 pound (3–4 medium) magenta beets

1 pound frozen mango chunks, defrosted, or 3 pounds fresh mangoes, pitted, peeled, and cut into chunks

1 tablespoon cider vinegar

Mango Vinaigrette (*recipe follows*)

Baby arugula leaves (optional)

1. Preheat the oven to 400°F, with a rack in the center. Line a baking sheet with foil.

2. Remove the beet greens (save, if nice) and trim the stems to within an inch of the beet. Lay the beets on the foil, add a tablespoon or two of water, and press together the edges of the foil to form a little beet packet. Roast for about 30 minutes, or until the beets are fork-tender. (Be careful when opening the packet. Steam will burst forth.)

3. Meanwhile, puree the mango into a smooth slush with an immersion or stand blender. Reserve 3 tablespoons for the vinaigrette and stir the cider vinegar into the rest.

4. Cool the beets completely, then peel them with your fingers and/or a sharp paring knife and slice them into bite-sized wedges. Transfer to a bowl and toss with 3 to 4 tablespoons of the vinaigrette.

5. To serve, spoon 3 to 4 tablespoons of the mango slush onto each of four salad plates, spreading it into a circle. Carefully, so as not to bleed the colors, place the beet wedges on top of the mango in an artful pattern. Top with a few leaves of baby arugula, if desired, and serve right away, passing the extra vinaigrette for individual applications.

MANGO VINAIGRETTE

MAKES ⅔ CUP ❀ VEGAN

This sparkler is plenty good made with all olive oil, but the combination of olive oil and roasted walnut oil will take it to insanely good.

❀ As with most vinaigrettes, this will keep for 3 weeks or longer in a tightly covered container in the refrigerator. Bring to cool room temperature and stir or shake to recombine before using.

½ teaspoon minced or crushed garlic

1 tablespoon cider vinegar

1 tablespoon fresh lemon juice

3 tablespoons reserved mango slush (see previous recipe, step 3)

¼ teaspoon salt

5 tablespoons extra-virgin olive oil and/or roasted walnut oil (see headnote)

1. Combine the garlic, vinegar, lemon juice, mango slush, and salt in a small bowl or a jar with a lid, and whisk to thoroughly blend.

2. Keep whisking as you drizzle in the oil. Store tightly covered in the refrigerator. Shake and/or stir from the bottom before each use.

Spiced Carrots in Thick Cranberry-Orange Vinaigrette

MAKES 4 TO 6 SERVINGS ❀ VEGAN

Compellingly aromatic from cumin and a beautiful shade of orange dotted with red, these carrots always elicit raves. Portable and reliably joy-inducing, they are my choice for dish-to-pass gatherings each holiday season.

❀ Make the vinaigrette up to a week ahead of time and store in an airtight container in the refrigerator.

2 tablespoons olive oil

½ teaspoon ground cumin

¼ teaspoon ground coriander

2½ pounds carrots, peeled and cut into diagonal slices about ⅛ inch thick

¼ teaspoon salt

3 tablespoons water

Thick Cranberry-Orange Vinaigrette (page 368)

Up to 1 cup lightly toasted whole almonds or Marcona almonds (optional)

1. Place a large, deep skillet with a lid over medium heat for about a minute, then add the oil and swirl to coat the pan. Sprinkle in the spices and cook them for just a few seconds, until fragrant.

2. Add the carrots and salt, stir to coat with the oil and spices, then cover the pan and cook for 5 minutes.

3. Stir in the water, cover the pan again, and continue to cook for another few minutes, or until the carrots are done to your liking. (If you prefer them very soft, you can cook them for as long as 8 to 10 minutes, stirring occasionally.)

4. Transfer the carrots to a bowl and add about ½ cup of the vinaigrette, mixing it in. Taste to see if you'd like to add a bit more (consider passing around the extra vinaigrette in a small bowl, so people can add a little extra). Top with the almonds, if desired, and serve at any temperature.

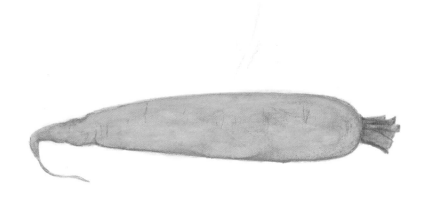

Cauliflower Salad with Salsa Verde

MAKES 4 OR 5 SERVINGS ❊ VEGAN

Cauliflower gets cooked in a panful of flavor, cooled in a haze of vinegar, and served in concert with Salsa Verde. This salad tastes best when the cauliflower is on the soft side. You can add some crunch back in with your selection of Enhancements.

As with many of the salads in this chapter, this can be served as a first course or a modular component to a larger plate. You can also choose any of the options below, to make this into more of a main event.

❊ Make the Salsa Verde well ahead of time. It lasts for up to a week, tightly covered and refrigerated.

3 tablespoons extra-virgin olive oil

1 heaping cup sliced or minced red onion

1 teaspoon cumin seeds

2 medium heads cauliflower (about 4 pounds total), trimmed and cut or broken into ¾-inch florets

½–1 teaspoon minced or crushed garlic

Up to ¾ teaspoon salt

4 teaspoons cider vinegar

Black pepper

Salsa Verde (page 357)

1. Place a large skillet with a lid over medium heat for about a minute, then add the olive oil and swirl to coat the pan. Add the onion and cumin and cook, stirring, for 3 to 5 minutes, or until the onion softens.

2. Stir in the cauliflower and as much of the garlic as you think you'd like, plus ½ teaspoon salt. Cover and cook, stirring occasionally, for 8 to 10 minutes, or until the cauliflower is as soft

as you prefer. (It's OK if it sticks to the pan a little; just scrape as you stir. This is flavor in the making.)

3. Transfer the cauliflower to a bowl, scraping in every last bit and sprinkle with the vinegar while it is still hot. Cover the bowl with foil or a plate and let it cool to room temperature, steaming further in its own heat.

4. Taste the cooled cauliflower to see if it needs more salt, and add a good amount of black pepper. You can stir in a few tablespoons of Salsa Verde at this point, or save it all for the top. This is also the time to add any of the Enhancements that need mixing in.

5. Cover and chill, if you like things cold, or serve right away, at room temperature. Top each serving with a dab of Salsa Verde.

OPTIONAL ENHANCEMENTS

Lemon wedges ❊ Cubes or crumbles of fresh cheese (feta, manouri, ricotta salata) ❊ Mayonnaise (1–2 tablespoons) mixed in with step 4, and/or a touch of Cucumber Mayonnaise (page 373) on top ❊ Pickled Red Onions (page 395) heaped on top ❊ Finely minced celery, fennel, and/or watercress ❊ Minced bell pepper ❊ Pair with Grated Carrot Salad (page 62) and Olive Oil Toasts (see page 409) ❊ An Herb Tangle (page 76) on top ❊ Browned Potatoes and Onion (page 391) on top ❊ Cherry tomatoes, halved or quartered ❊ Crispy Fried Lemons (page 389) for garnish ❊ Sliced radishes ❊ Hard-cooked egg halves or quarters or Egg "Noodles" (page 398) ❊ A scattering of capers

Grilled Ratatouille Salad

MAKES 6 OR 7 MODEST MAIN-DISH SERVINGS ❧ VEGAN

Just-grilled, still-hot eggplants and zucchini head directly for a vinaigrette landing strip, permitting generously deep flavor absorption as they cool. This newfangled approach to the classic recipe is so ridiculously good, I don't know why I didn't think of it a few decades sooner. If you use enough of the many Optional Enhancements, the salad expands into its own bona fide appetizer sampler.

❀ There are several tricks to this, none of them complicated. First, plan on making this well ahead of serving. It takes some time (I won't lie) to cut and grill all the vegetables, and then they'll need to marinate.

❀ Second, repeat this mantra: "Sliced, not cubed." This is the secret to imparting maximum flavor to maximum surface area. You can use a food processor with the slicing attachment for both the zucchini and the eggplant.

❀ Tongs are the best tool for vegetable grilling.

❀ And finally, the zucchini should be on the al dente side, but make sure the eggplant is truly soft. This allows each vegetable to be at its textural best. It's not difficult; just pay attention.

1 pound zucchini (4–5 small)

3 pounds eggplant (2 large)

3 tablespoons red or white wine vinegar or cider vinegar

6 tablespoons finely minced shallots

1½ teaspoons minced or crushed garlic

1 teaspoon salt, or more to taste

¼ teaspoon sugar

¼ teaspoon *each* dried thyme and dried oregano

Black pepper

About 6 tablespoons extra-virgin olive oil

1. Trim and discard the ends of the zucchini and eggplants. Cut each zuke into thirds crosswise. Peel the eggplants and cut them crosswise into quarters. One at a time, set each vegetable piece on a flat end and cut thin (⅛-inch-thick) slices lengthwise. You will end up with a large pile of elegant, slender, long bite-sized-ish pieces.

2. Combine the vinegar, shallots, garlic, ¾ teaspoon of the salt, sugar, thyme, oregano, and a few shakes or grinds of black pepper in a 9-x-13-inch baking dish. Whisk to blend and keep whisking as you drizzle in 5 tablespoons of the olive oil until it is incorporated. Place the dish near the stove.

3. Place a ridged grill pan or a large skillet over medium heat for about a minute, then brush or slick with the remaining 1 tablespoon olive oil. (You can also set up two pans to streamline operations.) Add the zucchini slices in a single layer and cook on both sides for a few minutes, or until just tender and emblazoned with brown grill marks (or, if using a skillet, until appetizingly golden). Transfer the cooked zucchini directly to the marinade, sprinkle lightly with salt and let it sit there in a pile for now. You might need to do this in several shifts.

4. Grill the eggplant slices just as you did the zucchini. (Make sure the cooked eggplant is very soft.) You don't need to be dainty with this—it's OK if the slices break up a bit as they cook. Pile the cooked eggplant on top of the zucchini in the marinade and sprinkle lightly with salt. When all the vegetables are cooked, stir gently to coat.

5. Let the vegetables rest in the marinade for at least 30 minutes (and up to an hour, or ideally even longer) to absorb the flavors, turning and rearranging every 5 minutes or so, for maximum absorption. After 30 minutes, taste to adjust the salt and pepper. (If you're going to let it stand for longer than an hour, cover it tightly and refrigerate.)

6. Serve cold or at cool room temperature.

OPTIONAL ENHANCEMENTS

Sweet cherry tomatoes (halved or quartered if large) ❋ High-quality extra-virgin olive oil drizzled on top at serving time ❋ Top with an Herb Tangle (page 76) of fresh marjoram, thyme, and/or oregano ❋ Roasted Red Pepper Pesto (page 358) ❋ Pine nuts and/or pomegranate seeds sprinkled on top ❋ Feta cubes or crumbled goat cheese ❋ Basic Tahini-Lemon Sauce (page 361) underneath or on the side ❋ Slow-Roasted Roma Tomatoes (page 393) on top ❋ Olive Oil Toasts (see page 409) ❋ Olives ❋ Lightly toasted walnuts, chopped or halved ❋ Add up to 2 cups cooked elbow macaroni, small shells, ditalini, or your own favorite pasta shape to expand this into a pasta salad

Roasted Eggplant Salad with Coconut-Lime Vinaigrette

MAKES 3 OR 4 MODEST MAIN-DISH SERVINGS ❋ VEGAN

Roasted eggplant readily soaks up a quietly exotic (but not difficult) vinaigrette, elevating this salad to focal-point status for a light summer lunch. Consider pairing it with Hot-Sweet-Sour Soup with Tofu and Pineapple (page 42) and some freshly cooked jasmine rice. Or, if you have the time, serve this with a batch of Yellow Coconut Rice with Chilies, Ginger, and Lime (page 187).

❋ Taste the cucumber before it goes in, to be sure it is very sweet.

Nonstick cooking spray

1½ pounds eggplant, peeled if large and cut into ½-inch cubes

Coconut-Lime Vinaigrette (page 108)

Salt

1 small (6-inch) cucumber (peeled if the skin is bitter), diced

1 small or ½ medium sweet bell pepper (orange or purple are especially nice), diced

Handful of very sweet cherry tomatoes, halved or quartered if large

About 10 fresh mint leaves, minced

Crushed red pepper (optional)

1. Preheat the oven to 400°F, with a rack in the center position. Line a baking sheet with parchment paper or foil and spray it with nonstick spray. Arrange the eggplant pieces on the baking sheet and roast for 15 minutes. Use tongs or a small metal spatula to loosen and turn the pieces, then roast for another 15 to 20 minutes, until the eggplant pieces are completely tender and even somewhat shriveled.

2. Meanwhile, place ¼ cup of the vinaigrette in a shallow dish large enough to hold the eggplant.

3. Remove the baking sheet from the oven, sprinkle the eggplant very lightly with salt, then transfer the still-hot eggplant directly to the vinaigrette in the dish. Let it sit and absorb as it cools to room temperature.

4. Stir in the cucumber, bell pepper, and tomatoes, along with another 2 tablespoons or so of the vinaigrette. Cover and refrigerate for at least 1 hour and up to 2 days. Serve cold or at cool room temperature, stirring the mint leaves in immediately before serving, and topping with a light sprinkling of crushed red pepper, if desired.

OPTIONAL ENHANCEMENTS

Stir in a touch of minced jalapeño and/or lime zest ❋ Top with an Herb Tangle (page 76) of minced scallions, cilantro, Thai basil, and mint ❋ Toss on some peanuts for garnish ❋ Top with Tofu "Noodles" (Coconut Version, page 399)

COCONUT-LIME VINAIGRETTE

MAKES ABOUT ¾ CUP ✿ VEGAN

In addition to the accompanying eggplant dish, this goes swimmingly with any tossed green salad.

✿ The vinaigrette can be made ahead of time and stored for up to a week in a tightly covered jar in the refrigerator. Let it come to room temperature and stir from the bottom or just shake it before using.

✿ After you've used the mere 3 tablespoons of coconut milk for this recipe, preserve the remainder of the can by freezing it in an ice cube tray. Once firm, transfer the cubes to a heavy zip-style plastic bag (label it!) for longer storage. Pull out what you need, when you need it, and you will have wasted not.

½ teaspoon minced or crushed garlic

3 tablespoons fresh lime juice

3 tablespoons reduced-fat coconut milk

½ teaspoon salt

1½ teaspoons agave nectar or sugar

5 tablespoons grapeseed or peanut oil

1. Combine the garlic, lime juice, coconut milk, salt, and sweetener in a small bowl or a jar with a lid, and whisk to thoroughly blend.

2. Drizzle in the oil, whisking as you go, until it is fully incorporated.

3. Store tightly covered in the refrigerator. Shake and/or stir from the bottom before use.

Marinated Grilled Zucchini with Corn and Tomatoes

MAKES 4 OR 5 MODEST MAIN DISH SERVINGS ❀ VEGAN

In this summer special, zucchini gets smacked out of its introversion with a good dose of grill time and a slick of oil. It then heads directly into a garlic- and shallot-infused vinaigrette, sealing the deal on its newfound personality upgrade. Cue some maximally sweet, in-season corn and tomatoes, and the makeover is complete.

❀ The zucchini should be sliced very thinly and then cooked very quickly, so it becomes almost like sturdy vegetable ribbons. Use a very sharp knife so you can get fairly uniform slices. You can also use the slicing attachment of a food processor.

❀ This tastes best at room temperature, within an hour of being made. If you want to prepare it further in advance, it's fine to let the zucchini sit in the marinade (covered tightly and refrigerated), but hold off on adding the corn and tomatoes until shortly before serving.

1½ pounds zucchini (about 6 small)

3 tablespoons finely minced shallot

Up to 1 teaspoon minced or crushed garlic

2 tablespoons red or white wine vinegar or cider vinegar

About ¾ teaspoon salt

Pinch of sugar

¼ teaspoon dried thyme

¼ teaspoon dried oregano

¼ cup extra-virgin olive oil, plus more for the pan

About 2 dozen sweet cherry tomatoes

Kernels from 2–3 freshly shucked ears of corn (2–3 cups)

Black pepper

1. Trim and discard the ends of the zucchini, then cut each squash into thirds crosswise. Set each cylinder on a flat end and cut thin (⅛-inch) slices lengthwise. (Alternatively, you can run the thirds through a food processor with the slicing attachment.) You will end up with a pile of elegant, slender, more or less bite-sized pieces.

2. Combine the shallot, garlic, vinegar, ¼ teaspoon salt, sugar, and herbs in a large, shallow bowl. Whisk to blend and keep whisking as you drizzle in ¼ cup olive oil until it is incorporated. Place the bowl near the stove.

3. Set a ridged grill pan or a cast-iron skillet over medium heat and brush it lightly with olive oil. Heat for about a minute, then add the zucchini slices in a single layer and sprinkle lightly with salt. Cook on both sides until just tender and decorated with golden grill marks (in the ridged pan) or just plain golden. Transfer the cooked zucchini directly to the marinade. You may need to do this in a couple of shifts.

4. Let the zucchini rest in the marinade to absorb the flavors for a minimum of 30 minutes.

5. Just before serving, stir in the tomatoes and corn and add black pepper to taste. Serve warm or at room temperature, with a scattering of any or all of the Optional Enhancements.

OPTIONAL ENHANCEMENTS

Stir in some minced bell pepper ❀ Sprinkle with pine nuts or minced walnuts ❀ Add small cubes of feta or crumbled goat cheese on top or Grilled Haloumi Cheese (page 406) on the side ❀ Garnish with Pickled Red Onions (page 395)

Endive, Jicama, and Wild Rice Salad with Blue Cheese–Yogurt Dressing

MAKES 4 SERVINGS

It's easy to eat a lot of this light, refreshing winter salad, so go ahead and be generous with the portions. It works its magic at any point in the meal—as a starter, a between-course palate cleanser, or even a final course. It's also a lively lunch partner for your favorite soup.

❀ At least 1 hour ahead of time, combine ¼ cup wild rice and about 2 cups water in a small saucepan. Bring to a boil and simmer uncovered for 45 to 50 minutes, or until the rice is tender. Drain thoroughly.

❀ If you can find both red and green Belgian endive, use a combination in this salad.

❀ For more about jicama, see page 381.

❀ Toss the salad right before serving.

4 Belgian endives (about 1 pound), sliced crosswise into ribbons

½ medium jicama (about ¾ pound), peeled and cut into matchsticks or other bite-sized pieces

1 medium red apple, cored and sliced

¾ cup cooked wild rice (see note)

Blue Cheese–Yogurt Dressing (*recipe follows*)

Black pepper

½ cup coarsely chopped pecans, lightly toasted

Pomegranate seeds (optional)

1. Toss the vegetables, fruit, and rice together in a medium bowl.

2. Keep tossing as you add the dressing until everything is coated as you like it. You may or may not end up using all the dressing.

3. Grind in some black pepper toward the end of the tossing. Serve right away, topped with the pecans and a scattering of pomegranate seeds, if desired.

BLUE CHEESE–YOGURT DRESSING

MAKES ¾ CUP

This is a silky, apple-themed flavor messenger. Use any kind of blue cheese that you love.

¼ cup plain yogurt

1 heaping tablespoon finely minced shallot

¼ teaspoon salt

2 tablespoons apple juice

1 teaspoon cider vinegar

1 teaspoon pure maple syrup

3 tablespoons extra-virgin olive oil

2 tablespoons crumbled blue cheese, or more to taste

Black pepper

1. Combine the yogurt, shallot, salt, apple juice, vinegar, and maple syrup in a medium bowl or jar with a lid. Whisk until thoroughly blended.

2. Keep whisking as you drizzle in the olive oil.

3. Stir in the blue cheese, then taste the dressing. Add more cheese, if you like. Season with black pepper to taste.

4. Cover tightly and refrigerate until use. Shake or stir from the bottom before using.

GRAIN SALADS

A grain salad should be immersed in deep flavor (good oil, a touch of vinegar and/or citrus juice, and a minced representative of the onion clan) and punctuated with colorful bits of vegetables, herbs, and sometimes fruit, nuts, or cheese. The challenge is to achieve a textural balance where the grains are completely cooked through but still thirsty enough to absorb the dressing without becoming swamp-like. So, in most of these recipes, the grains are cooked (or soaked in water, as in the case of the bulgur in Pomegranate Tabbouleh) until just done, and then combined with the dressing. The rest-soak period is an important part of the process, so plan to make all of these recipes at least several hours (and in many cases, up to a day) before you intend to serve them, so they can achieve their personal best. This can be a very good thing for the cook in many ways, not the least of which is that you get to share in the sense of novelty and surprise along with everyone else, having had a bit of a break from the salad while it sat.

Many people are intimidated by getting the right ratio of grain to water. I've alleviated the problem here: Just boil the grains as you would pasta. Drain when the grains are still slightly chewy, and they will drink up the dressing, becoming perfectly infused in the process.

Scattered Sushi-Style Rice Salad (Gomokuzushi)

MAKES 6 TO 8 MODEST MAIN-DISH SERVINGS

Rice is exuberantly stippled with pickled ginger, variously hued vegetables, and bright yellow flecks of egg, creating a busy, freestanding bowlful that can be served cold or at room temperature.

Gomokuzushi means "five-item sushi." (And "sushi" indicates rice, not fish, just to get that cleared up.) In this recipe, I've gone beyond five items. (It's difficult to avoid getting carried away.)

This is perfect picnic food or portable lunch. It will keep for 4 to 5 days, tightly covered and refrigerated—ideally with the vegetables kept separate until shortly before serving.

❀ If you are daunted by the prospect of buying an entire bottle of mirin (Japanese rice wine) in order to add just 3 tablespoons of it to this dish, rest assured that it will keep indefinitely in your cupboard, and you will likely use it again when this salad enjoys an encore or in the Misoyaki Sauce on page 362, to give just two examples.

❀ Seasoned rice vinegar is the kind that comes laced with a little salt and sugar. Check the label.

❀ Streamline preparations by getting the vegetables and egg ready while the rice cooks, or even further ahead of time.

❀ The instructions have you cooking the rice pasta-style, in plenty of boiling water, which I find easiest. That said, you can also just cook it in your usual manner, if you prefer—in measured water and/or in a rice cooker. Just make sure it is fluffy and dry before you proceed with the rest of the recipe.

10 slender green beans, trimmed and cut into ½-inch pieces

1–2 cups green peas (freshly shelled or frozen)

1 small yellow summer squash, minced

2 cups short-grain brown rice

6 tablespoons seasoned rice vinegar

3 tablespoons mirin (Japanese rice wine)

½ teaspoon salt, or more to taste

¼ cup minced pickled ginger

Nonstick cooking spray

1 teaspoon grapeseed or peanut oil

1 large egg, lightly beaten

1 medium carrot, minced

1 small (6-inch) cucumber (peeled if the skin is bitter), minced

A few snow peas, trimmed and cut into ½-inch pieces

2 scallions, whites very finely minced, greens cut into thin ovals

3 tablespoons sesame seeds

1. Place one colander on a plate next to the stove and another one in the sink. Have a skimmer near the stove as well. Fill a large saucepan with water and bring it to a boil.

2. Add the green beans to the water and cook for about 4 minutes, or until almost tender. Add the peas and squash and cook together for just 1 minute longer. Lift them out of the water with the skimmer, transferring them directly to the colander on the plate to drain.

3. Add the rice to the same water and cook, uncovered, at a gentle boil over medium heat for about 40 minutes, or until tender. (Check the water level during the cooking.) Drain thoroughly in the colander in the sink when done, then shake dry. You can help this along by patting the grains with a kitchen towel.

4. Take the colander of vegetables to the sink and run them under cold water for a minute or two to cool. Drain thoroughly, then shake dry and set aside.

5. Transfer the rice to a large bowl (a wide, shallow one, if possible). Sprinkle in the vinegar, mirin, salt, and pickled ginger, stirring to combine.

6. Lightly coat a 7- or 8-inch omelet pan with nonstick spray and heat over medium heat for about a minute. Add the oil and swirl to coat the pan. Wait another 30 seconds or so, then pour in the beaten egg. Tilt the pan in all directions to let the egg flow to the edges, lifting the cooked edges to allow the uncooked egg to flow underneath. (You are making an omelet.) Flip it over for a second, then transfer to the plate. When it cools a bit, cut the omelet into small pieces.

7. Add the egg, plus the cooked vegetables and all the remaining ingredients, to the rice and mix gently but thoroughly. Taste to see if it needs more salt, then serve right away at cool room temperature. If you wish to serve this later and/or cold, hold off on adding the vegetables until shortly before serving, and refrigerate everything in the meantime.

OPTIONAL ENHANCEMENTS

Crumbled nori seaweed (lightly toasted in a toaster oven if desired) ❋ Extra pickled ginger for the top ❋ A dab of Wasabi Mayonnaise (page 372) ❋ A drizzle of Soy Caramel (page 364) ❋ Extra omelet or Egg "Noodles" (page 398) for the top ❋ A tangle of chopped spinach, shiso, and/or watercress ❋ A topping of Tofu "Noodles" (page 399) ❋ A sprinkling of black sesame seeds on top ❋ Shelled, lightly steamed edamame mixed in or on top

Green Rice with Grapes and Pecans

MAKES 6 TO 8 MAIN-DISH SERVINGS ❧ VEGAN (WHEN MADE WITH AGAVE NECTAR OR MAPLE SYRUP)

Back by popular demand, this is a retooling of the very popular Jeweled Rice Salad from *Still Life with Menu*. Sweet juicy grapes pop (both visually and in your mouth) from the embrace of rice that has been stained a lush green by a fine mince of parsley and scallions. I love the way sweet fruit balances out savory herbs and grassy olive oil, especially when garlic whispers prompts from the sidelines. It covers all the flavor bases.

This is a good choice to include in a portable lunch. It's also great picnic food.

❋ The finished salad needs about 4 hours in the refrigerator after it's prepared, so the flavors can meld. It will continue to keep well for another 4 to 5 days.

❋ Put on the rice about 40 minutes ahead of time and get everything else ready while it cooks.

❋ The instructions have you cooking the rice pasta-style, in plenty of unmeasured boiling water, which I find easiest. That said, you can also just cook it in your usual manner, if you prefer, in measured water or in a rice cooker. Just make sure it is fluffy and dry before it enters the marinade.

2 cups long-grain brown rice (plain or basmati)

1 teaspoon minced or crushed garlic

6 tablespoons fresh lemon juice

1 tablespoon light-colored honey, agave nectar, or pure maple syrup

1 teaspoon salt, or more if needed

¼ cup extra-virgin olive oil

6 scallions, whites and light greens cut into 2-inch lengths

½ (packed) cup fresh flat-leaf parsley, larger stems removed

2 cups seedless grapes, halved

Black pepper

1 cup chopped pecans, lightly toasted, or to taste

Lemon wedges (optional)

1. Fill a large saucepan with water and bring it to a boil. Add the rice and cook, uncovered, at a gentle boil over medium heat for about 40 minutes, or until tender. (Check the water level during the cooking.) Drain thoroughly in a colander in the sink when done, then shake dry. You can help this along by patting the grains with a kitchen towel.

2. Meanwhile, combine the garlic, lemon juice, sweetener, and 1 teaspoon salt in a large bowl (a wide, shallow one, if possible) and whisk to blend. Keep whisking as you drizzle in the oil.

3. Add the freshly cooked, drained rice (it's OK if it's still hot or warm) to the dressing, mixing it in gently with a fork until completely coated.

4. Put the scallions in a mini food processor with the parsley, and buzz until feathery. If you don't have a small food processor, just go at the herbs on a cutting board with a very sharp knife until finely minced.

5. Add the herbs to the rice mixture, stirring gently with a fork until well combined. (The rice will turn a lovely shade of green.) Gently stir in the grapes, then taste to adjust the salt if needed and add some black pepper.

6. Cover tightly and chill well before serving. Serve cold or at cool room temperature. Stir in the pecans shortly before serving or just sprinkle them on top. Serve with lemon wedges, if desired.

OPTIONAL ENHANCEMENTS

Chopped or grated lemon zest for the top (zest the lemons before juicing) ❈ Up to ½ cup minced fresh mint leaves added to the herbs ❈ Chopped apple or other fruit in addition to the grapes

Wild Rice, Basmati, and Kidney Bean Salad

MAKES 6 TO 8 MAIN-DISH SERVINGS ❧ VEGAN

Freshly cooked grains marinate with kidney beans in a tasty vinaigrette before being joined by a colorful, crunchy chorus of bell pepper, cucumber, tomatoes, artichoke hearts, and parsley. The resulting salad is beautiful and satisfying enough to redefine main-dish possibilities. It also travels well.

❀ Any shade of sweet bell pepper will work, but an orange one is especially pretty in here. If you happen to find very sweet peppers of other hues and/or adjacent varieties at the market, feel free to experiment with them.

❀ This salad is easy, but needs to be made well ahead, since it tastes best if marinated for at least 2 hours. Consider putting it together the day before you intend to serve it.

❀ Put on the wild rice and basmati about an hour ahead of time, and get everything else ready while the grains cook.

❀ Taste the cucumber before adding it, to be sure it is delicious and sweet.

❀ You don't need to drain the artichoke hearts. Just lift them out of the jar with a fork and transfer them to a cutting board to slice them into bite-sized pieces.

❋ A stellar main course for lunch, this keeps very well for up to 5 days if covered tightly and refrigerated. It actually gets better as it sits, so you can eat it incrementally over a period of time.

1 cup wild rice

1 cup brown basmati rice

3 tablespoons red or white wine vinegar

1 tablespoon fresh lemon or lime juice

1 teaspoon minced or crushed garlic

1 teaspoon salt, or more to taste

5 tablespoons extra-virgin olive oil

¾ cup finely minced red onion

Black pepper

1 15-ounce can red kidney beans, rinsed and drained

1 medium sweet bell pepper, diced small

1 small (6-inch) sweet cucumber (peeled if the skin is bitter), diced

1–2 scallions, minced (whites and greens)

1 cup small cherry tomatoes, halved or quartered if large

Marinated artichoke hearts (from a 6-ounce jar), sliced or chopped into bite-sized pieces

1 large handful fresh flat-leaf parsley, finely minced (about ⅓ cup)

1. Fill 2 medium saucepans with water and bring to a boil. Add the wild rice to one pot and the basmati to the other. Cook, uncovered, at a gentle boil over medium heat until tender. (The wild rice will take up to 50 minutes to cook; the brown rice should take about 40 minutes.) Drain thoroughly in a colander in the sink (it's OK to use the same one for both grains), then shake dry. You can help this along by patting the grains with a kitchen towel.

2. Meanwhile, combine the vinegar, lemon or lime juice, garlic, and 1 teaspoon salt in a large bowl (a wide, shallow one, if possible), and whisk to blend. Keep whisking as you drizzle in the oil. Stir in the onion and grind in a generous dose of black pepper.

3. Add the hot or warm rice and the beans to the dressing, mixing gently with a fork until completely coated.

4. Let the rice and beans cool to room temperature. Add the bell pepper, cucumber, scallions, tomatoes, and artichoke hearts. Taste to adjust the salt and pepper, then cover and chill for at least 2 hours before serving.

5. Stir in the minced parsley shortly before serving and enjoy cold or at cool room temperature.

OPTIONAL ENHANCEMENTS

You can take this salad in a veg-tropic direction by adding diced or sliced carrot, celery, fennel, radicchio, endive, and/or other chopped vegetables ❋ Serve on a bed of lightly dressed baby arugula or other salad greens

Pomegranate Tabbouleh

**MAKES 4 TO 6 MODEST MAIN-DISH SERVINGS
(OR MORE, DEPENDING ON OPTIONAL ENHANCEMENTS)** ❧ VEGAN

Deep red, juicy punctuation reframes a familiar story, greatly refreshing the plotline. This enhanced tabbouleh is worthy of any winter holiday table, celebrating the fact that pomegranates are at their peak in December, and providing consolation for the waning days leading up to the solstice.

❀ Pomegranate molasses and concentrate are thick reductions of pure pomegranate juice. Find either or both (they keep forever in your cupboard) in Middle Eastern grocery stores or online.

❀ Make this the day before you plan to serve it, so the bulgur has time to absorb moisture and flavor.

❀ Here's the cleanest way to extract the seeds from a pomegranate so that your kitchen will not look like a murder scene: Quarter the fruit with a sharp knife on a cutting board and transfer the pieces to a large bowl of water, so you can aquatically hand-wrangle the seeds from their casing. The skins and pith will float to the surface, while the seeds will sink. Scoop out and discard the upper layer and you're good to go with the jewels on the floor.

❀ You can quickly mince the parsley and mint together in a food processor. Aim for getting them truly tiny.

❀ This keeps well for up to 5 days and is at its best when the minced green herbs are added shortly before serving.

½ cup finely minced red onion

1 cup bulgur

2 tablespoons extra-virgin olive oil

½ teaspoon minced or crushed garlic

½ teaspoon salt

1 tablespoon fresh lemon juice

1 tablespoon pomegranate molasses or pomegranate concentrate (see note)

Seeds from 1 pomegranate (see note)

1 bunch fresh flat-leaf parsley, larger stems removed (2–3 packed cups)

1–2 bunches fresh mint (about 1 cup leaves)

Black pepper

1. Put a kettle of water on to boil. Put the onion in a colander in the sink and the bulgur in a medium bowl, with a dinner plate handy.

2. Pour 2½ cups boiling water over the bulgur. Cover the bowl with the plate, then pour the remaining hot water over the onion and set aside to drain. When the bulgur is tender—at least 30 minutes—fluff it thoroughly with a fork.

3. Place the olive oil in a small bowl and add the garlic. Cover with a small plate and microwave on high for 30 seconds. Scrape the mixture into the bulgur, along with the salt, mixing to thoroughly combine.

4. Mix together the lemon juice and pomegranate molasses or concentrate in the same bowl you used for the garlic and olive oil and sprinkle it into the bulgur along with the onion, continuing to toss with a fork, and adding the pomegranate seeds. When it's well combined, cover the bowl tightly (or transfer to a container with a tight-fitting lid) and refrigerate for a minimum of 4 hours or overnight to let the flavors develop.

5. Within an hour or so before serving, very finely mince the parsley and mint. Add to the tabbouleh, along with black pepper to taste. Serve cold or at cool room temperature.

OPTIONAL ENHANCEMENTS

1 medium scallion (whites and light greens), finely minced along with the parsley and mint ❋ High-quality extra-virgin olive oil to drizzle on each serving ❋ Lightly toasted pine nuts or finely chopped walnuts mixed in or on top ❋ More pomegranate seeds for sprinkling on top ❋ Minced sweet cucumbers and/or bell peppers ❋ Additional minced vegetables: carrot, celery, sweet bell pepper ❋ A scattering of chickpeas ❋ Crumbled cheese (feta, manouri, ricotta salata) on top, or Grilled Haloumi Cheese (page 406) on the side

Summary Corn and Barley Salad

MAKES 4 TO 6 MODEST MAIN-DISH SERVINGS ❋ VEGAN (WHEN MADE WITH AGAVE NECTAR)

Deeply marinated barley is strewn with crunchy in-season vegetables, featuring large and small bursts of cherry tomatoes and fresh corn. The more I eat raw corn zipped straight from the cob, the less I want it any other way.

❋ Needless to say, this tastes best when made with the best ingredients—the newest corn, bell pepper, cucumbers, and cherry tomatoes that summer farmers' markets have to offer.

❋ Instead of the sweet red or orange bell pepper called for, you can use sweet peppers of other hues, if you can find them. Also feel free to use orange cherry tomatoes, which can be the absolute sweetest.

❋ It's important to taste the cucumbers before adding them to the salad. (I always buy a few extras, just in case one might be deal-breakingly bitter.) This makes all the difference, as does a very good, fruity extra-virgin olive oil, so use the best available.

❋ You can make this up to a day ahead, short of adding the vegetables, then cover and refrigerate. The corn should be cut off the cobs and added as last-minute as possible so it will be maximally fantastic.

1 cup pearl barley

1 tablespoon white wine vinegar

1 teaspoon minced or crushed garlic

¾ teaspoon salt, or more to taste

1 teaspoon agave nectar or light-colored honey

2 tablespoons fresh lemon or lime juice, or more to taste

¼ cup extra-virgin olive oil

½ heaping cup finely minced red onion

3–4 scallions, minced most of the way up (whites and greens)

1 small, very sweet red or orange bell pepper, finely minced

Black pepper

2 sweet (6-inch) sweet cucumbers (peeled if the skin is bitter), diced

1 cup very sweet cherry tomatoes, halved or quartered if large

Kernels from 4–5 freshly shucked ears of corn (about 4 cups)

1. Fill a medium saucepan with water (at least 3 cups; more is OK) and bring to a boil. Add the barley and cook at a gentle boil over medium heat for 40 to 45 minutes, or until tender.

2. Meanwhile, combine the vinegar, garlic, ½ teaspoon salt, agave or honey, and 2 tablespoons lemon or lime juice in a large bowl (a wide, shallow one, if possible) and whisk to thoroughly blend. Keep whisking as you drizzle in the olive oil until it is completely incorporated, then stir in the onion.

3. When the barley is cooked to your liking, thoroughly drain off any excess water and add the hot barley to the dressing in the bowl, so the onion and garlic can cook a little upon contact. Sprinkle with ¼ teaspoon salt, toss to thoroughly combine, then spread the mixture around in the bowl to cool and air out a little.

4. When the mixture has cooled to approximately room temperature, stir in the scallions and bell pepper and taste to see if it needs more salt or lemon/lime juice. Add some black pepper to taste as well.

5. Shortly before serving, gently mix in the cucumbers, tomatoes, and corn.

OPTIONAL ENHANCEMENTS

Shelled lightly steamed edamame on top ✻ Up to 2 tablespoons mayonnaise mixed in with the cucumbers, tomatoes, and corn ✻ Minced cilantro ✻ Minced fresh flat-leaf parsley ✻ Chunks or slices of firm, ripe avocado ✻ A dab of Salsa Verde (page 357) ✻ Up to 1½ cups (a 15-ounce can, rinsed and drained) chickpeas or black beans

Farro, Barley, Soybean, and Plum Salad

MAKES 6 TO 8 MODEST MAIN-DISH SERVINGS

If I had to choose one dish that personifies my cooking, it would probably be this one: a big bowlful of chewy farro and barley, crunchy soybeans, juicy plums, salty spots of cheese, and feathery strips of mint scattered throughout.

Make it for a crowd and/or enjoy the leftovers over a period of several days. Just be sure you hold off on adding the mint, plums, and cheese until shortly before serving.

❋ Soak 1 cup dried soybeans for at least 4 hours or overnight, then cook the soybeans and grains at least an hour before assembling the salad.

❋ If you don't have either of the roasted nut oils, it's fine to use all olive oil. That said, I hope you will decide to make roasted nut oils a staple in your kitchen.

❋ My favorite cheese for this is Mexican queso fresco, but choose whichever kind you like.

❋ The salad keeps, covered and refrigerated, for up to 5 days.

1 cup dried soybeans, soaked (see note)

1 cup farro, whole spelt, or white wheat berries

1 cup pearl barley

½ cup finely minced red onion

½ teaspoon minced or crushed garlic

1 tablespoon fresh lemon juice

1 tablespoon cider vinegar

¾ teaspoon salt, or more to taste

1 tablespoon agave nectar or light-colored honey

2 tablespoons extra-virgin olive oil

2 tablespoons roasted walnut oil or roasted almond oil

About 25 fresh mint leaves

1–2 firm, ripe plums (any kind)

1 cup crumbled fresh cheese (Mexican queso fresco, ricotta salata, or feta)

Black pepper

½ cup chopped almonds, lightly toasted (optional)

1. Drain the soybeans and place them in a pot with enough fresh water to cover by 2 inches. Bring to a boil, turn the heat to its lowest setting, and simmer, partially covered, for about an hour, or longer if necessary, until the soybeans are pleasantly tender. (They will retain some crunch.) Drain and set aside.

2. Fill a large saucepan with water and bring it to a boil. Add the farro and barley and cook at a gentle boil over medium heat for 40 to 45 minutes, or until tender.

3. Meanwhile, place the onion in a colander in the sink. When the grains are done to your liking, drain them directly into the onion, cooking it slightly in the process. Leave everything there for a few minutes to drain while you prepare the dressing.

4. Combine the garlic, lemon juice, vinegar, salt, and agave or honey in a bowl large enough to hold everything and whisk together until blended. Keep whisking as you drizzle in the oils until fully incorporated.

5. Add the grain mixture and the soybeans (it's OK if they're still hot or warm) to the bowl of dressing and mix to thoroughly combine. Let sit for a good hour for the flavors to develop and soak into the grains and beans.

6. You can serve the dish at room temperature or refrigerate it for up to several days and then serve cold or at cool room temperature. Shortly before serving, chop the mint (or snip it with scissors) and pit and thinly slice the plums and gently stir them in, along with the cheese. Season to taste with a little more salt, if desired, and some black pepper, and either stir in the almonds or sprinkle them on top as you serve, if desired.

Egg Salad with Rye Berries

MAKES 2 OR 3 MODEST MAIN-DISH SERVINGS (DOUBLES EASILY)

Welcome to the non-sandwich version of egg salad on rye. In this dish, chewy, pleasantly bitter whole rye berries—a relatively uncommon, highly nutritious grain—mingle with contrasting, complementary textures: hard-cooked eggs, minced fennel fronds, and Pickled Red Onions. This recipe also calls for a deeply flavored roasted nut or seed oil of your choice. Possible supporting players include a selection of minced fresh vegetables and toasted nuts or seeds, to add crunch to the chewiness.

❀ You can find whole rye berries in the bulk bins of natural food stores, usually near the other large whole grains (wheat berries, farro, spelt, etc.).

❀ Make a batch of Pickled Red Onions (page 395) up to several days ahead.

❀ I always look for ways to use the fronds of fresh fennel after the bulb has been employed. This is one such opportunity. Other cases can include any recipe that calls for fresh dill, for which fennel fronds can be a refreshing substitute.

½ cup rye berries (see note)

About ¼ cup finely minced fennel fronds, plus a bit of the top stem

¼ cup Pickled Red Onions (page 395), minced, with some juice

½ celery stalk, finely minced

2 large eggs, hard-cooked, finely chopped

¼ teaspoon salt, or more if needed

1 tablespoon roasted walnut, hazelnut, pumpkin seed, or pecan oil

Black pepper

1. Cook the rye berries in a generous amount of boiling water (as you would pasta) for up to 1 hour, or until done to your liking. When they pass your bite test, drain them into a colander, keeping in mind that regardless of cooking time, they will remain somewhat chewy. Spread out the drained, cooked grains in a single layer on a kitchen towel and pat dry.

2. Combine everything in a bowl large enough to permit mixing, starting with a little less salt, working your way up to ¼ teaspoon or possibly a touch more, as your taste indicates, and seasoning with black pepper to taste. Serve.

OPTIONAL ENHANCEMENTS

Minced carrot mixed in ❀ Chopped sweet bell pepper mixed in ❀ Chopped cucumber mixed in ❀ Lightly toasted pumpkin seeds on top ❀ A topping of minced walnuts, hazelnuts, or pecans, lightly toasted ❀ Minced cooked beets (any color) or grated raw, peeled beets for garnish ❀ Fresh, crisp salad greens or a Belgian endive "boat" for serving ❀ Shaved fennel or a Frond Tuft (page 76), lightly piled on top

Ravioli-Kale Salad

MAKES 2 OR 3 MODEST MAIN-DISH SERVINGS (DOUBLES EASILY)

Thin shreds of kale coated with olive oil and Parmesan surround freshly cooked ravioli, which mostly stays undercover. Then, suddenly, your fork spears something soft amid the crispy green toss, and out pops a mini UFO of filled pasta.

This is a good way to use some of that fresh artisanal ravioli that you may have been eyeing for a while, but finding beyond your budget. The salad extends it, adding volume and keeping things light and affordable. As an additional perk, the salad is neutral enough to partner well with various flavors, so go ahead and choose a ravioli whose filling is odd and creative, if it piques your interest.

❋ If you don't have access to good fresh ravioli, you can also use tortellini—fresh or dried, large or tiny (like the kind they sell at Trader Joe's).

❋ Look for exceedingly fresh lacinato kale with smallish, very dark green leaves for a more tender result. Cutting the kale before washing and drying it ensures it will all fit into your salad spinner and become drier. You can refrigerate the clean, dry kale until shortly before serving.

❋ This works best with coarsely shredded Parmesan, rather than finely grated.

1 large or 2 small bunches lacinato kale (½ pound total)

1–2 tablespoons shredded Parmesan

2 tablespoons extra-virgin olive oil

Salt

About 8 large (about 2-inch) ravioli (depending on the size and whether this is a main dish or an appetizer), with any kind of filling

A touch of fresh lemon juice or red wine vinegar (about 1 teaspoon)

Black pepper

1. Put a pot of water on to boil.

2. Hold each kale leaf by the stem and use a sharp knife to release the leaf from the base (it's OK to leave the narrow part of the stem that blends into the leaf farther up). Make a pile of the leaves, roll them tightly, and cut them crosswise into superthin strips. Transfer to a large bowl of cold water and swish around to clean. Spin dry and transfer to a large bowl.

3. Sprinkle the kale with the shredded Parmesan and the olive oil. Toss to completely coat, adding a little salt as you go.

4. Meanwhile, cook the ravioli per the package instructions. When they are done, fish them out of the pot with a skimmer.

5. Add the still-hot, drained ravioli directly to the salad, lifting clusters of kale from the bottom to cover and coat the pasta, very slightly wilting the kale in the process.

6. Toss in a drizzle of lemon juice or vinegar, season lightly with black pepper, and serve warm or at cool room temperature.

OPTIONAL ENHANCEMENTS

If you're using boutique ravioli, you can add touches of filling elements to the salad, as an echo: diced roasted butternut squash to match squash ravioli, sliced pear to match pear-Pecorino ravioli, or artichoke hearts to match artichoke ravioli ❋ If you are using a more standard filled pasta (such as cheese or pesto), add touches of ripe tomato, bell pepper, or onion

Coconut-Mango Rice Noodle Salad

MAKES 3 OR 4 MODEST MAIN-DISH SERVINGS ❧ VEGAN

Green beans, cashews, mint, carrot, cucumber, and lime shine through the pearly noodles in this pretty, uplifting dish. The noodles will seem undercooked at first, but they will soften as they absorb the marinade and the moisture from the other ingredients. If you cook them all the way, the finished dish will be mushy.

❈ Rice noodles of various thickness can be purchased inexpensively in most Asian-themed grocery stores, some supermarkets, and online. Use medium-thin ones for this recipe.

❈ You can freeze the unused coconut milk in an ice cube tray, then transfer the cubes to a heavy plastic zip-style bag for making this (or something else) in the future. Don't forget to label the bag.

❈ This tastes best within a few hours of being assembled, so plan accordingly.

❈ Make sure the cucumber is sweet.

2 tablespoons fresh lime juice

¼ teaspoon minced or crushed garlic

Up to 2 teaspoons agave nectar or sugar

½ teaspoon salt

2 tablespoons grapeseed or peanut oil

¾ cup reduced-fat coconut milk (half a 14- to 15-ounce can)

3 cups water

4 ounces medium-thin rice noodles

⅓ pound slender green beans, trimmed and halved either lengthwise or crosswise

½ cup Pickled Red Onions (page 395)

1 small (6-inch) cucumber (peeled if the skin is bitter), diced

1 medium carrot, coarsely grated

1 ripe, sweet mango, peeled, pitted, and cut into ½-inch dice, or 1 heaping cup diced defrosted frozen mango (see note, page 40)

About 10 fresh mint leaves, cut into thin strips

1 cup lightly toasted cashews, chopped or whole

1. Combine the lime juice, garlic, agave or sugar, and salt in a large bowl and whisk to blend. Keep whisking as you drizzle in the oil until it is completely incorporated; set aside.

2. Place a colander on a plate next to the stove and have a pair of tongs or a spider skimmer handy.

3. Combine the coconut milk and water in a medium saucepan and bring to a boil. Add the noodles and cook for exactly 3 minutes (best to use a timer). Use the skimmer or tongs to lift them out (leaving the pot on the heat) and transfer them to the colander. (They will be noticeably al dente.) Shake the colander over the plate to drain and dry the noodles, then transfer them directly to the marinade in the bowl. Turn and lift with tongs and/or a fork to get them coated.

4. Return the colander to the plate (emptied of any water) near the stove. Add the green beans to the simmering water–coconut milk mixture. Cook them for about 5 minutes, or until just tender. Use the skimmer or tongs to lift them into the colander to drain. You can save the coconut broth to make a little soup snack for yourself (see opposite page).

5. Add the green beans (it's OK if they're still hot) along with the Pickled Red Onions to the noodle mixture, mixing gently until combined. (Use a fork to grab the onions, leaving their liquid behind.)

6. Let the salad cool to room temperature, then add the cucumber and carrot. Cover and chill until serving time; the optimal marinating-chilling time is about 2 hours.

7. Stir in the mango, mint, and most of the cashews shortly before serving. Serve topped with the remaining cashews and any combination of the Enhancements.

OPTIONAL ENHANCEMENTS

Minced jalapeño scattered through ✳ Touch of lime zest mixed in to give it more zing ✳ Lime wedges ✳ Toasted unsweetened coconut on top ✳ Minced fresh basil (regular or Thai) and/or cilantro on top ✳ Chili paste or Sriracha on the side

LITTLE SOUP SNACK

Don't discard any leftover coconut-graced cooking liquid. Instead, make it into a cook's snack by adding tiny touches of lime juice, sugar, salt, and garlic, and a torn basil leaf. Sip happily while finishing the recipe.

Kale–Angel Hair Tangle with Orange-Chili Oil and Toasted Almonds

MAKES 4 MODEST MAIN-DISH SERVINGS ❋ VEGAN

Strips of fresh lacinato kale cook on contact with hot noodles, then they marinate together in orange-garlic-chili oil. Fresh orange sections and almonds are introduced at serving time. This salad tastes so exotic that you'll forget just how straightforward it was to prepare. Even the most labor-intensive preparations (cutting the kale, zesting and removing the orange sections from their membranes) are not difficult and can be done in advance.

❋ I use Lee Kum Kee Chili Garlic Sauce, which is widely available. That said, if you have your own favorite brand on hand, go ahead and use it.

❋ The range of orange zest allows you to customize both the labor and the flavor. However much you decide to use, you will be all the happier for remembering to zest the oranges before you peel and section them.

❋ Remove the orange sections from their membranes by first peeling the fruit completely with a serrated knife, and, holding each orange over a bowl, sawing in and out of the membranes with the same knife to release the sections. Squeeze in the juice and discard the membrane left behind. This is a wet, yet worthwhile, procedure. (Just keep a few damp kitchen towels handy.)

❋ This tastes best within 2 hours of being made. It does not need to be all-the-way chilled, and in fact, tastes best at cool room temperature.

2 tablespoons Chinese chili sauce

1 teaspoon minced or crushed garlic

Up to 1 teaspoon grated orange zest

2 teaspoons agave nectar or sugar

¼ heaping teaspoon salt, or more to taste

2 teaspoons cider vinegar or unseasoned rice vinegar

½ teaspoon soy sauce, or more to taste

¼ cup grapeseed or peanut oil

2 large or 4 small bunches very fresh lacinato kale (1 pound total)

6 ounces angel hair pasta

2 oranges, peeled, sectioned, and sections removed from membranes (see note)

½ cup sliced almonds, lightly toasted

1. Put on a large pot of water to boil.

2. Combine the chili sauce, garlic, zest, agave or sugar, salt, vinegar, and ½ teaspoon of the soy sauce in a large bowl. Whisk to blend, then keep whisking as you drizzle in the oil until it is completely incorporated. Set aside while you prepare the other ingredients.

3. Slice off and discard the larger kale stems, then make a uniform pile of the leaves and roll them tightly into a kale cigar. Make thin slices crosswise with an extremely sharp knife. Transfer to a large colander in the sink. Rinse and drain the kale, then leave the whole setup in the sink to await the hot noodles.

4. Add the pasta to the boiling water, keeping the heat high. Cook for the amount of time recommended on the package, tasting the pasta toward the end of the suggested time to be sure it is not getting overcooked. When it is just tender enough to bite into comfortably, but not yet mushy (better to err on the al dente side), dump the pasta plus all its water into the kale in the colander. Shake hard a few times to drain, then transfer the pasta and kale, still hot, directly into the bowl of dressing.

5. Use a fork or tongs to mix all the ingredients, lifting from the bottom of the bowl to distribute the dressing evenly. Let cool to room temperature and then taste to adjust the seasonings, if necessary.

6. If not serving immediately, cover tightly and let stand at room temperature, or in the refrigerator if your kitchen is too hot and/ or you prefer your salad chilled. Serve within 2 hours, ideally in individual bowls, gently mixing in the orange sections and most of the almonds and sprinkling the remaining almonds over the top.

Marinated Shiitakes with Cold Bean Thread Noodles

MAKES 4 TO 5 MODEST MAIN-DISH SERVINGS ❦ VEGAN

Shiitake mushroom lovers, this salad is dedicated to you. It's hard to stop nibbling on it as you prepare it. Fortunately, it takes a lot of nibbling to make even the smallest dent in these chewy noodles. This recipe is especially nice paired with Asian Slaw (page 62) or Mushroom Wonton Soup (page 38). At least 3 hours of marination will ensure deliciousness. You can also do it it a day ahead. If you plan to serve it with Asian Slaw, you can start them both at the same time and let them rest together.

❀ Soak the dried mushrooms at least 30 minutes ahead of time. After they are drained, you can use their soaking water to add to stock or to rice-cooking water.

❀ Seasoned rice vinegar is the kind that is laced with a little salt and sugar.

❀ Bean thread noodles can be found in Asian grocery stores, and usually come coiled in 2-ounce nests. If yours are in that format, use 3 of them.

7 cups water

3 ounces dried shiitake mushrooms (*not* presliced)

6 tablespoons seasoned rice vinegar, or more to taste

2 tablespoons grapeseed or peanut oil

1 teaspoon Chinese sesame oil, or more to taste

1 teaspoon soy sauce, or more to taste

½ teaspoon minced or crushed garlic

¾ teaspoon salt, or more to taste

1 heaping teaspoon agave nectar or sugar, or more to taste

6 ounces bean thread noodles

6 scallions, whites finely minced, greens cut into very thin ovals; whites and greens kept separate

3 tablespoons sesame seeds

Black pepper

Crushed red pepper

1. Put the water in a large saucepan and bring to a boil.

2. Place the mushrooms in a medium bowl and pour in 3 cups of the boiling water. Cover with a plate and let sit until the mushrooms are soft, about 30 minutes.

3. Meanwhile, combine the vinegar, oil, sesame oil, soy sauce, garlic, salt, and the heaping teaspoon of agave nectar or sugar in a large bowl and whisk to blend.

4. Return the pot with the remaining 4 cups hot water to the heat, bring it back to a boil, and add the noodles. (If they are in nest format, simply place the nests in the boiling water, then gently loosen and pull apart with tongs.) Cook the noodles for just 1 minute, then drain in a colander in the sink. Rinse under cold running water, then drain again thoroughly and add to the marinade, tossing to coat.

5. Drain the mushrooms gently but completely, hand-squeezing to expel as much of the water as you can.

6. Remove and discard the mushroom stems, then slice the caps very thin. Add the caps to the noodles, along with the scallion whites, 2 tablespoons of the sesame seeds, and big pinches of black and red pepper to taste. Toss to combine, cover, and refrigerate for at least 3 hours to marinate. After an hour or two, taste to see if it needs additional salt or sweetener.

7. Serve cold or at cool room temperature, topped with the scallion greens and the remaining 1 tablespoon sesame seeds. Pass additional sesame oil, soy sauce, crushed red pepper, and seasoned rice vinegar, if desired, for possible customization.

Soba-Seaweed Salad

MAKES 4 TO 6 MODEST MAIN-DISH SERVINGS ❈ VEGAN

Vegetarians get a rare chance to taste the ocean in this cross between a slaw and a noodle salad. I highly recommend topping it with Egg "Noodles" (page 398), which take less than 5 minutes to prepare.

❈ Hijiki is a thin and salty seaweed that comes dried in inexpensive smallish packages in most Asian grocery stores. All you need to do is soak it in cold water, then squeeze out the excess moisture, and it's ready to use. Do this at least 30 minutes ahead of time.

❈ Soba is a skinny, dark Japanese buckwheat pasta. Look for it in natural food stores as well as Asian groceries.

❈ Seasoned rice vinegar is the kind that comes laced with a little sugar and salt.

❈ You can possibly make this with no added salt, since the hijiki and the seasoned rice vinegar both contain some.

❈ This tastes best freshly made, but will keep well for up to a day, tightly covered and refrigerated.

1 ounce hijiki seaweed

6 ounces soba noodles

3 tablespoons grapeseed or peanut oil

3 tablespoons seasoned rice vinegar

1 medium carrot, coarsely grated

4 large radishes, cut into thin strips or grated

1 cup finely shredded or grated purple cabbage

1 small (6-inch) sweet cucumber (peeled if the skin is bitter), diced

2 scallions, whites finely minced, greens cut into very thin ovals; whites and greens kept separate

Up to ¼ teaspoon salt, or to taste

1. Place the hijiki in a small bowl with enough cold water to cover. Let it stand for 30 minutes to soften, then drain, thoroughly squeezing out and discarding all the excess water.

2. Put on a large pot of water to boil. When it boils, add the noodles, keeping the heat high. Cook for just 3 minutes, then drain, rinse in cold water, and drain thoroughly. Transfer the noodles to a medium bowl and toss with the oil and hijiki. Add all the remaining ingredients, except the scallion greens, mixing thoroughly to blend.

3. The salad is now ready to eat, or you can cover and chill it for up to a day. Serve topped with the scallion greens and as many of the Optional Enhancements as desired.

OPTIONAL ENHANCEMENTS

Sesame seeds, in or on top ❈ Roasted walnut oil or roasted almond oil swapped in for some or all of the other oil ❈ Toasted walnuts or almonds (to match the nut oil) ❈ Additional radishes ❈ Shelled, lightly steamed edamame on top ❈ A tangle of chopped shiso and/or thinly sliced snow peas ❈ A dab of Misoyaki Sauce (page 362) ❈ A dot of chili paste

STEWS
and
Their Accessories

***

Stews and soups are neighbors that share a balcony. At the soup end of the continuum, everything is brought together and simmered in added liquid, and on the stew side, the vegetables are, in large part, cooked from the inside, with their internal essence called up and sweated out. You could say the vegetables stew in their own juices; that they (quite literally) express themselves. The result can be as profound and complex as Sweet Potato–Black Bean Stew with Sweet Peppers and Peanut Sauce — or as satisfying as Very Simple Lentil Stew.

Any soup can be called a stew if the liquid reduces and the result becomes thick, and any stew can be turned into a soup, if a matching, delicious stock is added. If a stew becomes so thick that it is mostly a medley of tasty solids, you can mash it and serve it as a side on day two or three and tag that recipe as an honorary member of the Cozy Mashes chapter.

My goal was to make these stews filling without being heavy, maintaining interest and color while balancing flavors. Some (Black-Eyed Pea, Squash, and Shiitake Stew; Peruvian Potato-Bean Stew) are beany enough to border on chili, others (Kimchi Stew; Root Vegetable Stew with Ginger and Pears) surprise with unexpected guest ingredients, and a few (Mushroom Stroganoff over Cabbage "Noodles," Ribollita) are twists on traditional themes.

Almost all of these stews get their own accessory—a little something extra welcoming you in and promising novelty and contrast. (The sole exception is Ribollita, in which the toast is built into the recipe.) Whether mini biscuits, corn cakes, or puffed rice noodles, the accompaniments are wonderful but not essential: Every one of these stews, freestanding, can be dinner. And on their own, the accessories can be snacks or breakfast.

Curried Cauliflower Stew

ONION PAKORAS (optional; page 139)

MAKES 6 TO 8 SERVINGS

Yogurt, curry spices, carrots, cashews—this is the company cauliflower loves to keep. Get a batch of brown basmati rice going before you begin, and it will all come together easily. Then, have fun making it your own personal dish with a selection of the many Optional Enhancements.

❋ If you are accustomed to low-fat yogurt, that will work fine, but consider using whole-milk yogurt for a richer taste. A thicker, Greek-style yogurt, including nonfat, will also work well.

❋ Timing: You can prepare the pakora ingredients while the stew is cooking and keep the finished stew warm while you make the pakoras.

[continues]

1–2 tablespoons peanut, coconut, canola, or grapeseed oil

2 cups minced red or yellow onion (1 large)

1 tablespoon minced fresh ginger

2 teaspoons mustard seeds

1 teaspoon cumin seeds

¾ teaspoon salt, or more to taste

2 teaspoons ground cumin

1 teaspoon turmeric

½ teaspoon *each* ground cardamom and coriander (optional)

2 teaspoons minced or crushed garlic

2 medium heads cauliflower (about 4 pounds total), trimmed and cut into 1-inch florets

4 medium carrots (about 1 pound total), cut into half circles about ⅛ inch thick

Up to ¼ cup water (optional)

1 cup plain yogurt, at room temperature (see note)

1 15-ounce can chickpeas, rinsed and drained

Cayenne

1½ cups cashews, lightly toasted

Cooked brown basmati rice

1. Place a soup pot, large saucepan, or Dutch oven over medium heat for about a minute. Add the oil and swirl to coat the pan. Add the onion, ginger, mustard seeds, cumin seeds, and ½ teaspoon of the salt. Cook, stirring, for about 5 minutes, or until the onion becomes translucent and the spices begin to snap. Add the ground spices and garlic and cook over low heat, stirring often, for another 5 minutes.

2. Add the cauliflower and carrots, along with another ¼ teaspoon salt, stirring until the vegetables become coated with the good stuff in the pan. (If the mixture appears dry, splash in the water, a tablespoon at a time.) Cover and cook over medium-low heat, stirring occasionally, until the vegetables are just tender, 15 to 20 minutes, depending on the size of the pieces and your taste in vegetable texture.

3. When the vegetables are done to your liking, gently stir in the yogurt and chickpeas, mixing until thoroughly combined. Taste to adjust the salt and add cayenne to taste.

4. Stir in the cashews just before serving. Serve hot or warm over rice.

OPTIONAL ENHANCEMENTS

Finely chopped fresh spinach, added in step 3 ❋ Sliced ripe cherry tomatoes, stirred in or on top ❋ A scattering of torn cilantro leaves ❋ Golden raisins on top ❋ Raita (page 371) or extra yogurt ❋ Chopped Indian pickles (many choices at Indian grocery stores) ❋ A spot of your favorite authentic Indian chutney (found at Indian grocery stores) ❋ A drizzle of pomegranate molasses or Pomegranate-Lime Glaze (page 369) ❋ Crushed red pepper or chili oil

ONION PAKORAS

MAKES ABOUT 2 DOZEN (3 OR 4 PER SERVING)
❋ VEGAN

Chunks of onion are coated in an easy, spiced chickpea flour batter and fried into savory, crisp tidbits.

❋ You can buy chickpea flour at any Indian grocery store and at many natural food stores. It's also widely available online.

❋ For best results, sauté these in coconut oil (solid at room temperature), grapeseed oil, or high-oleic safflower oil, any of which can be safely heated to high temperatures. You can get a deep-fat-fried effect with a lot less oil if you get the pan and the oil really hot before adding the food, and by paying careful attention.

1 cup chickpea flour

½ heaping teaspoon salt, plus more for finishing if desired

1 teaspoon cumin seeds

1 teaspoon mustard seeds

Big pinch or two of crushed red pepper

⅔ cup water

2 medium onions, cut into 1-inch squares

Coconut, grapeseed, or high-oleic safflower oil for frying

1. Combine the chickpea flour, salt, seeds, and crushed red pepper in a medium bowl.

2. Add the water and stir until uniform. Stir in the onion pieces, turning them until they are completely coated.

3. Heat 2 tablespoons oil in a large skillet over medium heat until it is hot enough to instantly sizzle a bread crumb. Drop the batter by rounded teaspoons into the hot oil and fry on all surfaces (as much as possible—they're lumpy) for about 5 minutes, or until crisp. Drain on several layers of paper towels. Salt the pakoras lightly while still hot, if desired, and serve right away. (If you need to fry these in batches, keep the finished ones warm in a 200°F oven while you cook the rest, adding small amounts of additional oil as needed.)

OPTIONAL ENHANCEMENTS

Pomegranate molasses or Pomegranate-Lime Glaze (page 369) ❋ Sweet-Sour Dipping-Drizzling Sauce (page 370) ❋ Any favorite commercially prepared chutney and/or Indian pickles ❋ Yogurt or Raita (page 371)

Black-Eyed Pea, Squash, and Shiitake Stew
GINGER-PECAN MINI BISCUITS (optional; page 142)

MAKES 4 TO 6 SERVINGS ❧ VEGAN (WITHOUT THE BISCUITS)

Creamy black-eyed peas and chewy mushrooms play off beautifully against golden, sweet cubes of roasted butternut squash, while lemon and mustard infuse everything with sparkle and edge. I just plain love this recipe—it's one of my favorites—and the nutty, slightly sweet biscuits are a treat. There's nothing like sitting around a table after dinner with everyone silently and happily contemplating what they just experienced. Be prepared for that to happen here.

❀ The black-eyed peas can be cooked and the squash can be roasted well ahead of time. You can also use two 15-ounce cans of black-eyed peas, rinsed and thoroughly drained, instead of soaking and cooking dried ones.

❀ For more on roasting squash, see page 351.

❀ Timing: Make and cut the biscuit dough before you begin the stew. (The dough can be made the day before.) You can bake the biscuits after roasting the squash, while the stew finishes. You

can also have the biscuits all made and baked ahead of time and reheat them in an oven or toaster oven just before serving, if desired.

1 cup (½ pound) dried black-eyed peas, soaked in cold water for at least 4 hours (see note)

3 tablespoons grapeseed or olive oil or a combination

1 medium butternut squash (about 3 pounds), peeled, seeded, and cut into ¾-inch dice

3 tablespoons fresh lemon juice

2 cups chopped red onion (1 large)

2 teaspoons dry mustard

1 teaspoon salt, or more to taste

20 medium (2-inch cap) fresh shiitake mushrooms, stemmed, wiped clean, and thinly sliced

1½ teaspoons minced or crushed garlic

2 tablespoons cider vinegar

Black pepper

Lemon wedges

1. Drain and rinse the soaked black-eyed peas, then transfer them to a medium saucepan and cover with water by at least 2 inches. Bring to a boil, turn the heat way down, and simmer, partially covered, until pleasantly tender but not too soft, about 30 minutes. Drain, reserving ½ cup of the cooking water, and set aside.

2. Preheat the oven to 375°F, with a rack in the center position. Line a baking sheet with parchment paper or foil and slick it all over with 1 tablespoon of the oil. (You can use a piece of cut squash to do this.)

3. Spread out the squash in a single layer and roast for about 30 minutes, or until fork-tender and nicely browned around the edges. (Check on the roasting squash every 10 minutes or so; shake the baking sheet from time to time and/ or use tongs or a spatula to loosen and move the pieces around during roasting. You don't want the bottom surfaces to burn.) When the squash is done, sprinkle it with 2 tablespoons of the lemon juice. Let it sit and soak this up as it cools.

4. Meanwhile, place a soup pot, large saucepan, or Dutch oven over medium heat for about a minute. Add the remaining 2 tablespoons oil and swirl to coat the pan. Add the onion, mustard, and ½ teaspoon of the salt. Cook over medium heat, stirring often, for 8 to 10 minutes, or until the onion becomes very soft.

5. Stir in the mushrooms, garlic, and another ½ teaspoon salt. Cook, covered, over medium heat for 10 minutes, stirring often.

6. Add the beans to the vegetable mixture, along with the remaining 1 tablespoon lemon juice and the vinegar. Taste to adjust the salt and grind in a generous amount of black pepper. Stir from the bottom of the pot gently, so as not to break the beans, but thoroughly enough to mix everything. If it seems dry, add 1 cup or more of the reserved bean-cooking water. Cook over low heat for 5 minutes or so, just long enough to heat through.

[continues]

7. Carefully fold in the squash shortly before serving and heat gently without cooking the stew further, so the texture remains varied and interesting. Serve hot.

OPTIONAL ENHANCEMENTS

Lemon wedges ✳ Crystallized ginger, finely minced ✳ Minced pecans, lightly toasted (salted are OK) ✳ Grated or chopped lemon zest ✳ Fresh bread crumbs, pan-toasted in olive oil and/or butter ✳ Finely minced fresh flat-leaf parsley and/or scallions ✳ Serve with a cheese platter

GINGER-PECAN MINI BISCUITS

MAKES ABOUT 3 DOZEN (3 OR 4 PER SERVING)

Plus-size flavor and serious texture are loaded into tiny, scrumptious units. I don't use the "Beware: Habit-forming" cliché very often, but I feel it's my duty to invoke it here.

✳ You can make the dough up to a day in advance and store it, tightly wrapped, in the refrigerator.

✳ Baked biscuits last for at least a week in the refrigerator if wrapped airtight. They are easily reheated in a toaster oven. In a heavy zip-style plastic bag, they'll last a month or longer in the freezer.

1 cup unbleached all-purpose flour, plus more for handling

1 teaspoon baking powder

Scant ½ teaspoon salt

½ cup pecans

½ cup sliced crystallized ginger

⅓ cup buttermilk, plus more if needed

¼ cup grapeseed, canola, or peanut oil

Nonstick cooking spray (optional)

1. Preheat the oven to 375°F, with a rack in the center position. Have ready an ungreased baking sheet.

2. Combine the dry ingredients, nuts, and ginger in a food processor. Buzz for a few long pulses until the mixture is mostly uniform and resembles a coarse meal.

3. Pour the buttermilk and the oil into a liquid measuring cup. Whisk briefly to blend and then pour this into the feed tube while the machine is still running. Carefully remove the dough, pressing it into a disk.

4. Dust a clean, dry work surface with a little flour or spray it with nonstick spray and press or roll the dough into a square uniformly ½ inch thick. Use a dinner knife to cut into 1-inch squares or diamonds and transfer them to the baking sheet. Re-shape and keep cutting as needed until you've used all the dough. The pieces can be very close together, since they will not spread out while baking.

5. Bake for 8 to 12 minutes, or until lightly golden on the bottoms and edges. Let the biscuits cool on the baking sheet for about 5 minutes before devouring.

Ribollita

MAKES 6 SERVINGS ❧ VEGAN (WHEN CHEESE IS OMITTED)

Here is a relatively quick way to make what will taste gratifyingly like the old-fashioned, long-cooked, authentic Tuscanish bowl of hearty goodness. Kale, cabbage, beans, and an assortment of simple vegetables simmer into a soulful stew, creating a perfect soaking opportunity for thick slices of bread. A topping of cheese and good olive oil (and a glass of big red wine) will make this quiet dinner luxurious and complete.

❀ Start soaking the beans the night before and put them on to cook at least 2 hours before you begin cooking the Ribollita. It's important to begin with dried beans for this, rather than using canned, as you will be seasoning both the beans and the cooking water, and both will be included in the stew.

❀ Broil a little grated aged cheese on top just before serving.

THE BEANS (DO THIS WELL AHEAD OF TIME)

1 cup dried cannellini beans, soaked for at least 4 hours (preferably overnight)

3 large garlic cloves, peeled and halved

3 fresh sage leaves

1 3-inch sprig fresh rosemary

Several sprigs of fresh thyme

1 medium Parmesan rind (up to 4 ounces; optional)

1. Drain the soaked beans and place them in a large pot along with enough fresh water to cover by at least 2 inches (3 inches is even better). Add the garlic and herbs and bring to a boil.

2. Lower the heat to a simmer and cook, partially covered, for 1½ hours, or until the beans are as soft as they can get while still keeping their shape. (Make sure they are truly soft. No undercooked beans!) If you like, you can add the Parmesan rind about 45 minutes into the simmering.

3. Remove from the heat and drain in a strainer set over a large heatproof bowl, saving the cooking water. (Fish out the herbs and Parmesan rind, if using; it's OK to leave in the garlic.)

THE STEW

3 tablespoons olive oil

2 cups chopped onion (1 large)

2 celery stalks, diced

1 large carrot, cut into half circles about ⅛ inch thick or into bite-sized chunks

¾ teaspoon salt, or more to taste

2 tablespoons minced or crushed garlic

½ pound green cabbage, cut into bite-sized pieces (2 heaping cups)

1 large or 2 small bunches lacinato kale (½ pound total), stemmed and chopped fairly small (4 packed cups)

Black pepper

About 6 slices artisan bread (day-old is fine), such as ciabatta or Pugliese, toasted

Grated aged Parmesan, Pecorino, or Asiago (optional)

1. Place a soup pot or Dutch oven over medium heat for about a minute, then add 2 tablespoons of the oil and swirl to coat the pan. Add the onion and cook, stirring frequently, for 5 minutes, or until the onion begins to soften.

Stir in the celery, carrot, ¼ teaspoon of the salt, and 1 tablespoon of the garlic and cook for another 5 minutes, stirring often.

2. Stir in the cabbage, kale, and remaining 1 tablespoon garlic, sprinkling them with another ½ teaspoon salt as you go. The pot will be crowded at first, but the vegetables will cook down. Cover and cook, stirring frequently, until the vegetables are all tender, about 10 minutes. Add small amounts of the bean cooking water (½ cup at a time) if needed to prevent sticking, but otherwise try to force-cook the vegetables in their own moisture, adding as little water as possible.

3. When the vegetables are done to your liking, add the beans, stirring them in gently so they don't break. Add a little more bean-cooking water, if you wish. Cover again and cook for just a few more minutes. Taste to adjust the salt and add a good amount of black pepper.

4. Serve hot, drizzled with the remaining 1 tablespoon olive oil and topped with the toasted bread. If you want to enjoy a cheese-encrusted experience, spoon the stew into ovenproof ceramic bowls (as you would French onion soup), top with the bread slices, sprinkle some cheese over the bread, and broil briefly.

OPTIONAL ENHANCEMENTS

Diced tomatoes (ideally fresh, sweet ones) ✳ Chopped zucchini, chard or other greens, or fennel ✳ Diced boiled potatoes, plus some of their cooking water ✳ An Herb Tangle (page 76) of fresh flat-leaf parsley and snippets of fresh thyme

STREAMLINING A SLOW-FOOD CLASSIC

Describing the traditional preparation of Ribollita is akin to reciting a food version of "This Little Pig Went to Market." To wit:

FIRST DAY: A vegetable soup is in a pot on the stove.

SECOND DAY: The leftover vegetable soup is layered with stale bread and baked.

THIRD DAY: The leftover leftover-layered-with-bread vegetable soup is baked yet again, this time spending hours in the oven, topped with a pile of thinly sliced onions lightly drizzled with olive oil.

FOURTH DAY: The full-fledged ribollita finally emerges, this time from a frying pan, where its now-thick self has become deliciously encrusted on all available surfaces through slow cooking and patient turning in a slick of olive oil.

All of this sounds so good that clearly you and I both want to go fry ourselves some four-day-old, twice-baked bread and onion-layered soup right this minute. While the much quicker recipe above offers immediate gratification, you can also eat little bits at a time and then bake and fry the leftovers forward over the next number of days and enjoy the best of both worlds, old and new.

Very Simple Lentil Stew
COTTAGE CHEESE DUMPLINGS (optional)

MAKES 4 OR 5 SERVINGS ❧ VEGAN (WHEN MADE WITHOUT BUTTER AND DUMPLINGS)

It's good to be reminded from time to time that you can hold back and let ingredients speak for themselves. Lentils, in particular, are delicious quite plain. You'll do very little to the lentils, allowing them to bask in their own quiet merits.

❋ If you have some high-quality extra-virgin olive oil that you have been waiting to use, this is its moment. Just a subtle drizzle on top of each steaming bowlful of stew makes all the difference.

❋ Timing: You can make the dumplings through the poaching stage while the lentils simmer. When the stew is done, let it sit and wait while you do the quick, final sauté of the dumplings.

1 cup brown lentils

3 cups water

3 large garlic cloves, peeled and halved

2 sprigs fresh thyme or ½ teaspoon dried

1 tablespoon olive oil

1 teaspoon unsalted butter (optional)

1 cup minced onion

1 large very sweet carrot, finely chopped

½ teaspoon salt, or more to taste

Pinch *each* of dried thyme and rubbed dried sage

Black pepper

Splash of vegetable stock (page 22) or low-sodium store bought or red wine (optional)

High-quality extra-virgin olive oil

Crispy Sage Leaves (optional; page 394)

1. Combine the lentils and water in a medium saucepan. Add the garlic and thyme and bring to a boil over medium heat. Lower the heat to a simmer, partially cover, and cook until tender, about 30 minutes. Remove the thyme sprigs.

2. Meanwhile, place a medium skillet over medium heat for about a minute. Add the olive oil and swirl to coat the pan and, if you like, melt in the butter. Add the onion and carrot and cook, stirring, for 5 minutes. Add the salt and the herbs and cook, stirring often, for another 8 to 10 minutes, or until the vegetables are soft. (You can cover the pan to speed this along, if you wish.)

3. When everything is just right, stir the vegetables into the lentils, adding some black pepper as you go. Continue stewing, covered, over low heat, for another 5 to 10 minutes, to let the flavors mingle. (You can add a little more water during this time, if you like, or a splash of vegetable stock or red wine.)

4. Taste to see if it needs more salt, adjust if necessary, and serve hot, topped with a drizzle of extra-virgin olive oil, a few Cottage Cheese Dumplings, if using, and some Crispy Sage Leaves, if using.

OPTIONAL ENHANCEMENTS

Top with a tangle of minced watercress on any Little Salad (page 76) ❋ Serve on or with Quinoa-Couscous Pilaf with Carrot, Roasted Almond Oil, and Pickled Red Onions (page 220) and Orange-Olive-Fig Saladita (page 385)

COTTAGE CHEESE DUMPLINGS

MAKES ABOUT 16 DUMPLINGS (3 OR 4 PER SERVING)

I speak from experience when I say that these creamy dumplings are very good by themselves, served plain on a plate (or straight from the pan) as a light appetizer or lunch (or whatever you call the meal you eat standing at the stove).

The batter is superquick. Just mix it together and spoon it into simmering water. After the poaching process, the dumplings are finished in a skillet with some oil (and a little butter if you like), becoming golden and crisp on the outside while remaining soft and chewy within.

❀ If you substitute ricotta for the cottage cheese, the result will be slightly milder (less tart and tangy).

❀ You can make and poach the dumplings several days ahead of time and store them in an airtight container in the refrigerator. They can go, still cold, directly into the hot pan for the final step, and will emerge as tender as if they'd just been thrown together minutes before.

❀ Use a very clean pan and a small metal spatula with a thin blade to strongly assert the boundary between the dumplings and the skillet. Any bumps or debris in the pan will disturb the integrity of these delicate dumplings.

❀ Leftover sautéed dumplings can be successfully reheated in a microwave.

2 large eggs

⅔ cup cottage cheese (low-fat is OK)

6 tablespoons unbleached all-purpose flour

¼ teaspoon salt, plus more for the cooking water

2–3 fresh chives, snipped tiny with scissors (optional)

Grapeseed, canola, or peanut oil for the pan

Butter for the pan (optional)

1. Use a fork to beat together the eggs and cottage cheese in a medium bowl. In a small bowl, combine the flour, salt, and chives, if using. Sprinkle the dry mixture into the wet, stirring briefly with a spoon until blended. The batter will be soft. (*You can form and cook the dumplings right away, or chill the batter, tightly covered, for up to 24 hours.*)

2. Heat a wide, shallow saucepan of lightly salted water to boiling, then lower the heat to a simmer. Drop in rounded teaspoons of the batter and let them poach for 10 minutes, swishing the water a bit and turning them slightly as they cook. You will likely need to simmer them in batches, as they shouldn't crowd and will puff up a bit. If any of the dumplings seem to be sticking to the bottom, gently loosen them with a spatula. Remove with a slotted spoon and drain well on a bed of kitchen towels.

3. Meanwhile, heat a large skillet over medium heat for about a minute. Add a small slick of oil and about a teaspoon of butter, if using, and swirl to coat the pan. Cook the dumplings for about 5 minutes, turning frequently, until they become lightly golden all over. (It's OK if the pan is somewhat crowded.) They will crisp up on the outside and became condensed and chewy on the interior, while remaining tender. Serve them hot, straight out of the pan.

Sweet Potato–Black Bean Stew with Sweet Peppers and Peanut Sauce

BANANA-CHEESE EMPANADAS (optional; page 150)

MAKES 6 SERVINGS ❀ VEGAN (WHEN MADE WITH AGAVE NECTAR AND SERVED WITHOUT THE EMPANADAS)

I think this is one of the more beautiful dishes in my repertoire. The preparation is also intensely (but not too) gingery and just peanutty enough to hit that certain spot.

❀ Roasted peanut oil is an aromatic finishing oil that is also stable enough to cook with. Go ahead and use it in combination with another oil—or on its own—if you love a good, deep peanutty flavor.

❀ Use bright orange sweet potatoes, not white ones, which are too dry and starchy.

❀ Use a smooth, natural peanut butter for best results. The kind I use is lightly salted.

❀ To cook the black beans from scratch, soak 1 cup dried beans in plenty of water for at least 4 hours (and as long as overnight). Drain and simmer in fresh water to cover by at least 2 inches for about 1½ hours, or until tender. (Make sure they are truly soft!) You can slip a few thick slices of ginger plus some whole garlic cloves into the simmering water to give the beans a head start on the spirit of this stew.

❀ Timing: Assemble the empanadas (short of the final step) before making the stew. When the stew is cooked, keep it warm while you sauté the empanadas, so they can be served fresh and hot from the pan.

2 tablespoons grapeseed, olive, or roasted peanut oil, or a combination

2 cups minced red onion (1 large)

2 tablespoons finely minced fresh ginger

1¼ teaspoons salt, or more to taste

2 teaspoons minced or crushed garlic

2 pounds sweet potatoes, peeled and cut into ¾-inch cubes (7 cups)

½ cup water

1 large sweet red bell pepper, cut into ¼-inch dice (2 cups)

2 tablespoons fresh lime juice, or more to taste

3 cups cooked black beans or two 15-ounce cans, rinsed and drained

Nonstick cooking spray

⅓ cup peanut butter

½ cup boiling water

1½ teaspoons cider vinegar or unseasoned rice vinegar

1½ teaspoons agave nectar or light-colored honey

Crushed red pepper (optional)

1. Place a soup pot, large saucepan, or Dutch oven over medium heat for about a minute. Add the oil and swirl to coat the pan. Add the onion, ginger, and ½ teaspoon of the salt. Cook, stirring often, for about 3 minutes. Add 1 teaspoon of the garlic and sauté for about 5 minutes longer, or until the onion becomes translucent.

2. Stir in the sweet potatoes, plus the remaining 1 teaspoon garlic and another ½ teaspoon salt. Cover the pot and cook for 5 minutes, then add ½ cup water, cover again, and cook over low heat for about 30 minutes, or until the sweet potatoes are almost done. Stir from time to time to be sure they're cooking evenly.

3. Add the bell pepper and lime juice, stirring to get everything coated with everything else. Cover again and continue cooking for about 10 more minutes, or until the sweet potatoes are perfectly fork-tender. Check occasionally to see if anything is sticking, and if so add a little more water or lime juice as necessary. Gently stir in the beans during the last few minutes of cooking.

4. Meanwhile, lightly spray a ⅓-cup measure with nonstick spray (makes things easier), then measure the peanut butter and place in a medium bowl. Slowly stir in the boiling water, followed by the vinegar, sweetener, and the remaining ¼ teaspoon salt. When the sauce is completely blended, taste to see if it needs more salt, and adjust if necessary.

5. Use a rubber spatula to scrape all the peanut sauce into the stew, then stir gently to get it completely distributed. Taste it one more time to make sure the lime juice and salt are right, and to see if you might want to add some crushed red pepper. Serve hot, with the Enhancements of your choice and freshly cooked Banana-Cheese Empanadas on the side.

OPTIONAL ENHANCEMENTS

Roasted peanuts ❋ Lime wedges ❋ Torn cilantro leaves

BANANA-CHEESE EMPANADAS

MAKES 6 EMPANADAS (1 PER SERVING)

Odd-seeming, perhaps, but so surprisingly good that the first five minutes of dinner conversation will likely be devoted to empanada exclamations. And then people will probably ask you for the recipe.

❀ For best results, sauté these in grapeseed oil or high-oleic safflower oil. You can melt in a little piece of butter for extra flavor and color, if you like.

❀ These taste best when freshly cooked, but the filled empanadas will keep on a floured plate in a single layer—keep them dry—in the refrigerator for a couple of days before getting sautéed.

1 cup unbleached all-purpose flour, plus more for handling

½ teaspoon salt

Up to 1 teaspoon grated lime zest (optional)

½ cup buttermilk

1 teaspoon grapeseed or peanut oil

Nonstick cooking spray

2 ounces Jack cheese (plain or pepper Jack)

1 large banana (firm but not green)

1 tablespoon fresh lime juice

Crushed red pepper (optional)

Grapeseed or high-oleic safflower oil for the pan (see note)

Butter for the pan (optional)

1. In a medium bowl, thoroughly combine the flour, salt, and some grated lime zest, if desired. Make a well in the center.

2. In a liquid measuring cup, stir together the buttermilk and the oil and pour into the well in the dry ingredients. Mix with a spoon (and your lightly floured hand) to make a smooth, uniform dough, then spray the top lightly with nonstick spray and let it rest for 15 minutes.

3. Meanwhile, cut the cheese into thin slices and slice the banana diagonally into ¼-inch-thick pieces. Place the banana slices on a plate and douse them with the lime juice and a little crushed red pepper, if you like.

4. Divide the dough into 6 equal parts and briefly knead/shape each one into a perfectly round ball. Lightly coat a clean dry work surface with nonstick spray or a little extra flour, then use a rolling pin to roll each ball into a 3- to 4-inch circle.

5. Divide the cheese and banana pieces evenly among the 6 circles, placing them on one half of each circle and leaving about a ¼-inch border at the outer edge. (You can make them quite tall but not wide, since the dough is stretchy and can accommodate more than you might think (the pocket will expand). If you don't make them full enough, there will be an air pocket above the filling when you take a bite.

6. Use your finger or a pastry brush to apply a little water to the edge of the filled half, then fold over the empty half to cover. Use a fork to tightly crimp the edges closed. (*At this point, you can sauté the empanadas, or store them in the refrigerator in a single layer on a floured plate, covered with plastic wrap. Don't be shy with the flour; you can shake off any excess later and it's OK if some of it clings. Better this, than having the empanadas stick together.*)

7. Shortly before serving, heat a medium skillet over medium heat and wait about a minute. (During this minute, prepare a plate with a pile of four paper towels.) Add about a tablespoon of oil and about a teaspoon of butter, if desired, and swirl to coat the pan. Working in batches, cook the empanadas in a single layer for 2 to 3 minutes on each side, or until golden, crisp, and blistered in as many places as possible. Watch carefully, as they brown (and can burn) quickly. Transfer to the paper towels to drain for a couple of minutes before serving. (If eating these right away, be careful, as the very hot banana in the center can burn your mouth.)

Peruvian Potato-Bean Stew

TINY QUINOA-SPECKLED BUTTERMILK CORN CAKES
(optional; page 154)

MAKES 6 SERVINGS ❧ VEGAN (WHEN SERVED WITHOUT THE CORN CAKES)

A spicy potato infusion is very much at home with a bean-themed backstory, and for good reason. All these ingredients (the chilies and tomatoes included) originated in the New World, so their association, going back centuries, is truly ancestral. You can taste the purity and rightness of that in this soulful dish.

The colors of this stew are beautiful (especially if you can find blue potatoes) when accented by the little, bright yellow corn cakes, so I hope you will try them. They can perch directly on top, or slightly to one side, for a beret effect. (Wrong culture, but attractive nonetheless.)

✽ In a perfect world, you will be making this with blue potatoes and Mayacoba beans—a beautiful, yellow, genuinely Peruvian variety (also called Canario or Peruano). I like to Internet-order them from Rancho Gordo. As Steve Sando, R.G. honcho, notes: "It's a small but meaty thin-skinned bean that will take on all the flavors you can throw at it." And we are throwing a few in this recipe. That said, pinto beans can be substituted to similar effect.

✽ If you can't get blue potatoes, use red creamers or a waxy type, such as Yukon gold.

✽ If you are chili adventurous, please feel free to increase and vary the fresh chilies (in addition to the poblanos or Anaheims) and also to throw in touches of like-minded spices (ground chipotle powder, New Mexico chili powder) to customize. (Wash your hands and equipment after handling hot chilies.)

✽ If using dried beans, you'll need to soak and cook them ahead of time (see page 148; save the cooking water). You can also use canned pinto beans, but you will lose out on being able to include some bean-cooking water in the stew, which adds depth.

✽ Timing: The corn cake batter can be thrown together in about 5 minutes; it cooks quickly. So make the complete stew first and let it rest while you prepare the corn cakes, so they can be served fresh and hot from the pan.

2 tablespoons olive oil

2 cups chopped onion (1 large)

2 teaspoons chili powder

½ teaspoon ground cumin

1 large sweet red bell pepper, minced

1–2 medium poblano and/or Anaheim chilies, seeded and minced

2 teaspoons minced or crushed garlic

1½ teaspoons salt, or more to taste

4 medium potatoes (about 1½ pounds; see note), peeled if desired and cut into 1-inch chunks (5 cups)

Up to 1 cup water or reserved bean-cooking water (see note)

3 cups cooked Mayacoba or pinto beans (see note) or two 15-ounce cans pinto beans, rinsed and drained

1 pound ripe tomatoes, diced, with juice, or 1 cup Slow-Roasted Roma Tomatoes (page 393) or one 15-ounce can diced tomatoes

Black pepper

Up to 2 tablespoons fresh lime juice

1. Place a soup pot or Dutch oven over medium heat for about a minute, then add the oil and swirl to coat the pan. Add the onion, chili powder, and cumin and cook for 5 minutes, stirring often. Stir in the bell pepper and chilies, garlic, and 1 teaspoon of the salt and cook for another 5 minutes.

2. Stir in the potatoes and another ½ teaspoon salt. Cook, covered, over low heat, stirring occasionally, for 5 minutes. Add ½ cup of the water or bean-cooking water, cover again, and continue to cook for 10 to 15 minutes, or until the potatoes are completely tender but not mushy. If additional liquid seems necessary, go ahead and add up to ½ cup more water or bean-cooking liquid.

3. Carefully (so as not to break them) stir in the beans, along with the tomatoes and their juice. Heat to boiling, lower to a simmer, and cook for 5 minutes longer. Taste to see if the stew needs more salt, add black pepper and lime juice to taste, and serve hot.

OPTIONAL ENHANCEMENTS

Grated mild white cheese ✸ Torn or minced cilantro leaves ✸ Top with a sprinkling of quinoa (leftover from making the corn cakes, page 154) ✸ Lime wedges ✸ Fire-Roasted Bell Pepper Saladita (page 380) ✸ Toasted pumpkin seeds or Chili Pepitas (page 401) ✸ A dab of sour cream or Mexican crema on top ✸ Lime-Drenched Sweet Corn and Pepper (page 337) on the side, or corn on the cob with Chili-Cilantro Mayonnaise (page 373)

TINY QUINOA-SPECKLED BUTTERMILK CORN CAKES

MAKES ABOUT 4 DOZEN TINY CAKES (8 PER SERVING)

Cooked quinoa is stirred into a simple batter with otherworldly results. These cakes are a reliable crowd-pleaser for any meal, including breakfast.

❀ Use finely milled yellow cornmeal, not the coarser polenta.

❀ To cook quinoa, about 45 minutes ahead of time, combine ½ cup rinsed quinoa and ¾ cup water in a small saucepan. Bring to a boil and lower the heat to the slowest possible simmer (with a heat diffuser, if you have one, underneath). Cover and simmer for 30 minutes, or until all the water is absorbed. Fluff with a fork, then measure out a packed ½ cup to use for this recipe. You can sprinkle the leftover quinoa on top of the Peruvian Potato-Bean Stew (page 152).

❀ The batter can be made as much as a day ahead and refrigerated in a tightly covered container. Stir to recombine before cooking.

½ cup unbleached all-purpose flour

½ cup cornmeal (see note)

½ (packed) cup cooked quinoa (see note)

2 teaspoons sugar

Scant ½ teaspoon salt

½ teaspoon baking powder

¼ teaspoon baking soda

1 cup buttermilk

2 large eggs

2 teaspoons grapeseed or canola oil

Butter for the pan

1. In a medium bowl, whisk together the flour, cornmeal, quinoa, sugar, salt, baking powder, and baking soda. Make a well in the center.

2. Measure the buttermilk into a liquid measuring cup and break in the egg. Whisk until well blended, adding the oil as you go. Pour this mixture into the well in the dry ingredients.

3. Using a spoon or rubber spatula, mix with a few swift strokes until the batter is pretty much uniform. (A few lumps are OK.) Don't overmix.

4. Melt a little butter in a medium skillet over medium heat and swirl to coat the pan. When the butter is hot enough to instantly sizzle a bread crumb, use a teaspoon to drop small dots of batter into the pan. Cook for 2 to 3 minutes on each side, until golden. Serve right away. (You will likely need to cook these in batches; keep the finished ones warm in a 200°F oven until the rest are ready.)

Mushroom Stroganoff over Cabbage "Noodles"

TOASTED BARLEY DUMPLINGS (optional; page 156)

MAKES 5 OR 6 SERVINGS

A trio of mushrooms and a pair of onions are gently stewed in a smoky sour cream–lemon-wine sauce and arranged on a simple bed of butter-laced cooked cabbage strands. Toasted Barley Dumplings are placed on top like tiny caps of soothingness, allowing you to imagine you are having a winter dinner by the hearth of a Northern European cabin in a previous century. Sound like a plan?

❋ Smoked paprika can vary in potency from one brand to another. So try to find one with a predictable, pleasant smokiness that matches your palate.

❋ Regarding the Toasted Barley Dumplings: Put on some barley to cook before you do anything else. You can even make the full dumpling batter and poach the dumplings ahead of time.

1 tablespoon grapeseed, canola, or peanut oil

1 tablespoon unsalted butter, plus about 1 teaspoon for the cabbage

3 cups minced onions (2 medium)

1¼ teaspoons salt, or more to taste

1 tablespoon smoked paprika

1 teaspoon minced or crushed garlic

12 medium (2-inch cap) shiitakes, stemmed, wiped clean, and thinly sliced

2 pounds mushrooms (domestic and/or cremini), stemmed if necessary, wiped clean, and quartered

2 tablespoons unbleached all-purpose flour

¾ cup dry white wine, at room temperature

1 pound green or napa cabbage, thinly sliced

½ cup sour cream, at room temperature

Up to 2 tablespoons fresh lemon juice (optional, depending on the tartness of the wine)

Black pepper

1. Place a soup pot, large saucepan, or Dutch oven over medium heat for about a minute. Add the oil, melt in the 1 tablespoon butter, and swirl to coat the pan. Add the onions and ¼ teaspoon of the salt and cook, stirring, for 5 minutes, or until the onions become translucent. Sprinkle in the paprika and garlic and cook, stirring, for another minute. Add the shiitakes and stir until they are coated. Cook, stirring often, for another 3 minutes.

2. Add the mushrooms, along with another ½ teaspoon of the salt. Stir to combine, then cover and cook, stirring occasionally, for 5 to 8 minutes, or until the mushrooms have cooked down a bit, expressing their juices. Whisk the flour into the juices with a large whisk, so the mushrooms won't get caught in the wires.

3. Pour in the wine and bring to a quick boil. Lower the heat to a simmer, partially cover, and let stew for 10 minutes.

4. Steam or blanch the cabbage over or in simmering water until it becomes very tender, about 5 minutes. Drain, if necessary, then transfer to a bowl or platter and toss with about 1 teaspoon of butter and ½ teaspoon salt.

5. Stir the sour cream into the stew. Keep the heat low and continue cooking, stirring occasionally, for 5 to 8 minutes, or until everything melds.

[continues]

Taste to adjust the salt (it will likely need another ¼ teaspoon or so), and also to see if it might want some lemon juice. Add a generous amount of black pepper and serve hot, over and/or surrounded by the "noodles."

OPTIONAL ENHANCEMENT

You can smuggle a modest amount of freshly cooked real noodles into the cabbage "noodles" for additional heft ❋ Dust the top with more paprika ❋ Scatter on some minced fresh dill

TOASTED BARLEY DUMPLINGS

MAKES ABOUT 20 DUMPLINGS (3 OR 4 PER SERVING)

Gloriously chewy, these provide a most unusual format for whole grains. They're a tad homely, but so good that they will become beautiful to you after you taste one. The poached dumplings are fried directly in the cooked onions. This contact browning is a lovely way to extend flavor and color—and to confer additional intrigue.

❋ Cook the barley well ahead of time. You don't need to measure the water. Just simmer ⅓ cup pearl barley in a small saucepan with plenty of water to cover until done to your liking, about 40 minutes.

Then drain off any excess water and shake the barley seriously dry.

❄ For enhanced flavor, you can dry-toast the uncooked barley on the stovetop before simmering it. Just toss it around attentively for a few minutes in a dry cast-iron skillet over medium heat until it gives off a toasty aroma.

❄ You can make the batter a few days ahead, and you can also poach the dumplings up to 2 days ahead, if you store everything tightly covered in the refrigerator. Be sure to save the final sautéing step for just before serving, so the dumplings can go to the table fresh and hot from the pan.

1 cup cooked barley (see notes)

1 cup unbleached all-purpose flour

½ teaspoon salt, plus more for the cooking water and onion

2–3 fresh chives, snipped tiny with scissors (optional)

6 tablespoons milk

2 large eggs

Up to 1 tablespoon grapeseed or canola oil

Butter for the pan (optional)

1 cup finely minced onion

1. Combine the cooked barley, flour, ½ teaspoon salt, and chives, if using, in a medium bowl.

2. Measure the milk in a liquid measuring cup, then beat in the eggs with a fork or small whisk until smooth.

3. Heat a wide, shallow saucepan of lightly salted water to boiling, then lower the heat to a simmer. Drop in rounded teaspoons of the batter and let the dumplings poach for 10 minutes, swishing the water a bit and turning them slightly as they cook. You will likely need to simmer them in batches, as they shouldn't crowd and they will puff up a bit. If any of the dumplings seem to be sticking to the bottom, gently loosen them with a small metal spatula with a thin blade. Remove with a slotted spoon and drain well on a bed of kitchen towels.

4. Meanwhile, place a large skillet over medium heat and wait about a minute. Add a scant ½ tablespoon oil, then melt in about 1 teaspoon of butter, if desired, and swirl to coat the pan. Add the onion and sauté for 8 minutes, or until deeply golden. Sprinkle lightly with salt and spread out the onion in the pan.

5. Add a little more oil and/or butter to the pan. Add the dumplings and cook, turning them gently in the onion, for about 5 minutes, or until they become lightly golden and onion-coated all over. (It's OK if the pan is somewhat crowded.) The dumplings will crisp up on the outside and become condensed and chewy on the interior, while remaining tender. Serve them straight from the pan.

Kimchi Stew

MAGICALLY PUFFED RICE NOODLES (optional; page 160)

MAKES 6 TO 8 SERVINGS ❧ VEGAN

Delightfully slippery noodles, creamy tofu, ever-so-slightly crunchy cabbage, chewy mushrooms, and hot and sour kimchi make this a sensuous, even mysterious texture-fest. Take it over the top by adding the crunchy rice noodle topping, which is one of the most entertaining cooking projects you'll ever encounter.

❀ Bean thread, aka "cellophane," noodles are commonly (and inexpensively) available in most Asian grocery stores and well-stocked supermarkets as well as on the Internet. (And while you're there, pick up the other ingredients, too—including the rice noodles for the accessory.) The noodles cook up quickly.

❀ There are many kinds of kimchi, and some are hotter or sweeter than others. (Flavor characteristics are usually indicated on the label.) Taste around to discover your preferred brand. I like the hot kind for this. Whichever kind you use, be careful when opening the jar. Because it is fermented (and still active) it's a lot like opening a bottle of beer or sparkling wine, creating its own little celebration. In other words, do this over the sink.

❀ Consider using roasted peanut oil for the initial sautéing—and also to drizzle on afterward in addition to or instead of Chinese sesame oil (see the Optional Enhancements). It's an aromatic oil usually used for finishing, but sturdy enough to cook with.

3–4 ounces bean thread noodles (see note)

2 tablespoons peanut oil (roasted or plain) or grapeseed oil

4 cups chopped onions (2 large)

¾ pound shiitake mushrooms, wiped clean, stemmed, and sliced

½ pound very firm tofu, cut into thin strips

1 teaspoon salt, or more to taste

1 pound or more domestic mushrooms, wiped clean, stemmed if necessary, and quartered

½ pound savoy cabbage, cut into thin strips (4 cups)

1 14-ounce jar kimchi (see note)

1. Cook the bean threads in boiling water for 1 minute, then drain and rinse in cold running water. Set them aside in a container of cold water to keep them separate until ready to use.

2. Place a soup pot, large saucepan, or Dutch oven over medium heat for about a minute. Add the oil and swirl to coat the pan. Add the onions, shiitakes, tofu, and ¼ teaspoon of the salt. Over medium or medium-high heat, cook, stirring, for about 5 minutes, or until the onions begin to soften. Stir in the domestic mushrooms and ¼ teaspoon of the salt and cook for another 5 minutes, stirring often.

3. Add the cabbage and another ¼ teaspoon of the salt, stirring from the bottom to bring up the cooked vegetables as you incorporate the cabbage. When it looks well blended, cover, reduce the heat to medium-low, and cook for 10 minutes, adding another ¼ teaspoon salt after the first 5 minutes or so.

4. Add the kimchi with all its liquid, possibly going in with scissors to cut any too-large pieces into bite-sized ones. (It's also OK to leave them large.) Stir to blend, then thoroughly drain. Drain the bean threads, then stir them in with a fork. Taste for salt; it might want just a touch more.

5. Serve hot or warm, with any of the Optional Enhancements and the Magically Puffed Rice Noodles, if using.

OPTIONAL ENHANCEMENTS

Torn cilantro leaves ✻ A drizzle of Chinese sesame oil or roasted peanut oil ✻ A few drops of seasoned rice vinegar ✻ Sriracha or chili oil or another chili sauce ✻ Crushed red pepper ✻ Chopped toasted peanuts or cashews ✻ Shelled, lightly steamed edamame on top ✻ Cooked green beans (thin ones or halved lengthwise) ✻ Egg "Noodles" (page 398) on top ✻ Rice underneath

MAGICALLY PUFFED RICE NOODLES

MAKES ABOUT 6 SERVINGS AS AN ACCESSORY FOR A STEW; 3 TO 4 SNACK SERVINGS ✿ VEGAN

Enjoy the thrilling experience of watching a panful of inert rice sticks spring to life and puff into action as they hit the hot oil, as if suddenly possessed by a spirit.

✿ Rice noodles of various thicknesses can be purchased inexpensively in Asian-themed grocery stores, some regular supermarkets (in the "imported foods" section), and online. Use thin ones for this recipe.

✿ For best results, use high-oleic (also sometimes called "high heat") safflower oil or regular grapeseed oil.

✿ It takes just seconds for the noodles to puff. Have a paper towel–lined plate ready beside the stove.

✿ Very thin strands of fresh ginger (from about a 1-inch knob), expertly sliced with your sharp knife, can fry along with the noodles. If you add the ginger to the pan first, giving it a few seconds' head start, it will infuse the oil with its inimitable flavor, which will then extend, with subtlety, to the noodles.

3–5 tablespoons high-oleic safflower oil or grapeseed oil

3–4 ounces slender dried rice noodles

Salt (optional)

1. Heat about 3 tablespoons oil in a large skillet over medium-low heat. Place a plate with a triple pile of paper towels, plus tongs, by the stove. Separate the noodles with your hands, if they are clumped together.

2. When the oil is hot enough to instantly sizzle a dry noodle, use a fork or tongs to carefully lay in about one third of the noodles—however many will fit in a single layer. It's OK if they are touching.

3. The noodles will shimmy and inflate immediately upon contact with the hot oil and within a few seconds they'll be light and puffy, like popcorn. Make sure that every part of every noodle gets its chance to meet the oil, as any unpuffed parts will be too crunchy to bite.

4. Transfer the transformed noodles to the paper towels to drain and repeat with one or two more batches (per pan capacity), adding more oil as needed and making sure it returns to instant-sizzle temperature before anything goes in.

5. Lightly salt the finished noodles, if you wish, and use as desired.

Root Vegetable Stew with Ginger and Pears

MINI BUTTERMILK ROSEMARY-WALNUT BISCUITS (optional; page 163)

MAKES 4 OR 5 SERVINGS ❧ VEGAN (WITHOUT THE BISCUITS)

A pleasant surprise unfolds as rutabaga, parsnip, sweet potato, and onion simmer with fresh pears in ginger- and lemon-infused pear nectar. The result is a gentle, sunny stew—soft and soothing enough to qualify as comfort food, but also compelling enough to spark and maintain interest.

If you have any left over, try mashing it into a vibrant side dish or winter lunch or snack. It reheats beautifully in the microwave.

A bit of prep is involved. Coring the parsnip is important, since the core is comprised of incorrigibly tough fiber. It seems like you're losing a lot of the vegetable (those cores can be huge!) but you'd end up picking those bits out later anyway, so you're paving the way for a smooth eating experience. The positive part is that parsnip cores make a lovely stock. Get them into a pot filled with water and boil it up (or down) with a touch of salt.

[continues]

* Kern's Pear Nectar is available pretty much everywhere. If you have any left over, I'm sure you'll find a use for it. (Smoothie? Newfangled cocktail?)

* You can substitute carrots for the parsnips. All you need to do is peel and cut them—no coring needed. (But then you don't get the stock.)

* Use any kind of pear other than Asian or Bosc, which are too crunchy for this dish.

* Timing: Make and cut the biscuit dough before you begin. (The dough can be made the day before.) Preheat the oven after step 1 and bake the biscuits during step 4. You can also have the biscuits all made and baked ahead of time, and reheat them in an oven or toaster oven just before serving, if desired.

2 tablespoons grapeseed or canola oil

2 cups minced red onion (1 large)

2 tablespoons finely minced fresh ginger

1¼ teaspoons salt, or more to taste

1 pound rutabaga (1 large or 2 small), peeled, cored, and diced (about 2 cups)

1 pound parsnips (about 3 medium), peeled, cored, and diced (about 2 cups)

1½ cups pear nectar

2 pounds sweet potatoes (2–3 medium), peeled and diced (6 cups)

½ cup water

2 firm but ripe pears, cored and sliced (peeling optional)

3 tablespoons fresh lemon juice, or more to taste

Cayenne or crushed red pepper

Lemon wedges (optional but recommended)

1. Place a soup pot or Dutch oven over medium heat for about a minute. Add the oil and swirl to coat the pan. Add the onion and ginger, plus ¾ teaspoon of the salt, and cook, stirring, for about 5 minutes, or until the onion becomes translucent.

2. Stir in the rutabaga and parsnips, cover, and cook for about 10 minutes, stirring occasionally, until mostly tender but not yet soft.

3. Stir in 1 cup of the pear nectar and cook for 5 minutes. Add the sweet potatoes and the remaining ½ cup pear nectar. Cover and simmer for another 10 minutes. Add the water and simmer for 10 to 15 minutes, or until the sweet potatoes are done to your liking.

4. Gently stir in the pear slices, 3 tablespoons lemon juice, and the remaining ½ teaspoon salt. Turn the heat to low and simmer for another 8 to 10 minutes, just long enough to slightly cook the pears and let everything meld. Taste to adjust the lemon juice and salt, if necessary, and add cayenne or crushed red pepper to taste. Serve hot, in bowls, with lemon wedges, if desired.

OPTIONAL ENHANCEMENTS

Extend the stew into a soup by adding vegetable stock (and possibly a touch of cream) to taste; adjust the salt ❁ Puree (or just fork-smash) it and serve as you would any of the mashes on pages 164 to 185 ❁ Lay out a wedge of aged cheddar or some fabulous goat cheese (herb- or lavender- or wasabi-infused)

MINI BUTTERMILK ROSEMARY-WALNUT BISCUITS

MAKES ABOUT 3 DOZEN (3 OR 4 PER SERVING)

Four cornerstones of healthy flavor—olive oil, buttermilk, walnuts, and rosemary—dance their inimitable quadrille in these rough-hewn and fantastic biscuits.

❀ Easily reheated in a toaster oven, these last for at least a week in the refrigerator if wrapped airtight. In a heavy zip-style plastic bag, they'll last a month or longer in the freezer.

1 cup unbleached all-purpose flour, plus more for handling

1 teaspoon baking powder

2 teaspoons sugar

Scant ½ teaspoon salt

¾ cup walnut pieces

2 tablespoons minced fresh rosemary or 1 teaspoon dried

⅓ cup buttermilk, plus more if needed

¼ cup olive oil

Nonstick cooking spray (optional)

1. Preheat the oven to 375°F, with a rack in the center position.

2. Combine the dry ingredients, walnuts, and rosemary in a food processor. Buzz for a few long pulses until the mixture is mostly uniform and resembles a coarse meal.

3. Pour the buttermilk and the oil into a liquid measuring cup. Whisk briefly to blend and then, while still running the machine, pour this into the feed tube. Carefully remove the dough, pressing it into a disk.

4. Dust a clean, dry work surface with a little flour or spray it with nonstick spray and press or roll the dough into a square ½ inch thick. Cut into 1-inch squares or diamonds and transfer them to an ungreased baking sheet. (Re-shape and keep cutting the dough as needed until you've used all of it.) The biscuits can be very close together since they will not spread out during baking.

5. Bake for 10 to 12 minutes, or until lightly golden on the bottoms and edges. Let the biscuits cool on the baking sheet for about 5 minutes before enjoying.

COZY MASHES

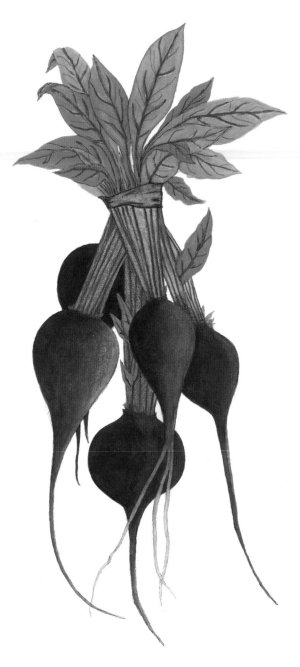

✳ ✳ ✳

With this embracing collection of soft, savory foods (mostly vegetables, but also lentils, beans, and polenta, and all of them deeply soothing), you will now have a series of quietly grand opportunities to spoon-feed your inner child.

Mashes might seem like side-dish material at first glance, and they are, in the old-school meat-and-potatoes approach to dinner. These recipes are happy to continue occupying that spot on that kind of plate—and then some, as our sense of plates is evolving. In a vegetarian setting, a cozy mash can be served solo, as a little bowlful of pure comfort on its own, and it can also be spread or spooned thickly as a substantial topping over, or a bed underneath, other dishes. The important thing to realize about mashes is that much of your overall vegetarian menu planning and plate design can be based upon them—literally.

The possibilities are many. I hope you will feel emboldened to augment and expand the optional enhancements that I suggest after each recipe, pulling additional ideas from other chapters (Sauces, Vinaigrettes, Toppings, and Other Meaningful Touches, page 352, in particular) and trying your hand at a series of grand (or small) experiments. You will discover that cozy mashes can be an end in themselves, or just the beginning.

BUILDING OUT A COZY MASH

Consider using a Cozy Mash as the base of a layered plate. Begin by making a lovely mound or wide circle in the center. Expand it with simple, contrasting items, such as grilled vegetables, some slaw or a few spoonfuls of a salad, and a garnish of sliced fruits or Pickled Red Onions (page 395). Some stripes of glaze (Soy Caramel, for example, page 364) or dabs of a sauce or dip, perhaps, around the edge of the plate can lend color and interest. Crown the whole arrangement with one or more saladitas (pages 381 to 386) or a slaw (pages 64 to 66), plain toasted nuts, Pistachio Smash (page 402), Fried Lentils (page 404), a touch of shaved cheese, Tofu "Noodles" (page 399), or Tempeh Croutons (page 405). This is a loose template.

Consider making more than one of these mashes (just rinse out the food processor in between) and serve several juxtaposed, for contrasting colors and flavors.

MASHES WORK BEAUTIFULLY AS

- nests for fried or poached eggs
- platforms for pilafs
- edible baskets for grilled or roasted complementary vegetables
- the bottom layer of your own modular plate arrangement

OTHER IDEAS

- A generous slice of toast or grilled bread can provide a sense of completion to a bowl of cozy mash, as can Crispy Polenta Triangles (page 185). Use them as scoops or spoon the mash on top.
- Use mashes as you would any pesto, stirred into or heaped on top of freshly cooked pasta, or nestled under it. Olive oil, a little extra garlic, and some shredded Parmesan could be compatible here as well. You can make this up as you go.

- You can also transform all of these but the polenta into soup by thinning with stock and adjusting the salt to taste. Or head in the other direction, and fork-mash a leftover soup or stew that might have thickened a bit as it sat around. (My favorite choice for this is Root Vegetable Stew with Ginger and Pears, page 161.)

OTHER MASHED THINGS

BAKED POTATOES, unzipped, mashed inside their skins, and seasoned with olive oil, salt, and pepper. A spoonful of Greek yogurt, perhaps, and maybe a crown of roasted broccoli.

MASHED POTATOES, laced with butter, milk, salt, and pepper. You can add (or swap in):

> good-quality olive oil
>
> buttermilk
>
> Roasted Garlic Paste (page 173)
>
> goat cheese
>
> wasabi paste or regular horseradish
>
> minced fresh parsley and/or chives

MASHED SWEET POTATOES: Try holding back on the butter, brown sugar, and marshmallows and go down the revelatory path of lime juice (a lot) and salt (a little). Nothing more. Try this same treatment for mashed winter squash (any kind).

FAVA BEANS: Cook shelled, peeled favas (see page 265) in water until very soft, then drain and puree them in a food processor, using some of their cooking water (as needed), and add salt and pepper to taste. Drizzle the top with a good-quality extra-virgin olive oil and serve with a lemon wedge. A little chopped fresh mint on top is very nice.

AVOCADO: A perfectly ripe avocado tastes amazing with nothing more than lime juice and salt. Spread it thickly on toast. Divine!

BRILLIANT BEET ARRANGEMENT

1. Spread a modest layer of thick yogurt (Greek or otherwise) on a plate.

2. Heap on some room-temperature Beet Crush (opposite page).

3. Sprinkle the top with Pistachio Smash (page 402).

4. Toss on some Fried Lentils (page 404).

5. Scatter a few leaves of baby arugula on top and/ or serve some olive-oil-and-garlic-sautéed beet greens on the side or underneath.

Beet Crush

MAKES ABOUT 4 SERVINGS ❄ VEGAN

Summer beets, recently harvested, are best for this recipe, which has you doing so little to them that they get a chance to show their true essence. I like to use yellow beets for this—they are so pretty and unexpected. That said, beets of any color will do just fine. And if the leaves are fresh, crisp, and unfaded, you're in for a treat. Stemmed, cleaned beet greens cook very quickly over medium-low heat in garlic and olive oil with a little salt and pepper and are delicious served alongside or on top of the Beet Crush.

❄ The beets need to be put into the oven to roast at least 90 minutes (and up to several days) beforehand. This will allow them the time they need to cook, cool until comfortable to handle, and get peeled—an unpredictable process. Sometimes the peel lifts right off, and other times it needs guidance from a paring knife. You can also simply boil the beets until soft enough to slide a fork into, if you don't feel like heating your oven. The flavor will be less intense, but still fine. The peels will rub off easily after the beets are drained, refreshed under cold running water, and cooled.

❄ This will keep for 3 to 4 days in a tightly covered container in the refrigerator. It also freezes beautifully and reheats well, covered, in a 250°F oven or in a microwave.

3 pounds (9–12 medium) beets

2 tablespoons olive oil

1 teaspoon minced or crushed garlic

4 teaspoons champagne vinegar or white wine vinegar, or more to taste

¾ teaspoon salt, or more to taste

1. Remove the beet greens (save them to cook separately, if they're nice) and trim the stems to within an inch of the beet. Cook the beets, whole and unpeeled, either in simmering water until fork-tender, about 30 minutes, or by roasting. To roast them, preheat the oven to 400°F, with a rack in the center position. Line a baking sheet with foil. Lay the beets on the foil, add a splash of water (a tablespoon or two), and press together the edges of the foil to form a packet. Roast for about 30 minutes, or until the beets are fork-tender. (Be careful when opening the packet. There will be steam.)

2. Place the olive oil and garlic in a small, microwave-worthy bowl and cover it with a plate. Zap for 30 seconds, then remove from the microwave and carefully remove the plate. Let the mixture cool until safe to handle.

3. When the beets are cool enough to handle, peel them and cut into quarters and transfer to a food processor. Scrape in the oil-garlic mixture and add the vinegar and salt. Buzz into a coarse crush a few degrees short of completely smooth.

4. Taste to adjust the salt and vinegar and serve hot, warm, or at room temperature.

Curried Mashed Carrots and Cashews

MAKES 4 OR 5 SERVINGS ❧ VEGAN (WHEN MADE WITHOUT THE HONEY)

Moderately spicy from the ginger and with just the right degree of richness from the cashews, this mash is intensely satisfying—a good kind of Code Orange. You can eat it plain for lunch, stacked for dinner (see page 215), or simply as a bolstering afternoon snack, reheated in a microwave.

❀ The sweeter the carrots, the better this will taste.

❀ Stock option: If you put a few slices of ginger, some onion, and a clove or two of garlic into the carrot-cooking water, you'll end up with a lovely broth. You can heat it and serve it straight as a very light appetizer or a nourishing snack—or add it to any soup you might deem compatible. You can also use it to thin this mash into a soup.

❀ This will keep for 4 to 5 days in a tightly covered container in the refrigerator. It also freezes beautifully and reheats well, covered, in a 250°F oven or in a microwave.

2 pounds carrots

2 tablespoons oil (I use half olive oil and half grapeseed)

1 cup chopped red onion

1 tablespoon minced fresh ginger

1 teaspoon curry powder

½ teaspoon salt, or more to taste

1 teaspoon minced or crushed garlic

½ cup unsalted cashews, lightly toasted

Up to 2 tablespoons fresh lemon juice

1 teaspoon light-colored honey (optional, depending on the sweetness of the carrots)

1. Peel the carrots and cut them into 1-inch chunks, then place them in a large saucepan with enough water to cover. Bring to a boil, lower the heat to a simmer, and cook until the carrots become fork-tender, 8 to 10 minutes.

2. Meanwhile, place a medium skillet over medium heat for about a minute, then add the oil and swirl to coat the pan. Toss in the onion and cook, stirring, for about 3 minutes, or until it begins to soften. Add the ginger and cook, stirring, for another couple of minutes, then sprinkle in the curry powder and the ½ teaspoon salt. Sauté for another minute or so, then reduce the heat to medium-low, add the garlic, and cook, stirring often, for another 8 to 10 minutes, or until everything is very soft. (You can add up to a few tablespoons of the carrot-cooking water to the mix, to augment the process.)

3. Drain the carrots in a strainer or colander over a bowl in the sink, saving the water. Transfer the carrots (it's fine if they're still hot or warm; just be careful) to a food processor, along with the onion mixture, scraping in every last drop of flavor—plus any and all liquid—from the pan. Add the cashews.

4. Puree to your desired consistency, adding 2 to 3 tablespoons of the cooking water, as needed, to move things along and to keep the mixture spoon-soft.

5. Transfer to a bowl and season to taste with lemon juice and a little more salt as desired, and adding a touch of honey, if you'd like it sweeter. Serve hot, warm, or at room temperature.

OPTIONAL ENHANCEMENTS

Heap onto toast and top with a few shelled, lightly steamed edamame or fava beans (page 256) ✳ Pair this with a second piece of toast, topped with Golden Lentils with Soft, Sweet Onions (page 182) and a few Crisp, Ethereal Onion Rings (page 387) ✳ Spread as a bed under Spiced Basmati Pilaf with Nuts and Raisins (page 192) ✳ Spread as a bed under an arrangement of Forbidden Rice with Beluga Lentils and Mushrooms (page 214), Mashed White Beans (page 183), possibly left whole and scattered on top, and Pan-Grilled Mushroom Slices (see page 349)

Roasted Garlic–Mashed Cauliflower

MAKES 4 OR 5 SERVINGS ✻ VEGAN (WHEN MADE WITH SOY MILK)

Seasoned and mashed on its own terms, cauliflower holds its ground and commands respect.

✻ Roast some garlic—or make the Roasted Garlic Paste—well in advance.

✻ More of a head of cauliflower is edible than you might think. Trim it minimally—you can include pretty much all the white parts, including the bulk of the center. Just remove and discard the leaves and take one thin slice from the base. Then use a sharp knife to cut out the first 2 or 3 inches of the core to remove a triangular plug from the bottom. Use everything else. You'll get more final volume this way and it's all pure cauliflower.

✻ Transform this into a gratin: Spread it in an oiled or sprayed small baking dish or a pie pan and top with some grated cheese (your choice) and fresh bread crumbs. Place in the upper half of a 350°F oven until heated through and browned on top.

✻ This will keep for 4 to 5 days in a tightly covered container in the refrigerator. It also freezes beautifully and reheats well, covered, in a 250°F oven or in a microwave.

1 large head cauliflower (about 3 pounds)

1 head roasted garlic or 3 tablespoons Roasted Garlic Paste (page 173)

2 tablespoons olive oil

¾ teaspoon salt, or more to taste

Up to 3 tablespoons milk, half-and-half, cream, or soy milk

Black pepper

1. Trim the cauliflower (see note) and chop it into 1-inch pieces. You should end up with about 8 cups.

2. Place the cauliflower in a soup pot or a large saucepan with enough water to cover. Bring to a boil, lower the heat to a moderate simmer, and cook until very tender, 8 to 10 minutes. Drain into a strainer or colander over a bowl in the sink, saving some of the water.

3. Transfer half the cauliflower (it's fine if it's still hot or warm; just be careful) to a food processor. Squeeze in or add half the garlic, 1 tablespoon of the olive oil, and ½ teaspoon of the salt and begin to process.

4. Keep the machine going as you add a tablespoon or two of the cooking water— just enough to smooth things out. When this first batch packs down, add the rest of the cauliflower, along with the remaining garlic, the remaining tablespoon olive oil, ¼ teaspoon salt, and 2 tablespoons milk or cream.

5. Buzz further, adding water as needed to achieve your desired consistency, then scrape the mash into a bowl.

6. Taste to adjust the salt and possibly the remaining milk or cream and add some black pepper. Serve hot, warm, or at room temperature.

OPTIONAL ENHANCEMENTS

Top with Caramelized Onion and Lemon Marmalade (page 375) or Fire-Roasted Bell Pepper Saladita (page 380) ✻ Festoon with Crisp, Ethereal Onion Rings (page 387) ✻ Dab with Maple-Mustard Glaze (page 370) ✻ Spread as a bed under Simple Buckwheat Pilaf (page 230) or Kasha Varnishkes (page 231) ✻ Serve spooned into a portobello mushroom cap, prepared for stuffing (page 350)

ROASTED GARLIC PASTE

MAKES 6 TABLESPOONS ✿ VEGAN

Roasting garlic completely transforms its flavor. It's still pungent, but the sharpness is greatly softened. Use Roasted Garlic Paste for mashing into soups, potatoes, sauces, or dressings; spreading on crackers or little toasts as an appetizer; topping grilled chicken, fish, or steak; or tossing into cooked vegetables.

✿ Topped with a slick of olive oil and packed into a small, tightly covered container, this will keep well for up to 3 weeks in the refrigerator—or indefinitely in the freezer.

3 heads garlic

3 tablespoons olive oil, or more for topping

1. Preheat the oven, with a rack in the center position, or a toaster oven to 375°F. Line a small baking pan with foil.

2. Slice off the very topmost tip of each garlic head. Discard the tips and stand the heads cut side up on the prepared pan. Carefully pour about 1 teaspoon of the olive oil onto the cut surface of each head.

3. Roast for 30 to 40 minutes, or until the heads feel soft when gently pressed. (Larger heads will take longer.) When they are cool enough to handle, break each head into individual cloves and squeeze the pulp onto a plate.

4. Use a fork to mash the garlic as well as possible. It will still have some lumps. As you mash, gradually add the remaining 2 tablespoons olive oil, mixing and mashing it into the garlic pulp. Use right away or coat the top surface with a thin layer of olive oil and refrigerate or freeze. (Do not store at room temperature—it needs to stay cold.)

Mashed Celery Root

MAKES 4 OR 5 SERVINGS ❀ VEGAN (WHEN MADE WITH SOY MILK)

Celery root is the vegetable version of a big dog that looks threatening from a distance, but is all puppy love up close. Once you get past the gnarly, prehistoric-seeming exterior, which trims off surprisingly easily with a sharp paring knife, the interior of this often-overlooked vegetable is as gentle-flavored as anything you could wish for, especially when whipped up with touches of olive oil and milk or cream.

❀ The "4 pounds celery root" refers to the whole vegetable, as you'd buy it in the store. Once trimmed, the roots will weigh a bit less. At that point, just focus on the volume.

4 pounds celery root

2 tablespoons olive oil

½ teaspoon salt, or more to taste

Up to 3 tablespoons milk, half-and-half, cream, or soy milk

Black pepper

1. Use a sharp paring knife to trim the rough outer skin of the celery root and cut what remains into chunks. You should have about 8 cups. Place the chunks in a soup pot or a large saucepan with enough water to cover. Bring to a boil, lower the heat to a moderate simmer, and cook until very tender, 8 to 10 minutes. Drain into a strainer or colander over a bowl in the sink, saving some of the water.

2. Transfer the celery root to a food processor (it's fine if still hot or warm; just be careful). Add the olive oil, salt, and 2 tablespoons milk or cream and buzz until "mashed." (If it seems dry, you can add an additional tablespoon of milk or cream, and/or a tablespoon or two of the cooking water to help smooth things out.) When it reaches the desired consistency, taste to see if it needs additional salt and possibly a touch more milk or cream. Add black pepper to taste.

3. Scrape the mash into a bowl and serve hot, warm, or at room temperature.

OPTIONAL ENHANCEMENTS

Top with Crisp, Ethereal Onion Rings (page 387) ❀ Add a dab of Caramelized Onion and Lemon Marmalade (page 375) or Beet, Orange, and Ginger Marmalade (page 374) on top ❀ Drizzle with Balsamic Reduction or any of the Sweet-Sour Glazes (pages 369 to 370) ❀ Top with a green salad tossed with Sherry-Honey-Tarragon Mustard Vinaigrette (page 367)

Smoky Mashed Caramelized Eggplant and Onions

MAKES 3 OR 4 SERVINGS (EASILY DOUBLED) ❈ VEGAN

Garlic and well-done onions meet again, and this time the setting is eggplant, baked or grilled into blissful, smoky oblivion. Puree everything together with some salt and lemon juice, and you will have a lip-smacking reminder that simple ingredients can become downright remarkable when cooked with loving patience.

❈ You can cook the onions and eggplants at the same time, all of which can be done well ahead of the final assembly.

❈ This will keep for 4 to 5 days in a tightly covered container in the refrigerator. It also freezes beautifully and reheats well, covered, in a 250°F oven or in a microwave.

2 tablespoons olive oil

2½–3 cups minced onions (1 pound)

1 teaspoon minced or crushed garlic

¾ teaspoon salt, or more to taste

2 large globe eggplants (about 2 pounds)

1 teaspoon fresh lemon juice

Black pepper

1. Preheat the oven to 400°F, with a rack in the center position, and line a baking sheet with foil, or fire up the coals in a grill.

2. Meanwhile, place a large (10- to 12-inch) skillet over medium heat for about a minute, then add the oil and swirl to coat the pan. Toss in the onions, spreading them out in the pan. Cook, stirring often, for 10 minutes, or until softened. Add the garlic and ½ teaspoon of the salt and reduce the heat to medium-low. Continue to cook, stirring frequently, for another 10 to 15 minutes, or until the onions are golden and very soft. Set aside.

3. Meanwhile, prick the eggplants in ten or so places with a fork and place them, still whole, on the baking sheet (or directly on the grill grate, over white coals, covered, if possible, to increase the smoky flavor) and cook until utterly collapsed and soft and the skin has pulled away from the flesh, 30 to 45 minutes, depending on the size of the eggplants. Remove the collapsed eggplants from the heat and let them cool until comfortable to handle.

4. Strip off and discard the eggplant skins and transfer the flesh to a food processor. Scrape in every last drop of the onions and add the lemon juice, plus another ¼ teaspoon salt. Puree until smooth. Taste to see if it needs more salt, and season with black pepper.

5. Scrape the mash into a bowl and serve hot or warm.

OPTIONAL ENHANCEMENTS

Add cayenne or crushed red pepper ❈ Serve with lemon wedges ❈ Drizzle with good-quality olive oil ❈ Top with Crunchy Chickpea Crumble (page 403) ❈ Sprinkle pine nuts or sesame seeds over the top ❈ Decorate with very sweet cherry tomatoes ❈ Drizzle with pomegranate molasses and top with pomegranate seeds ❈ Garnish with radishes, whole, quartered, or sliced ❈ Add a topping of Grated Carrot Salad (page 62) ❈ Toss on torn fresh flat-leaf parsley

Mashed Parsnips

MAKES 4 SERVINGS ❀ VEGAN

Have you ever been surprised by the sheer benevolence of a parsnip? You're not alone; the unabashed sweetness of this vegetable seems to catch everyone off guard. So be prepared for this delicious mashed treatment to make you as unexpectedly happy as you could possibly be, having just read this spoiler.

❀ There is no way to tenderize the fibrous core of a parsnip. After slicing the tender sides off the central cylinder, you may end up with a disappointing net volume of actual vegetable. The silver lining is that those pesky cores simmer readily into one of the world's more delicious stocks, so they don't need to go to waste. Three pounds of parsnips will yield about 2 pounds of usable vegetable.

❀ Black pepper is often taken for granted, but I want to give it a shout-out here, as it plays beautifully against the melodious parsnips.

❀ This will keep for 4 to 5 days in a tightly covered container in the refrigerator. It also freezes beautifully and reheats well, covered, in a 250°F oven or in a microwave.

3 pounds parsnips (any size, although large ones are less work)

2 tablespoons extra-virgin olive oil, or more to taste

1 tablespoon balsamic vinegar, or more to taste

¾ teaspoon salt, or more to taste

Black pepper

1. Trim off the ends of the parsnips, then peel what's left and slice the tender sides from the tough cores. You should end up with at least 6 cups.

2. Place the parsnips in a soup pot or a large saucepan with enough water to cover. Bring to a boil, lower the heat to a moderate simmer, and cook until very tender, about 8 minutes. Drain into a strainer or colander over a bowl in the sink, saving some of the water.

3. Transfer the parsnips to a food processor. Add the oil, vinegar, and salt and buzz. (If the mixture seems dry, you can also drizzle in a tablespoon or two of the cooking water to help smooth things out.) When it reaches the desired consistency, taste to adjust the salt, oil, and vinegar and add some black pepper.

4. Scrape the mash into a bowl and serve hot, warm, or at room temperature.

OPTIONAL ENHANCEMENTS

Serve topped with or surrounded by grilled summer squash, onions, and/or radicchio wedges ❀ Drizzle with Pomegranate-Lime Glaze (page 369) ❀ Top with Crispy Fried Lemons (page 389) ❀ Let it share the plate with Hazelnut–Wilted Frisée Salad with Sliced Pear (page 84)

Mashed Broccoli

MAKES 4 OR 5 SERVINGS ❧ VEGAN (WHEN MADE WITH OLIVE OIL AND SOY MILK)

Perched in a relaxed position at the far end of the texture spectrum from the raw broccoli spears that were once fashionable as party dip scoops, this comfort-food version of the noble green vegetable is designed to eat in a bowl with a spoon. It is possibly one of the best rainy-day snacks ever.

❈ Note that this mash will not come out completely smooth, since tiny specks of broccoli floret will still be detectable after their run through the food processor. Enjoy the subtle dottedness.

❈ This will keep for 4 to 5 days in a tightly covered container in the refrigerator. It also freezes beautifully and reheats well, covered, in a 250°F oven or in a microwave.

2 pounds broccoli

2 tablespoons unsalted butter or olive oil

1 teaspoon minced or crushed garlic

¾ teaspoon salt, or more to taste

2 tablespoons milk, half-and-half, cream, or soy milk, or more if needed

Black pepper

1. Trim the base of the broccoli, leaving most of the stalks. Shave the outer tough skin from the stalks with a sturdy vegetable peeler, then chop the entire bunch, peeled stems and all, into small (approximately ¾-inch) pieces. You should end up with a heaping 8 cups.

2. Place the broccoli in a soup pot or a large saucepan with enough water to cover. Bring to a boil, lower the heat to a moderate simmer, and cook until very tender, 5 to 8 minutes. (Don't worry if the broccoli loses some of its color as it cooks. That's normal.) Drain into a strainer or colander over a bowl in the sink, saving some of the water.

3. Transfer the broccoli to a food processor, add the butter or oil, garlic, salt, and milk or cream, and buzz. (If the mixture seems dry, you can drizzle in a tablespoon or two of the cooking water to help smooth things out, although I don't usually find it necessary.) When it reaches the desired consistency, taste to see if it needs additional salt (and possibly a touch more milk or cream) and add black pepper to taste.

4. Scrape the mash into a bowl and serve hot, warm, or at room temperature.

OPTIONAL ENHANCEMENTS

Spread thickly on toast and top with Egg "Noodles" (page 398) ❈ Spoon into portobello mushrooms (see page 350), sprinkle a little cheese on top, and broil ❈ Mix into freshly cooked pasta ❈ Spread as a bed under Bulgur and Spaghetti (page 222) ❈ For color and flavor contrast, top with a dab of Roasted Red Pepper Pesto (page 358) or Romesco Sauce (page 359)

Bright Green Mashed Peas

MAKES 4 OR 5 SERVINGS ❋ VEGAN (WHEN MADE WITH OLIVE OIL AND SOY MILK)

Did you smash your peas with the back of your fork when you were a kid, because you instinctively knew they would taste better that way? Have you secretly longed to continue the ritual all these years, but have refrained, because adults aren't supposed to be mashing things on their dinner plate? Well, now you can revisit your original relationship with peas through this lightly creamy, scallion- and garlic-laced iteration that has been officially mashed on grown-up terms (i.e., in a food processor prior to being served). It's easy and quick, and surprisingly good—and you can feel like your old/young self again.

❋ This recipe was designed for frozen peas, due to the large volume. You don't need to defrost them ahead of time.

❋ The above notwithstanding, you can swap in fresh peas, if you want to shuck about 4 pounds (which is what you'd need to get the 1 pound called for here). In step 2, cook until soft. (More about fresh peas on page 208.)

❋ At first glance, this might seem like a large volume of ingredients, but they will cook down to 4 or 5 servings.

✼ This will keep for 4 to 5 days in a tightly covered container in the refrigerator. It also freezes beautifully and reheats well, covered, in a 250°F oven or in a microwave.

3–4 tablespoons unsalted butter or olive oil

6–8 medium scallions, chopped (whites and trimmed greens)

2 teaspoons minced or crushed garlic

2 pounds (8 cups) frozen green peas

Up to 1 teaspoon salt

2–3 tablespoons milk, half-and-half, cream, or soy milk (optional)

Black pepper

1. Melt the butter or heat the olive oil in a large (10- or 12-inch) skillet over medium-low heat. Stir in the scallions and garlic, reduce heat to low, and cook for about 5 minutes, or until the scallions are soft and shiny.

2. Add the peas and ½ teaspoon of the salt. Cover and cook over medium-low heat for about 5 minutes. When the peas have defrosted—or just softened, if you have heroically shucked a pile of fresh ones—stir to coat them with everything else.

3. Cover again and cook for another 5 minutes or so—just long enough for the peas to become completely tender while remaining bright green. Stir once or twice during this time.

4. Transfer the mixture to a food processor and buzz until smooth, adding milk or cream, if desired, a tablespoon at a time as you blend. Play with the seasoning. There's a good chance you will want up to another ½ teaspoon salt and a modest amount of black pepper.

5. Scrape the mash into a bowl and serve hot or warm.

OPTIONAL ENHANCEMENTS

Serve surrounded by Crispy Polenta Triangles (page 185) ✼ Top with a spoonful of Curried Mashed Carrots and Cashews (page 170) or Grated Carrot Salad (page 62) crowned with a dab of Thick Cranberry-Orange Vinaigrette (page 368) ✼ Tuck in some lemon wedges ✼ Broil some Parmesan on top ✼ Crown with freshly steamed peas for textural contrast ✼ Pile on some Pickled Red Onions (page 395) ✼ Scatter with Crisp, Ethereal Onion Rings (page 387) ✼ Dab with Beet, Orange, and Ginger Marmalade (page 374) ✼ Top with fresh mint, basil, or tarragon ✼ Make this into a nest for Browned Potatoes and Onion (page 391)

Soft Cuban-Style Black Beans

MAKES 5 OR 6 SERVINGS ✻ VEGAN

Authentic and straightforward, these utterly reliable black beans will (I hope) taste exactly as you expected. And that's my true definition of comfort food: familiar, as in conferring a sense of place, and altogether spoon-worthy.

This dish is also ridiculously inexpensive, which makes it taste even better (and more comforting). Affordability is a highly underrated seasoning in and of itself.

✻ If you look at black beans closely, they are more of a deep maroon or purple than actual *noir*. Very pretty, especially in this dish, with the luminous mince of carrot speckled in.

✻ If you're making this with dried beans, allow plenty of time (6 hours or so) to prepare them before you begin the recipe. Soak 1 cup dried beans in plenty of water for at least 4 hours (and as long as overnight). Drain, add enough fresh water to cover by at least 2 inches, and simmer—not rapidly boil—for about 1½ hours, or until tender. (Make sure they are truly soft.) Save the cooking water.

✻ If you're using canned beans, choose an organic brand; you won't need to rinse or drain them. The packing liquid can be flavorful and helps achieve the desired soft texture.

1 scant tablespoon olive oil

1 cup finely minced onion

1 medium carrot, finely minced

2 teaspoons ground cumin

1 teaspoon minced or crushed garlic

¼ teaspoon salt, or more to taste

3 cups cooked (see note) black beans or two 15-ounce cans, liquid reserved

¼ cup water (optional)

2 teaspoons fresh lime juice, or more to taste

Black pepper

1. Place a large (10- to 12-inch) skillet over medium heat for about a minute, then add the oil and swirl to coat the pan. Toss in the onion and cook, stirring, for just a minute or so, then add the carrot and cumin and sauté for 5 to 8 minutes more, or until the carrot begins to soften.

2. Stir in the garlic and ¼ teaspoon salt and sauté for another minute or so. Add the beans and about ¼ cup of their cooking liquid, if you prepared them from scratch, or the liquid they were packed in (or ¼ cup water), if canned.

3. Turn the heat to medium-low and cook, mashing slightly as you stir, until heated through and all the vegetables and seasonings are distributed throughout.

4. Season to taste with additional salt, if needed. Add the lime juice and black pepper to taste. Serve hot or warm.

OPTIONAL ENHANCEMENTS

Serve with Goat Cheese–Stuffed Piquillo Peppers (page 85) ✳ Top with sliced avocado, drizzled with fresh lime juice ✳ Minced or torn cilantro leaves ✳ Toasted pumpkin seeds or Chili Pepitas (page 401) ✳ Sprinkle with finely crumbled fresh cheese ✳ Serve with Crunchy Cucumber and Red Onion with Fresh Cheese (page 73) ✳ Garnish with hard-cooked eggs, chopped or in wedges ✳ Lime wedges ✳ A spoonful of sour cream, thinned by whisking slightly, or crème fraîche ✳ A scattering of in-season sweet corn ✳ Serve with Orange Rice (page 190) ✳ Add roasted squash to the plate

Golden Lentils with Soft, Sweet Onions

MAKES ABOUT 6 SERVINGS ❋ VEGAN (WHEN MADE WITHOUT THE BUTTER)

Red lentils, which are actually orange, cook up quickly into a mustardy yellow mash that is quite tasty even before you add anything to it. A generous batch of long-cooked dark, sweet onions casts its spell on the entire potful and possibly, also, on you.

❋ Get the onions going at least 45 minutes before you hope to have the finished dish, then start simmering the lentils, so both can cook at the same time.

❋ This will keep for 4 to 5 days in a tightly covered container in the refrigerator. It also freezes beautifully and reheats well, covered, in a 250°F oven or in a microwave.

1½ tablespoons olive oil

2 teaspoons unsalted butter (optional)

3 cups minced onions (2 medium)

½ teaspoon salt, or more to taste

Up to 3 tablespoons balsamic vinegar

2 cups red lentils

5 cups water

Black pepper

Cayenne

1. Place a large (10- to 12-inch) skillet over medium heat for about a minute, then add the oil and swirl to coat the pan. Melt in the butter, if desired, then toss in the onions. Stir and/or shake the pan to get the onions wilted, about a minute. Reduce the heat to medium-low and cook, stirring often, for 20 minutes.

Add the ½ teaspoon salt and cook for 10 to 20 minutes, until the onions are supersoft and very sweet. Douse with 2 tablespoons of the vinegar during the last 2 to 3 minutes.

2. Meanwhile, place the lentils in a soup pot or large saucepan with the water. Bring to a boil, lower the heat to the slowest possible simmer (with a heat diffuser, if you have one, underneath), and partially cover. Cook quietly for about 40 minutes, or until the lentils are perfectly and mindlessly soft. (The mash will be supple at this stage. If you'd like it stiffer, simmer uncovered for a little longer.)

3. Add the lentils to the onions, stirring to thoroughly blend, then add more salt and vinegar if needed. Season further with black pepper and cayenne and serve hot, warm, or at room temperature.

OPTIONAL ENHANCEMENTS

Top with finely diced ripe heirloom tomatoes or sliced cherry tomatoes if in season ❋ Slow-Roasted Roma Tomatoes (page 393) mixed in or on top ❋ Dab with Fire-Roasted Bell Pepper Saladita (page 380) ❋ A drizzle of Balsamic Reduction (page 369) ❋ Chopped or sliced olives (any kind) ❋ Spread thickly on toast and top with Crisp, Ethereal Onion Rings (page 387) ❋ Top with pomegranate seeds and a dollop of thick yogurt ❋ For a beautiful vegetarian plate, begin with this soothing mash and add Couscous with Dates, Pistachios, Pine Nuts, and Parsley (page 217) and Flash-Fried Kale with Garlic, Almonds, and Cheese (page 346)

Mashed White Beans

MAKES 5 OR 6 SERVINGS ❈ VEGAN

Just a touch of savory seasoning enhances the flavor of these beans, letting their essence shine through. This lightly infused dish can be made with dried or canned beans, and can be the easygoing center of a winter lunch or a light dinner.

❈ I like to use flageolet beans, but you can use any light-colored variety, from navy or pea beans to cannellini. You can also try a less common heirloom variety about which you may have been curious.

❈ If you're making this with dried beans, allow plenty of time (6 hours or so) to prepare them before you begin the recipe. Soak 1 cup dried beans in plenty of water for at least 4 hours (and as long as overnight). Drain, add enough fresh water to cover by at least 2 inches, and simmer—do not rapidly boil—for about 1½ hours, or until tender. (Make sure they are truly soft.) Save the cooking water for mashing the beans or for augmenting vegetable stock or rice-cooking water.

❈ Despite this recipe's title, you can also serve the beans whole.

2 tablespoons olive oil

1 cup minced onion

¼ teaspoon salt, or more to taste

¼ teaspoon dried thyme, or more to taste

1 teaspoon minced or crushed garlic

3 cups cooked (see note) white or light-colored beans or two 15-ounce cans cannellini, rinsed and drained

Up to ¼ cup water (if using canned beans)

Black pepper

1. Place a medium skillet over medium heat for about a minute, then add the oil and swirl to coat the pan. Add the onion and cook, stirring, for 5 minutes. Add the salt and thyme and continue cooking, stirring, until the onion is brown around the edges, 8 to 10 minutes longer. When it is just about done, stir in the garlic, and cook it briefly (about 20 seconds), then turn the heat down to low.

2. Gently stir in the beans, and cook, stirring, for 3 to 5 minutes—long enough for them to absorb the flavors. Use a potato masher or a fork to mash the beans to your desired state, adding small amounts of the bean-cooking liquid or water as needed to reach your preferred texture.

3. Taste to see if it needs more salt or thyme, and add black pepper to taste. Serve hot, warm, or at room temperature.

OPTIONAL ENHANCEMENTS

A final drizzle of high-quality extra-virgin olive oil—plain or lemon-infused ❈ Grated lemon zest ❈ A touch of Maple-Mustard Glaze (page 370) ❈ Slow-Roasted Roma Tomatoes (page 393) ❈ Crispy Sage Leaves (page 394) ❈ Lemon wedges ❈ You can also leave the beans whole and scatter them as a topping on other dishes

Soft Polenta

MAKES 3 OR 4 SERVINGS (ABOUT 3½ CUPS) ❧ VEGAN

When your heart and instinct (and stomach, schedule, and cupboard) say "polenta," don't analyze. Because clearly, at this moment, you need a bowlful of yellow calm. Melt in some cheese or crown it with a single poached egg. Heap on a mound of mushrooms or top with a weave of garlicky greens or something red, such as a preparation of tomatoes or peppers, perhaps. Many suggestions follow.

❀ Soft polenta cooks up in 15 minutes. If you make it firmer and spread it out to cool on a plate, it will become sliceable. You can then fry the pieces until crisp (recipe follows).

❀ Polenta will keep for 4 to 5 days in a tightly covered container in the refrigerator. Reheat it in a microwave or by mashing it in a bowl and adding hot water or warmed milk until it is restored to your chosen consistency.

4 cups water

½ teaspoon salt, or more to taste

1 cup polenta (coarse cornmeal)

1. Pour 3 cups of the water into a medium saucepan. Add the salt, cover, and bring to a boil. Meanwhile, place the polenta in a bowl with the remaining 1 cup water and stir until it is completely moistened.

2. When the water boils, turn down the heat to a simmer and spoon in the wet polenta. Cook over medium-low heat, stirring slowly and often with a wooden spoon, until it turns creamy-thick, about 15 minutes.

3. Taste, adjust the salt, then serve hot with any combination of toppings.

OPTIONAL ENHANCEMENTS

Melt in a little butter ❋ Top with grated or sliced hard cheese, such as Parmesan or Pecorino Romano ❋ Crumble on some Gorgonzola and drizzle lightly with honey ❋ Adorn with chopped, toasted walnuts ❋ Top with a freshly poached egg and some salt and pepper ❋ Cover with Mixed Mushroom Ragout (page 348) or some Grilled Mushroom Slices (see page 349) ❋ Dab on Fire-Roasted Bell Pepper Saladita (page 380) or Romesco Sauce (page 359) ❋ Top with Salsa Verde (page 357) or basil pesto ❋ Add some minced ripe heirloom tomatoes or Slow-Roasted Roma Tomatoes (page 393)

CRISPY POLENTA TRIANGLES

VEGAN (WHEN MADE WITH OLIVE OIL)

Polenta made with less water yields a firmer result that can be cut into shapes and sautéed. My favorite is the ever-mystical triangle. You can also cut diamonds or squares.

❋ You can store these in a tightly covered container in the refrigerator for 4 to 5 days before frying them.

1. Follow the Soft Polenta recipe, but put on only 1¾ cups water to boil. When you add the wet polenta to the boiling water, it will become thick right away. Keep cooking and stirring over medium-low heat for 2 to 3 minutes, then remove it from the stove.

2. Turn the polenta out onto 2 dinner plates, spreading it into an 8-inch circle, ½ inch thick, on each plate. It will stiffen as it cools. Let it sit for 1 hour, then cut it into 2-inch triangles (or your own preferred shape). Separate the pieces and let them stand for another 30 minutes or longer to dry out.

3. Fry the pieces until crisp in a hot pan coated with melted butter and/or olive oil—about 10 minutes on each side, or until golden. Serve hot, with any savory dish—or as a snack, with any kind of salsa.

RICE and OTHER GRAINS

***

Whole grains open doors to colorful dishes that are key to your beautiful, satisfying vegetarian plate. If you can boil water, the process of cooking whole grains is simple. And because they are terrific team players, this is a good place to start, if your improvisational spirit is stirring (in all senses of the word).

Until recently, most grains have been beyond the realm of the typical American dinner plate. There might have been barley in the soup or buttered white rice on the side, but that was about the extent of it. Fortunately, we've come to understand that rice and its grain cousins can be and do so much more. They are overdue for prime time now, stepping up eagerly to their central role on the plate—not as "starch," but as a highly textured, aromatic, pleasantly complex delivery system for protein, fiber, minerals, and vitamins, and most important, for flavor, texture, and your creativity.

Cooked grains can run the spectrum from plain (with maybe just a little olive oil or nut oil and some salt and pepper), to slightly augmented (flecks of onion and minced herb, dots of nuts or dried fruit), to fully loaded main-course vegetable (and sometimes fruit) collaborations. Stir some freshly cooked grains into any cooked vegetable dish—or layer them underneath or sprinkle them on top.

The recipes in this chapter reflect my own flights of grain fancy, often with the vivid support of vegetables and legumes. These are tiny broccoli dots flecked generously into millet; cauliflower pulverized into a couscous doppelganger; a subtle intersection of black rice, beluga lentils, and minced mushrooms; and an expansion of the universal rice-and-beans meme into colorful, playful combinations: yellow rice with red beans, black rice with white beans, red rice with green beans, orange rice with black beans, and more. You will also find quinoa, farro, buckwheat, and bulgur in this chapter and in various other groupings throughout the book, especially in Salads and Burgers and Savory Pancakes.

Risotto inhabits its own world, and thus gets its own section. Enter there, and be prepared to stir your way into a new repertoire of soothing one-bowl meals.

COOKING RICE

Just as you can't simply order a cup of tea anymore without combing through pedigreed options, rice is no longer just rice. There are many fascinating kinds available, both in good food shops and online, and it's fun to experiment with the various colors, sizes, and subtle flavors. I recommend you head out on a rice shopping expedition and see what new possibilities present themselves. Find out what you love and adopt your own signature blends. Rices are often interchangeable, and they all cook basically the same way, although their cooking times vary.

MY OWN RICE-COOKING METHOD

I like to cook rice in measured water, in a ratio of 2 parts raw rice to 3 parts water. (I neither rinse the rice nor salt the water, but many of my chef friends do both of these things—all with good results.) I put everything into the pot at once, bring it to a boil, cover the pot, insert a heat diffuser underneath,

and lower the heat to the slowest available simmer. Depending on the cooking instructions for the various types of rice, I lift the cover and do a taste test at the earliest recommended cooking time—but not before, so as not to disturb the rice and compromise the all-important steam buildup. When it's done to my liking, I fluff the cooked rice with a fork to let the steam escape and allow the grains to separate. This cooking step can often be done well in advance.

You may already have your own way of cooking rice (an electric rice cooker that you love, perhaps?) that works well for you. If so, there is no need to change it. On the other hand, if you would rather not measure the water and you want a safety net, you can simply boil rice in a generous amount of unmeasured water, as you would pasta, draining it when a taste test tells you it's ready. This works just fine for most recipes, and yields fluffy separate grains. Your call.

Orange Rice

MAKES 5 OR 6 SERVINGS ❈ VEGAN

As autumn rolls in and the compression of light and time prods us toward an earlier dinner hour, we need some color on our plate to match the scenery while the leaves are still attached, and to remind us of it after they have fallen.

Orangeing up a batch of rice is an apt center-of-the-plate plan for the season of diminishing sunlight. There is no limit to the beautiful gold accents you can pack into—and pile onto—this dish. And the more Enhancements you choose, the more of a complete meal it becomes. The full-

plate version (below) includes black beans, taking it into Halloween mode.

❈ You can prepare and cook the other ingredients while the rice simmers.

❈ The large skillet might seem oversized at first, when you are cooking just vegetables, but you will need the space to accommodate the cooked rice.

❈ This will keep for 3 to 4 days in a tightly covered container in the refrigerator. It reheats well, covered, in a 250°F oven or toaster oven or in a microwave.

1½ cups brown basmati rice

Up to 2½ cups water

1 tablespoon grapeseed or olive oil

1 heaping cup minced onion

1 teaspoon mild paprika

¾ teaspoon salt, or more to taste

¼ teaspoon ground coriander (optional)

1 teaspoon minced or crushed garlic

1 heaping cup finely minced carrots

1 heaping cup finely minced orange bell pepper

1 tablespoon fresh lemon juice

Splash of fresh orange juice (optional)

Crushed red pepper

1. Combine the rice and 2¼ cups water in a medium saucepan. Bring to a boil, lower the heat to a simmer, cover, and cook undisturbed (with a heat diffuser, if you have one, underneath) for 40 minutes. If the rice is not tender enough at this point—or if it appears to be sticking—splash in up to ¼ cup additional water and cook it a little further. When the rice is done to your liking, fluff it with a fork to let steam escape and to separate the grains.

2. Meanwhile, place a large (10- to 12-inch) skillet over medium heat for about a minute, then add the oil and swirl to coat the pan. Toss in the onion, paprika, ¼ teaspoon of the salt, and the coriander, if using, and cook, stirring, for 5 to 8 minutes, or until the onion softens.

3. Stir in the garlic, carrots, and bell pepper and cook, stirring, for another 5 minutes, or until the vegetables are just tender.

4. Turn the heat to low and begin forking the rice into the vegetables, stirring it in with a large fork and fluffing as you go. Sprinkle with the lemon juice and add another ½ teaspoon salt. When the salt is completely mixed in, taste to see if it's the right amount. You can also splash in some orange juice, if you like—just a whisper—for an extra flavor layer, and sprinkle on crushed red pepper to taste.

5. Continue to cook the rice in the vegetables, keeping the pan over the heat for just as long as it takes to get the rice incorporated. You want to impart flavor without letting things get mushy.

6. Serve right away.

OPTIONAL ENHANCEMENTS

Top with any of the following: ❋ Small dice of roasted butternut squash (see page 351) ❋ Orange zest, grated or in long strands ❋ Thinly sliced kumquats ❋ Diced papaya or mango ❋ Slices of firm, ripe avocado ❋ Crumbled fresh cheese ❋ Golden raisins ❋ Toasted cumin seeds ❋ Toasted pumpkin seeds ❋ Torn cilantro leaves

ORANGE RICE AND BLACK BEANS

Serve next to Soft Cuban-Style Black Beans (page 180), with any or all of the above accoutrements, and possibly with a simple green salad or Crunchy Cucumbers and Red Onion with Fresh Cheese (page 73).

Make the black beans and roast the diced squash well ahead of time. Everything reheats beautifully.

Spiced Basmati Pilaf with Nuts and Raisins

MAKES 6 SERVINGS ❧ VEGAN (WHEN MADE WITHOUT BUTTER)

The irresistible fragrance of basmati sets sail into full resonance with measured touches of ginger, garlic, and spice. Harmonics of fruit enter, followed by a cascade of nuts. You did the usual things and with fairly ordinary ingredients, yet something unusual has come of it—to wit: a raga of rice. This is why we love to cook.

❀ The large skillet might seem oversized at first, when you are cooking just the onion and seasonings, but you will need the space to accommodate the cooked rice.

❀ This will keep for 3 to 4 days in a tightly covered container in the refrigerator. It reheats well, covered, in a 250°F oven or toaster oven or in a microwave. Keep the nuts separate until shortly before serving.

2 cups brown basmati rice

Up to 3¼ cups water

2 tablespoons grapeseed, peanut, or canola oil

1½ cups minced onion (1 medium)

1 tablespoon minced or crushed garlic

1 tablespoon minced fresh ginger

1 teaspoon fennel seeds or cumin seeds (whole or ground)

½ teaspoon salt, or more to taste

Up to 1½ cups sliced almonds and/or pistachios

1 tablespoon unsalted butter (optional)

½ cup raisins (dark or golden, or a combination)

Up to 2 teaspoons grated orange or lemon zest (or a combination)

1. Combine the rice and 3 cups of the water in a medium saucepan. Bring to a boil, lower the heat to a simmer, cover, and cook undisturbed (with a heat diffuser, if you have one, underneath) for 40 minutes. If the rice is not tender enough at this point—or if it appears to be sticking—splash in up to ¼ cup additional water and cook it a little further. When the rice is done to your liking, fluff it with a fork to let steam escape and to separate the grains.

2. While the rice is cooking, place a large (10- to 12-inch) skillet over medium heat for about a minute, then add the oil and swirl to coat the pan. Toss in the onion, garlic, ginger, fennel or cumin seeds, and ½ teaspoon salt. Cook, stirring, over medium-low heat for about 15 minutes, or until the onion becomes very soft. Turn off the heat.

3. Meanwhile, get the nuts ready. You can either toast them in a 250°F oven or toaster oven until fragrant (10 to 15 minutes), or sauté them in butter over low heat in a medium skillet for about 5 minutes, stirring frequently. Watch them carefully, so they don't burn. Set the nuts aside.

4. Begin adding the rice to the onion mixture, working it in with a fork to thoroughly combine. Add the raisins, citrus zest, and additional salt, if desired, while you stir. If you're serving this right away, stir in the nuts. If not, hold off on adding them until shortly before serving, after the rice is reheated. Serve hot or warm.

OPTIONAL ENHANCEMENTS

Yogurt on top and/or mixed in slightly ✳ Lemon wedges ✳ A chai tea bag added to the rice-cooking water ✳ Whole cardamom (4 pods) plus a cinnamon stick added to the rice-cooking water (fish them out later) ✳ Diced carrots and/or sweet bell peppers sautéed with the onion, added after 5 minutes ✳ Very thin strips of fresh mint leaves on top

BROWN RICE AND YELLOW BEANS

Make this into an Indian-style version of rice and beans by serving it over, under, or surrounding Yellow Split Pea Dal (page 28) and/or Curried Eggplant Slap-Down with Yogurt, Onion Relish, and Pomegranate (page 341). Round out the meal with Raita (page 371) and a garnish of fresh orange wedges.

Green Rice

MAKES 6 SERVINGS ❧ VEGAN

Generously coated with cumin- and garlic-infused olive oil, brightened with fresh lemon juice, and flecked green with cilantro, this beguiling combination tastes far more complex than the relatively short ingredient list might lead you to believe. Serve it anywhere you want a spoonful of tasty, savory rice, as it is versatile and lends itself readily to many contexts. My favorite setting for this is in a hollowed-out sweet bell pepper half that has been seared first in hot olive oil for a few minutes on each side, until lightly blistered. Spoon in the warm rice, sprinkle with crumbly fresh cheese and some chopped toasted walnuts, and you have a complete little meal.

❀ Jade rice is a delicate-tasting variety that has been infused with green bamboo juice and is therefore rich in chlorophyll. This very pretty grain has gradually been making its way into many good grocery stores, and is also available online. It cooks more quickly than brown basmati, and because it is a short-grain rice, it becomes stickier and softer. (Brown basmati will cook up drier and more separate.) I love this dish made with both kinds of rice and tend to alternate between them.

❀ You can add any amount of chopped cilantro—up to 2 bunches. That translates into roughly a cup or so per bunch. Go by feel and visuals and green up the rice per your own taste (and the amount of cilantro you have on hand). Remember that herbs are also vegetables, so when you pack them into any dish, you are increasing your vegetable consumption while making the food taste incredible.

❀ This will keep for 3 to 4 days in a tightly covered container in the refrigerator. It reheats well, covered, in a 250°F oven or toaster oven, or in a microwave.

2 cups brown basmati rice or jade rice (see note)

Up to 3¼ cups water

3 tablespoons olive oil

1½ teaspoons minced or crushed garlic

1 teaspoon ground cumin

1 teaspoon salt, or more to taste

3 tablespoons fresh lemon juice, or more to taste

1–2 bunches cilantro, chopped (up to 2 cups, loosely packed)

1. Combine the rice and 3 cups water in a medium saucepan. Bring to a boil, lower the heat to a simmer, cover, and cook undisturbed (with a heat diffuser, if you have one, underneath) for 20 minutes for jade rice or 40 for brown basmati. If the rice is not tender enough at this point—or if it appears to be sticking—splash in up to ¼ cup additional water and cook it a little further. When the rice is done to your liking, fluff it with a fork to let the steam escape and to separate the grains.

2. Meanwhile, stir together the olive oil, garlic, and cumin in a small, microwave-safe bowl. Cover and zap on high for 30 seconds. Carefully uncover (when you deem it cool enough to safely do so) and scrape all of this mixture into the rice, mixing with a fork to thoroughly combine.

3. Add the salt and lemon juice to taste and toss until everything is evenly distributed. Mix in the cilantro, and it's ready to serve.

OPTIONAL ENHANCEMENTS

Top with minced, lightly toasted walnuts (highly recommended) or lightly toasted pine nuts ❋ Sprinkle over crumbled fresh cheese, such as Mexican queso fresco (also highly recommended) ❋ Make a complete plate by serving Green Rice stuffed into lightly seared pepper halves (see headnote) and surrounding with grilled squash and some plain cooked beans, topped with dabs of guacamole and salsa

VARIATION

If cilantro is a no-go (most people either love it or hate it), substitute a combination of fresh flat-leaf parsley and mint leaves.

Yellow Coconut Rice with Chilies, Ginger, and Lime

MAKES 6 TO 8 SERVINGS ❄ VEGAN

Turmeric is basmati's first stop on the flavor highway leading to one of the feistier (and most popular) pilafs in my repertoire. From there, the rice takes a spin down chili lane, picking up a significant cargo of lime juice, garlic, and ginger before arriving at coconut. You can stop there or take it all the way to Yellow Rice and Red Beans as in the photo below.

Emboldened by the popularity of this dish among my family and friends, I once ventured so far as to prepare it for a children's birthday party. It disappeared in minutes!

❋ The large skillet might seem oversized at first, when you are cooking just the onion, chilies, and seasonings, but you will need the space to accommodate the cooked rice.

❋ Fresh chilies vary greatly in heat, and it's impossible to gauge their strength until they are actually in play. So add half of them with the other seasonings, and the rest—gradually—at the end, carefully tasting the mixture (not straight chilies!) as you go. Keep in mind that sometimes cut jalapeños ease up after they've been sitting awhile, so what's very hot today might have gone mildish by tomorrow. Be sure to wash your hands, knife, and cutting board between chili handling and touching anything else (your eyes and face, especially).

❋ This will keep for 3 to 4 days in a tightly covered container in the refrigerator. It reheats well, covered, in a 250°F oven or toaster oven or in a microwave.

2 cups brown basmati rice

Up to 3¼ cups water

½ teaspoon turmeric

1 tablespoon grapeseed, peanut, or canola oil

2 cups minced onion (1 large)

Up to 3 tablespoons finely minced serrano or jalapeño chilies, or crushed red pepper to taste

2 tablespoons minced fresh ginger

2 tablespoons minced garlic

¾ teaspoon salt, or more to taste

1¼ teaspoons grated lime zest

¼ cup fresh lime juice (from about 2 limes), or to taste

1 cup shredded unsweetened coconut, lightly toasted

1. Combine the rice with 3 cups of the water and the turmeric in a medium-large saucepan. Bring to a boil, lower the heat to a simmer, cover, and cook undisturbed (with a heat diffuser, if you have one, underneath) for 40 minutes. If the rice is not tender enough at this point—or if it appears to be sticking— splash in up to ¼ cup additional water and cook it a little further. When the rice is done to your liking, fluff it with a fork to let steam escape and to separate the grains.

2. Meanwhile, place a large (10- to 12-inch) skillet over medium heat for about a minute, then add the oil and swirl to coat the pan. Toss in the onion and cook, stirring, over medium heat for 5 to 8 minutes, or until it softens. Stir in 1 tablespoon of the chilies (or a pinch of crushed red pepper), plus the ginger, garlic, and ½ teaspoon salt, then turn the heat to low and continue to cook very slowly for about 10 minutes longer, until everything is soft and blended. If the mixture appears to be sticking, splash in a little water.

3. Turn off the heat and begin forking the rice into the onion mixture, stirring and fluffing it as you go. Gradually add another ¼ teaspoon salt, the lime zest, lime juice to taste, and most of the toasted coconut, saving some for the top. Stir in additional chilies or crushed red pepper, staying on the shy side if you are chili-shy, or treading on the generous side if you have a heat-inclined palate. Taste (carefully) as you go, and while you're doing that, check to see if it needs more salt.

4. Serve hot, warm, or at room temperature, topped with the reserved coconut.

YELLOW RICE AND RED BEANS

Add up to 3 cups cooked red chili beans or kidney beans (one or two 15-ounce cans, rinsed and thoroughly drained), stirring them in gently, so the rice becomes evenly studded with ovals of dark red.

Cranberry Rice

MAKES 6 SERVINGS ❧ VEGAN

Keep the winter holiday spirit going between those large feasts with this delicious, tart, very easy burgundy pilaf. And for a fun, Christmasy rice-and-beans treatment, consider expanding it into a full-on arrangement of Red Rice and Green Beans (instructions follow the recipe).

You begin with red rice, and then take it deeper into garnet-hued territory with cranberry-infused red onion: a little sweet, a little salty.

❀ There are several kinds of whole-grain red rices available in natural food stores and gourmet shops and online. I tend to alternate between Bhutanese and Wehani.

❀ Wehani rice is a ruddy basmati relative, developed by the Lundberg family of Richvale, California, and named for brothers Wendell, Eldon, Homer, and Harlan. A dark reddish brown, it looks like a plump, blushing version of wild rice. The Lundbergs describe Wehani's aroma as reminiscent of "hot, buttered peanuts."

❀ Bhutanese red rice is exported from Bhutan in the Himalayas. The American importers, Lotus Foods, have done double good, providing Bhutanese farmers with access to the global marketplace while protecting this beautiful, once-rare whole-grain rice from extinction. It's relatively quick-cooking (20 minutes).

❀ The large skillet might seem oversized at first, when you are cooking just the onion and cranberries, but you will need the space to accommodate the cooked rice.

❀ Cranberries need to be sweetened, even if just minimally, in order to be palatable. Both agave nectar and sugar will work, and I like to use a combination, usually 2 tablespoons agave nectar and 1 tablespoon sugar. You can customize per your own inclinations.

❀ Not only is it OK to make this dish ahead, it's actually better that way. If you're serving it with Green Beans, Edamame, and Peas (page 330), make the rice ahead and reheat it just before serving.

❀ This will keep for 3 to 4 days in a tightly covered container in the refrigerator. It reheats well, covered, in a 250°F oven or toaster oven, or in a microwave.

2 cups Bhutanese or Wehani red rice (see notes)

Up to 3¼ cups water

2 tablespoons grapeseed or canola oil

1½ cups finely minced red onion (1 medium)

½ teaspoon salt, or more to taste

1½–2 cups coarsely chopped cranberries (fresh or frozen)

Up to 3 tablespoons agave nectar and/or sugar

1. Combine the rice and 3 cups water in a medium saucepan. Bring to a boil, lower the heat to a simmer, cover, and cook undisturbed (with a heat diffuser, if you have one, underneath) for 20 minutes for Bhutanese rice or 40 minutes for Wehani. If the rice is not tender enough at this point—or if it appears to be sticking—splash in up to ¼ cup additional water and cook it a little further. When the rice is done to your liking, fluff it with a fork to let steam escape and to separate the grains.

2. Meanwhile, place a large (10- to 12-inch) skillet over medium heat for about a minute, then add the oil and swirl to coat the pan. Toss in the onion and ¼ teaspoon salt and cook, stirring, for 5 to 8 minutes, or until the onion begins to soften.

3. Stir in the cranberries and sauté for another 5 minutes, or until the cranberries have softened. Add the sweetener, stirring to distribute it as evenly as possible.

4. Turn off the heat and begin forking the rice into the cranberry mixture, stirring it in with a large fork, sprinkling in another ¼ teaspoon salt, and fluffing as you go. When all the rice is incorporated, taste to see if you're happy with the salt and sweetening and adjust accordingly. Serve hot or warm.

OPTIONAL ENHANCEMENTS

A few dried cranberries tossed in with the fresh ones
❉ Pomegranate seeds in addition to the cranberries
❉ Finely chopped pecans, lightly toasted

RED RICE AND GREEN BEANS

Serve Cranberry Rice in artful combination with Green Beans, Edamame, and Peas (page 330). I like to use a large star-shaped cookie cutter as a template to fashion a red star center with a green background. It takes only a little maneuvering to get everything in place, and it's worthwhile, especially when you see the delighted response when you bring it to the table. You can do this in larger format on a serving platter or in smaller versions on individual plates. Kids will love it.

Serve with Radicchio Salad with Oranges and Pistachios (page 78).

Blueberry Rice

MAKES 6 SERVINGS ❧ VEGAN

Something compelled me to combine a savory blueberry sauce with a batch of freshly cooked aromatic rice. To make the sauce, I simply added a bag of frozen unsweetened blueberries to sautéed, minced red onion, and then let it reduce and thicken. I then added two small batches of rice—brown basmati and black rice (which cooks into a lovely shade of dark violet)—and the result was a beautiful amethyst pilaf, stippled with plum.

Although it seemed like a wild and crazy idea at first, the taste is subtle, tart, and utterly dignified in its deliciousness. The blueberry essence is unmistakable, yet completely harmonious with both kinds of rice.

❀ You can use any kind of frozen unsweetened blueberries.

❀ There's more information about black rice on page 214.

❀ It's OK, and actually desirable, if the rice comes out a little on the dry side, as it will absorb moisture from the sauce.

* You can double the sauce recipe, if you like—incorporating half into the rice and serving the other half as an extra luxury, spooned around the edges and/or on top.

2 cups brown basmati rice or black (Forbidden) rice or 1 cup each

3 cups water

1 tablespoon grapeseed or canola oil

1½ cups minced red onion (1 medium)

¾ teaspoon salt, or more to taste

10–12 ounces frozen unsweetened blueberries (defrosting is optional)

Fresh lemon or lime juice (optional)

1. Combine the rice and water in a medium saucepan. (If you are using half basmati and half black rice, place 1 cup each in separate, smaller saucepans with 1½ cups water.) Bring to a boil, lower the heat to a simmer, cover, and cook undisturbed (with a heat diffuser, if you have one, underneath) for 40 minutes. When the rice is done to your liking, fluff it with a fork to let the steam escape and to separate the grains.

2. Meanwhile, place a large (10- to 12-inch) skillet over medium heat for about a minute, then add the oil and swirl to coat the pan. Toss in the onion and ¼ teaspoon of the salt and cook, stirring, for 8 to 10 minutes, or until the onion becomes soft.

3. Add the blueberries, breaking them up with a spoon if they are still frozen, and stirring them into the onions. When all becomes liquidy, turn up the heat to medium-high and let it bubble

away, occasionally stirring from the bottom of the pan to prevent sticking. The sauce will reduce and thicken over the next 10 minutes or so. Keep an eye on it to be sure it doesn't burn. When it reaches the consistency of very soft jam, remove the pan from the heat.

4. Add all the rice to the blueberry mixture, stirring it in with a large fork, sprinkling in another ½ teaspoon salt, and fluffing as you go. When everything is combined, taste to see if you're happy with the salt and adjust accordingly, adding a little lemon or lime juice to taste, if desired. Serve hot or warm, in an artful arrangement, to your delighted and intrigued guests.

OPTIONAL ENHANCEMENTS

Lemon or lime wedges * Extra sauce spooned around and on top (from a double batch) * Pomegranate seeds sprinkled on top * Lime wedges * Lime zest, grated or in long strands * Fresh and/or dried blueberries * Lightly toasted pine nuts * Stuff it into a baked acorn squash half (see page 350)

PURPLE RICE, YELLOW BEANS

Serve Blueberry Rice juxtaposed, in your own inimitable way, with steamed yellow wax beans tossed with brown butter and a little fresh mint or dried thyme. Round out the meal and expand the rainbow theme with a side of Citrusy Beets (page 98). A platter of cheeses is also welcome.

RELAXING INTO RISOTTO

There is much mystique surrounding the making of a risotto, but in fact, no unusual techniques are required. You simply need to pay attention to a few choice ingredients and allow yourself some time in the kitchen getting it ready—stirring, waiting, and maybe sipping some wine. The result, if you are in the zone, will be a dreamy bowlful of subtle texture and warmth.

So what does it mean to be in the risotto zone? You have carefully selected the rice, wine, stock, and cheese, and you've prepared the ingredients for a tasty filling or topping (or both). A commitment to the following will get you there.

RICE

Arborio and the less common Vialone Nano and Carnaroli are the risotto rices. They are short-grained and round and high in starch. As they cook, their starch releases into the stock, so the grains soften while the liquid thickens.

WINE

Use a good, dry white wine that you enjoy drinking. It doesn't need to be expensive, just crisp and tasty. Since you will be using only ½ cup per batch, keep it in the refrigerator until next time (which might well be soon) or simply enjoy the rest of the bottle with the meal.

STOCK

The stock is very important, since it becomes the body of the risotto. Taste around and find (or make) one that you love (see page 22). My own preference, when I don't have time to make my own stock from scratch, is Kitchen Basics Unsalted Vegetable Stock. It's available in many grocery stores and online.

CHEESE

Splurge on the best Parmesan for these recipes. It goes in at the end and you won't need much, but its effect will be important, so don't skimp on the quality of the cheese. You can freeze it between risottos.

POINTERS

- Be sure everything is prepped and measured and near the stove before you begin.
- You'll need a pot of at least a 2½-quart capacity (ideally about 8 inches in diameter and 4 inches deep). You should have a trusty wooden spoon at the ready.
- Heat and simmer the stock (covering between dips, so it doesn't evaporate) in a second pot nearby. A ladle is handy.
- Don't overcook it! Remove the risotto from the heat while the grains are still slightly chewy and the stock is thickened but sloppy-soft. This can take anywhere from 20 to 50 minutes, depending on your saucepan, stove, and the rice itself. Always make sure the guests are ready ahead of time, because this wants to get served right away. Sip wine while you wait.
- Bonus detail: Treat yourself to some dedicated risotto bowls that are cozy, sturdy, and somewhat shallow.
- Nice touch: Give your guests both forks and spoons for the fullest risotto experience. Every time I do this, we all happily use both.

Mushroom Risotto

MAKES 5 OR 6 SERVINGS

Rice dives headlong into the deep end of mush-room flavor, as though the pot has a mystical false bottom. Porcini-infused stock contributes to a profoundly tasty backdrop, layering it to the nth (or should I say mth?) degree. Invite your die-hard mushroom-infatuated friends for dinner.

❋ Soak the dried mushrooms at least 30 minutes ahead of time. They need to soften and then cool until comfortable to handle. Save the water as you drain them, since it will be added to the stock.

❋ You may end up with more stock than you need for the recipe. If so, you can add the extra to any compatibly flavored soup or to the cooking water for another batch of grains.

❋ You can use a food processor to mince the fresh mushrooms.

1 ounce dried porcini mushrooms

2 cups boiling water

1 quart vegetable stock (page 22) or low-sodium store-bought

2 tablespoons unsalted butter

1 heaping cup minced onion

1 teaspoon minced or crushed garlic

¼ teaspoon dried thyme

½ pound fresh mushrooms (domestic and/or cremini), wiped clean, stemmed if necessary, and minced

1 teaspoon salt, or more to taste

1½ cups risotto rice (see page 202)

½ cup dry white wine or dry sherry, at room temperature

¾ cup shredded Parmesan, or more if needed

Black pepper

1. Place the porcini in a medium bowl and pour over the boiling water. Cover with a plate and let sit until the mushrooms are soft, about 30 minutes.

2. Place a strainer over a second bowl and drain the mushrooms into it, gently but completely hand-squeezing them to expel (and save) as much of the water as you can. Mince the drained mushrooms.

3. Strain the mushroom-soaking water through a fine strainer or a coffee filter into a medium saucepan and add the stock. Cover the pot, bring to a boil over medium-low heat, then reduce the heat to low. Have a ladle ready, resting on a plate. Keep the simmering stock covered between applications.

4. Melt the butter in a heavy-bottomed medium saucepan over medium-low heat, then swirl to coat the pan. Toss in the onion and cook, stirring, for about 2 minutes, then add the garlic and thyme. Cook, stirring, for another 2 to 3 minutes, or until the onion begins to soften.

5. Stir in the porcini and fresh mushrooms and ½ teaspoon of the salt, then cover and let everything cook undisturbed for 5 to 8 minutes, or until the mushrooms have cooked down and given off some liquid.

[continues]

Butternut Risotto

MAKES 5 OR 6 SERVINGS

6. Add the rice and stir over medium heat for about a minute to coat it with everything else in the pan. Add the remaining ½ teaspoon salt and the wine or sherry and stir until the wine is absorbed, about 30 seconds.

7. Ladle in enough hot stock to cover, stirring until most of the liquid is absorbed. Repeat this process until the mixture is creamy and a bit loose; the rice should still have some chew to it, but should not taste at all raw. You may not need to add all the stock. Remove from the heat while the grains still show some resistance. Don't overcook.

8. Turn off the heat and stir in the Parmesan. Taste to see if the rice needs more salt and/or cheese and season to taste with black pepper. Serve right away.

OPTIONAL ENHANCEMENTS

A little fresh lemon juice drizzled in, to taste, when you add the cheese ❀ A garnish of lemon zest, grated or in long strands ❀ Decorate with Crispy Fried Lemons (page 389) ❀ Top with sprigs of fresh thyme or an Herb Tangle (page 76) ❀ Salad pairing: Wilted Spinach Salad with Crispy Smoked Tofu, Grilled Onion, Croutons, and Tomatoes (page 82)

I have two recipes for butternut squash risotto, and I go back and forth between them, depending on whether I feel like heating the oven and roasting the squash or cooking it on the stovetop for a softer, less dramatic effect. I like them equally.

In the first method, you make everything in a single pot. In the second, you roast the squash separately ahead of time and then fold it into a plain risotto. The roasting itself imparts a certain extra essence—"hot oven" is actually a kind of seasoning—but the rest of the flavor profile (brown butter, sage, sharp cheddar) is the same.

❀ The squash can be made as much as a day ahead and stored in an airtight container in the refrigerator. Be sure it is warmed at least to room temperature before you begin the risotto.

❀ The recipe uses only part of what you'll end up with when you peel and chop an average-sized (3½-pound) butternut squash. Save any extra and use it for another dish (see page 267) and/or freeze it for later.

2 tablespoons unsalted butter

1 heaping cup minced onion

1 teaspoon rubbed dried sage

2 generous cups diced (¾-inch) butternut squash

¾ teaspoon salt, or more to taste

1 quart vegetable stock (page 22) or low-sodium store-bought

1½ cups risotto rice (see page 202)

½ cup dry white wine, at room temperature

½ cup (packed) grated sharp cheddar

Black pepper

STOVETOP VERSION

1. Melt the butter in a large (10- to 12-inch) skillet over medium-low heat. Swirl to coat the pan, then wait another few seconds for the butter to brown slightly. Add the onion and sage and cook, stirring, over low heat for about 3 minutes, or until the onion just begins to soften.

2. Add the squash and ½ teaspoon of the salt. Stir briefly to coat the squash, then cover and cook over low heat for 6 to 8 minutes, or until the squash softens slightly. (The squash will finish cooking in the risotto.)

3. Meanwhile, bring the stock to a boil in a covered saucepan over medium-low heat, then reduce the heat to low. Have a ladle ready, resting on a plate. Keep the simmering stock covered between applications.

4. Add the rice to the skillet with the squash and stir over medium heat for about a minute to coat it with everything else in the pan. Add another ¼ teaspoon salt and the wine and stir until the wine is absorbed, about 30 seconds.

5. Ladle in enough hot stock to cover, stirring until most of the liquid is absorbed. Repeat this process until the mixture is creamy and a bit loose; the rice should still have some chew to it, but should not taste at all raw. (If you run out of stock and the risotto seems to need a little more cooking, you can add some water at this point, ½ cup at a time.) Remove from the heat while the grains still show some resistance. Don't overcook.

6. Turn off the heat and stir in the cheese. Taste for salt and season to taste with black pepper. Serve right away.

ROASTED SQUASH VERSION

1. Prepare a batch of roasted butternut squash (see page 351) well ahead of time.

2. Make the risotto as described in the stovetop version, but using a heavy-bottomed medium saucepan and cook the onions for 5 minutes. Skip step 3. Add the salt in step 4. When you get to the end, fold in about 2 cups of the roasted squash when you add the cheese. Serve the remaining roasted squash on top or on the side, as desired.

OPTIONAL ENHANCEMENTS

Top with Crispy Sage Leaves (page 394) ✳ Extra cheddar on top ✳ Top with a dab of Thick Cranberry-Orange Vinaigrette (page 368) ✳ Lemon wedges ✳ Sprinkle with toasted walnuts ✳ Celery-Almond-Date Saladita (page 376) ✳ Apple-Parsley Saladita (page 386) ✳ Endive, Jicama, and Wild Rice Salad with Blue Cheese–Yogurt dressing (page 110) ✳ Grilled Mushroom Slices (see page 349) scattered or placed on top

Roasted Cauliflower Risotto

MAKES 5 OR 6 SERVINGS

Cauliflower is roasted at a high temperature ahead of time, emerging from the oven with golden edges and a baked-on fontina coating. Once folded into the risotto, it both blends in and stands out, retaining its definition just enough to provide distinct bursts of vegetable-cheese texture against the serenity of the rice. Extra fontina joins Parmesan in the sauce, yielding a complex cheesy flavor.

❁ You can roast the cauliflower immediately before assembling the risotto, or as much as a day ahead, if you store it in an airtight container in the refrigerator. Be sure it is warmed at least to room temperature before continuing.

THE CAULIFLOWER

1 tablespoon olive oil

1 medium head cauliflower (about 2 pounds), trimmed and cut or broken into ¾-inch florets

¼ cup (packed) grated fontina

¼ teaspoon salt

1. Preheat the oven to 400°F, with a rack in the center position. Line a baking sheet with parchment paper or foil and slick it with the olive oil. (You can use a chunk of cauliflower to spread it around.)

2. Arrange the cauliflower pieces on the baking sheet. Roast for 15 minutes, then shake the baking sheet and/or use tongs to loosen and redistribute the pieces.

3. Roast for another 5 to 10 minutes, until the cauliflower is becoming uniformly golden, then push the pieces together in the center of the sheet, keeping them in a single layer. Sprinkle evenly with the fontina.

4. Roast for 10 or so minutes longer, or until the cheese is thoroughly melted and a compelling goldenness rules. Remove the sheet from the oven, sprinkle the cauliflower with the salt, and set aside. (You can also turn off the oven and leave the cauliflower in there with the oven door ajar to keep things warm.)

THE RISOTTO

1 quart vegetable stock (page 22) or low-sodium store-bought

1 tablespoon olive oil or unsalted butter or a combination

1 heaping cup minced onion

1½ cups risotto rice (see page 202)

½ teaspoon salt

½ cup dry white wine, at room temperature

½ cup (packed) grated fontina

½ cup grated Parmesan

Black pepper

1. Bring the stock to a boil in a covered saucepan over medium-low heat, then reduce the heat to low. Have a ladle ready, resting on a plate. Keep the simmering stock covered between applications.

2. Place a heavy-bottomed medium saucepan over medium heat for about a minute, then add the olive oil and/or butter and swirl to coat the pan. Toss in the onion and cook, stirring, for about 5 minutes, or until the onion begins to soften.

3. Add the rice and stir over medium heat for about a minute to coat it with everything else in the pan. Add the salt and the wine and stir until the wine is absorbed, about 30 seconds.

4. Ladle in enough hot stock to cover, stirring until most of the liquid is absorbed. Repeat this process until the mixture is creamy and a bit loose; the rice should still have some chew to it but should not taste at all raw. (If you run out of stock and the risotto seems to need a little more cooking, you can add some water at this point, ½ cup at a time.) Remove from the heat while the grains still show some resistance. Don't overcook.

5. Turn off the heat and stir/fold in the fontina, Parmesan, as much of the roasted cauliflower as seems to fit, and a generous amount of black pepper. Serve right away, topped with any additional cauliflower that you might not have folded in.

OPTIONAL ENHANCEMENTS

This goes beautifully with a side of Orange-Olive-Fig Saladita (page 385) ❋ Salad pairing: Kale Caesar (page 68)

Risotto Primavera with Asparagus and Green Peas

MAKES 5 OR 6 SERVINGS

Dots and dashes of peas and asparagus transmit their delicious code from within the creamy rice, contributing little pops of texture. This is a spring dish, in every sense of the word.

❀ You can use asparagus of any thickness. For this recipe, I like to use thinner spears. Peeling the bottom half, after snapping off and discarding the tough bottoms, is optional. While peeling, lay the asparagus as flat as possible to prevent breakage.

❀ For each cup of fresh peas, you'll need to shuck about a pound of pods. It's fun and it goes pretty fast. Frozen peas are fine, too, and they don't need to be defrosted.

❀ Wherever and whenever asparagus and fresh English peas meet up, fresh fava beans are also welcome. If you can get your hands on some and are willing to go through the ritual of getting them ready (see page 256), feel free to add however many you desire. The same goes for edible-pod peas (sugar snaps or snow peas)—whole or cut, raw or lightly cooked, in or on top.

❀ Consider making and using your own stock for this by simmering the pea pods in about 6 cups water with a few slices of onion and ½ teaspoon salt for 15 to 20 minutes, partially covered, over medium heat. Strain, and it's ready for risotto.

❀ The vegetables can be prepared and cooked up to an hour in advance and kept at room temperature. If you're going to make them further in advance (up to a day ahead is OK), cover and refrigerate, then bring them back to room temperature before making the risotto.

THE VEGETABLES

1 tablespoon unsalted butter

1 pound asparagus, trimmed, peeled (if desired), and cut into 1½-inch pieces

½ teaspoon minced or crushed garlic

¼ teaspoon salt

1–2 cups green peas (freshly shelled or frozen)

1. Melt the butter in a heavy-bottomed medium saucepan over medium-low heat, then swirl to coat the pan. Stir in the asparagus, garlic, and salt, cover, and cook for just a minute or two, or until the asparagus is not quite tender—neither too crunchy nor all-the-way soft—as it will cook further upon contact with the hot risotto.

2. When the asparagus is almost where you want it (about 2 minutes short of ready), stir in the peas. Cover again and cook for just a couple of minutes longer. Transfer the mixture to a medium bowl, scraping from the bottom of the pan. Without washing the pan, return it to the turned-off stove to wait for the risotto.

THE RISOTTO

1 quart vegetable stock (page 22) or low-sodium store-bought

1 tablespoon olive oil and/or unsalted butter

1½ heaping cups minced onion

1½ cups risotto rice (see page 202)

½ teaspoon salt, or more to taste

½ cup dry white wine, at room temperature

½ cup grated Parmesan, or more to taste

Black pepper

PEAS

Fresh peas are better than frozen ones only when they are truly fresh, not recently fresh or past fresh, or fresh-ish. "Fresh" can mean weary, if the peas have been sitting in the case for two days.

I learned this the hard way, after I purchased a (not cheap) packaged pound of organic peas in pods that seemed in retrospect as though they'd lost their commitment to the color green. In a rush, I grabbed them anyway. When I got them home and opened the mottled pods, most of the peas were overdeveloped and tough. But because they were labeled "fresh," I shucked a full pound of them before I realized I should wake up and taste one. And?

Awful! Bitter enough to ruin my entire risotto. So the "fresh" peas were assigned to compost and the understudies in my freezer got the call. Disaster averted and lesson learned. Oh, and frozen peas make really good risotto.

1. Bring the stock to a boil in a covered saucepan over medium-low heat, then reduce the heat to low. Have a ladle ready, resting on a plate. Keep the simmering stock covered between applications.

2. Place the same saucepan you used for the vegetables over medium heat for about a minute, then add the olive oil and/or butter and swirl to coat the pan. Toss in the onion and cook, stirring, for about 5 minutes, or until it begins to soften.

3. Add the rice and stir over medium heat for about a minute to coat it with everything else in the pan. Add the salt and the wine and stir until the wine is absorbed, about 30 seconds.

4. Ladle in enough hot stock to cover, stirring until most of the liquid is absorbed. Repeat this process until the mixture is creamy and a bit loose; the rice should still have some chew to it, but should not taste at all raw. (If you run out of stock and the risotto seems to need a little more cooking, you can add some water at this point, ½ cup at a time.) Remove from the heat while the grains still show some resistance. Don't overcook.

5. Turn off the heat and add the Parmesan and the vegetable mixture, stirring and folding them in gently. Taste to possibly add more salt and cheese, and season to taste with black pepper. Serve right away.

OPTIONAL ENHANCEMENTS

Fava beans added to the vegetable mixture or dotting the top ✳ Sugar snap peas, chopped and added to the vegetable mixture ✳ Snow peas, trimmed and cut lengthwise into thin strips, piled on top ✳ Snipped fresh tarragon on top ✳ Minced fresh mint ✳ Extra cheese on top ✳ Lemon wedges ✳ Lemon zest in long strands ✳ For a lovely spring meal, serve this with Olive Oil–Buttermilk Sherbet and Strawberries on Green Salad (page 80)

Winter Risotto with Escarole, Leeks, and Dried Figs

MAKES 6 TO 8 SERVINGS

A large-scale batch of an unusual vegetable-fruit combination surrounds this risotto—and it's enough to serve a crowd. You won't need much else, since it's kind of a main dish, side, and salad all rolled into one.

The chicory category includes sturdy, pleasantly bitter leafy greens (and purples and reds)—radicchio, frisée, endive, and escarole—used most commonly in salads. They go in a sterner direction on the stove, needing to be lightened up by touches of sweet and sour. In this case, those touches show up in the form of dried figs macerated in balsamic vinegar with a good amount of lemon zest. This recipe makes a generous amount of vegetables. The idea is to heap them around and on top of the dense risotto, providing a contrasting lightness.

❋ If fresh figs are in season, you can slice some as a garnish. But dried ones work better for the rest of the dish.

❋ You can begin soaking the figs up to a day ahead. Cover them and leave them at room temperature.

❋ Usually when I use lemon zest, I like to grate it fine on a rasp, for subtle effect. But once in a while, as with this recipe, I want the lemon zest to be more of a presence. The easiest way to do this (and to get a full tablespoon of it) is to remove the zest (yellow part only) from a medium organic lemon with a sturdy vegetable peeler and chop it fine with a very sharp knife.

❋ The best way to clean leeks is to slice them first (rinsing off any dramatically visible dirt as you go) and then place the slices in a large bowl of cold water. Swish the leeks around, then lift them out into a waiting colander. Change the water and repeat once or twice, or until the water remains clean after swishing. Drain and dry the leeks.

❋ If you are in the mood to gild this lily, make some Crispy Fried Lemons (page 389) ahead of time and serve them alongside or as a crowning touch.

THE VEGETABLES

12 dried Calimyrna figs, stemmed and sliced into rounds or slim wedges (see notes)

1 tablespoon chopped lemon zest (see note)

1 tablespoon balsamic vinegar

1 tablespoon olive oil

1 pound leeks (about 3 medium), cut into thin rings, cleaned, and dried (3 cups)

1 pound escarole, trimmed, washed, dried, and chopped (about 9 cups)

½ pound radicchio, coarsely chopped (4–5 cups)

About ½ teaspoon salt

Black pepper

1. Place the figs in a small, shallow bowl or a plate with a rim and sprinkle with the lemon zest and vinegar. Stir to mingle, then let it sit while you prepare the rest of the dish, stirring a little from time to time. (*The figs can macerate up to a day ahead.*)

2. Place a large (10- or 12-inch) skillet over medium heat for about a minute, then add the oil and swirl to coat the pan. Toss in the leeks and cook, stirring often, for 5 minutes, or until they become shiny and soft.

3. Add about a third of the escarole and half the radicchio, sprinkling it with ¼ teaspoon salt. The pan will be crowded, but the vegetables will cook down quickly. To help this along,

[continues]

use tongs to lift the cooked vegetables from the bottom, allowing the raw vegetables on top to rotate down to the heat. Keep things moving to make room for more. You can also cover the pan in between stirrings to give the vegetables some steam.

4. Add the rest of the escarole and radicchio in batches, sprinkling with the remaining ¼ teaspoon salt, continuing to turn with tongs as everything cooks. When the vegetables are wilted to your liking, stir in half the figs, add black pepper to taste, and turn off the heat while you make the risotto.

THE RISOTTO

1 quart vegetable stock (page 22) or low-sodium store-bought

1 tablespoon olive oil and/or unsalted butter

1 heaping cup minced onion

1½ cups risotto rice (see page 202)

½ teaspoon salt, or more to taste

½ cup dry white wine, at room temperature

½ cup grated Parmesan

Black pepper

1. Bring the stock to a boil in a covered saucepan over medium-low heat, then reduce the heat to low. Have a ladle ready, resting on a plate. Keep the simmering stock covered between applications.

2. Heat the olive oil or melt the butter in a heavy-bottomed medium saucepan over medium heat for about a minute, then swirl to coat the pan. Toss in the onion and cook, stirring, for about 5 minutes, or until it begins to soften.

3. Add the rice and stir over medium heat for about a minute to coat it with everything else in the pan. Add the salt and wine and stir until the wine is absorbed, about 30 seconds.

4. Ladle in enough hot stock to cover, stirring until most of the liquid is absorbed. Repeat this process until the mixture is creamy and a bit loose; the rice should still have some chew to it, but should not taste at all raw. (If you run out of stock and the risotto seems to need a little more cooking, you can add some water at this point, ½ cup at a time.) Remove from the heat while the grains still show some resistance. Don't overcook.

5. Reheat the vegetables if necessary. Add the Parmesan and about half of the vegetable-fig mixture to the risotto, stirring and folding them in gently. Taste to possibly add more salt and season to taste with black pepper. Serve right away, on rimmed plates, surrounded by and/or topped with the rest of the vegetables and the remaining figs.

OPTIONAL ENHANCEMENTS

Crispy Fried Lemons (page 389) ❋ Extra Parmesan

INSTANT FLAVOR TRICKS FOR GRAINS

Cooked grains are the perfect tabula rasa—a neutral and willing springboard for improvisation. Clutter them up or keep them plain. Follow a recipe or follow your instincts. Let whole grains occupy the center of your plate or spread (or sprinkle) them as a bed, side, or topping.

Here are some suggestions for making cooked grains special without too much extra labor. After you try a few of these touches, have fun experimenting with some of your own ideas.

- Save leftover cooked vegetables—any amount. Chop them small if the pieces are large and combine with rice, spelt, or farro (freshly cooked or left over), and reheat, if necessary. A microwave works just fine for this.
- Drizzle any freshly cooked grain with a modest amount of any roasted nut oil and adorn the top with matching nuts, chopped and lightly toasted.

- Sauté some finely minced shallot in olive oil or butter over low heat until soft. Lightly salt and add it to freshly cooked barley, buckwheat, or any kind of rice.
- Chopped dried fruit and a touch of grated lemon, orange, or lime zest are great additions to wild rice, quinoa, couscous, bulgur, or wheat berries. Toss in some finely minced scallions or chives.
- Sprinkle any cooked grain, large or small, onto a green salad just before tossing. Some of the grains will cling to the dressed leaves; others will migrate to the bottom of the bowl, where their brief encounter with the dressing will coat them beautifully.
- Top grains with dabs of (m)any of the sauces on pages 356 to 386.
- Use cooked grains as a bed for fried or poached eggs.

Forbidden Rice with Beluga Lentils and Mushrooms

MAKES 5 OR 6 SERVINGS ❧ VEGAN

Once upon a time in China, precious black rice was permitted only to emperors. (At least, that's how the legend goes.)

Flash forward a few centuries, and that once-illicit delicacy is now available in natural food stores and gourmet shops and online—designated (and trademarked as) "Forbidden Rice" by a company based in El Cerrito, California. The evocative name matches the subtle, dark grapey grain, but lucky for us, that moniker is now purely symbolic.

In this "fade into black" dish, tiny black lentils and minced mushrooms disappear into the shadows of the mysterious, nightlike grain. Depending on the ambient light and the angle, there may also be undertones of purple, dreamily nocturnal. The subtle, deep flavor of the finished dish echoes the soothing, dark theme, like a reverie of umami.

❀ Black rice is available in bulk in many natural food stores and also packaged (look for Lotus Foods Forbidden Rice) in gourmet shops and online.

❀ Beluga lentils are found in similar shops (and sometimes Trader Joe's) or online. If you can't find them, French green lentils (*lentilles du Puy*) can be swapped in.

❀ The large pan might seem oversized at first, when you are cooking just the shallots or onion and the mushrooms, but you will need the space to accommodate the cooked rice and lentils.

❀ This will keep for 4 to 5 days in a tightly covered container in the refrigerator. It reheats well, covered, in a 250°F oven or toaster oven or in a microwave.

1 cup black (Forbidden) rice

1 cup beluga (small black) lentils

Scant 3 cups water

½ teaspoon salt, or more to taste

1 tablespoon grapeseed, canola, or peanut oil

½ cup finely minced shallots or red onion

½ pound domestic or cremini mushrooms, wiped clean, stemmed if necessary, and finely minced (can use a food processor)

½ teaspoon minced or crushed garlic

1 tablespoon fresh lemon juice

Black pepper

Lemon wedges or extra fresh lemon juice for sprinkling on top (optional)

White truffle oil (optional)

1. Combine the rice, lentils, water, and ¼ teaspoon salt in a medium saucepan. Bring to a boil, lower the heat to a simmer, cover, and cook undisturbed (with a heat diffuser, if you have one, underneath) for 40 minutes. If the rice is not tender enough at this point, splash in up to ¼ cup additional water and cook it a little further. (The lentils will remain somewhat al dente.) When it's done to your liking, turn off the heat and fluff with a fork to let the steam escape.

2. Meanwhile, place a large (10- to 12-inch) skillet over medium heat for about a minute, then add the oil and swirl to coat the pan. Toss in the shallots or onion and cook, stirring, for 5 minutes. Stir in the mushrooms and garlic

[continues]

and the remaining ¼ teaspoon salt, and cook for 5 minutes, stirring often. Splash in the lemon juice and continue to cook for just 1 to 2 minutes longer, or until the liquid evaporates and the mushrooms are nicely dried out and beginning to brown and stick slightly to the pan. Mix from the bottom of the pan, scraping up and including whatever might have stuck (always the most flavorful part) and turn off the heat.

3. Transfer the cooked rice and lentils to the mushroom mixture, stirring and fluffing with a fork as you go. Adjust the salt, if necessary, and add black pepper to taste.

4. Serve hot or warm, with lemon wedges tucked in or lemon juice sprinkled on top, if desired. You also might want to pass around some white truffle oil to drip delicately on top.

BLACK RICE AND WHITE BEANS

Make this beautiful by arranging it around Curried Mashed Carrots and Cashews (page 170), topping with white beans (see page 183) and framing with Grilled Mushroom Slices (page 349) and halved cherry or grape tomatoes. It's a very unusual combination that is homey, yet surprising. The carrots, rice, and beans can all be made ahead and reheated. The mushrooms can be cooked quickly as the other items are heating. A green salad of your own design will make this into a complete meal.

A QUICK LITTLE WEEKDAY MEAL: BROWN RICE "SOUFFLÉ"

Add a beaten egg or two to freshly cooked long- or short-grain brown rice while it's still in the pot. Beat vigorously with a fork as you mix in the egg. Cover the pot, remove it from the heat, and let it sit for 5 minutes. Add salt and pepper and maybe some finely minced scallions. That's all!

Couscous with Dates, Pistachios, Pine Nuts, and Parsley

MAKES 4 OR 5 SERVINGS ❋ VEGAN

Couscous flirts with dates, pine nuts, and pistachios, yet still revels in the traditional olive oil, lemon, scallions, and parsley. This dish straddles that ambiguous border where savory and sweet touch shoulders.

Quick-cooking whole-wheat couscous is hardly authentic to Moroccan cuisine, but it is a godsend to busy modern cooks. And the accents in this dish are Mediterranean enough for any purist, especially when you build out the plate with the easy extras listed after the recipe. (Yogurt, especially, rounds this out and qualifies it as a bona fide light main dish.) Try this with Lablabi (page 30), and a new favorite dinner awaits you.

❋ If pine nuts exceed your budget, you can make this with just pistachios—or finely chopped walnuts.

❋ If you're making this more than 2 hours ahead of time and/or your kitchen is hot, cover the dish tightly and refrigerate it until about an hour before you plan to serve it. It will then need to come to room temperature (at least) to be at its best. Heat it further, if desired, covered, in a 250°F oven or toaster oven, or in a microwave.

2 cups whole-wheat couscous

2 cups boiling water

2 tablespoons extra-virgin olive oil, plus more for finishing

Up to 2 tablespoons fresh lemon juice

¼ teaspoon salt, or more to taste

1 cup dried dates, pitted and chopped

2–3 scallions, finely minced

A handful of fresh flat-leaf parsley, finely minced (thicker stems discarded; about ¼ cup)

¾ cup pine nuts, lightly toasted

¾ cup pistachios, lightly toasted

1. Place the couscous in a medium-large bowl and pour in the boiling water. Cover the bowl with a plate and let it stand for 15 to 20 minutes, or until the water is completely absorbed. Fluff with a fork to separate the grains.

2. Stir in the olive oil, 1 tablespoon of the lemon juice, ¼ teaspoon salt, and the dates, mixing with a fork to thoroughly combine. (*The dish can be finished and served at this point, or you can replace the plate and let it stand for up to an hour or two, until shortly before serving time.*)

3. Stir in the scallions, parsley, and nuts shortly before serving, then taste to adjust the salt and lemon juice. Serve hot, warm, or at room temperature, finished with a drizzle of olive oil.

OPTIONAL ENHANCEMENTS

Lemon wedges ❋ Chopped, pitted olives ❋ A dollop of yogurt, seasoned with salt and pepper, underneath or on top ❋ A few wedges of perfect fresh figs on top or tucked into the side ❋ Minced fresh chives and/or mint ❋ Minced sweet cucumber, celery, or sweet bell peppers ❋ Crushed red pepper ❋ Serve surrounded with an assortment of roasted vegetables (see page 336) ❋ This is also delicious heaped on top of Mashed Celery Root (page 174), Smoky Mashed Caramelized Eggplant and Onions (page 175), or Golden Lentils with Soft, Sweet Onions (page 182)

Cauliflower Couscous

MAKES 4 TO 6 SERVINGS ❧ VEGAN

Cauliflower is so convincing when pulverized into its couscous impersonation that you can hardly see it when the two are combined—even when the vegetable out-volumes the grain, as it does here.

Sometimes, especially in summer, it's possible to find cauliflower in various shades of green, "cheddar," and purple. I tried this recipe with a purple one, and the whole dish turned a beguiling shade of lavender. When I sprinkled on the lemon juice at the end, little spots of gorgeous bright pink immediately appeared wherever the citrus drops had landed.

❀ Spraying the food processor with nonstick cooking spray will make any wayward cauliflower crumbs obey you.

❀ Skillet size always makes a difference, and this recipe is a good example. Wider than 10 inches is better, since the more you can spread out the cauliflower, the more efficiently it can cook. Your chosen pan should have a lid.

❀ This will keep for 4 to 5 days in a tightly covered container in the refrigerator. It reheats well, covered, in a 250°F oven or toaster oven or in a microwave.

Nonstick cooking spray

1 small head cauliflower (about 1½ pounds), trimmed

1 tablespoon olive oil

1 heaping cup finely minced onion

Up to 1 teaspoon minced or crushed garlic

¾ teaspoon salt, or more to taste

1 cup whole-wheat couscous

½ cup water

Black pepper

Juice from 1 medium lemon or lemon wedges

1. Spray the interior of a food processor, including the steel blade attachment and the lid, with nonstick spray.

2. Cut the cauliflower into 2- to 3-inch chunks and place them in the processor. Buzz for just a few seconds, or until the cauliflower is in couscous-sized crumbs. You should have about 4 cups.

3. Place a large (10- to 12-inch) skillet over medium heat for about a minute, then add the oil and swirl to coat the pan. Toss in the onion and cook over medium-low heat, stirring often, for 5 minutes. Add the garlic and ¼ teaspoon salt, and cook, stirring, for another 5 minutes.

4. Scrape in all the cauliflower using a rubber spatula and add the remaining ½ teaspoon salt. Turn up the heat to medium and cook, stirring often with a fork, for 8 to 10 minutes. (It's OK if the cauliflower browns and sticks a little, but be sure to scrape the bottom of the pan often.)

5. Add the couscous and stir it in with the fork so that everything is evenly distributed. Cook, stirring, for 1 to 2 minutes. Add the water, cover the pan, and turn off the heat. Let it sit for about 5 minutes, then fork through to fluff, scraping in whatever bits may have stuck to the sides and bottom of the pan and doing your best to avoid leaving any of it behind. Taste to see if it needs more salt, and season with black pepper.

6. Serve hot or warm, topped with a sprinkling of lemon juice, or with lemon wedges on the side.

OPTIONAL ENHANCEMENTS

Finely minced scallions or chives, mixed in or on top ❋ Good-quality extra-virgin olive oil or toasted nut oil (or even a touch of butter) for finishing ❋ Pistachios, pine nuts, sunflower seeds, or cashews ❋ Finely minced fresh parsley ❋ Cheese (any) crumbled in (feta) or broiled on top ❋ Sweet cherry tomatoes (halved, if not tiny) on top ❋ Dab of Tahini-Ginger-Pomegranate Sauce (page 360) or Almond Faux Aioli (page 356) ❋ Serve as a bed or frame for Crispy-Coated Eggplant Parmesan "Burgers" (page 308) ❋ Stuff into a large, partially hollowed-out tomato and heat gently, and also consider broiling some cheese on top

Quinoa-Couscous Pilaf with Carrot, Roasted Almond Oil, and Pickled Red Onions

MAKES 4 OR 5 SERVINGS ❧ VEGAN

My original vision for this recipe was more complicated, but things took an unexpected turn toward the simple when, midway through, I took a taste and realized the dish was complete. Now the crowd of possible ingredients is consigned to the Optional Enhancements lists. You can expand this into a grain-themed salad bar for a dinner party by laying out the full array, so that your guests get a visual preview of the flavor layers they're about to enjoy.

The colors will enchant: pale yellow strewn with bright orange, crosshatched with an unnameable electric blueish pink from the onions.

❀ The key ingredient is roasted almond oil. It makes this dish, and I recommend you buy an entire bottle for just it. Keep it refrigerated, and you will find yourself

a) making this repeatedly

b) using roasted almond oil in salad dressings, to finish vegetables, finishing, brushed onto toast (see page 409), and for many other things.

❀ You can make this with all quinoa, if you prefer a gluten-free option. Use 2 cups rinsed quinoa cooked in 2 cups water for the same amount of time.

❀ The Pickled Red Onions (page 395) are nicely crunchy and turn each mouthful into a lively bite. Begin pickling the onions at least an hour (or as much as a week) ahead of time.

❀ This will keep for several days in a tightly covered container in the refrigerator. It reheats well, covered, in a 250°F oven or toaster oven or in a microwave.

1 cup quinoa, rinsed

1 cup water, plus 1 cup boiling water

1 cup whole-wheat couscous

½ teaspoon salt

1 fat, sweet carrot, peeled and minced, cut into small dice, or coarsely grated

2 tablespoons roasted almond oil

Black pepper

Pickled Red Onions (page 395)

1. Combine the quinoa and 1 cup water in a small saucepan. Bring to a boil, lower the heat to a very slow simmer, and cook undisturbed (with a heat diffuser, if you have one, inserted underneath) for 20 minutes, or until all the water is absorbed. Fluff with a fork to let the steam escape and set aside. (The grains will be on the dry side.)

2. Meanwhile, place the couscous in a medium-large bowl and pour in the 1 cup boiling water. Cover with a plate and let it stand for 15 to 20 minutes, or until the water is completely absorbed. Fluff with a fork to separate the grains.

3. Transfer the quinoa into the couscous, fork-fluffing as you go to keep the grains distinct, and continue to fluff as you mix in the salt, carrot, and almond oil.

4. Add black pepper to taste and lay the Pickled Red Onions on top. Bring it to the table this way and then stir in the onions just before serving for a dramatic effect. Enjoy hot, warm, or at room temperature.

OPTIONAL ENHANCEMENTS

Dot with cooked chickpeas and/or Fried Lentils (page 404) or frame with Crunchy Chickpea Crumble (page 403) ✹ Top with an Herb Tangle of parsley, baby arugula, mint, and/or cilantro (page 76) or a scattering of minced radicchio, radish, and/or shaved fennel ✹ Drizzle on some good-quality extra-virgin olive oil and/or additional roasted almond oil ✹ Garnish with peeled, sliced or diced Fuyu persimmon, or unpeeled chopped apple ✹ Crumble on some fresh cheese (feta, Mexican queso fresco, manouri, ricotta salata) ✹ Decorate the top with a few roasted whole almonds or chopped toasted almonds ✹ Serve this alongside a steaming bowlful of Lablabi (page 30) ✹ Serve Orange-Olive-Fig Saladita (page 385) alongside

Bulgur and Spaghetti

MAKES 4 TO 6 SERVINGS ❋ VEGAN

My food writer friends like to joke about how "nutty" is the default adjective when you run out of words for "delicious." I could possibly think of other ways to describe this recipe, but it actually *is* nutty-tasting, so I'll rest my case right there regarding the flavor. Texture is another story. Fluffy, slightly chewy bulgur surrounds pieces of broken spaghetti, a call-and-response of whole-grain heartiness and unabashed simple-carbohydrate comfort.

The fun begins earlier, when you brown the raw spaghetti in a generous amount of onions, imparting the flavor royally. The bulgur also benefits from a ride through the oil before settling down with the water or stock.

❋ Use a large skillet with a tight-fitting lid.

❋ Leftovers keep for 5 days or longer in a tightly covered container in the refrigerator. The dish reheats beautifully and serves as a perfect side or surround for cooked vegetables, beans, eggs . . . anything. It's also a contrasting warm bed for a heap of freshly tossed, cold green salad.

Up to 2 tablespoons olive oil

4 cups minced onions (2 large)

½ teaspoon salt, or more to taste

1½ cups broken (1½-inch pieces) spaghetti or vermicelli

1½ cups bulgur

2½ cups water or vegetable stock (page 22) or low-sodium store-bought

Black pepper

1. Place a large (10- to 12-inch) skillet over medium heat for about a minute, then add 1 tablespoon of the oil and swirl to coat the pan. Toss in the onions and ¼ teaspoon salt and cook over medium heat, stirring, for about 5 minutes, or until the onion softens.

2. Add the spaghetti or vermicelli to the onions and sauté for about 10 minutes, or until coated and lightly browned. (You might need to drizzle in small amounts of additional oil if it begins to stick.)

3. Stir the bulgur into the pasta, along with the remaining ¼ teaspoon salt, and let it brown a little for 5 minutes or so before pouring in the water or stock. Bring to a boil, cover the pan, and lower the heat to the slowest possible simmer, with a heat diffuser, if you have one, underneath. Open the lid after 15 minutes and fluff from the bottom of the pan with a fork.

4. Cover the pan again and cook for about 10 more minutes. Leaving the cover on, remove the pan from the heat and let sit for another 10 minutes.

5. Fluff with a fork and taste to see if it needs more salt. Add black pepper to taste. Transfer to a bowl and serve right away.

OPTIONAL ENHANCEMENTS

Scatter on some chopped fresh flat-leaf parsley ❋ Drizzle with additional olive oil ❋ Spoon Crunchy Chickpea Crumble (page 403) around the edges ❋ Top with a big dab of Caramelized Onion and Lemon Marmalade (page 375) or Romesco Sauce or Muhammara (page 359) ❋ Crown with Crisp,

Ethereal Onion Rings (page 387) and/or Crispy Fried Lemons (page 389) ✽ Fork on some Pickled Red Onions (page 395) ✽ Sprinkle with Fried Lentils (page 404) and/or serve with Very Simple Lentil Stew (page 146) ✽ Top with a Miniature Tossed Salad (page 76) ✽ Crumble in (or on) some feta ✽ Decorate with very sweet cherry tomatoes (halved or quartered, if large) or Slow-Roasted Roma Tomatoes (page 393) ✽ Sprinkle with chopped, toasted walnuts ✽ Serve this double-decker over, under, or side by side with Mixed Mushroom Ragout (page 348) or Smoky Mashed Caramelized Eggplant and Onions (page 175) ✽ Build it out by adding any or all of these after step 1, cooking them for about 5 minutes before you add the pasta: sliced mushrooms, chopped spinach, torn kale leaves, minced or crushed garlic (add small amounts of additional oil and salt, to taste, as needed)

MAKING FRIENDS WITH LESS FAMILIAR GRAINS

Getting to know farro, wheat berries, spelt, quinoa, millet, buckwheat, bulgur, couscous, and barley will expand your grain vocabulary, affording a greater range of texture and flavor for you to enjoy. You can find these grains near the rice in the bulk bins of natural food stores and good grocery stores, and I hope you will buy a few at a time and take them into your kitchen to try them. All they need is contact with boiling water, and they will be ready for use in any number of ways.

The larger grains (farro, wheat berries, spelt) remain spunky regardless of how long they're simmered. I use them interchangeably, depending on availability, as they have similar properties: earthiness and a nutty kind of neutrality that blends readily with other flavors—sweet, tart, or bright. (Rye berries are similar in texture, but more bitter in flavor, so I use them more as an accent than as the body of a dish.) To expedite cooking these larger grains, some cooks soak them first and/or use pressure cookers. My own preferred method is to simply simmer them, without presoaking, in boiling water until al dente, pasta-style. Then I drain and mix them with other ingredients (vegetables, seasonings, beans).

Barley is a great grain, and even when refined into the "pearl" version, it remains a good source of fiber. I buy the darkest colored pearl barley I can find. You can also use the rougher hulled kind, but keep in mind it takes a bit longer (up to 90 minutes) to cook.

Smaller grains provide more diverse results, and can be cooked to a much softer state (if you like) than the larger ones. Quinoa is soft and very slightly (and pleasantly) bitter; millet is drier and lends a sunny demeanor with an earthy flavor. Buckwheat has a distinct taste that people either love or hate, and it mixes beautifully with anything related to onion. Bulgur and couscous (which is technically a pasta but treated in most cases as a grain) are precooked wheat iterations that simply need to soak in hot water to come fully to life. Once cooked or soaked, these grains lend themselves to many combinations, including medleys with one another.

All of the above grains are easy to prepare and require very little attention beyond remembering to check in to see when they're done.

Spring Farro

MAKES 6 TO 8 SERVINGS ❋ VEGAN (WHEN MADE WITHOUT THE FETA)

Simmer some farro, add green peas, and then toss it with olive oil, garlic, and sliced leek. Touches of feta, salt, lemon, and pepper round everything out. This lovely, light dish then heads straight to the table without additional primping. No fuss, no fanfare, just good food. It's a wonderful choice for a potluck, as it travels well and is good at any temperature.

Thread-slender leek slices are a revelation in this dish. We so rarely think of adding them straight to a dish without first cooking them into buttery softness. Yet they are a completely different vegetable when treated in this manner, poised for newfound appreciation. Make sure, as always (but especially now), that your excellent knife is gleamingly sharp, and you will hear a gratifying whisper-like sound effect when it slices through the leek.

❋ Prepare the leek and other ingredients while the farro is cooking, so everything is ready and waiting when it is done. If you use spelt or wheat berries, the simmering will take longer.

❋ This will keep for 3 to 4 days in a tightly covered container in the refrigerator. It reheats well, covered, in a 250°F oven or toaster oven or in a microwave.

1 slender, fresh leek (about ¾ inch diameter)

½ teaspoon minced or crushed garlic, or more to taste

3 tablespoons extra-virgin olive oil, or more to taste

1½ cups farro, spelt, or wheat berries

1 cup green peas (freshly shelled or frozen)

½ teaspoon salt, or more to taste

Up to 1 cup diced or minced feta (optional)

Lemon juice (optional)

Black pepper

1. Fill a medium-large saucepan with water and bring it to a boil.

2. Meanwhile, trim the leek and cut it into super-thin rings. Transfer the leek rings to a bowlful of cold water, swishing around to clean. Lift out the leek rings and drain them in a colander in the sink, then shake and/or pat them dry. (You might want to do this process twice, with a change of water in between, if the leek needs extra cleaning.) Transfer to a medium-large bowl and return the colander to the sink. Add the garlic and 2 tablespoons of the olive oil to the leek rings and stir to blend.

3. When the water boils, add the farro, spelt, or wheat berries and cook, uncovered, at a gentle boil over medium heat for 20 to 25 minutes for farro (70 to 75 minutes for spelt, and anywhere from 50 to 75 minutes for wheat berries), or until chewy-tender. If using fresh peas, add them to the water during the last couple of minutes or so. If using frozen peas, place them, still frozen, in the colander.

4. When the grains are done to your liking (they will retain some chewiness), drain everything into the colander. Shake emphatically to dry, then immediately transfer the entire contents of the colander to the bowl with the leek rings.

5. Stir from the bottom of the bowl to bring up the leek, garlic, and olive oil, sprinkling in the ½ teaspoon salt, plus the remaining 1 tablespoon olive oil as you go. Gently mix until everything is thoroughly combined, to avoid breaking the peas.

6. Stir in the feta, if using, then taste to adjust the salt and add some lemon juice and black pepper. You might also want to add more olive oil or simply to pass some around for drizzling at the table. Serve warm, at room temperature, or cold (as a grain salad).

OPTIONAL ENHANCEMENTS

1 to 2 cups fresh fava beans (see page 256) added with the fresh peas ✳ Lemon wedges ✳ Thin strips of fresh mint on top or minced fresh mint mixed in ✳ A scattering of lightly toasted pine nuts ✳ Crumbled goat cheese in place of feta

VARIATION: SPRING COUSCOUS

You can make this with couscous instead of farro.

To do so, place 1½ cups whole-wheat couscous in a medium-large bowl and pour in 1½ cups boiling water. Cover the bowl with a plate and let it stand for 15 to 20 minutes, or until the water is completely absorbed. Fluff with a fork to separate the grains. If using fresh peas, cook them; if using frozen, defrost. Then proceed with the recipe, beginning with step 2. Serve the finished dish with an extra drizzle of olive oil over the top to keep it moist.

Farro and Tuscan White Beans

MAKES 6 TO 8 SERVINGS ❧ VEGAN

Joyful, large-scale texture abounds in this generously chewy main-dish combo, making it a very satisfying meal-in-a-bowl.

❋ Farro lives in the same grain neighborhood as wheat berries and spelt and can be used interchangeably. Wheat berries and spelt will take longer to cook, so plan accordingly.

❋ For maximum flavor, begin with dried beans, which you need to soak ahead of time, and then simmer in garlic-and-herb-infused water. You can use canned, but this will not really save time, as you'll be waiting for the farro to cook anyway. For dried beans, soak 1 cup in plenty of water well ahead (4 hours, minimum; overnight is fine). If you cook the beans ahead of time, any reserved bean-cooking water can be used as part of the grain-cooking water. Additional flavor layers will ensue.

❋ Use a combination of various-colored cherry tomatoes, if available. Not only will they be beautiful, they will provide a juicy pop-in-the-mouth contrast to the more staid grain-bean backdrop.

❋ The large skillet might seem oversized at first when you are cooking just the onion, but you will need the space to accommodate the cooked farro.

❋ This will keep for 4 to 5 days in a tightly covered container in the refrigerator. It reheats well, covered, in a 250°F oven or toaster oven or in a microwave.

1 cup soaked dried cannellini (white kidney) beans or two 15-ounce cans cannellini beans

4 large garlic cloves, halved (peeling optional)

1 bay leaf

2–3 fresh sage leaves

1½ cups farro, spelt, or wheat berries

2 tablespoons olive oil

2 cups minced onion (1 large)

½ teaspoon *each* dried rubbed sage, thyme, oregano, crushed red pepper

¾ teaspoon salt, or more to taste

2 teaspoons minced or crushed garlic

1½ tablespoons white wine vinegar

Black pepper

Crushed red pepper (optional)

2 cups sweet cherry tomatoes or diced ripe heirloom tomatoes (about ¾ pound) or Slow-Roasted Roma Tomatoes (page 393)

1. Drain the soaked beans (if using canned, just rinse and thoroughly drain, then reserve) and transfer them to a pot with enough fresh water to cover by 2 inches, adding the garlic halves, bay leaf, and sage leaves. Bring to a boil, lower the heat to a simmer, partially cover, and cook gently (so as not to break the beans) until tender—about 50 minutes. Drain (save the water for soup, if you like), fishing out and discarding the leaves and the spent garlic cloves.

2. Meanwhile, fill a medium-large saucepan with water and bring it to a boil. When the water boils, add the farro, spelt, or wheat berries and

cook, uncovered, at a gentle boil over medium heat for 20 to 25 minutes for farro (70 to 75 minutes for spelt and anywhere from 50 to 75 minutes for wheat berries), or until chewy-tender. Drain in a colander and shake dry.

3. Place a large (10- to 12-inch) skillet over medium heat for about a minute, then add the oil and swirl to coat the pan. Toss in the onion and cook for about 2 minutes. Add the dried herbs and ¼ teaspoon salt and continue to cook for another 5 minutes. Stir in the minced or crushed garlic and turn the heat to medium-low. Cover the skillet and cook for about 15 minutes, stirring often, until the onion is very soft.

4. Turn the heat to low and mix the farro in with a fork, adding the remaining ½ teaspoon salt. When all the farro is incorporated, add the drained beans, very gently mixing them in until combined. Splash in the vinegar and taste for salt, then season with black pepper and more crushed red pepper, if desired. Delicately stir in the tomatoes or just lay them on top and serve hot, warm, cold, or at room temperature.

OPTIONAL ENHANCEMENTS

Top with Crispy Sage Leaves (page 394) ❈ Pile on a tangle of baby arugula ❈ A drizzle of high-quality extra-virgin olive oil ❈ Lightly toasted walnuts ❈ Crumble on some white cheese (ricotta salata or feta)

Broccoli Millet

MAKES 4 TO 6 SERVINGS

In this modestly glorious twofer, tiny pieces of green are flecked into even tinier, sunny dots of whole grain. It's quick and straightforward—especially if you use a food processor to mince the broccoli.

❋ Look for a crown-heavy bunch of broccoli, as you will be using the florets, not the stems. Save whatever stems happen to be there and grate them into a slaw (see page 66) or peel and slice them and add to Pickled Red Onions (page 395).

❋ Prepare the other ingredients while the millet cooks.

❋ Butter is a great millet partner, balancing its flavor perfectly.

❋ This dish will keep for 4 to 5 days in a tightly covered container in the refrigerator. It reheats well, covered, in a 250°F oven or toaster oven or in a microwave.

1 cup millet

Up to 1¾ cups water

Nonstick cooking spray

1 pound broccoli

1–2 tablespoons butter or a combination of butter and grapeseed oil

1 cup very finely minced shallots and/or red onion

½ teaspoon salt, or more to taste

1. Rinse the millet a couple of times in a fine-mesh strainer, then transfer it to a medium-large saucepan with a tight-fitting lid. Add 1½ cups water and bring to a boil, then lower the heat to a simmer, cover, and cook undisturbed, with a heat diffuser, if you have one, underneath, until tender, about 30 minutes. (If it's not quite tender enough at this point—or if it appears to be sticking—splash in up to ¼ cup additional water and cook it a little further.) When it is done to your liking, remove it from the heat and fluff it with a fork to separate the grains and let the steam escape. Set aside.

2. Meanwhile, spray the interior of a food processor, including the steel blade attachment and the lid, with nonstick spray. Remove the stems from the broccoli (saving them for another use), then cut the florets into large chunks and buzz them in the processor for just a few seconds, or until the broccoli is rendered into millet-sized crumbs. You should have about 3 cups.

3. Melt the butter and heat the oil, if using, in a 10-inch skillet over low heat. When it froths, add the shallots or onion and ¼ teaspoon of the salt and cook, stirring often, until very soft, about 10 minutes.

4. Stir in the broccoli and the remaining ¼ teaspoon salt, and cook, stirring, over medium heat for 5 to 8 minutes, or until the broccoli is bright green and tender.

5. Gently stir the millet into the broccoli with a fork, combining thoroughly. Remove from the heat and taste to adjust the salt. Serve hot or warm.

OPTIONAL ENHANCEMENTS

Lemon or lime wedges ✳ Sliced oranges on top or as a frame ✳ A little cheese broiled on top ✳ Nuts and seeds ✳ Make this a main dish by stuffing it into 4 to 6 portobello mushroom caps (see page 350) ✳ Serve as a bed for fried or poached eggs for a nice little supper

Simple Buckwheat Pilaf

MAKES 4 TO 6 SERVINGS ❊ VEGAN (WHEN MADE WITHOUT THE BUTTER)

Triangular seeds of buckwheat cook up quickly into a tender, highly fragrant pilaf. Given its many attributes (convenience, affordability, wonderful vegetable-compatible flavor, zero gluten), this superfood deserves more renown and wider appreciation. Let's get that going here and now.

These tasty groats add a flavorful, nutritious layer when sprinkled on salads, soups, or just about any cooked vegetable. You can pull them out and spontaneously toss them onto your favorite savory food, rendering simple things complex with just a flick of the wrist. When something can be described as both earthy and exotic, you know you're in the goodness zone.

❊ "Kasha" simply refers to buckwheat that has been dry-roasted. Kasha and plain buckwheat groats can be used interchangeably.

❊ Your chosen pan should have a lid.

❊ This dish will keep for up to 5 days in a tightly covered container in the refrigerator. It reheats well—covered, in a 250°F oven or toaster oven or in a microwave.

1 tablespoon olive oil

1 teaspoon unsalted butter (optional)

1 heaping cup minced onion

½ teaspoon salt

1½ cups buckwheat groats

1½ cups boiling water or hot vegetable stock (page 22) or low-sodium store-bought

Black pepper

1. Place a large (10- to 12-inch) skillet over medium heat for about a minute, then add the oil and swirl to coat the pan. You can also melt in the butter, if you like. Toss in the onion and ¼ teaspoon of the salt and cook over medium-low heat, stirring often, for 8 to 10 minutes, or until the onion is very soft and verging on brown.

2. Add the buckwheat and the remaining ¼ teaspoon salt. Sauté for about 5 minutes to toast the groats. When you can smell the results, pour in the water or stock.

3. Cover the pan and let it simmer over lowest possible heat (with a heat diffuser, if you have one, underneath) for up to 20 minutes, or until all the liquid is absorbed. (Check after 10 minutes, as the absorption time can vary.)

4. When the water is absorbed and the buckwheat is puffy, fluff it with a fork, sprinkle with a little pepper, and it's ready to serve.

OPTIONAL ENHANCEMENTS

Serve with Mixed Mushroom Ragout (page 348) ❊ Top with Grilled Mushroom Slices or Mushroom "Bacon" (see page 349) ❊ Veg it up by adding up to 2 cups chopped cabbage, cauliflower, carrots, spinach, broccoli, or shredded Brussels sprouts to the onion halfway through its cooking in step 1 ❊ Sprinkle with minced scallions or fresh dill ❊ Adorn with Pickled Red Onions (page 395) ❊ Top with Egg "Noodles" (page 398) or chopped hard-cooked egg ❊ Scatter with toasted sunflower seeds ❊ Dab on some yogurt, crème fraîche, or sour cream, possibly with a little horseradish mixed in

VARIATION: KASHA VARNISHKES

An Ashkenazic Jewish classic returns. Actually, it never left. But now it's trendy, which theoretically would have gratified my Grandma Minnie. The dish she loved, kasha varnishkes, is simply a buckwheat pilaf combined with farfalle (bow-tie pasta).

Prepare Simple Buckwheat Pilaf, and at the same time put on a pot of water to boil. When it does, add 2 cups (about 8 ounces) small farfalle and cook according to the package directions, or until done to your liking. Drain, toss with a little salt and olive oil, and stir this into the pilaf at the end of step 4.

PASTA and
ASIAN NOODLES

*** *** ***

A plateful of simply rendered spaghetti (or any of its cousins) can be the easiest, most dependable weeknight dinner solution, especially when you are crunched for time and challenged for ideas (and hungry). Assuming you already have some well-loved routines for throw-together pasta-based meals in your repertoire, I decided to focus this chapter on a few more structured main courses—my own takes on some traditional favorites, which, unsurprisingly, will have you packing in more vegetables than you might have imagined possible.

Cheese is relegated to a backup player (and, in some cases, sidelined altogether) to make room for the extra greenery and flavor. These are pasta dishes flipped into vegetable dishes, with their character not only intact, but enhanced.

First, I'm happy to present a quartet of mac and cheese recipes that embrace combinations such as paprika, cauliflower, and cheese; Gorgonzola and caramelized onions; and a rarebit-like beer and white cheddar sauce cloaking not only the "mac," but also a generous complement of spinach and mushrooms. These preparations are perfect for Sunday suppers and/or for making on weekends to enjoy, reheated, during the week.

Next up, a selection of lasagnas, one for each season, designed for when you have a

little extra time to craft a handsome stack to celebrate a special occasion. In each of these recipes, a generous volume of seasonal vegetables is lovingly layered with more modest amounts of noodles and cheese (or, in vegan variations, the same vegetables and noodles are served in a bowl of broth, with crumbled tofu standing in for the cheese). An all-season, full-out mushroom lasagna joins the group, making this selection into a quintet.

Rounding out the collection, I've chosen two Italian-style dishes, each featuring a single green vegetable and a nut-based sauce, and three of my best-loved Asian noodle recipes. You will find more cold noodle ideas in the salad chapter (pages 59 to 133), so don't forget to look there as well.

And speaking of looking elsewhere

in the book, don't forget the many tasty touches, sauces, and vegetable dishes (plus cozy mashes and even some soups) that work beautifully as cloaks or bases for plain cooked pasta of any shape, so you can customize your own tossed-together pasta meals. There are no rules, and this category is so expandable and forgiving that you will now have additional opportunities to inch up the vegetable ratio in your cooking, bit by delicious bit, while still enjoying the soothing effect of good old trusty noodles.

TIPS FOR SUCCESSFUL MAC AND CHEESE

- You can improvise your choice of cheeses and pasta shapes. I have listed my preferred kinds.

- Whole milk makes the best-tasting sauce, and low-fat milk is also acceptable. I can't guarantee the best results if you use skim.

- Before you preheat the oven, set the rack in the topmost position that will fit the baking pan. This helps the top brown nicely.

- "Shredded" and "grated" Parmesan are not the same thing. The former is little lines and the latter is more of a powder. The look and the texture differ, especially when the cheese goes on top, where it is visible. Use whichever kind you prefer.

- It's not necessary to salt the pasta water, but you can if you want. These recipes were tested with unsalted water, so if you salt the water, consider going lighter on the salt in the rest of the recipe.

- Make sure the saucepan is large enough to hold the cheese sauce and the pasta, plus the other ingredients. A too-small pan is a pain, and you will end up having to transfer everything to a larger one and then need to wash two pans.

- The easiest way to warm and add the milk is to measure it directly into a microwave-safe liquid measuring cup and zap for 1 minute in the microwave. Then put it near the stove so it's ready to pour at the proper moment.

- The best cheese sauce utensils are a whisk to get things smooth early in the process and a wooden spoon for when they thicken.

- Each of these recipes fits perfectly into an 8-inch square pan.

- To make delicious, fresh whole-wheat bread crumbs, simply toast slices of your favorite whole-wheat bread until they are crisp, then break them into pieces and grind to the desired consistency in a food processor or blender. If you want to keep a nice stash in your freezer, spread the crumbs in a single layer on a baking sheet and freeze for about 20 minutes, then transfer to a heavy zip-style plastic bag. (This method helps prevent them from freezing into a solid clump.) Keep them frozen for optimal freshness, taking out just what you need. Two average slices of whole-wheat bread will usually yield a generous cup of crumbs.

- If you need a shortcut, know that the pasta can be cooked up to 3 days ahead, lightly oiled, and refrigerated in a covered container.

- All of these recipes reheat beautifully, covered, in a 250°F oven or in a microwave. The top might need recrisping, which you can do under the broiler.

- An elegant way to serve any mac and cheese is to spoon it into a freshly cooked vegetable vessel such as acorn squash or a portobello mushroom cap prepared for stuffing (see page 350), or a seared bell pepper.

Lemony Caramelized Onion Mac and Gorgonzola

MAKES 5 OR 6 SERVINGS

Intensely sweet, lemony, long-cooked onions meet up with tangy, salty, unapologetically pungent Gorgonzola in this unusual mac and cheese. Appreciators of umami will find taste resonance here.

❁ Read the Tips for Successful Mac and Cheese on page 235 before you begin.

❁ The onions take at least 20 minutes to cook properly, as they need time to truly caramelize. They can do that mostly on their own, with just some occasional stirring from you. The bigger project is getting them minced, which can be done in a food processor, if you pulse them carefully rather than giving them a long buzz, which would liquefy them. It might seem like a large amount of onions when you begin, but they will cook down dramatically.

4 tablespoons olive oil, plus a little more for the pasta

4 cups minced onions (2 large)

1 teaspoon salt, or more to taste

1 tablespoon balsamic vinegar

1 teaspoon grated lemon zest

1 tablespoon fresh lemon juice

Nonstick cooking spray

½ pound orecchiette, elbow macaroni, or equivalent-sized shells

2 cups milk (low-fat is OK)

1 tablespoon unsalted butter

1 teaspoon dry mustard

2 tablespoons unbleached all-purpose flour

1½ cups crumbled Gorgonzola (6–8 ounces)

Black pepper

¾ cup fresh whole-wheat bread crumbs (see page 235)

1. Place a medium-large saucepan over medium heat for about a minute, then add 2 tablespoons of the olive oil and swirl to coat the pan. Toss in the onions, spreading them out in the pan. Cook, stirring often, for about 10 minutes, then add ½ teaspoon of the salt and reduce the heat to medium-low. Continue to cook, stirring frequently, for another 10 to 15 minutes, or until the onions are golden and very soft. Add the vinegar during the last 2 minutes or so. Remove from the heat, stir in the lemon zest and juice, and scrape everything into a bowl. Set aside, keeping the pan handy. (There's no need to clean it.)

2. Preheat the oven to 350°F, with a rack in the highest position that will fit your baking pan. Lightly spray a 2-quart baking dish or an 8-inch square pan with nonstick spray.

3. Put on a medium-large pot of water to boil. When the water boils, add the pasta and cook until just tender enough to bite into comfortably, then drain and transfer to a bowl. Toss with a little olive oil and set aside.

4. Heat the milk—ideally in a spouted measuring cup in a microwave—until it is steaming and too hot to touch, but not boiling. Set the hot milk near the stove.

5. Return the saucepan you used for the onions to the stove over low heat. After about a minute, add the remaining 2 tablespoons oil, scraping up any onion remnants. Toss in the butter, let it melt into the oil, then swirl to coat the pan. Whisk in the dry mustard and sprinkle in the flour as you whisk constantly; they will quickly become a paste. Continue to whisk for another 15 seconds or so.

6. Keep the pan over low heat as you drizzle in the hot milk, whisking constantly. (It might take as long as 5 minutes to incorporate the milk into the paste.) When the mixture is smooth, add the remaining ½ teaspoon salt and cook, stirring with a wooden spoon, for about 5 minutes longer, until the mixture becomes a thick sauce.

7. Remove the sauce from the heat, then stir in the onions (you might need some help from a fork), cooked pasta, and cheese, along with a good dose of black pepper. Taste for salt, then transfer the mixture to the prepared baking pan.

8. Top with the bread crumbs and bake, uncovered, for 15 to 20 minutes, or until bubbly around the edges and crisp and golden on top. Serve hot.

OPTIONAL ENHANCEMENTS

Top with Crisp, Ethereal Onion Rings (page 387) and Crispy Fried Lemons (page 389) ✳ Serve with a salad of arugula, sliced fresh pears, dried figs, and toasted walnuts dressed with Pomegranate Vinaigrette (page 367) ✳ Serve spooned into an acorn squash, prepared for stuffing (see page 350)

Mac, Chili, and Cheese

MAKES 5 OR 6 SERVINGS

Beany and slightly spicy, this recipe combines two traditional American favorites. The tawny effect from combining red kidney beans, colorful peppers and chilies, and chili powder is further enhanced if you use an orange cheddar. Not essential, but lovely.

❋ Glance over the Tips for Successful Mac and Cheese on page 235 before you begin.

❋ This calls for a standard chili powder. They all differ, so find and adopt your own favorite. Depending upon your palate, you could add touches of New Mexico chili powder (ground whole, dried New Mexico chilies) and/or chipotle chili powder (ground whole, dried smoked jalapeños) in addition to the regular chili powder.

❋ One 15-ounce can of kidney beans will do it for this recipe. If you happen to have 1½ or so cups of home-cooked beans lying around, go ahead and use them.

Nonstick cooking spray

½ pound orecchiette, elbow macaroni, or equivalent-sized shells

2 tablespoons olive oil, plus a little more for the pasta

2 cups milk (low-fat is OK)

1 cup minced onion

1 small red, orange, or yellow bell pepper, diced (1 cup)

1 medium Anaheim or poblano chili, minced (½ cup)

1 teaspoon minced or crushed garlic

1 tablespoon chili powder

½ teaspoon ground cumin

1 teaspoon salt

1½ tablespoons unbleached all-purpose flour

1½ (packed) cups grated sharp cheddar (6 ounces)

6 tablespoons grated or shredded Parmesan

1 15-ounce can red kidney beans, rinsed and drained

Black pepper

Cayenne or crushed red pepper

1. Preheat the oven to 350°F, with a rack in the highest position that will fit your baking pan. Lightly spray a 2-quart baking dish or an 8-inch square pan with nonstick spray.

2. Put on a medium-large pot of water to boil. When the water boils, add the pasta and cook until just tender enough to bite into comfortably, then drain and transfer to a bowl. Toss with a little olive oil and set aside.

3. Heat the milk—ideally in a spouted measuring cup in a microwave—until it is steaming and too hot to touch, but not boiling. Set the hot milk near the stove.

4. Place a medium-large saucepan over medium heat for about a minute, then add the oil and swirl to coat the pan. Toss in the onion and cook, stirring often, for about 3 minutes, or until it just begins to soften. Stir in the bell pepper, chili pepper, and garlic, along with the chili powder and cumin and ½ teaspoon of the salt. Cook, stirring often, for 5 minutes.

5. Turn the heat to low and sprinkle in the flour, whisking constantly; it will quickly become a paste. Continue to whisk for another 15 seconds or so.

6. Keep the pan over low heat as you drizzle in the hot milk, whisking constantly. Add the remaining ½ teaspoon salt and cook, stirring with a wooden spoon, for about 2 minutes, until the mixture is thick and smooth. Sprinkle in ¾ cup of the cheddar and 4 tablespoons of the Parmesan, stirring until the cheese is fully incorporated.

7. Remove the sauce from the heat, then add the cooked pasta, along with the beans and the remaining 2 tablespoons Parmesan. Stir until all the pasta and beans are well coated, being careful to avoid breaking the beans. Sprinkle in some black pepper, plus touches of cayenne or crushed red pepper to taste, as you go.

8. Transfer to the baking pan. Sprinkle with the remaining ¾ cup cheddar. Bake uncovered for 15 to 20 minutes, or until bubbly around the edges and crisp and golden on top. Serve hot.

OPTIONAL ENHANCEMENTS

Crown with Fried Green Tomato "Burgers" (page 310), crisply coated with Parmesan and cornmeal, fresh from the pan ✳ Top the unbaked dish with Parmesan-sprinkled tomato slices ✳ Serve spooned into seared bell pepper halves or acorn squash, prepared for stuffing (see page 350)

Roasted Cauliflower Mac and Cheese

MAKES 5 OR 6 SERVINGS

Cauliflower and cheese are natural mates, as are mac and cheese. So why not add them all together? Roasting the cauliflower and onion, then coating them both with cheese, takes the flavor two steps deeper.

❋ For smooth sailing, read the Tips for Successful Mac and Cheese on page 235 before you begin.

❋ The roasting of the cauliflower can be done as much as a day or two ahead. If you follow this route, store the roasted cauliflower in an airtight container and let it come to room temperature before proceeding.

2 tablespoons olive oil, plus a little more for the pasta

1½ pounds cauliflower (1 small head), trimmed, and broken or cut into small (¾-inch) pieces (about 6 cups)

2 cups minced onion (1 large)

¾ cup grated or shredded Parmesan

2½ (packed) cups grated sharp cheddar (10 ounces)

1 teaspoon salt

Nonstick cooking spray

½ pound orecchiette, elbow macaroni, or equivalent-sized shells

2 cups milk (low-fat is OK)

1 tablespoon unsalted butter

1 teaspoon minced or crushed garlic

2 tablespoons unbleached all-purpose flour

Black pepper

¾ cup fresh whole-wheat bread crumbs (see page 235)

Paprika (sweet or smoked) for the top

1. Preheat the oven to 425°F, with a rack in the center position. Line a baking sheet with parchment paper or foil and slick it with a tablespoon of the olive oil. (You can use a chunk of cauliflower to spread the oil around.)

2. Arrange the cauliflower pieces on the baking sheet, sprinkle them with the minced onion, and roast for 15 minutes. Shake the baking sheet and/or use tongs to loosen and redistribute the pieces (do this gently, so they don't escape). Return to the oven.

3. Meanwhile, put on a medium-large pot of water to boil.

4. Roast the cauliflower for another 5 to 10 minutes, or until the cauliflower is becoming uniformly golden, then push the pieces together in the center of the baking sheet, keeping them in a single layer. Sprinkle evenly with ½ cup each of the two cheeses. Continue roasting for about 15 minutes longer, or until the cheese is thoroughly melted and a compelling goldenness rules. Remove from the oven, sprinkle with ½ teaspoon of the salt, and set aside.

5. Reduce the oven temperature to 350°F and carefully reposition the oven rack in the highest position that will fit your baking pan. Lightly spray a 2-quart baking dish or an 8-inch square pan with nonstick spray.

6. When the water boils, add the pasta and cook until just tender enough to bite into comfortably, then drain and transfer to a bowl. Toss with a little olive oil and set aside.

7. Heat the milk—ideally in a spouted measuring cup in a microwave—until it is steaming and too hot to touch, but not boiling. Set the hot milk near the stove.

8. Place a medium saucepan over medium heat for about a minute. Add the remaining 1 table-spoon olive oil and swirl to coat the pan, then add the butter, letting it melt into the oil. Turn the heat to low and whisk in the garlic, letting it cook for just a few seconds, then sprinkle in the flour, as you whisk constantly; it will quickly become a paste. Continue to whisk for another 15 seconds or so.

9. Keep the pan over low heat as you drizzle in the hot milk, whisking constantly. Add the remaining ½ teaspoon salt and cook, stirring with a wooden spoon, for 2 to 3 minutes, until the mixture is thick and smooth. Sprinkle in 1½ cups of the remaining cheddar and the remaining ¼ cup Parmesan, stirring until the cheese is fully blended in. Remove from the heat.

10. Add the cooked pasta to the sauce, along with the cauliflower and all its specks of goodness from the baking sheet. Grind in some black pepper to taste as you go.

11. Transfer to the baking pan and sprinkle with the bread crumbs and the remaining ½ cup grated cheddar. Dust the top with paprika. Bake, uncovered, for 15 to 20 minutes, or until bubbly around the edges and crisp and golden on top. Serve hot.

OPTIONAL ENHANCEMENTS

Serve with a simple salad of thickly sliced in-season ripe tomatoes drizzled with good-quality olive oil or topped with Slow-Roasted Roma Tomatoes (page 393) ❋ Another excellent pairing: Asparagus Salad with Roasted Red Peppers and Chickpeas (page 94)

Spinach-Mushroom Mac and Cheese

MAKES 5 OR 6 SERVINGS

A golden path to popularity, this is a great use for leftover flat beer. It can also be made with present-tense, still-perky beer—in the unlikely event that "leftover" means the other half of the one you're drinking while you read this.

❀ Glance over the Tips for Successful Mac and Cheese on page 235 before you begin.

❀ Different beers can yield vastly different flavors, and it's fun to experiment with various light and dark varieties when making beer-cheese sauces, such as this one (which is a riff on Welsh rarebit). Continuing the theme, plan to drink something that matches (chilled bottles from the same six-pack, perhaps?) with your dinner.

❀ In a pinch, you can use a 10-ounce package of frozen chopped spinach instead of the fresh. Defrost thoroughly and squeeze as dry as possible ahead of time.

Nonstick cooking spray

½ pound orecchiette, elbow macaroni, or equivalent-sized shells

1 tablespoon olive oil, plus a little more for the pasta

1 cup milk (low-fat is OK)

1 tablespoon unsalted butter

½ pound mushrooms, wiped clean, stemmed as necessary, and cut into ½-inch dice

1 teaspoon salt, or more to taste

1 teaspoon minced or crushed garlic

1 teaspoon prepared Dijon or plain yellow mustard

2 tablespoons unbleached all-purpose flour

1 cup room-temperature beer (your choice)

1 pound fresh spinach, stemmed as necessary and chopped (4 packed cups)

1½ (packed) cups grated sharp white cheddar (6 ounces)

¾ cup fresh whole-wheat bread crumbs (see page 235)

½ cup minced walnuts (optional)

1. Preheat the oven to 350°F, with a rack in the highest position that will fit your baking pan. Lightly spray a 2-quart baking dish or an 8-inch square pan with nonstick spray.

2. Put on a medium-large pot of water to boil. When the water boils, add the pasta and cook until just tender enough to bite into comfortably, then drain and transfer to a bowl. Toss with a little olive oil and set aside.

3. Heat the milk—ideally in a spouted measuring cup in a microwave—until it is steaming and too hot to touch, but not boiling. Set the hot milk near the stove.

4. Place a medium-large saucepan over medium heat for about a minute, then add the oil and swirl to coat the pan. Toss in the butter, letting it melt into the oil. Add the mushrooms and ½ teaspoon of the salt and cook, stirring, over medium-low heat for 5 minutes.

5. Whisk in the garlic and mustard, then turn the heat to low and sprinkle in the flour, whisking constantly; it will quickly become a paste. Continue to whisk for another 15 seconds or so.

6. Keep the pan over low heat as you drizzle in the hot milk, whisking constantly. When the milk is incorporated, whisk in the beer. Turn up the heat to medium and stir constantly with a wooden spoon as you add the chopped spinach and the remaining ½ teaspoon salt. Cook for about 5 minutes, or until the spinach wilts its way into the sauce. Remove the pan from the heat and stir in both the cooked pasta and the cheese.

7. Taste for salt, add a touch more if you wish, then transfer the mixture to the baking pan. Top with the bread crumbs and walnuts, if desired, and bake uncovered for 15 to 20 minutes, or until bubbly around the edges and crisp and golden on top. (It might look loose on its way into the oven, but it will pull itself together by the time it comes out.) Serve hot.

OPTIONAL ENHANCEMENTS

Serve with Apple-Parsley Saladita (page 386) or Nectarine-Thyme Saladita (page 386) ❋ A good first (or second) course for this meal is Citrusy Beets (page 98) or Roasted Beets Surrounded by Mango (page 100) ❋ Serve in a portobello "vessel" (see page 350)

Mushroom Lasagna

MAKES 6 TO 8 SERVINGS

Some mushroom lasagnas seem to be competing in an Olympics of richness and complicatedness. My goal is to head in the opposite direction and deconstruct the dish down to its essentials: mushrooms and noodles and something tasty to hold them together. No ricotta, no mozzarella, just a lightly herbed white sauce and some Parmesan, framing—not masking—the many wonderful mushrooms.

This is where you can get adventurous, if you feel like it (and if the produce market complies), by experimenting with unusual wild or wildish mushrooms. Go ahead and swap them in for some of the domestic or cremini mushrooms or cram them in as extras, making this a one-dish mushroom festival.

❋ Slicing the mushrooms a bit on the thick side will make this dish more texturally interesting. Wipe them clean first with a damp towel, trim the stems as necessary, and then go at it with a sharp knife.

❋ The noodles go in completely raw and get cooked in the oven. Regular noodles will do this just fine—no need to buy a "no bake" variety. You must believe. It really works.

Olive oil

1 quart whole or 2-percent milk

3 tablespoons unsalted butter

2 pounds domestic and/or cremini mushrooms, wiped clean, stemmed as necessary, and sliced

Up to ½ pound other mushrooms (optional), wiped clean, stemmed as necessary, and chopped (or left whole, if small)

1 tablespoon minced or crushed garlic

½ teaspoon dried thyme

1½ teaspoons salt

Black pepper

½ cup dry sherry or dry white wine

5 tablespoons unbleached all-purpose flour

10 2¼-inch-wide lasagna noodles (about ¾ pound)

1 cup grated or shredded Parmesan

Paprika (sweet or smoked)

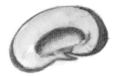

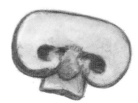

1. Preheat the oven to 375°F, with a rack in the center position. Coat a 9-x-13-inch pan (or its equivalent) with a light layer of olive oil.

2. Pour the milk into a saucepan and place it over low heat until it becomes hot to the touch. Remove from the heat before it boils and set aside.

3. Melt the butter in a medium-large saucepan over medium-low heat. Add the mushrooms, garlic, thyme, salt, and some black pepper and cook, stirring, for about a minute. Cover and cook for another 5 to 8 minutes, or until the mushrooms have expressed some liquid. Splash in the sherry or wine, cover again, and cook for another minute or so.

4. Sprinkle in the flour, whisking constantly. When all the flour is incorporated, drizzle in the hot milk, whisking constantly to keep the sauce smooth. Continue to cook, stirring with a wooden spoon, until the mixture is smooth and slightly thickened. (It will be thinner than a traditional béchamel.) Remove from the heat.

5. Ladle a little of the sauce into the baking pan (just enough to cover the bottom) then add a layer of 5 uncooked noodles. It's OK if they overlap slightly and don't perfectly fit the pan.

6. Ladle half the remaining sauce on the noodles, spreading it into place, then sprinkle with ½ cup of the Parmesan.

7. Repeat with a layer of the remaining 5 noodles, followed by the remaining sauce. (Reserve the remaining Parmesan for later.) Cover the pan tightly with foil and bake for about 35 minutes, or until the noodles are soft enough to be pierced easily with a fork. Be careful not to get a steam burn!

8. At this point, sprinkle the top with the remaining ½ cup Parmesan and some paprika. Return the pan to the oven, this time uncovered, and bake until the top becomes crusty and golden, 20 to 30 minutes. Remove from the oven and let sit for at least 15 minutes before cutting and serving. (It may look wet when it comes out of the oven, but will reabsorb the sauce while sitting.) Serve hot or warm.

Indian Summer Lasagna Stacks

MAKES 4 LARGE OR 8 SMALLER SERVINGS ❄ VEGAN (WHEN MADE AS DIRECTED IN THE VARIATION)

Swelter-free, this no-bake treatment (which is like a lasagna salad or a double-decker lasagna tostada) will be a happy addition to your summer dinner repertoire. First you pan-grill and marinate zucchini and/or summer squash with herbs and fresh corn. Then you layer the vegetables generously with a pesto-laced cheese filling, cooked noodles, and a tomato "sauce," which is simply a bowlful of diced, fresh tomatoes that have been given the opportunity to (literally) express themselves.

Prepare all the components well in advance and assemble the stacks on a platter or on individual plates just before serving. After a brief heat-up in the microwave, the lasagna is ready to serve. Added bonus: There is no lasagna pan to wash afterward.

I've divided this recipe into two parts, to make it easier to follow.

❈ Note that the zucchini need at least an hour to marinate in part 1.

❈ With your good, sharp knife, you'll find your own preference for the thickness of the squash—neither too thick nor too thin.

❈ Go ahead and use a good store-bought basil pesto, unless you feel like making your own favorite recipe well ahead of time. You can also just add ½ teaspoon minced or crushed garlic and a handful of minced fresh basil to the ricotta, if you don't have any pesto on hand.

PART 1

2 tablespoons olive oil, plus more for the pan

1 teaspoon white wine vinegar

½ teaspoon minced or crushed garlic

½ teaspoon salt, or more to taste

Dried thyme

Dried rosemary, crumbled

1 pound small (4- to 6-inch) zucchini and/or yellow summer squash, cut into circles about ¼ inch thick

Black pepper

3 tablespoons grated or shredded Parmesan

Kernels from 1 freshly shucked ear of fresh, sweet corn

1. Combine the 2 tablespoons olive oil, the vinegar, garlic, and ½ teaspoon salt in a large, shallow bowl. Whisk to blend and place the bowl near the stove.

2. Set a ridged grill pan or a cast-iron skillet over medium heat, brush it lightly with olive oil, and sprinkle with a little thyme and rosemary. Place the zucchini on the hot, herbed surface in a single layer and cook on medium-high on both sides until browned and just tender, about 5 minutes. (You will likely need to cook the zucchini in several shifts, adding thyme and rosemary before each batch.) Sprinkle it lightly with salt and pepper as it cooks. When it is tender and golden, transfer the cooked squash directly to the marinade, spreading it out so all surfaces can get flavor exposure. Sprinkle with 1½ tablespoons Parmesan while it is still warm.

[continues]

3. Without cleaning it, heat the pan again, brushing with a touch more oil, if necessary. Toss in the corn and a little more thyme and rosemary and cook for just a minute or two to heat. Scrape the corn and all the flavor from the pan into the marinating squash and toss to coat. Add the remaining 1½ tablespoons Parmesan, season with more salt and pepper, if desired, and set aside to marinate for at least an hour—and ideally, for several. (If it's going to be much longer and your kitchen is hot, cover the bowl and refrigerate until it's time to assemble the lasagna.)

PART 2

1 tablespoon olive oil

1 pound ripe but firm, sweet, in-season tomatoes

½ teaspoon salt

Nonstick cooking spray (optional)

8 2¼-inch-wide lasagna noodles (½ pound)

1 pound ricotta (preferably whole-milk)

Up to 6 tablespoons basil pesto (store-bought or homemade)

Black pepper

¼ cup grated or shredded Parmesan

10 or more fresh basil leaves, cut into thin strips (optional)

1. Fill a large pot with water, add the oil, and bring to a boil.

2. Core the tomatoes and cut them into small (¼-inch) dice. Transfer them to a bowl, sprinkle with ¼ teaspoon of the salt, cover, and set aside.

3. Lay out a kitchen towel on a counter near the sink, or spray a baking sheet with nonstick spray. Add the noodles to the boiling water, using a dinner knife or something similar to swish in a gentle slicing motion between and among them, to prevent their sticking together. Boil for exactly 7 minutes, then carefully drain the noodles in a colander. Immediately use tongs or a pasta gripper to gently lift them out, laying them flat in a single layer on the waiting towel or baking sheet.

4. Combine the ricotta and pesto to taste in a medium-large bowl. Season with the remaining ¼ teaspoon salt and black pepper to taste.

5. To assemble the lasagna, have ready four or eight broiler- or microwave-proof plates. Place a noodle—long, or cut shorter (or in half, if going for 8 servings) with scissors—on each, then spread it with about a thin layer of the ricotta mixture. Add spoonfuls of the vegetable mixture and the tomatoes (about

half of each), then repeat with a second tier. (Don't worry if things tumble down—that's part of the charm.) You'll end up with beautiful stacks, topped with a preponderance of vegetables.

6. Sprinkle with the Parmesan and then broil to heat through and possibly brown the top or microwave each stack on high power for 1 minute. Serve hot or warm, topped with strips of fresh basil leaves if desired.

VEGAN VARIATION

Omit the Parmesan and ricotta. Place the vegetables from part 1 in a bowl with the cooked noodles (cut to fit, if necessary), along with a crumble of firm tofu, if desired, and ladle in some hot vegetable stock (any kind you prefer). Add the chopped tomatoes and top with a vegan pesto (see page 257) and a few grinds of black pepper.

Autumn Vegetable Lasagna

MAKES 6 SERVINGS ❀ VEGAN (WHEN MADE AS DIRECTED IN THE VARIATION)

Fall vegetables paint the plate in this hybrid of landscape and abstraction, themed in toasted butternut orange, striated scarlet, onion mauve, and chard-leaf green. Swirls of Balsamic Reduction complete the design (and the flavor).

❀ If you can find spinach lasagna noodles, this will be even prettier.

❀ You can prepare the reduction while the lasagna bakes.

6–7 tablespoons olive oil

3 pounds butternut squash (1 medium)

3 tablespoons balsamic vinegar

1 pound red onions (about 2 medium), cut into ¼-inch-thick slices or rings

¾ teaspoon salt

½ pound ruby chard, leaves removed from stems and chopped

Nonstick cooking spray (optional)

8 2¼-inch-wide lasagna noodles (½ pound)

1 pound ricotta (preferably whole-milk)

1 (packed) cup grated or chopped mozzarella (about 6 ounces)

2 teaspoons minced or crushed garlic

Black pepper

⅓ cup grated or shredded Parmesan, plus more for topping

Balsamic Reduction (page 369)

1. Preheat the oven to 400°F, with a rack in the center position. Line one or two baking sheets (however many are needed to accommodate the squash) with foil or parchment paper and slick each with about 1 tablespoon of the olive oil.

2. Peel and seed the squash and cut it into rounds (or half rounds) a scant ½ inch thick. Arrange the slices in a single layer on the baking sheet(s) and bake for 20 to 30 minutes, or until the squash becomes tender. Check the squash during the roasting, so you can loosen—and possibly flip—the slices with a small metal spatula, if they seem to be sticking or burning.

3. Remove the squash from the oven, sprinkle it with 1 tablespoon of the vinegar, and let it rest. Turn the oven down to 375°F.

4. Place a large (10- to 12-inch) skillet over medium heat for about a minute, then add 1 tablespoon olive oil and swirl to coat the pan. Increase the heat to medium-high, toss in the onions and ¼ teaspoon of the salt, and cook, stirring, until the onions are bright pink and shiny, about 3 minutes.

5. Fill a large pot with water, add about 1 tablespoon olive oil, and bring to a boil.

6. Stir the remaining 2 tablespoons vinegar into the onions, along with the chard and ¼ teaspoon of the salt. Turn off the heat, and let it rest.

7. Meanwhile, slick a 9-x-13-inch pan (or its equivalent) with a little olive oil. Lay out a kitchen towel on a counter near the sink or spray a baking sheet with nonstick spray. Add the noodles to the boiling water, using a dinner knife or something similar to swish in a gentle slicing motion between and among them, to prevent their sticking together. Boil for exactly 4 minutes, then carefully drain the noodles in a colander. Immediately use tongs or a pasta gripper to gently lift out 4 of the noodles, laying them directly in the oiled baking pan in a single layer. Place the other 4 noodles in a single layer on the towel or baking sheet.

8. Combine the ricotta and mozzarella in a medium-large bowl. Place 2 tablespoons of the olive oil and the garlic in a small, microwave-safe bowl, cover, and zap for 30 seconds, then stir into the ricotta. Season with the remaining ¼ teaspoon salt and black pepper to taste.

9. To assemble the lasagna, spoon half the ricotta here and there on the noodles in the pan. Try to get the cheese fairly evenly distributed. (There will be gaps.) Cover the cheese with a layer of half the squash, followed by half the chard and onion mixture, and sprinkle with the ⅓ cup Parmesan. Lay the remaining 4 noodles on the Parmesan, then repeat the layers, ending with a light dusting of Parmesan.

10. Bake uncovered for 30 minutes, or until heated through and lightly golden on top. Serve hot or warm, drizzled with the Balsamic Reduction. Drizzle the plates decoratively and serve.

VEGAN VARIATION

Place the cooked noodles (cut to fit, if necessary) and vegetables in a bowl, along with a crumble of firm tofu, if desired, and ladle in some hot vegetable stock (any kind you prefer). Drizzle the top with Balsamic Reduction, if desired.

Winter Lasagna

MAKES 6 SERVINGS ❄ VEGAN (WHEN MADE AS DIRECTED IN THE VARIATION)

Brimming with Brussels sprouts, mushrooms, bell pepper, leeks, and cabbage, this soothing lasagna is a perfect match for a big Cabernet or mug of spicy hot cider. Or both. You will likely want to follow it with a chocolate dessert.

❄ The best way to clean the leeks is to slice them first and then swish the slices around assertively in a large bowl of cold water. Lift them out, change the water, and repeat. Drain thoroughly and pat dry with a towel.

4 tablespoons olive oil, plus more for the pan

Nonstick cooking spray (optional)

8 2¼-inch-wide lasagna noodles (½ pound)

1 pound Brussels sprouts, trimmed and sliced about ⅛ inch thick

½ pound thinly sliced, cleaned leeks (3 cups) or thinly sliced red onion (1 medium)

¾ teaspoon salt

¾ pound green cabbage, sliced

1 tablespoon minced or crushed garlic

½ pound mushrooms, wiped clean, stemmed as necessary, and sliced

½ pound red bell pepper, sliced (1 large)

Black pepper

1 pound ricotta (preferably whole-milk)

1 (packed) cup grated or chopped mozzarella (about 6 ounces)

⅓ cup grated or shredded Parmesan, plus more for topping

1. Fill a large pot with water, add 1 tablespoon olive oil, and bring to a boil.

2. Preheat the oven to 375°F, with a rack in the center position. Slick a 9-x-13-inch pan (or its equivalent) with a little olive oil. Lay out a kitchen towel on a counter near the sink or spray a baking sheet with nonstick spray.

3. Add the noodles to the boiling water, using a dinner knife or something similar to swish in a gentle slicing motion between and among them, to prevent their sticking together. Boil for 2 minutes, then add the Brussels sprouts to the water. Boil for another 2 minutes, then drain the noodles and sprouts in a colander. (The total cooking time is 4 minutes.) Immediately use tongs or a pasta gripper to gently lift out 4 of the noodles, laying them directly in the oiled baking pan in a single layer. Place the other 4 noodles in a single layer on the towel or baking sheet. Leave the Brussels sprouts in the colander.

4. Place a large (10- to 12-inch) skillet over medium heat for about a minute, then add 1 tablespoon of the olive oil and swirl to coat the pan. Toss in the leeks or onion, along with ¼ teaspoon of the salt, and cook, stirring, for about 3 minutes for the leeks or 5 minutes for the onion, or until softened.

5. Add the cabbage and 1 teaspoon of the garlic and cook, stirring, for another 2 minutes, or until the cabbage wilts slightly. Add another ¼ teaspoon of the salt and the mushrooms and bell pepper and cook for 8 to 10 minutes longer,

or until everything is tender, but still a touch spunky. Stir in the Brussels sprouts during the last minute or so, along with some black pepper. Remove from the heat and set aside.

6. Combine the ricotta and mozzarella in a medium-large bowl. Place the remaining 2 tablespoons olive oil and the remaining 2 teaspoons garlic in a small, microwave-safe bowl, cover, and zap for 30 seconds, then stir into the ricotta. Season with the remaining ¼ teaspoon salt and black pepper to taste.

7. To assemble the lasagna, spoon half the ricotta here and there on the noodles in the pan. Try to get the cheese fairly evenly distributed. (There will be gaps.) Cover the cheese with half the vegetables and a little more than half the Parmesan. Lay the remaining 4 noodles on the Parmesan, then repeat the layers, ending with a light dusting of the remaining Parmesan.

8. Bake uncovered for 30 minutes, or until heated through and lightly golden on top. Serve hot or warm.

VEGAN VARIATION

Place the cooked noodles (cut to fit, if necessary) and vegetables in a bowl, along with a crumble of firm tofu, if desired, and ladle in some hot vegetable stock (any kind you prefer).

Spring Lasagna

MAKES 6 SERVINGS ❧ VEGAN (WHEN MADE AS DIRECTED IN THE VARIATION)

Greenness, noodles, cheese: my kind of trifecta. This qualifies as the lightest lasagna ever. I will not lie: It takes a bit of prep. (Less if you use frozen peas, but the fresh ones are so good.) Make it a relaxation ritual. Snapping asparagus, for example, can be as satisfying as popping bubble wrap, replete with crisp sound effects.

❋ You can use asparagus of any thickness. For this recipe, I like to use thinner spears. Peeling the bottom half or so, after snapping off and discarding the tough bottoms, is optional. While peeling, lay them as flat as possible, to prevent breakage.

❋ You can use fresh or frozen green peas. To get 1 cup of fresh ones, shuck a pound of pods.

❋ If you are including the favas, use up to a pound of whole pods, and prepare the beans well ahead of time. Details are on page 256.

❋ Pea and Mint Pesto is ideal, but any other green pesto you think would be compatible is fine, especially a traditional basil version. For an unusual and dramatically colorful effect, you can use Bright Green Mashed Peas (page 178) in place of the pesto. Whichever you're using, have it ready ahead of time.

❋ It's especially nice to use long-shredded rather than finely grated Parmesan for this dish, to confer crunchy, crosshatched cheese lines on the top.

3 tablespoons olive oil, plus more for the pan

Nonstick cooking spray (optional)

8 2¼-inch-wide lasagna noodles (½ pound)

1½ pounds asparagus, trimmed, peeled (if desired), and cut into 1½-inch pieces

1 cup green peas (freshly shelled or frozen)

Up to 1 cup shelled, peeled fresh fava beans (optional)

½ pound sugar snap peas, trimmed and halved lengthwise

1 pound ricotta (preferably whole-milk)

1 (packed) cup shredded, grated, or chopped mozzarella (about 6 ounces)

2 teaspoons minced or crushed garlic

About ¼ teaspoon salt

Black pepper

Pea and Mint Pesto (page 257) or a green pesto of your choice

⅓ cup shredded Parmesan, plus more for topping

1. Fill a large pot with water, add 1 tablespoon olive oil, and bring to a boil.

2. Preheat the oven to 375°F, with a rack in the center position. Slick a 9-x-13-inch pan (or its equivalent) with a little olive oil. Lay out two kitchen towels on a counter near the sink or use one towel for the vegetables and spray a baking sheet with nonstick spray for the noodles.

3. Add the noodles to the boiling water, using a dinner knife or something similar to swish in a gentle slicing motion between and among them, to prevent their sticking together. Boil for 2 minutes, then add the asparagus, fresh green peas (if using), and favas (if using). (If you are using frozen green peas, just place them in a colander in the sink.) Boil for 1 minute, then add the sugar snaps and boil for 1 minute longer. (The total cooking time is 4 minutes.) Drain into a colander (directly over the frozen peas, if using). Immediately use tongs or a pasta gripper to gently lift out 4 of

[continues]

the noodles, laying them directly in the oiled baking pan in a single layer. Place the other 4 noodles in a single layer on one of the towels or the baking sheet. Leave the vegetables in the colander.

4. Refresh the vegetables under cold running water until they are no longer hot, to lock in the bright green. Shake off all the excess water and lay them on a towel and pat them dry.

5. Combine the ricotta and mozzarella in a medium-large bowl. Place 2 tablespoons of the olive oil and the garlic in a small microwave-safe bowl, cover, and zap for 30 seconds, then stir into the ricotta. Season to taste with the salt and black pepper.

6. To assemble the lasagna, spread half the pesto over the noodles in the pan with a rubber spatula, then spoon half the ricotta mixture here and there over the pesto. Try to get the cheese fairly evenly distributed. (There will be gaps.) Scatter half the vegetables over the cheese and sprinkle with a little more than half the Parmesan. Lay the remaining 4 noodles over the Parmesan, then repeat the layers, ending with a light scattering of the remaining Parmesan.

7. Bake uncovered for 30 minutes, or until heated through and lightly golden on top. Serve hot or warm.

VEGAN VARIATION

Place the cooked noodles (cut to fit, if necessary) and vegetables in a bowl, along with a crumble of firm tofu, if desired, and ladle in some hot vegetable stock (any kind you prefer). Add a dab of the pesto (made with vegetable stock rather than dairy), some minced fresh tarragon, and a few lightly toasted pine nuts, if desired.

PREPPING FAVA BEANS

Getting fava beans ready for eating is not the most efficient kitchen endeavor, but for me, it is among the most enjoyable. I love the calm meditative state I find myself in when fiddling with them alone—although it is also time well spent to make this a shared project with others. The fleetingness of fava season and the sensual transcendence they bring to any plate, make everything worthwhile. For every pound of whole pods, you can expect to get about 1 cup of beans.

Here's what to do:

- Put on a pot of water to boil. Have a colander in the sink.
- Slit the fava pods with a sharp paring knife, then unzip them to liberate the beans.
- Plunge the beans into the simmering water for exactly 1½ minutes.
- Drain the beans, then immediately refresh them under cold running water.
- Remove and discard the outer skin from each bean (one stroke of the fingernail, and the bean should just slip out).

PEA AND MINT PESTO

MAKES ABOUT 1 CUP
❧ VEGAN (WHEN MADE WITH STOCK)

This pesto showcases the wonderful affinity of mint and peas. My favorite use is to slather it into freshly cooked pasta, adding a big splash of half-and-half or cream, a generous amount of Parmesan, and some black pepper. Pea and Mint Pesto is also wonderful mashed into baked potatoes or used as a topping for soups—in particular Fresh Corn Soup (page 32).

❀ If you're using fresh peas, shuck a full pound and then steam them over (or simmer them in) boiling water for about 5 minutes, or until just tender and very bright. If you're using frozen peas, simply place them in a strainer or colander and run them under room-temperature tap water for a few minutes to defrost, then drain and dry them.

❀ If you don't use this pesto right away, the top surface will lapse into a dull, gray cast, but everything underneath will remain the original green. Just mix that oxidized part back in and it will all blend as if nothing ever faded.

❀ Store the pesto in a tightly covered container in the refrigerator. It will keep for about 3 days.

½ **teaspoon minced or crushed garlic**

2 **tablespoons extra-virgin olive oil**

1 **heaping cup green peas (see note)**

Up to 1 **(packed) cup fresh mint leaves**

2 **slender scallions, chopped**

½ **teaspoon salt, or more to taste**

About 3 **tablespoons milk, half-and-half, or cream, or vegetable stock (page 22) or low-sodium store-bought**

1. Combine the garlic and 1 tablespoon of the olive oil in a small microwave-safe bowl. Cover and microwave for 15 seconds.

2. Combine the peas, garlic oil, remaining 1 tablespoon olive oil, mint, scallions, and salt in a food processor (or a mini processor). Process to get everything as smooth as possible, adding the milk, half-and-half, cream, or stock a tablespoon at a time, as needed.

3. When it reaches the desired texture, taste to see if it needs more salt. Store in a tightly covered container in the refrigerator.

OPTIONAL ENHANCEMENTS

A few drops of fresh lemon or lime juice ❀ A touch of grated lemon or lime zest ❀ Freshly grated Parmesan ❀ A small amount of finely minced fresh tarragon ❀ Additional garlic ❀ Pine nuts, lightly toasted ❀ Black pepper

Linguine and Green Beans in Pesto Trapanese

MAKES ABOUT 1½ CUPS PESTO, 4 TO 6 SERVINGS ❀ VEGAN (WHEN MADE WITHOUT THE CHEESE)

Less well known than the classic basil pesto from Genoa is this Sicilian gem that similarly involves basil, garlic, and olive oil, but only as backup players. Ground almonds, moistened with fresh tomato and lightly sparked with crushed red pepper, are the main event, delivering texture and a subtle flavor. It makes a luxurious coating for long strands of pasta and shorter lengths of green beans—a quietly substantial main dish, crowned with fresh cherry tomatoes.

❀ The traditional pasta shape for Pesto Trapanese is trenette, akin to a chubby, square-edged spaghetti. It is traditional in Trapani, but hard to find here. If you can find trenette instead of linguine, all the better.

❀ The ratio of sauce to pasta and vegetables is generous and the sauce is thick. You can make the sauce thinner by adding an extra tomato in step 3 and/or by splashing in some of the pasta cooking water. You can also increase the green beans for a more vegetable-centric dish. Another option, if you'd like to keep things light, is to simply toss the pasta and green beans with a little olive oil and garlic and serve with a modest dab of pesto on top of each serving. You can pass more pesto at the table.

❀ Because Pesto Trapanese is less intense than its more famous green counterpart, you can use it straight—as a dip for vegetables, for example, or as a thick spread on an open-faced sandwich.

❀ This delightful sauce will keep for up to a week in a tightly covered container in the refrigerator. Let it come to room temperature before applying it to hot pasta.

¾ cup blanched almonds, lightly toasted

12 large fresh basil leaves

1 teaspoon minced or crushed garlic

½ teaspoon salt, or more to taste

½ teaspoon crushed red pepper, or more to taste

2 teaspoons red wine vinegar, or more to taste

2 medium ripe tomatoes (about ½ pound), cored and roughly chopped

4 tablespoons extra-virgin olive oil

½ pound linguine or trenette (see note)

½ pound fresh green beans (slender, if available), trimmed

¼ cup grated or shredded Parmesan, or more to taste (optional)

12 or more sweet cherry tomatoes, halved or quartered if large

1. Put on a large pot of water to boil.

2. Meanwhile, combine the almonds, basil, garlic, ½ teaspoon salt, crushed red pepper, and vinegar in a food processor. Pulse into a coarse meal.

3. Add the tomatoes, buzzing a few times to blend them into the mix. With the machine still running, drizzle 2 tablespoons of the olive oil through the feed tube until it is incorporated. Transfer to a wide serving bowl, taste to adjust the salt, and let the pesto rest at room temperature.

4. When the water boils, add the pasta. Boil for 6 minutes, then toss in the green beans. When the pasta is tender (about 5 minutes later), drain everything together in a colander (it's fine to leave some water clinging) and transfer directly to the pesto in the bowl.

5. Drizzle with the remaining 2 tablespoons olive oil and sprinkle with the Parmesan, if using. Use tongs or a pasta gripper to mix from the bottom, getting everything as well combined as you can.

6. Taste to see if the dish wants a touch more vinegar, salt, or crushed red pepper (or just pass shakers of these at the table). Top with the cherry tomatoes and serve pronto.

Farfalle and Rapini in Creamy Walnut Sauce

MAKES 4 TO 6 SERVINGS ❧ VEGAN (WHEN MADE WITH SOY MILK)

Lightly toasted ground walnuts make an opulent, slightly sweet sauce that is pure luxury.

❀ Rapini (also known as broccoli rabe) is a tender-stalked, mostly leafy, tiny-floret brassica cousin to broccoli. It is pleasantly bitter and goes beautifully in any context where olive oil, garlic, and salt are also involved. If you can't find rapini, look for broccolini (baby broccoli), which is an increasingly available cross between broccoli and Chinese broccoli. You can also use Chinese broccoli, or if none of these is evident in your produce market, go with regular broccoli, coarsely chopped.

❀ The best way to toast nuts is in a 250°F oven or toaster oven for 10 to 15 minutes, or until fragrant. Watch them carefully, so they don't become too dark or burn.

❀ The ratio of sauce to pasta and vegetables is generous, and the sauce is thick. You can thin the sauce by adding a little more milk and/or some of the pasta cooking water. You can also increase the rapini for a greener dish. Another option, if you'd like to keep things light, is to simply toss the pasta and rapini with a little olive oil and garlic and serve it with a modest dab of sauce on top of each serving. Pass more sauce at the table.

2 cups walnuts, lightly toasted

1 teaspoon minced or crushed garlic

Scant ½ teaspoon salt

1 teaspoon white wine vinegar or champagne vinegar

3 tablespoons olive oil or roasted walnut oil, or a combination

½ cup hot milk or soy milk, or more as needed

½ pound farfalle (bow-tie pasta)

½ pound rapini (broccoli rabe) or broccolini

Black pepper

1. Put on a large pot of water to boil.

2. Meanwhile, combine the walnuts, garlic, salt, and vinegar in a food processor and buzz until it turns into a coarse mash. Keep the machine going while you drizzle in the oil. When it's incorporated, transfer about two thirds of the sauce to a wide pasta serving bowl. Use a large whisk to blend in the hot milk, beating gently until uniform.

3. When the water boils, add the farfalle. Boil for 6 minutes, then toss in the rapini or broccolini. When the pasta is tender, 5 to 6 minutes more, drain everything together in a colander (it's fine to leave some water clinging) and transfer directly to the sauce in the bowl.

4. Use tongs or a pasta gripper to mix from the bottom of the bowl, sprinkling with black pepper as you go, until everything is completely coated. Serve right away, passing the extra sauce so people can add more if they wish.

NUT GRAVITAS

Nuts have been gradually upgrading their status from snack to ingredient, and that is very good news, especially for plant-based cooking. In addition to delivering body, flavor, and texture, they pack a good hit of healthy oil, fiber, and protein. Keep them in the freezer and use as needed.

Vegetarian Tan Tan Noodles

MAKES 4 OR 5 SERVINGS ❧ VEGAN (WHEN MADE WITH AGAVE NECTAR OR SUGAR)

Tan Tan (also called Dandan) refers to an across-the-shoulder pole carried by food peddlers in old Sichuan. Baskets—one with sauce and the other with noodles—dangled from each end of the pole, providing an inexpensive and nourishing meal to strolling locals. Eventually the noodles were named after the pole, coming to be known as "peddler's noodles"—street food from way back.

The traditional Chinese recipe is a chili-laced noodle soup strewn with ground pork, preserved vegetables, and scallions. My version combines minced vegetables and tofu with a black bean, garlic, and peanut butter sauce that coats the noodles with deep, dark essence and crunch.

❀ Use the least-processed, freshest-tasting peanut butter you can find. The salt measurement in the recipe is based on a creamy, lightly salted variety. If you are making the recipe with unsalted peanut butter, adjust the seasoning accordingly.

❀ Almond butter can be swapped in for the peanut butter.

❀ I alternate between Lee Kum Kee Black Bean Garlic Sauce and Chili Black Bean Sauce for this recipe, as they both work very well. You can also use a plain chili paste or any chili-garlic sauce.

❀ Use the firmest firm tofu you can find. If you have any doubts, you can firm it up further by boiling it, already diced, for about 10 minutes, well ahead of time. Drain and dry it thoroughly before adding to the stir-fry.

[continues]

½ cup creamy, lightly salted peanut butter

½ cup black bean–garlic sauce (see note)

1 tablespoon agave nectar, light-colored honey, or brown sugar

1 cup very hot water

1 tablespoon grapeseed, canola, or peanut oil, plus more as needed

1 heaping cup minced onion

½ pound shiitake mushrooms, wiped clean, stemmed, and minced (about 4 cups)

Scant ¼ teaspoon salt

1 celery stalk, minced

1 8-ounce can water chestnuts, drained and minced (1 cup)

12 ounces very firm tofu, cut into small dice

½ pound bucatini, linguine, or spaghetti or fresh long Chinese noodles, if available

1. Combine the peanut butter, black bean–garlic sauce, sweetener, and hot water in a medium-large bowl and whisk until blended. Set aside.

2. Put on a large pot of water to boil.

3. Meanwhile, heat a large (10- to 12-inch) skillet or a large wok over medium heat for about a minute. Add the oil, swirl to coat the pan, then toss in the onion and cook, stirring, for about 2 minutes, or until it just begins to soften. Add the shiitakes and salt, and cook, stirring, for another 2 or 3 minutes. Add the celery, water chestnuts, and tofu. Increase the heat to medium-high as you continue to stir-fry, allowing the mixture to stick to the pan a little and brown. Use a spatula with a thin metal blade to scrape the bottom of the pan, so the well-done bits can become incorporated. (You can add a touch more oil during this time, moving things over so it hits the pan directly.) Keep this process going for 5 minutes or so, until the vegetables and tofu are deeply browned, scraping as you go. Turn the heat down to low and stir in the peanut sauce.

4. When the water boils, add the noodles and cook until al dente, or done to your liking.

5. When the noodles are done, drain them thoroughly in a colander and transfer them to the sauce. Toss to coat and serve immediately.

OPTIONAL ENHANCEMENTS

Chili oil, crushed red pepper, or a dab of chili paste ❋ Steamed green peas and/or edamame (green soybeans) decorating the top ❋ A crown of cucumber, in thin strips or minced ❋ Thin ovals of scallion greens scattered around ❋ Lightly toasted peanuts or cashews on top

Stir-Fried Noodles with Asparagus, Mushrooms, Tofu, and Cashews

MAKES 4 OR 5 SERVINGS ❧ VEGAN

You never know ahead of time if a dish is destined to become a keeper. But if, after many bouts of enjoyment, it's still at the front of your repertoire, go ahead and invoke posterity: The dish will have earned such status.

This recipe, originally published in my book *Still Life with Menu*, is one of those for me. Tweaked slightly over time, it always grabs with its interplay of lemon, ginger, soy sauce, garlic, and sesame oil, and the textural triangle of asparagus, mushrooms, and tofu against cashew-coated noodles. The only significant change from the original recipe is the cashews, which used to be sesame seeds. Feel free to reclaim the sesame seeds, if you wish—tossing on a small handful before serving.

❀ Use the firmest firm tofu you can find. If you have any doubts, you can firm it up further by boiling it, already diced, for about 10 minutes, well ahead of time. Drain and dry it thoroughly before adding to the stir-fry.

❀ The tofu and mushrooms need at least 15 minutes (ideally 30—and up to 2 hours is fine) to marinate before the recipe is assembled. You can use this time to prepare the asparagus.

1 cup cashews, lightly toasted

8 scallions, minced (whites and greens kept separate)

1 tablespoon minced or crushed garlic

1 heaping tablespoon grated fresh ginger

2 tablespoons soy sauce

½ teaspoon grated lemon zest

¼ cup fresh lemon juice

2 tablespoons Chinese sesame oil

3 tablespoons water

3 tablespoons light or dark brown sugar

Up to 1 teaspoon salt

½ pound very firm tofu, cut into ½-inch dice

12–15 fresh mushrooms (about ¾ pound), wiped clean, stemmed, and sliced or quartered

1 pound asparagus

½ pound linguine, fettuccine, spaghetti, or fresh, long Chinese noodles, if available

2 tablespoons grapeseed, canola, or peanut oil

Crushed red pepper

1. Place the cashews in the food processor (or a mini processor) and pulse until they are coarsely chopped. Set aside.

2. In a 9-x-13-inch pan (or its equivalent), stir together the scallion whites, garlic, ginger, soy sauce, lemon zest and juice, sesame oil, water, brown sugar, and ¼ teaspoon of the salt. Stir in the tofu and mushrooms and let stand for at least 15 minutes or up to 2 hours.

[continues]

The marinade won't completely cover the tofu and mushrooms, so shake the pan and stir to redistribute the liquid every so often.

3. Meanwhile, put on a large pot of water to boil.

4. Snap off and discard the tough ends of the asparagus and, if desired, peel the remaining stalks about halfway up. Cut them diagonally into 1-inch lengths (they can be longer if the asparagus is very thin) and set aside.

5. When the water boils, cook the noodles until al dente, or until done to your liking. Drain, rinse in warm water, and then drain again—thoroughly this time. Leave them in the colander in the sink for now.

6. Place a large (10- to 12-inch) skillet or a large wok over medium heat for about a minute, then add the oil and swirl to coat the pan. Turn up the heat to medium-high, toss in the asparagus and ¼ teaspoon salt, and stir-fry until the asparagus is just tender, 5 to 7 minutes, depending on thickness.

7. Add the drained noodles and another ¼ teaspoon salt, mixing as best you can with tongs or a large fork. Stir-fry over medium-high heat for about 3 minutes, or until the noodles and asparagus entwine.

8. Pour in the entire panful of marinade, tofu, and mushrooms. Turn the heat to high and stir-fry for another 3 minutes, tossing in the ground cashews and a light touch of crushed red pepper as you go. When the sauce and cashews are well distributed and everything is heated through, taste to see if it needs more salt, and add ¼ teaspoon more if so. Serve immediately, topped with a scattering of the scallion greens.

Soba Noodles with Butternut Squash, Miso, Smoked Tofu, Pumpkin Seeds, and Basil

MAKES 4 OR 5 SERVINGS ❧ VEGAN

Sweet, pungent, smoky, herby, toasty—this dish will address your entire taste bud geography as you happily slurp the skinny noodles and butternut squash, cloaked with the mysterious fermented flavor of miso. Crunch, in the form of pumpkin seeds, and heat, from crushed red pepper, deliver your mouth to an altered state. Originally published in my book *Vegetable Heaven*, this straightforward one-dish meal has never receded from its privileged position at the front of my recipe file.

❀ One of the things I love most about this recipe is that the sauce is miso dissolved in water—nothing more. The light-colored miso called for here will be sweeter and more pleasantly subtle than a darker, more powerfully flavored kind. (With miso, as with honey, the darker the hue, the more assertive the taste.) If you love the darker types, please feel free to customize accordingly.

❀ Most butternuts will yield more than the 2 to 3 cups that fit into this dish. You can freeze the remaining squash or cook it into something else.

1 generous tablespoon white (shiro) or yellow miso

1½ cups hot water

1 tablespoon grapeseed, canola, or peanut oil

2 cups minced or sliced onion (1 large)

2–3 cups peeled, chopped (¾-inch cubes) butternut squash (about 1 pound)

½ teaspoon salt

½ (packed) cup fresh basil leaves

8 ounces smoked tofu, cut into small dice

8 ounces thin soba noodles

Crushed red pepper

Up to 1 cup pumpkin seeds, lightly toasted

1. Put on a large pot of water to boil.

2. Combine the miso and hot water in a small bowl and mash with a spoon until the miso dissolves. (It doesn't have to be perfectly smooth.) Set aside.

3. Place a large (10- to 12-inch) skillet over medium heat for about a minute, then add the oil and swirl to coat the pan. Toss in the onion and cook, stirring, for about 5 minutes, or until it softens. Add the squash and salt, cover, and cook for about 15 minutes, or until the squash is tender.

4. Coarsely chop the basil, or just tear the leaves, then stir the miso sauce, tofu, and basil into the onion and squash. Turn the heat to low, cover the pan, and let the mixture simmer while you cook the soba.

5. When the water boils, cook the noodles for 5 to 8 minutes, or until done to your liking. Drain them thoroughly in a colander, shaking off any excess water. Transfer to a serving bowl and pour in the vegetable-tofu-miso mixture. Gently toss with tongs or a large fork, so as not to break the noodles, adding crushed red pepper to taste as you go. Sprinkle the top with pumpkin seeds and serve hot, warm, or at room temperature.

SUPPERS from the OVEN

❋ ❋ ❋

When your dinner is a simple, peasanty dish that has spent some time melding and deepening in the oven, the overall effect will have taken on uplifting metaphysical qualities. (I call these mystical micronutrients.) One could get scientific or psychological about this, but I simply choose to get busy in the preparation and lost in the eating.

Early vegetarian cooking tended to center around heavy casseroles. I know; I was there. Flashing forward an approximate lifetime, my current oven repertoire for savory dishes is significantly more straightforward and quite a bit lighter. I have whittled it all down to the select list I now find myself making over and over—and always with fresh appreciation.

So what exactly are we talking about here? Potatoes, mushrooms, bread. Asparagus, zucchini, cauliflower. Milk, eggs, cheese. Homemade pizza, designed by you. Comfort food that presents itself in a soothing muffin shape or can be scooped from a pan with a spoon or cut into rectangles, wedges, or squares. The common denominators? Oven-to-table meals and a profoundly relieving sense of warmth and informality.

This is when you get to call dinner "supper." And that, in and of itself, is a comfort.

Vegetable Pizza

MAKES FOUR 8-INCH PIZZAS ❋ VEGAN (IF MADE WITHOUT CHEESE)

Vegetables are the main event in this pizza, and the modest amount of cheese serves as their anchor (and the cheese itself is optional). A high-temperature oven enables a very quick baking process that locks in the beautiful vegetable colors, allowing them to shine. You will feel like you are delivering a series of round abstract paintings to the table—hot, crisp, deeply flavorful, and no two alike.

Homemade pizza is more accessible than you might think with this quick, foolproof dough that's made in the food processor, especially if you keep a supply of dough in the freezer. If you make small pizzas (pizzettas), you can individualize the toppings and satisfy the various tastes of everyone in your household, without a whole lot of extra work.

❋ Prepare the topping ingredients while the dough rises.

❋ You can make several different pizzas and serve them together.

❋ In this pizza, I like to feature the subtle flavors of vegetables without overpowering them with tomato sauce. If you would be unhappy in its absence, feel free to spread a layer of your favorite kind in step 7, before adding the other toppings.

❋ One batch of dough divides perfectly into two 1-pound ricotta cheese containers—or fit a whole batch into a 1-quart yogurt container—for easy freezing. Take the container out of the freezer before you go to work in the morning, and it will be ready to roll, so to speak, when you get home.

DOUGH

2 cups unbleached all-purpose flour, plus more if needed

Nonstick cooking spray

½ cup whole-wheat flour

1 teaspoon salt

1 teaspoon active dry yeast (approximately ½ package)

2 tablespoons olive oil

1 cup lukewarm water

Cornmeal for the baking sheets (optional)

1. Prepare a work surface by either sprinkling a little flour on a clean counter or spraying the counter lightly with nonstick spray. Coat the inside of a medium bowl with nonstick spray.

2. Combine the flours, salt, and yeast in a food processor and pulse for about 5 seconds to blend.

3. Combine the olive oil and the water in a small bowl and, with the food processor motor running, pour this mixture through the feed tube. The dough will come together in a ball in about 20 seconds or less. Carefully remove the dough and transfer it to the prepared work surface.

4. Lightly spray your hands with nonstick spray (or flour your hands, if you prefer) and knead the dough for 2 to 3 minutes, or until it acquires a texture similar to your earlobe. The dough should be very soft, but not sticky. If it's sticky, knead in small amounts of additional flour, about a tablespoon at a time, until it

[continues]

no longer sticks. Transfer the dough to the prepared bowl, spray the top surface with a little more nonstick spray, cover the bowl with plastic wrap or a kitchen towel, and set it in a warm place to rise for about an hour, until its bulk increases by about 60 percent. (*You can also refrigerate the dough for up to a day, or freeze it for up to a month. Let it come to room temperature before proceeding.*)

5. Punch down the dough and return it to the freshly floured or sprayed surface. Divide it into 4 equal parts, knead each quarter for a few minutes, then let the balls of dough rest for about 10 minutes. (This allows the gluten to relax, so the dough will stretch easily into shape.)

6. Meanwhile, preheat the oven to 400°F, with a rack in the lower position.

7. Patiently stretch each ball into an 8-inch circle. Sprinkle two baking sheets with flour or cornmeal and place 2 circles on each. Top each pizza with a small amount of cheese, if desired, and then vegetables in any combination that appeals to you. If using nuts, make sure they land on top so they can toast. If omitting the cheese, be sure to gently but firmly press the vegetables into the dough, so they'll adhere.

8. Bake for 10 to 12 minutes, or until the edges are crispy and brown. Serve hot, warm, or at room temperature.

TOPPING POSSIBILITIES

Shredded Parmesan

Thin slices of mozzarella

Ripe tomato slices (large or cherry)

Thinly sliced red onion

Sliced mushrooms

Sliced bell peppers (various colors)

Cauliflower florets, cut thin

Broccoli florets, cut small

Canned artichoke hearts, drained and sliced

Olives (any kind), pitted and sliced

Fresh corn kernels

Pine nuts and/or coarsely chopped walnuts (highly recommended)

Crushed red pepper

Mushroom Popover Pie

MAKES 2 OR 3 SERVINGS (THIS RECIPE IS EASILY DOUBLED, IF YOU HAVE A SECOND SKILLET)

Knife, skillet, blender, oven—you will be delivering savory, puffy splendor to your humble table in just a few straightforward strokes. I hope someone remembered to chill a bottle of crisp white wine.

Crustless and replete with an airy, custardy pancake-like texture, this popover is baked in a skillet and then gets cut into wedges. This could well become the new dinner fallback plan, especially for mushroom lovers. I like to serve it with any Feathered Fennel Variation (page 75).

❀ The combination of fresh domestic and shiitake mushrooms results in layers of deep mushroom flavor. If you can't find shiitakes, it's OK to substitute cremini (brown) mushrooms or use all domestic ones.

2 tablespoons unsalted butter

½ cup finely minced onion

½ pound domestic mushrooms, wiped clean, stemmed as necessary, and thinly sliced

10 medium (2-inch cap) shiitake mushrooms, stemmed and minced

1 teaspoon minced or crushed garlic

1 teaspoon salt

½ teaspoon dried thyme

Black pepper

3 large eggs, ideally at room temperature

1 cup milk (low fat OK)

1 cup unbleached all-purpose flour

1. Preheat the oven to 375°F, with a rack in the center position.

2. Melt 1 tablespoon of the butter in a 9- or 10-inch cast-iron skillet over medium-low heat. Add the onion and cook, stirring, for 5 minutes, or until softened. Add the mushrooms, garlic, ¾ teaspoon of the salt, thyme, and a generous amount of black pepper and cook, stirring often, for about 15 minutes, or until the liquid the mushrooms have given off evaporates and the mushrooms are becoming golden around the edges. (It will seem like a lot of mushrooms at first, but they will cook down.)

3. Meanwhile, combine the eggs, milk, flour, and remaining ¼ teaspoon salt in a blender and whip them into a smooth batter. (If you don't have a blender, whisk them together in a medium bowl. It's fine if the mixture has a few lumps.) Set aside.

4. When the mushrooms are ready, transfer them to a bowl, then thoroughly wash and dry the pan and return it to the stove. Add the remaining 1 tablespoon butter and heat over low heat just until the butter melts and begins to foam. Immediately remove the pan from the heat and swirl to coat. (Be sure to get the edges.) Add the mushrooms, spreading them into a fairly even layer, then pour in the batter.

5. Bake for 25 to 30 minutes, or until the batter becomes dry on top and feels solid when touched lightly with a fingertip. The edges will have shrunk from the sides of the pan and become quite brown. Cut into wedges and serve hot or warm.

Mini Cauliflower Quiches

MAKES 6 LARGE OR 12 SMALL MINI QUICHES (ABOUT 6 SERVINGS)

It's always fun to be served something that was baked in individual units, as though you're receiving a personal party favor from the cook. This one delivers cauliflower, tomato, and feta, with a lovely parsley beret across the top (it floats upward in the batter). Instead of a crust, I've added bread crumbs to the light filling. These quiches are a perfect main course for brunch or a light supper and are highly portable for weekday lunch. (Just a quick reheat in a microwave will render them as good as new.)

✿ Room-temperature eggs acquire much more volume when beaten than do cold ones, so if you think of it—and your kitchen is not too hot—take the eggs out of the refrigerator a few hours ahead of time. Break them into a bowl while they are still cold and then cover the bowl with plastic wrap or a plate.

✿ If good, fresh, ripe tomatoes are unavailable, you can substitute 1 cup diced canned tomatoes, drained.

✿ For the bread crumbs, simply toast a slice of your favorite whole-wheat sandwich bread, then whirl it into fine crumbs in a mini food processor or a blender.

✿ Spray or grease the muffin pans generously to be sure the quiches come out easily. (Avoid paper liners—they will stick.)

✿ Mini Cauliflower Quiches make a perfect summer supper served with Fresh Corn Soup (page 32) and Gazpacho Salad (page 86). For a winter meal, pair them with Humble Potato-Leek Soup (page 24) and Grilled Bread and Kale Salad with Red Onions, Walnuts, and Figs (page 71).

✿ The quiches will keep in a zip-style plastic bag or container in the refrigerator for up to 5 days. Reheat for 30 seconds in a microwave.

Butter, oil, or nonstick cooking spray

1 tablespoon olive oil

2 cups minced onion (1 large)

1 teaspoon salt

1 teaspoon minced or crushed garlic

1 small head cauliflower (about 1½ pounds), trimmed and chopped into pea-size pieces

1 medium tomato, perfectly ripe

¼ cup fine fresh whole-wheat bread crumbs (see note)

1 cup crumbled feta (about ⅓ pound)

Black pepper

1 dozen large eggs, ideally at room temperature

¼ cup minced fresh flat-leaf parsley

1. Preheat the oven to 350°F, with a rack in the center position. Generously grease or spray the bottoms and sides of 6 jumbo (4-inch) muffin cups or 12 standard (2½-inch) muffin cups (preferably nonstick).

2. Place a large (10- to 12-inch) skillet over medium heat for about a minute, then add the olive oil and swirl to coat the pan. Add the onion and cook, stirring, for about 3 minutes, until the onion just begins to soften, then add ½ teaspoon of the salt. Sauté for 8 to 10 minutes longer, or until the onion is very soft.

3. Stir in the garlic and cauliflower, cover, and cook over medium heat until the cauliflower is tender, 8 to 10 minutes. Remove from the heat.

4. Core the tomato, cut it in half, and squeeze out and discard the seeds. Chop the tomato into ¼-inch dice and stir it into the cauliflower, along with the bread crumbs. Divide the vegetables evenly among the muffin cups and sprinkle with the feta and black pepper to taste.

5. Beat the eggs with a whisk or handheld electric mixer or in a blender until smooth and frothy. Stir in the remaining ½ teaspoon salt and the parsley. Ladle the egg mixture into the cups.

6. Bake for 35 to 40 minutes, or until the quiches are solid in the center when a knife is inserted.

7. Allow to cool in the pans for 10 minutes before removing and serving.

Savory Ricotta "Muffins"

MAKES 4 (2 APIECE FOR DINNER) TO 8 SERVINGS (1 APIECE FOR LUNCH)

Gentle ricotta, spiked with the fresh taste of minced scallions and a pungent edge of Parmesan, bonds with beaten egg to create lovely, puffy quiches on a bread-crumb base. Eat them on a plate with a fork or just pick one up and take a bite. They're highly portable. Consider pairing them with Wild Rice Chili-Mango Soup (page 40) and Wilted Spinach Salad with Crispy Smoked Tofu, Grilled Onion, Croutons, and Tomatoes (page 82).

❄ Break the eggs into the bowl while they are still cold; cover the bowl and let them come to room temperature.

❄ For the bread crumbs, simply toast a slice of your favorite whole-wheat sandwich bread, then whirl it into fine crumbs in a mini food processor or a blender.

❄ Spray or grease the muffin pans generously to be sure the muffins come out of the pan easily. (Avoid paper liners—they will stick.)

❄ You can store these for up to 5 days in a tightly covered container in the refrigerator. Reheat them for 30 seconds in a microwave, and they'll be as fresh as just-baked.

Nonstick cooking spray

About 2 tablespoons butter for the pans

⅓ cup fine fresh whole-wheat bread crumbs

8 large eggs, ideally at room temperature

1 cup ricotta (preferably whole-milk)

Scant ½ teaspoon salt

½ cup finely minced scallions

Black pepper

2 tablespoons grated or shredded Parmesan

1. Preheat the oven to 350°F, with a rack in the center position. Generously spray the bottoms and sides of 8 nonstick standard (2½-inch) muffin cups with nonstick spray, then place a slice of butter in each cup. Place the pans in the oven for a minute or so to melt the butter, then take them out and divide the bread crumbs among them.

2. Combine the eggs, ricotta, and salt in a medium-large bowl and whip until smooth with a whisk or immersion blender. Stir in the scallions and a generous amount of black pepper. Pour the egg mixture into the prepared cups, filling them right up to the rim.

3. Bake for 10 minutes, then reach in and carefully sprinkle the top of each muffin with a little Parmesan. Bake for another 10 minutes, or until the tops are puffy, golden, and delicately firm to the touch.

4. Remove the pans from the oven and let the muffins cool in the pans for 5 minutes, during which time they will deflate a little. Run a knife around the edges and lift or invert each muffin onto a cooling rack or a plate. Serve hot, warm, or at room temperature.

Mushroom Bread Pudding

MAKES 6 TO 8 SERVINGS

Bite-sized pieces of artisanal bread are drenched in a deeply flavored, savory custard and riddled with mushrooms, then baked until set in the center and slightly crunchy on top. This most luxurious star of brunch and Sunday supper can be served with just a simple green salad and a crisp white wine, and it will feel like a full banquet.

❈ For best results, use a country-style bread with a crisp crust and an airy, chewy interior (known in bread-speak as a "high crust-to-crumb ratio"). These breads are often called batard, ciabatta, or pugliese. If you can't find any of these, use stale French or Italian bread.

❈ Break the eggs into a bowl or container while they are still cold; cover and let them come to room temperature before using.

❈ This tastes best served warm or at room temperature, and reheats perfectly well in a microwave. In fact sometimes it tastes even better reheated, which should encourage you to make this dish at any time.

Nonstick cooking spray

2 tablespoons olive oil

1½ cups minced onion (1 medium)

½ teaspoon dried thyme

1 teaspoon salt

1½ pounds domestic mushrooms, wiped clean, stemmed if necessary, and sliced

12 medium (2-inch cap) shiitake mushrooms, wiped clean, stemmed, and thinly sliced

1 tablespoon minced or crushed garlic

¼ cup dry sherry

2 tablespoons fresh lemon juice

Black pepper

3 cups bite-sized bread cubes

5 large eggs, ideally at room temperature

2 cups milk (low fat is OK)

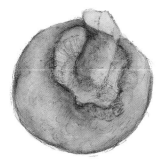

1. Preheat the oven to 350°F (325°F if using a glass pan), with a rack in the center position. Lightly spray a 9-x-13-inch baking pan with nonstick spray.

2. Place a large (10- to 12-inch) skillet over medium heat for about a minute, then add the oil and swirl to coat the pan. Toss in the onion, thyme, and ½ teaspoon of the salt and cook, stirring, for about 8 minutes, or until the onion is very soft.

3. Add all the mushrooms, garlic, and the remaining ½ teaspoon salt and continue to cook, stirring, for about 10 minutes, or until the mushrooms cook down.

4. Stir in the sherry and lemon juice. Cook, stirring, for 5 minutes longer, remove from the heat, and add black pepper to taste.

5. Arrange the bread cubes more or less evenly in the pan. Spread the mushroom mixture on top of the bread, scraping the pan to include every last bit.

6. Combine the eggs and milk in a blender or a food processor and process until smooth. Pour the liquid mixture over the bread and mushrooms and let sit for about 5 minutes. Use your finger or a spoon to poke the bread into the liquid until all the pieces are soaked.

7. Bake for 35 to 40 minutes, or until the custard is almost set and the top pieces of bread turn golden on the edges. (It's OK if the top is still moist, as it will continue to cook from its own heat for a few minutes after it comes out of the oven.)

8. Cool for at least 15 minutes before serving. Serve warm or at room temperature.

OPTIONAL ENHANCEMENTS

❋ Grated cheddar and/or Parmesan sprinkled on top before baking ❋ A little mound of sour cream or crème fraîche on top or on the side

VARIATION: ASPARAGUS-MUSHROOM BREAD PUDDING

Add ¾ pound asparagus, trimmed and cut into 1-inch pieces, to the mushrooms in step 3, after they've cooked for about 5 minutes. Cover and cook for about 10 minutes longer over medium heat, tossing in up to 1 teaspoon dried tarragon, if desired. Proceed with the rest of the recipe as written.

Asparagus Puff Pastry Tart

MAKES 4 OR 5 SERVINGS

I got the idea to pair asparagus and puff pastry from an entrancing photo of a dish created by the gifted British food writer Annie Bell. This is my own highly simplified version.

Three ingredients—one of them a total cheat—are all that stand between you and a sexy little gem of a dish 15 baking minutes later. My favorite salad partner for this is Radicchio Salad with Oranges and Pistachios (page 78).

❁ Use a good brand of frozen puff pastry, preferably one made with butter, such as Dufour, and allow it to defrost thoroughly before you unwrap and use it.

❁ The asparagus may need to be blanched in two installments. If so, set up a colander on a plate by the stove, take out the first batch with tongs, and blanch the second batch while you remove the colander to the sink to refresh the first batch. You can also use two pots. Prepare and blanch the asparagus far enough in advance that it dries thoroughly before you proceed.

❁ If you choose Parmesan, use shredded rather than grated, which is too powdery. You want the separate little lines on top of the tart.

1½ pounds medium-thick asparagus

1 8-inch square (or equivalent rectangle) unbaked puff pastry (⅟₁₆ inch thick)

1 packed cup grated Gruyère or shredded Parmesan (about ¼ pound)

1. Fill a large saucepan with water and bring it to a boil. Place a colander in the sink and have ready a bed of absorbent kitchen towels.

2. Meanwhile, trim or break off the tough asparagus bottoms, then use a vegetable peeler to peel the skin from the base about halfway up. Peeling works best if you lay each spear flat and work at it as horizontally as your wrists will permit. (Peeling is not essential, but does beautify the asparagus.)

3. When the water boils, turn the heat down to a simmer. Add the asparagus and cook for 1 minute, then drain and immediately refresh under cold running water until it cools to room temperature. Shake off all excess water, then lay the asparagus on the towels to thoroughly dry. (Some patting will help.)

4. Preheat the oven to 400°F, with a rack in the center position.

5. Place the pastry on an ungreased baking sheet. Distribute a little more than half the cheese evenly over the entire square of pastry, leaving no margin. (You want goldenness everywhere.)

6. Lay the asparagus over the pastry in a tight row, touching, and patch any spaces with pieces of the asparagus cut with scissors to fit. Sprinkle the remaining cheese on top of the asparagus (no need to make it even this time).

7. Bake for 15 minutes, or until golden. Cut into pieces with scissors and serve hot, warm, or at room temperature. It's nice to bring the entire thing to the table before cutting it, for dramatic effect.

Caramelized Onion Frittata with Artichoke Hearts, Zucchini, and Goat Cheese

MAKES 4 OR 5 SERVINGS

In my own personal food awards, frittatas win medals in these categories: Quick; Easy Supper; Vegetarian Entrées for All Tastes; and Everything That's Good About Eggs. In that last one, frittatas are to be commended for their ability to be both sturdy and tender at the same time, and for their willingness to be delicious at room temperature or even cold.

This frittata is like a crustless, vegcentric quiche. The zucchini, onion, and artichoke hearts—abstractly stacked like interlocking puzzle pieces, lightly spotted with goat cheese—provide the foreground. The eggs serve mostly just to hold them together. You don't have to walk on eggshells (sorry!) with this forgiving dish, as you might with an omelet, and if it breaks at any point, just piece it back together. This is a true keeper, and a confidence builder for any beginning cook.

8 large eggs

3 tablespoons olive oil

2 cups minced onion (1 large)

Pinch *each* of dried thyme and rubbed dried sage

2 small zucchini (½ pound total), cut into ⅛-inch-thick coins

8 ounces (1½ cups) canned quartered artichoke hearts, rinsed, drained, and thoroughly dried

1 teaspoon salt

1 tablespoon white wine vinegar

Black pepper

5 ounces soft, fresh goat cheese

Nonstick cooking spray

¼ cup grated or shredded Parmesan

1. Break the eggs into a large bowl, cover, and let them rest at room temperature while you prepare the other ingredients.

2. Place a medium (9- or 10-inch) ovenproof skillet over medium heat for about a minute, then add 1 tablespoon of the oil and swirl to coat the pan. Toss in the onion, spreading it out in the pan, and sprinkle in the herbs. Cook, stirring often, for about 10 minutes, or until translucent. Add the zucchini and artichoke hearts, plus ½ teaspoon of the salt, and continue to cook, stirring often, for another 8 to 10 minutes, or until the onion is golden and the zucchini is tender. Stir in the vinegar and black pepper to taste and remove from the heat.

3. Beat the eggs with a large whisk until smooth, adding the remaining ½ teaspoon salt as you go. Scrape in the sautéed vegetables, plus all the flavorful bits from the pan, then crumble in the goat cheese and stir until blended.

4. Clean and dry the skillet, spray it with nonstick spray, and return it to the stove over medium heat.

5. Preheat the broiler to 500°F, with a rack in the upper half of the oven.

6. When the skillet is hot, add the remaining 2 tablespoons olive oil, wait about 30 seconds, then swirl to coat the pan. Pour in the vegetable-egg mixture and let it cook undisturbed over medium heat for 3 to 4 minutes, or until the eggs are set on the bottom.

7. Sprinkle the top with the Parmesan, then transfer the skillet to the preheated broiler, and broil for about 3 minutes, or until the frittata is firm in the center and golden on top. Run a rubber spatula around the edge to loosen the frittata. Slide or invert it onto a large plate, and serve hot, warm, or at room temperature, cut into wedges.

OPTIONAL ENHANCEMENTS

For a beautiful color accent, add 2 or 3 finely chopped ruby chard leaves, including some of the stems ✿ Add 1 teaspoon minced or crushed garlic to the onion after the first 5 minutes of cooking ✿ Feta can substitute for the goat cheese; if so, consider reducing the salt to ¾ teaspoon ✿ Serve surrounded by halved (unless tiny) very sweet cherry tomatoes (orange ones, in summer, are especially great) ✿ Layer thinly sliced, cooked potatoes with the zucchini in addition to, or instead of, the artichoke hearts

Brussels Sprout Gratin with Potatoes and Spinach

MAKES 6 TO 8 SERVINGS ❈ VEGAN (WHEN MADE WITH ALL OLIVE OIL, SOY MILK, AND NO CHEESE)

When I decided on a meal of Brussels sprouts cooked with potatoes, onion, garlic, and spinach and baked under a lacy roof of grated cheese and coarse bread crumbs, I expected the results to be cozy, but lackluster. Except for the cozy part, I was so wrong.

❈ Gruyère cheese is ideal for this. You can also use Emmentaler.

❈ For the bread crumbs, toast 2 slices of your favorite whole-wheat bread, then coarsely crumble in a food processor.

❈ Round out the meal with Hazelnut–Wilted Frisée Salad with Sliced Pear (page 84).

2½ tablespoons olive oil, or 1½ tablespoons olive oil and 1 tablespoon unsalted butter

1 pound smallish potatoes, cut into ⅛-inch-thick half circles (peeling is optional)

1 pound Brussels sprouts, trimmed and cut into ⅛-inch-thick slices (include all the leaves that fall off while you're cutting them)

2 cups chopped onion (1 large)

1 teaspoon salt

2 teaspoons minced or crushed garlic

½ pound fresh spinach (baby leaves or coarsely chopped larger leaves)

Black pepper

¼ cup cream, milk, half-and-half, or soy milk

1 cup fresh whole-wheat bread crumbs (see note)

1 (packed) cup grated Gruyère (about ¼ pound; optional)

Paprika (optional)

1. Preheat the oven to 350°F, with a rack in the highest position that will fit your baking pan. Coat a 9-x-13-inch baking pan or equivalent gratin pan with about ½ tablespoon of the olive oil.

2. Fill a medium-large saucepan with water and put it on to boil. When the water boils, add the potatoes and Brussels sprouts and cook them for 8 to 10 minutes, or until they become fork-tender. Drain them in a colander and shake to thoroughly drain.

3. Meanwhile, place a large (10- to 12-inch) skillet over medium heat for about a minute, then add 1 tablespoon olive oil (2 tablespoons, if not adding butter) and swirl to coat the pan. Melt in the butter, if using, and swirl again. Add the onion and ¼ teaspoon of the salt and cook, stirring, for about 8 minutes, or until the onion becomes very soft, verging on golden.

4. Stir in the garlic and lay the spinach on top to wilt. (It will quickly oblige.) Stir it in, along with the drained potatoes and sprouts, the remaining ¾ teaspoon salt, a generous amount of black pepper, and the cream. Mix to get everything thoroughly distributed, then transfer to the prepared pan.

5. Sprinkle the top with the bread crumbs and cheese and dust it lightly with paprika, if desired. Bake for 15 to 20 minutes, or until the cheese is perfectly melted and turning golden. Serve hot or warm.

BURGERS
and SAVORY
PANCAKES

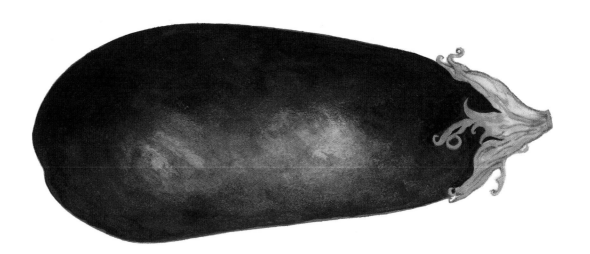

✳ ✳ ✳

How do you make a weeknight dinner feel fresh and exciting?

Grill something to order in a skillet and serve it straight from the pan. It can be a big slice of vegetable, like a thick eggplant circle, lightly coated in Parmesan and briefly sautéed until crisp, then served as a "burger." Or it can be thin zucchini coins and flecks of mint souffléd into dinner pancakes; corn cakes littered with diced vegetables and black beans, sautéed in sizzling butter; or mashed potatoes speckled with finely chopped broccoli, formed into thick and tender disks and browned.

Mash-ups of vegetables, spices, grains, beans, and/or nuts are as front burner as your willingness and imagination will allow. In my lexicon, you are allowed to call anything in individual round (or rectangular) units that have been cooked briefly into an artful interplay of exterior crispness and inner tenderness a "burger." As you will soon see, that definition can embrace everything from a generously proportioned fried green tomatoes, to a slab of spice- and seed-coated tofu, to a "batter burger," made from a combination of soft ingredients. They can all be served with the usual hamburger setup (toasted bun, ketchup, mustard, etc.), or you can serve them on a plate with an assortment of Enhancements.

Savory pancakes are among my favorite things to make. They are batter-based, similar to some of the burgers, but whereas the batter burgers are thick and dense and need some shaping, the pancakes are self-shaping and light.

All of these dinner solutions become yet more fantastic when topped with a slaw (see pages 62 to 66) or a saladita (a cross between a salad and a salsa; see pages 376 to 386), or dabs of flavor (see pages 356 through 375), or a touch of guacamole and salsa, or anything else that appeals to you. Browse through the book; be innovative and bold. No rules.

BATTER BURGER TIPS

Batter burgers—Cumin-Scented Black Bean Burgers, Caramelized Onion–Brown Rice–Lentil Burgers, Mushroom-Barley-Cashew Burgers, and Sweet Potato–Chickpea-Quinoa Burgers—are delicate going into the pan, yet firm up during cooking and come out sturdy. Because the batter is pliable, you can (and will often need to) reshape the burgers once they're in the pan. It's especially important to smooth the top surface while the first side cooks, so it cooks evenly after you turn it.

Thick batter burgers are most attractive when formed with a ⅓-cup measure. Be sure to spray the measure lightly with nonstick cooking spray ahead of time and between each use.

Let each burger become truly crunchy all around on the outer surface and flip it more than once, if necessary (it won't suffer from a lot of handling, as pancakes might). They're delicate, so I wouldn't recommend cooking them on an outdoor grill.

A very hot, oil-slicked pan—not flashed with high heat, but rather deeply heated over medium—will do the best job of cooking these burgers. You can use olive oil for cooking the burgers (as indicated in the ingredient lists) or you can use grapeseed or high-oleic safflower oil, both of which are good high-temperature players.

For best turning results, use a small spatula with an inflexible, thin, square-edged blade. This precise little tool will not only make for easier turning but is the best gadget for efficiently loosening the burger from the pan, so you won't leave any of it behind.

You can make the batter up to a day ahead of forming and cooking the burgers if you keep it covered and refrigerated. Cooked batter burgers also freeze and reheat perfectly. Wrap each burger individually in plastic wrap, then pack them up together and freeze in a heavy zip-style plastic bag. Defrost while still wrapped, then reheat in a toaster oven or in a lightly oiled pan over medium-low heat. You can also warm defrosted burgers in a microwave, but I recommend finishing them in an oil-slicked skillet over medium heat (even if for just a few minutes) so the outside surfaces can regain their crispness.

If you're cooking the burgers in batches, keep the finished ones warm on a baking sheet or an ovenproof plate in a 250°F oven while you make the rest.

Cumin-Scented Black Bean Burgers

MAKES 6 BURGERS

Full-throttle, authentic flavor and just the right amount of heft make these burgers a good choice for meat lovers who'd like a vegetarian burger experience once in a while but don't want to venture too far down Hippie Lane. These are especially wonderful served on warmed, buttered corn tortillas. And, of course, seriously consider the list of Optional Enhancements.

This recipe first appeared in my book *Get Cooking* (William Morrow, 2009).

✺ Whole-wheat bread crumbs "on the fine side" means crumbs that are no larger (and preferably smaller) than lentils. To get a generous cup of tasty crumbs, toast 4 average-sized slices good-quality whole-wheat bread, then pulverize them in a food processor.

✺ To save on cleanup, use the same skillet for sautéing the onion and cooking the burgers (just wipe it out in between—no need to wash it).

✺ If you're cooking the burgers in batches, keep the finished ones warm on a baking sheet or an ovenproof plate in a 250°F oven while you make the rest.

✺ These freeze and reheat beautifully after they've been cooked. Details are on page 291.

2–3 tablespoons olive oil

½ cup finely minced onion

2 teaspoons ground cumin

2 teaspoons minced or crushed garlic

½ teaspoon salt

2 15-ounce cans black beans, rinsed and thoroughly drained, or 3 cups cooked beans

1 large egg, beaten

1 cup whole-wheat bread crumbs
(on the fine side; see note)

Black pepper

Nonstick cooking spray

1. Place a large (10- to 12-inch) skillet over medium heat for about a minute, then add 1 tablespoon oil and swirl to coat the pan. Toss in the onion and cook, stirring often, for about 2 minutes, or until it begins to soften. Add the cumin, garlic, and ¼ teaspoon of the salt and sauté for another 2 to 3 minutes, or until the onion becomes translucent.

2. Transfer the drained beans to a medium-large bowl and use a potato masher or fork to smash them as smooth as possible. Stir in the beaten egg, bread crumbs, the remaining ¼ teaspoon salt, and some pepper. Add the onion (scraping in all its surrounding flavor) and mix until thoroughly combined.

3. Wipe out the skillet and return it to medium heat for another minute or so. When the pan is hot, add a scant ½ tablespoon oil and swirl to coat the pan. (No need to measure—you just want the pan to be thoroughly oil-slicked.) Heat for another minute or so, until the oil is hot enough to sizzle a crumb on contact.

4. Use a nonstick-sprayed ⅓-cup measure to scoop-shape the batter as uniformly as possible. Carefully transfer as many burgers as will fit in a single layer to the hot, oiled pan, knocking the cup handle assertively against the side of the pan or using the back of a spoon to release the batter. Smooth the top surface

with a dinner knife, so the burgers will crisp evenly, and push in the sides so they will hold together and keep their shape as they cook.

5. Reduce the heat to medium-low and cook for about 5 minutes, or until golden brown on the bottom. Use a small spatula with a thin blade to carefully loosen each burger and flip it over, adding a little more oil as needed and pushing the burgers back into shape if they slump or break.

6. Cook on the second side for about another 5 minutes, or until the bottoms are nicely browned. Continue to cook in batches, adding more oil as needed, until all the batter is used. Serve hot or warm.

OPTIONAL ENHANCEMENTS

Serve on a warmed tortilla or with tortilla chips ❋ Thick slices of ripe, in-season tomato or Slow-Roasted Roma Tomatoes (page 393) ❋ Pickled Red Onions (page 395) or Strawberry-Rhubarb Pickles (pages 396) ❋ Guacamole or Avocado "Mayo" (page 373) ❋ A dab of Salsa Verde (page 357) ❋ A dab of sour cream ❋ Jicama–Pink Grapefruit Saladita (page 381) ❋ A few torn cilantro leaves or an Herb Tangle (page 76) ❋ Crumbled feta or fresh cheese ❋ Top with shredded Jack or cheddar while the second side is cooking

Mushroom-Barley-Cashew Burgers

MAKES 8 BURGERS

The surefire match of mushrooms and barley is utterly, reliably satisfying, crunched up with minced cashews. I dub this duo the Ginger Rogers and Fred Astaire of the plant food world.

❋ You can use a standard commercial mozzarella or, if you're in splurge mode, fresh cheese—the kind that comes in a little tub of water. The former is firmer and can be chopped or loosely grated. Fresh mozzarella is too gorgeously soft to chop or grate, but easily tears into fine feathers after it's been patted somewhat dry. Although it's fine either way, fresh mozzarella, if you can swing it, is optimal.

❋ Cook the barley well ahead of time. You don't need to measure the water. Just simmer ½ cup pearl barley in a small saucepan with plenty of water (enough to amply cover) until done to your liking, about 40 minutes. Then drain off any excess water and shake the grains dry. It's fine if the barley is still warm when it enters the burger batter.

❋ To save on cleanup, use the same skillet for sautéing the onion and cooking the burgers (just wipe it out in between—no need to wash it).

❋ If you're cooking the burgers in batches, keep the finished ones warm on a baking sheet or an ovenproof plate in a 250°F oven while you make the rest.

❋ These freeze and reheat beautifully after they've been cooked. Details are on page 291, along with other pearls of burger-building wisdom.

1½ cups cooked barley (from ½ cup uncooked; see note)

2–3 tablespoons olive oil

¾ cup finely minced onion

¼ pound mushrooms (domestic or cremini), wiped clean, stemmed as necessary, and finely minced

½ teaspoon salt, or more to taste

1½ teaspoons minced or crushed garlic

1 tablespoon balsamic vinegar

2 large eggs, beaten

½ (packed) cup grated, chopped, or torn mozzarella

½ cup minced unsalted cashews, lightly toasted

6 tablespoons unbleached all-purpose flour

Black pepper

Nonstick cooking spray

1. Put the cooked barley in a medium-large bowl.

2. Place a large (10- to 12-inch) skillet over medium heat for about a minute, then add 1 tablespoon of the oil, and swirl to coat the pan. Toss in the onion and cook, stirring often, for about 2 minutes, or until it begins to soften. Add the mushrooms and ¼ teaspoon of the salt and continue to sauté for another 2 to 3 minutes, or until the onion becomes translucent.

3. Add the garlic and cook for another 5 to 8 minutes, or until the onion is very tender and the mushrooms have cooked down. Stir in the remaining ¼ teaspoon salt, plus the vinegar, then transfer this mixture to the barley.

4. Stir in the beaten eggs, mozzarella, cashews, and flour. Mix well, taste to correct the salt, and add black pepper to taste. (If you prefer not to ingest raw egg or flour, just "taste" with your inner sense or fry a tiny patty as a test.)

5. Wipe out the skillet and return it to medium heat for another minute or so. When the pan is hot, add a scant ½ tablespoon oil and swirl to coat the pan. (No need to measure—you just want the pan to be thoroughly oil-slicked.) Heat for another minute or so, until the oil is hot enough to sizzle a crumb on contact.

6. Use a nonstick-sprayed ⅓-cup measure to scoop-shape the batter as uniformly as possible. Carefully transfer as many burgers as will fit in a single layer to the hot, oiled pan, knocking the cup handle assertively against the side of the pan or using the back of a spoon to release the batter. Smooth the top surface with a dinner knife, so the burgers will crisp evenly, and push in the sides to help them keep their shape as they cook.

7. Reduce the heat to medium-low and cook for 5 to 8 minutes, or until the burgers are golden on the bottom. Use a small spatula with a thin blade to carefully loosen each burger and flip it over, adding a little more oil as needed and pushing the burgers back into shape if they slump or break.

8. Cook on the second side for another 5 to 8 minutes, or until the bottoms are nicely browned. Continue to cook in batches until all the batter has been used. Serve hot or warm.

OPTIONAL ENHANCEMENTS

Scatter with Crispy Sage Leaves (page 394) ❋ Guacamole or mashed avocado ❋ Your favorite store-bought salsa or Fire-Roasted Bell Pepper Saladita (page 386) ❋ An Herb Tangle (page 76) ❋ Grated Carrot Salad (page 62) on top or on the side ❋ Romesco Sauce (page 359) underneath or on top ❋ Slow-Roasted Roma Tomatoes (page 393)

Caramelized Onion–Brown Rice–Lentil Burgers

MAKES 8 TO 10 BURGERS ❧ VEGAN

Ordinary pantry staples would like to show you just what they can achieve without any additional fancy ingredients muscling their way in. All that's required from you is a little attention—and faith—and these most basic items from your cupboard will deliver beyond expectations.

❀ Short-grain brown rice works best for this recipe, as it cooks up soft and porridge-like, which is exactly what we want in a burger batter.

❀ Both the rice-lentil mixture and the onions need to cook separately for about 40 minutes. Beyond that, this recipe is very low maintenance.

❀ If you're cooking the burgers in batches, keep the finished ones warm on a baking sheet or an ovenproof plate in a 250°F oven while you make the others.

❀ These freeze and reheat beautifully after they've been cooked. Details are on page 291, along with other burger advice.

1 cup short-grain brown rice

1 cup brown lentils

3 cups water

3–4 tablespoons olive oil

4 cups finely minced onions (2 large)

1 teaspoon salt

Up to 2 teaspoons soy sauce

1 tablespoon balsamic vinegar

Black pepper

Nonstick cooking spray

1. Combine the rice, lentils, and water in a medium-large saucepan and bring to a boil. Lower the heat to a simmer, cover, and cook undisturbed (with a heat diffuser, if you have one, underneath) until everything is very tender and all the water is absorbed, about 40 minutes. If the mixture gets a bit mushy (and the lentils definitely will), that's perfectly fine.

2. Meanwhile, place a large (10- to 12-inch) skillet over medium heat for about a minute, then add 2 tablespoons of the oil and swirl to coat the pan. Toss in the onions and cook, stirring often, for about 5 minutes, or until the onions become soft. Add ½ teaspoon of the salt, reduce the heat to medium-low, and cook, stirring occasionally, for another 20 to 35 minutes, or until the onions are entirely soft and sweet.

3. Add the rice-lentil mixture to the onions and cook and mash together for another 10 minutes or so over very low heat. Gradually add the remaining ½ teaspoon salt, the soy sauce, vinegar, and a generous amount of black pepper.

4. Place a second large skillet over medium heat for about a minute, then add a scant ½ tablespoon oil and swirl to coat the pan. Heat for another minute or so, until the oil is hot enough to sizzle a crumb on contact.

[continues]

5. Use a nonstick-sprayed ⅓-cup measure to scoop-shape the batter as uniformly as possible. Carefully transfer as many burgers as will fit in a single layer to the hot, oiled pan, knocking the cup handle assertively against the side of the pan or using the back of a spoon to release the batter. Smooth the top surface with a dinner knife, so the burgers will crisp evenly, and push in the sides to help them keep their shape as they cook.

6. Reduce the heat to medium-low and cook for 3 to 4 minutes, or until golden on the bottom. Use a small spatula with a thin blade to carefully loosen each burger and flip it over, adding a little more oil as needed and pushing the burgers back into shape if they slump or break.

7. Cook on the second side for another 3 to 4 minutes, or until the bottoms are nicely browned. Continue to cook in batches, adding more oil as needed, until all the batter has been used. Serve hot or warm.

OPTIONAL ENHANCEMENTS

Pickled Red Onions (page 395) ❋ Strawberry-Rhubarb Pickles (page 396) ❋ Avocado "Mayo" (page 373) ❋ Wasabi Mayonnaise (page 372) ❋ Cantaloupe-Basil Saladita (page 386), Sweet Corn and Blueberry Saladita (page 383), or Celery-Almond-Date Saladita (page 376) ❋ Tahini-Ginger-Pomegranate Sauce (page 360) ❋ Crispy Fried Lemons (page 389)

Sweet Potato–Chickpea-Quinoa Burgers

MAKES 10 OR 11 BURGERS ❁ VEGAN

When it comes to sweet potatoes, American cuisine needs some imagination, and these irresistible burgers are here to help. Just throw a cooked sweet potato into your trusty food processor, along with chickpeas, scallions, and spices, and buzz it into orange tastiness.

Two complementary iterations of quinoa (whole cooked grains and flour) step in to balance the sweetness—and also to hold the burgers together—while upping the protein and calcium content. Green pea polka dots round it out in every way, making this taste and color fest even more fun and interesting.

❁ Be sure to use the moist, orange variety of sweet potato (not the drier, starchier white type).

❁ Regarding the quinoa flour: Don't panic. Just get out the inexpensive electric coffee grinder that you dedicated to spice grinding, wipe it out thoroughly, and add 6 tablespoons of whole quinoa. Buzz for less than 5 seconds, and you've got your ingredient—probably slightly more than the amount you'll need for the recipe.

❁ If you're using fresh peas, they'll need to be steamed or blanched for about 5 minutes. Frozen ones require only to be defrosted in a strainer—a brief encounter with room-temperature tap

[continues]

water, then a shake to dry. Either of these steps can be done ahead.

❋ Begin cooking the sweet potato well ahead of time, so it can cool before you assemble the batter. This is also a good use for leftover plain mashed sweet potatoes. You'll need 2 cups.

❋ Toasting cumin seeds is most easily done in a small, dry skillet over low heat. Shake the pan as you go and pay careful attention. It takes only a few minutes to toast them—and a blink of an eye beyond that to irreparably burn them. You can use the same pan (and same method) to toast the peanuts, if you wish.

❋ If you're cooking the burgers in batches, keep the finished ones warm on a baking sheet or an ovenproof plate in a 250°F oven while you make the rest.

❋ These freeze and reheat beautifully after they've been cooked. Details are on page 291, along with other burger-building tips.

⅓ cup quinoa

1 medium orange sweet potato (¾ pound)

1½ cups cooked chickpeas or one 15-ounce can, rinsed and thoroughly drained

1 heaping tablespoon finely minced fresh ginger

1 teaspoon minced or crushed garlic

3 scallions (whites plus light greens), cut into 1-inch pieces

¾ teaspoon salt, or more to taste

2 teaspoons cumin seeds, lightly toasted

2–3 tablespoons fresh lemon juice, or to taste

6 tablespoons quinoa flour (see note)

1 cup green peas (steamed fresh or defrosted frozen)

1 cup unsalted peanuts, lightly toasted (optional)

Crushed red pepper

About 2 tablespoons grapeseed or high-oleic safflower oil for frying

Nonstick cooking spray

1. Combine the quinoa and ½ cup water in a very small saucepan with a lid. Bring to a boil, cover the pot, and lower the heat to the slowest possible simmer, with a heat diffuser, if you have one, underneath. You'll have cooked quinoa in about 20 minutes. Uncover, fluff with a fork, and set aside.

2. Meanwhile, cut the sweet potato into rounds about 1½ inches thick and steam over or cook in boiling water until fork-soft, about 15 minutes. Cool until comfortable to handle. Strip off and discard the peels and transfer to a food processor.

3. Add the chickpeas, ginger, garlic, scallions, ¾ teaspoon salt, cumin, and 2 tablespoons of the lemon juice to the sweet potato and process until reasonably blended. It doesn't need to be completely smooth.

4. Transfer the mixture to a bowl, then sprinkle in the cooked quinoa and the quinoa flour. Stir until all the quinoa disappears into the mixture. Gently fold in the green peas and peanuts, if using. Taste to see if it needs more salt or lemon juice and add a few big pinches of crushed red pepper flakes to taste.

5. Place a medium skillet over medium heat for about a minute, then add a scant ½ tablespoon oil and swirl to coat the pan. Heat for a little longer, until the oil is hot enough to instantly sizzle a dot of the sweet potato mixture. Turn the heat to low.

6. Use a nonstick-sprayed ⅓-cup measure to scoop-shape the batter as uniformly as possible. Carefully transfer as many burgers as will fit in a single layer to the hot, oiled pan, knocking the cup handle assertively against the side of the pan or using the back of a spoon to release the batter. Smooth the top surface with a dinner knife, so the burgers will crisp evenly, and push in the sides to help them keep their shape as they cook.

7. Cook over low heat for 8 to 10 minutes, or until golden brown on the bottom. (Longer cooking is OK—just not hotter. The sugar content of sweet potatoes causes them to burn easily at higher temperatures.) Use a small spatula with a thin blade to carefully loosen each burger and flip it over, adding more oil as needed and pushing the burgers back into shape if they slump or break.

8. Cook on the second side for 8 to 10 minutes, or until the bottoms are nicely browned. Continue to cook in batches until all the batter has been used. Serve hot or warm.

OPTIONAL ENHANCEMENTS

Toasted peanuts on top ❋ Steamed peas on top ❋ An Herb Tangle (page 76) ❋ Yogurt or Raita (Indian-Style Yogurt Dip; page 371) ❋ Salsa Verde (page 357) ❋ A drizzle of pomegranate molasses (see note, page 118) or Pomegranate-Lime Glaze (page 369) on top ❋ Sweet-Sour Dipping-Drizzling Sauce (page 370) ❋ A touch of Pistachio Smash (page 402) ❋ A side of Asian Slaw (page 62) ❋ A topping of Tofu "Noodles," Coconut Version (page 399)

Cajun-Style Tofu Burgers

MAKES 4 BURGERS ❧ VEGAN

Creamy slabs of tofu encrusted with crunchy seeds and an assertive spice mix are cooked in the Cajun ("blackened") style: i.e., slapped into a very hot, unoiled pan, so the outside sears upon contact. You will be rewarded with a contrasting golden, smoky, texture-dense outer surface and a luxurious interior that slides down like the bona fide comfort food it is.

You can play with the spices, swapping in some others you might like to try and/or adjusting the ratio of what's already included to make this your own.

❀ Simmering the tofu helps make it even firmer, so it will hold up better during the coating and cooking process.

❀ Leftover burgers can be reheated in a toaster oven, a lightly oiled skillet over medium heat, or a microwave.

1 pound very firm tofu, cut into 4 slabs (about ¾ inch thick)

1½ tablespoons cumin seeds

1½ tablespoons sesame seeds

1 teaspoon dried thyme

1 teaspoon sweet paprika

1 teaspoon smoked paprika (optional)

¼ teaspoon garlic powder

¼ teaspoon black pepper

¾ teaspoon salt

1. Put on a medium-large pot of water to boil. When the water boils, turn the heat to low and add the tofu. Simmer for 10 minutes, then use a slotted spoon to gently slip the slabs into a colander to drain, being careful so they don't break.

2. Meanwhile, combine the spices and salt in a pie pan, mix to thoroughly blend, and spread in an even layer.

3. Place a large (10- to 12-inch), heavy skillet over medium heat for about a minute. (Turn on the stove fan and/or open a window if you can. This will be a bit smoky.)

4. Meanwhile, gently place the tofu, one piece at a time, into the spice mix, pressing it down to coat first one side and then the other. (You can also just leave it on the first side and sprinkle/press spice mix to coat the top.) Transfer the coated pieces to a clean plate.

5. When the pan is hot enough to instantly sizzle a speck of spice mix, carefully transfer as many coated tofu slabs to the heated pan as will fit in a single layer and cook undisturbed for about 2 minutes, or until golden underneath.

6. Use a sturdy spatula with a thin blade to carefully loosen each tofu slab and flip it over. Cook for another 2 minutes, or until the bottom surfaces match the tops. (If some of the spice mix falls off, just pick it up and put it back on. Most of it will stick. You can also push some of the fallen spices onto the sides of the tofu.) Continue to cook in batches until all the tofu is used. Serve hot.

OPTIONAL ENHANCEMENTS

There will be a lot of flavor left in the pan. You can retrieve it by pouring in 1 to 2 tablespoons olive oil (be careful—it will sizzle) to pick up all the leftover spice mix, plus its imparted essence. Spoon this over the tops of the burgers for a delightful finish. ❋ Serve on split, toasted baguettes, with a thick layer of hummus and/or mashed avocado on the other side of the bread. Garnish with fresh parsley, sliced cucumbers, and cherry tomatoes. ❋ Serve on a bed of Green Rice (page 94) ❋ Top with a spoonful of Beet, Orange, and Ginger Marmalade (page 374) ❋ Top or surround with Peanut Coleslaw (page 64) ❋ Pile on some Slow-Roasted Roma Tomatoes (page 393)

Grilled Tempeh and Tofu Fingers Infused with Miso Vinaigrette

MAKES 6 TO 8 SERVINGS ✿ VEGAN (WHEN MADE WITH AGAVE NECTAR OR SUGAR)

Pumped up with one of the more intense vinaigrettes in my playbook, these little fingers of grilled tofu and tempeh could well exceed anything you might be expecting.

Serve them as you would any tasty morsels from the grill at any barbecue: plain, with salads on the side, on top of or next to cooked grains or polenta. They are bound to attract new fans, even among the most vehement soy skeptics.

✿ The marinade is a bit sharper than the usual. That will serve to royally infuse the tempeh and tofu with the level of assertive flavor they need.

✿ Allow at least 90 minutes of marinating time before grilling. You can also marinate the tofu and tempeh 1 to 2 days ahead of time. Store them together in the marinating pan, covered with foil or plastic wrap, in the refrigerator.

✿ Tofu and tempeh have different rates of absorbing the vinaigrette, so it works best to marinate them sequentially. The tofu will pick up a ton of flavor but soak up very little of the liquid, all in a relatively short time. Put it in first and then take it out and marinate the tempeh, which hoovers up the marinade with gusto. For effective marination, use a baking dish or gratin pan that is a good fit for the volume of ingredients.

✿ If you have the equipment and don't mind the extra cleanup, consider running two pans of these at the same time.

✿ Soak the grill pan in hot water as soon as you're done cooking for easiest cleanup.

½ cup light (shiro) miso (see page 267) or any variety you prefer

¼ cup red or white wine vinegar

2 teaspoons agave nectar, light-colored honey, or sugar

2 teaspoons minced or crushed garlic

½ teaspoon dried thyme or 2 teaspoons minced fresh

½ teaspoon salt

Black pepper

6 tablespoons extra-virgin olive oil

¾ pound very firm tofu

½ pound tempeh

Nonstick cooking spray

1. Combine the miso, vinegar, sweetener, garlic, thyme, salt, and a generous amount of black pepper in a large, wide pan, such as a baking pan or gratin dish, and whisk to thoroughly blend.

2. Whisk in the olive oil a little at a time, allowing each application to become completely incorporated before adding the next.

3. Cut the tofu into ¼-inch-thick strips and arrange the strips in a single layer in the marinade. Spoon marinade over the top and let them sit at room temperature (or in the refrigerator, if your kitchen is very hot) for at least 30 minutes (and as long as an hour). Transfer them to a plate (it's OK if some of the thick vinaigrette adheres) and set aside.

4. Cut the tempeh into ½-inch-thick strips and arrange them similarly in the remaining marinade. Let them soak for about an hour (longer is fine).

5. Lightly spray a ridged grill pan or a large (10- to 12-inch) skillet with nonstick spray and heat the pan over medium heat for about 2 minutes. Lay on both kinds of marinated strips in a single layer—it's OK if they touch. (The tofu will splatter when it hits the hot pan, so stand back. Also, you might want to turn on your exhaust fan or open a window, as there will be significant vinegar fumes.)

6. Reduce the heat to medium-low and cook the strips on each side in batches for 3 to 5 minutes, or until grill marks show up and/or the surfaces darken appetizingly, being careful to prevent them from becoming too dark or burning. (Miso is sensitive to heat.) Use a small spatula with a thin blade to loosen the bottoms and the edge of a wooden spoon to scrape up and push to the side any solids that may stick to the pan.

7. Remove the strips from the pan and let them sit on a plate for about 10 minutes before you serve them, so they can reabsorb some of the marinade. Serve at any temperature.

OPTIONAL ENHANCEMENTS

Serve on a bed of freshly cooked brown basmati rice ✳ Frame with Sweet Corn and Blueberry Saladita (page 383) and top with Slow-Roasted Roma Tomatoes (page 393) ✳ Spoon on a big dab of Caramelized Onion and Lemon Marmalade (page 375) ✳ Top with a small dollop of Chipotle Cream (page 371)

Seitan Medallions in Good Gravy

MAKES 4 OR 5 SERVINGS ❋ VEGAN

Seitan is pure wheat gluten cooked up into a pleasantly chewy state, and it should win the prize in the vegetarian "tastes like chicken" sweepstakes. The protein content is high and the flavor is mild and highly diplomatic, which is to say it blends very well with other ingredients and is compatible with many taste themes.

You can buy seitan premade, but it is much more economical (and supereasy) to make your own from scratch. Here is my basic version, which comes with its own gravy, so it's more than ready for prime time. For a vegetarian rendition of an American nostalgia dinner, serve this over mashed potatoes with a side of Green Beans, Edamame, and Peas (page 330). In addition, I recommend you keep it around as a sturdy, reliable, and harmonious addition to the creative modular vegetarian plates that I hope you will invent.

❋ Gluten flour is available in 1-pound bags in natural food stores and online. The brand I use is Bob's Red Mill.

❋ This keeps for up to a week in your refrigerator and reheats seamlessly.

1 quart vegetable stock (page 22) or low-sodium store-bought

1 cup gluten flour (see note)

1 cup water

1 tablespoon olive oil

½ cup finely minced shallot or onion

About 6 medium mushrooms, wiped clean, stemmed, and finely minced (optional)

Big pinches of rubbed dried sage and dried thyme (and, if desired, marjoram)

½ teaspoon minced or crushed garlic

1 tablespoon unbleached all-purpose flour

Salt, soy sauce, or Bragg Liquid Aminos (see note, page 37; optional)

Black pepper

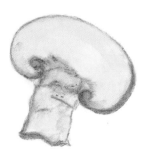

1. Put on the vegetable stock to boil in a medium covered pot over medium heat.

2. Meanwhile, in a medium bowl, combine the gluten flour with the water and whisk to combine. It should come together easily and will quickly form a spongy mass. Use your hands to shape it into a log about 8 inches long and 3 inches wide. Let the seitan rest while the stock comes to a boil.

3. Slice the seitan crosswise into medallions about ½ inch thick, add the slices to the boiling stock, reduce the heat to very low, and simmer, partially covered, for 45 minutes. Have a colander resting on a shallow plate near the stove.

4. Remove the seitan with a slotted spoon and transfer it to the colander to rest while you make the gravy. Let the stock continue to bubble away uncovered over low heat for about 15 minutes, until it is reduced to about 2½ cups. You can eyeball it, or measure it, if you'd like to be more exact.

5. Place a large (10- to 12-inch), deep skillet over medium heat for about a minute, then add the olive oil and swirl to coat the pan. Toss in the shallot or onion and the mushrooms, if using, and sprinkle with the herbs. Cook, stirring often, for about 3 minutes. Stir in the garlic and continue to cook, stirring frequently for 5 minutes, or until the shallot is very soft. If using the mushrooms, you may need to cook it for a few minutes longer, or until the mushrooms have cooked down and expressed their liquid.

6. Reduce the heat to low and whisk in the all-purpose flour. Continue whisking over low heat for a minute or two, or until the flour is evenly distributed and the mixture thickens.

7. Whisk in the reduced stock, then switch to a wooden spoon and stir over low heat until it becomes a thick gravy, about 10 minutes.

8. Season to taste with a little salt or a few drops of soy sauce or Bragg Liquid Aminos, if desired, and some pepper. Add the seitan to the hot gravy, stirring until it is completely coated, and serve.

Crispy-Coated Eggplant Parmesan "Burgers"

MAKES 4 TO 6 SERVINGS (2 OR 3 SLICES PER SERVING)

The burgerization of eggplant (appreciated by everyone, except, apparently, my spell-checker) is pro-vegetablism at its best. To that end, I've combined two well-loved standards—grilled eggplant and eggplant Parmesan—into a single recipe.

The overview: Hefty eggplant slices are egg-dipped, pressed into herbed Parmesan, and lovingly sizzled in a slick of hot oil. The result? Delightful, slightly salty, golden crispness covering a melted center—as good on a bun as it is just plain, forked up from a plate.

❋ Use a big, chubby eggplant, rather than the long, narrow kind, to ensure uniform, round slices of burger dimensions. You want it to be shiny, smooth, and tight-skinned—without soft spots or blemishes—since you will not be peeling it. (Eggplant peel is edible, although some recipes recommend removing it. Not this one.)

❋ An optional but very worthwhile first step, if you give yourself a little extra time: Salt the eggplant slices lightly and let them sweat ahead of time. This makes a flavor difference, although it is not essential. If you choose to do this, mop them with a paper towel when they are finished with their salt scrub.

❋ You'll likely need to cook these in batches. If you have the equipment and don't mind the extra cleanup, consider running two pans at the same time, so dinner can be ready sooner. If you get the pan(s) hot enough and work attentively, there should be very little, if any, scrubbing needed in the aftermath.

❋ Ideally, the oil will do its work from the outside without being absorbed by the eggplant. A thoroughly heated pan coated with just a slick of oil is key to keeping the eggplant from becoming a sponge.

❋ Although the burgers can be refrigerated and later reheated, they don't improve with age. Slightly puffed when freshly cooked, they will shrink with time. If you do store and reheat them (or just want to keep the early ones warm, as you make these in shifts), transfer them to a wire rack on a baking sheet in a 250°F oven to help keep them crisp. And consider doubling the recipe, as they'll be a good deal thinner later.

1 large eggplant (about 1¼ pounds), unpeeled

Salt

1½ cups finely grated Parmesan

Black pepper

Pinches of dried thyme, dried oregano, and/or rubbed dried sage (optional)

2 large eggs

2–3 tablespoons olive oil

1. Slice off and discard the eggplant's ends, then cut the rest crosswise into ½-inch-thick slices. You should end up with 10 or 11 rounds.

2. If you have time, salt the eggplant slices lightly and let them sit for 10 minutes or longer, then flip and do the other side. They can rest on the cutting board during this process—no need to drain. When they've sweated visibly, mop them gently all over with a paper towel.

3. On a dinner plate, combine the Parmesan, a dash or two of salt (if you didn't salt the eggplant), and some pepper. Add a few pinches of dried herbs, if you like, and mix to combine. Have ready another dinner plate or two, plus some damp paper towels to wipe your hands as needed.

4. Break the eggs into a pie pan and beat them with a fork or small whisk until smooth.

5. Place a large (10- to 12-inch) skillet over medium heat for about a minute, then add a tablespoon of the oil and swirl to coat the pan. Wait another minute or so, until the oil is hot enough to sizzle a crumb on contact.

6. Dip the eggplant slices, one at a time, into the egg, then let any excess egg drip off back into the bowl. (The eggplant will resist holding the egg beyond a slight dampening, and that is fine.) Put each moistened round into the Parmesan, pressing it down firmly so it adheres. Turn it over and press the second side into the cheese until it becomes completely coated all over. Resist the temptation to shake off the extra cheese, then transfer each coated slice to a plate (or directly to the pan).

7. Carefully transfer as many coated eggplant slices as will fit in a single layer to the hot pan. Cook undisturbed for 4 to 5 minutes, or until golden brown on the bottoms. Use a small spatula with a thin blade to carefully loosen each piece, keeping its coating intact (you don't want to lose any of it to the pan). Flip and cook on the second side for another 4 to 5 minutes, until the coating is evenly golden all over and the eggplant becomes fork-tender (or finger-tender, as you can tell if it's done by gently pressing). Cook the remaining eggplant, drizzling in additional olive oil as you go if the pan seems dry.

8. Transfer the cooked slices to a plate or a rack (see note) and repeat with the remaining slices. Serve as soon as possible.

OPTIONAL ENHANCEMENTS

Dabs of Salsa Verde (page 357) or basil pesto ❋ Serve open-faced on thick slabs of grilled garlic bread, then add a slice of heirloom tomato and some sliced or grated mozzarella and broil ❋ Top with a spoonful of Romesco Sauce or Muhammara (page 359) ❋ Make a platter with Browned Potatoes and Onion (page 391) and Flash-Fried Kale with Garlic, Almonds, and Cheese (page 346) ❋ Surround with a slaw (see page 66) ❋ Dab on a spot of Miso-Almond Sauce (page 361)

Fried Green Tomato "Burgers"

MAKES 3 OR 4 SERVINGS (2 OR 3 SLICES PER SERVING) ❦ **VEGAN (WHEN MADE WITHOUT THE BUTTER)**

Tart, cornmeal-crunchy, and dripping with juice, fried green tomatoes are traditionally served as an appetizer or side dish. In this recipe, we're making them burger-thick and serving them center stage, possibly with a fried egg on top or Tempeh Croutons (page 405) underneath. I also highly recommend these as a topping for Mac, Chili, and Cheese (page 238).

❦ The tomatoes don't have to be literally green, as long as they're unripe and hard. Some unripe tomatoes are a pale pink. But some heirloom varieties are bright green when perfectly ripe, and they will soften up so much during this cooking process that they will slip into shapelessness and you will have sauce.

❦ Use a small spatula with an inflexible, thin blade for turning the tomatoes, assertively scraping the surface of the pan as you lift them. This ensures that you won't accidentally separate the delicious cornmeal coating from the tomato. (And if that does happen, just shovel up the orphaned cornmeal and return it to the tomato.)

❦ Because the insides of the tomatoes become very hot and retain that heat for longer than you might think, allow up to 10 minutes between cooking and serving. The tomatoes will still be plenty warm, and no one will suffer a burnt mouth. If you like, place the cooked tomatoes on a wire rack during the waiting period, to retain crispness. In the meantime, you can fry another batch.

2 large or 3 medium unripe tomatoes
(about 1 pound; just this side of baseball-hard)

½ heaping cup cornmeal

¼ heaping teaspoon salt

1 tablespoon olive oil, plus more as needed

About 1 teaspoon butter, plus more as needed
(optional)

1. Core the tomatoes and thinly slice off the ends. Cut each tomato into three or four ½-inch-thick slices and set them aside.

2. Combine the cornmeal and salt on a dinner plate and mix until uniform.

3. Dredge the tomato slices in the cornmeal mixture, pressing the mixture into the cut surfaces to create a thick coating.

4. Place a large (10- to 12-inch) skillet over medium heat for about a minute, then add 1 tablespoon of the oil and swirl to coat the pan. Melt in the butter, if desired, and tilt the pan to distribute the butter. When it's hot enough to instantly sizzle a crumb, add as many of the coated tomatoes as will fit.

5. Fry as many tomatoes as will fit in a single layer for 8 to 10 minutes, or until crisp and golden, turning once and scraping from the bottom as you turn them over to include all the coating. Add more oil and/or butter as needed, to prevent sticking.

6. Remove the tomatoes from the pan, ideally placing them on a wire rack to stay crisp. Wait for at least 5 minutes (and up to 10) before serving, so the insides can cool down a little. Continue to cook in batches until all the tomatoes have been used.

7. Serve warm, with some or (m)any of the Optional Enhancements.

OPTIONAL ENHANCEMENTS

A fried or poached egg on top (plain or Olive Oil–Bread Crumb–Coated Fried Eggs, page 408) ✳ Tempeh Croutons (page 405) underneath ✳ Add 2 tablespoons grated or shredded Parmesan to the cornmeal ✳ Black pepper (a coarse grind is nice) ✳ A sprinkling of coarse salt on top after they're cooked ✳ Dab of Salsa Verde (page 357) ✳ Crumbled feta or Grilled Haloumi Cheese (page 406) ✳ A spot of crème fraîche or sour cream ✳ Chipotle Cream (page 371) ✳ A sprinkling of Chili Pepitas (page 401) ✳ Avocado "Mayo" (page 373) ✳ A side of Celery-Almond-Date Saladita (page 376)

Bulgur-Walnut Kibbeh Balls

MAKES 2 DOZEN KIBBEHS (4 SERVINGS AS A MAIN DISH; 6 SERVINGS AS AN APPETIZER)
❁ VEGAN (WHEN MADE WITHOUT THE BUTTER)

Exotic little faux meatballs made from finely ground bulgur, minced walnuts, and touches of spice are so satisfying that even fans of real meatballs will enjoy them.

My favorite way to serve these is on a small plate, in a modest pool of yogurt, Raita (page 371), or Tahini-Ginger-Pomegranate Sauce (page 360), with very sweet, small cherry tomatoes scattered all around. Add sliced radishes and a few olives and throw on some torn leaves of cilantro or mint, and welcome to your new favorite appetizer.

❁ It's important to use the fine-grade ("#1 grade") bulgur, in order for the kibbehs to hold together. This is commonly available in Middle Eastern groceries and online. (Sadaf is a reliably findable brand.) If you can't find it, buzz some coarser bulgur in a food processor until it resembles a coarse meal, like a very rough polenta.

❁ Make the kibbeh mixture far enough ahead to allow it to cool before you form it into balls. If you are inclined to plan, I recommend doing this the day before.

❁ Use a medium-large skillet with a tight-fitting lid.

❁ If you're cooking the kibbehs in batches, keep the finished ones warm on a baking sheet or an ovenproof plate in a 250°F oven while you make the rest.

❁ These reheat very well in a lightly oiled pan over medium heat or a toaster oven or microwave.

2 tablespoons olive oil, plus more for cooking the kibbehs

1 cup finely minced onion

½ teaspoon ground cumin

1 teaspoon minced or crushed garlic

1 cup fine (#1) bulgur (see note)

½ cup finely minced walnuts

Up to ½ teaspoon salt

Black pepper and/or crushed red pepper

2 cups boiling water

2 tablespoons pomegranate molasses (see note, page 118)

1 tablespoon fresh lemon juice

2 tablespoons tomato paste

A little butter for the pan (optional)

1. Place a medium-large skillet with a lid over medium heat for about a minute, then add 1 tablespoon of the oil and swirl to coat the pan. Add the onion and cumin and cook, stirring, over medium heat for about 3 minutes, or until the onion softens. Add the garlic and sauté for another 3 minutes.

2. Add another tablespoon of oil, then stir in the bulgur, walnuts, salt, and pepper(s). Cook, stirring, over medium heat for 5 to 8 minutes, or until toasty and aromatic, then add 1 cup of the boiling water. (It will steam and sizzle dramatically upon contact.) Give it a quick stir and it will disappear in just a few seconds.

3. Stir in the pomegranate molasses, lemon juice, and tomato paste. Add the remaining 1 cup boiling water and stir to combine. After all the liquid is absorbed (about 10 minutes), reduce the heat to low. Cook for another 2 minutes or so, then cover the pan, turn off the heat, and let it sit for 30 minutes.

4. Uncover the pan and let the mixture cool until comfortable to handle. (You can also transfer it to a container with a tight-fitting lid and chill until cold, for easiest handling.)

5. Have a dinner plate or two ready. Wet your hands and make little balls (about 1 inch in diameter) of the mixture, pushing the kibbeh into itself and rolling it slightly in your palms until round. Place the finished balls on the plate(s), cover with plastic wrap, and refrigerate until cooking time.

6. About 15 minutes before serving, heat a medium-large skillet over medium heat for about a minute, then add ½ tablespoon or so of olive oil and swirl to coat the pan. You can also melt in a little butter, if you like. Sauté the kibbehs, turning them with tongs to heat them through and allow all surfaces to brown and crisp, at least 10 minutes. Serve hot or warm.

OPTIONAL ENHANCEMENTS

Surround with Orange-Olive-Fig Saladita (page 385) ✵ Serve some Salsa Verde (page 357) or Pomegranate-Lime Glaze (page 369) on the side for dipping ✵ Make a meze plate with your favorite hummus, Slow-Roasted Roma Tomatoes (page 393), Grilled Haloumi Cheese (page 406), Crudité "Chips" (see page 77), and assorted olives ✵ Serve on a bed of Golden Lentils with Soft, Sweet Onions (page 182) or Smoky Mashed Caramelized Eggplant and Onions (page 175)

Walnut-Coated, Broccoli-Speckled Mashed Potato Cakes

MAKES 5 SERVINGS (2 CAKES PER SERVING) ❧ VEGAN (WHEN MADE WITHOUT THE BUTTER)

Green-flecked and soft on the inside, and darkly golden and crunchy on the outside, this is how to embed broccoli in mashed potatoes. I've served these many times to consistently exuberant reviews, with no one ever fully identifying all the ingredients.

✿ The mustard can be plain yellow or Dijon. It can also be wasabi paste. Needless to say, wasabi will take it into the hot zone, so exercise the mindfulness doctrine of the Tao of Zing.

✿ Grind the walnuts by pulsing them in short spurts in a food processor until they resemble bread crumbs (slightly coarser than polenta).

✿ Keep the finished cakes warm on a baking sheet or an ovenproof plate in a 250°F oven as you go.

✿ You can make and coat the patties up to a day in advance, storing them on a plate, tightly covered with plastic wrap, in the refrigerator. You can also finish them completely (frying included) and store them in the refrigerator overnight. Reheat the next day in a toaster oven (10 minutes at 300°F). Perfect!

✿ These freeze and reheat beautifully after they've been cooked. Defrost thoroughly before reheating.

2 cups finely minced broccoli florets and peeled stems (about 6 ounces)

2 medium russet potatoes (about 1 pound)

1–2 tablespoons prepared mustard or wasabi paste (less if using wasabi)

Up to 2 tablespoons minced fresh dill (optional)

1 teaspoon minced or crushed garlic

½ cup finely minced scallions

½ teaspoon salt, or more to taste

Black pepper

1¼ cups ground walnuts (see note)

2–3 tablespoons olive oil or grapeseed oil

A touch of butter (optional)

1. Put a medium pot of water on to boil. Have the minced broccoli waiting in a strainer or colander perched over a second pot in the sink. When the water boils, pour it over the broccoli to cook it slightly, reserving the water. Drain the broccoli well, shaking off all the excess water, then transfer it to a kitchen towel, spreading it out and patting it completely dry. Return the second pot of water to the stove and return the colander to the sink (there's no need to clean it).

2. Peel the potatoes, then cut them into 1-inch chunks. Add them to the pot of water, making sure there's enough water to more than cover the potatoes. Bring it to a boil, then lower the heat and simmer until the potatoes become very soft, about 15 minutes. Use a ladle to scoop out and save about ½ cup of the cooking water, then drain the potatoes into the colander (it's OK if some water clings).

3. Return the potatoes to the pot and mash with a hand masher or immersion blender until smooth, adding about a tablespoon of the cooking water if needed. You should have about 1½ cups mashed potatoes.

4. Transfer the mashed potatoes to a medium bowl. Add the broccoli, mustard or wasabi, dill (if using), garlic, scallions, ½ teaspoon of the salt, and some black pepper. Mix until everything is thoroughly blended, then taste to see if it needs more salt.

5. Use your hands (wet them, if you like, for easier handling) to form the mixture into ten 3-inch cakes—about ¼ cup apiece.

6. Place the ground walnuts on a dinner plate. Press each cake gently but firmly into the ground walnuts to generously coat the entire surface on both sides.

7. Place a large (10- to 12-inch) skillet over medium heat for about a minute, then add a scant tablespoon of the oil and swirl to coat the pan. If you'd like, you can also melt in a touch of butter. When the oil is hot enough to instantly sizzle a dot of the mixture, turn the heat to medium-low. Fry the cakes in batches (wiping out the pan in between and adding more oil and butter), for 2 to 3 minutes on each side, until the walnuts are golden and crisp all over (but not too dark) and the cakes are heated through. Serve hot or warm.

OPTIONAL ENHANCEMENTS

Serve with Apple-Parsley Saladita (page 386) or Citrusy Beets (page 98) ✹ Top with a Feathered Fennel Variation (page 74) ✹ Top with a generous spoonful of Fire-Roasted Bell Pepper Saladita (page 380) or your favorite store-bought salsa ✹ Dab with Wasabi Mayonnaise (page 372) ✹ Spoon on some Raita (page 371)

Fully Loaded Buttermilk Corn Cakes

MAKES 3 OR 4 SERVINGS (3 OR 4 CAKES PER SERVING)

Brimming with bell pepper, jalapeño, black beans, and corn kernels, these cakes are a reliable crowd-pleaser. Once the vegetables are minced, the rest comes together fast.

❋ Use regular, finely milled yellow cornmeal, not the coarser polenta.

❋ Ideally, you will be making this with fresh, sweet corn recently shaved from the cobs. Frozen corn is also OK. Defrost it in a strainer under room-temperature tap water for about 25 seconds. Shake off the water and dry completely.

❋ Wash your hands, knife, and cutting board with warm, soapy water after handling the jalapeños.

❋ To keep the corn cakes warm, transfer them to a wire rack on a baking sheet in a 200°F oven until serving time. (The rack keeps them crisp.)

1 tablespoon olive oil

¼ cup finely minced red bell pepper

Up to ¼ cup finely minced jalapeño (optional)

2 cups corn kernels (from about 4 freshly shucked ears) or defrosted frozen corn (see note)

¾ cup cooked black beans (about half a 15-ounce can), rinsed, drained, and blotted dry with a towel

¼ cup finely minced scallions

½ cup cornmeal

½ cup unbleached all-purpose flour

½ teaspoon salt

1 teaspoon baking powder

½ teaspoon baking soda

1 cup buttermilk

2 large eggs

Nonstick cooking spray

Up to 3 tablespoons unsalted butter

1. Place a medium skillet over medium heat for about a minute, then add the oil and swirl to coat the pan. Toss in the bell pepper, jalapeño (if using), and corn, reduce the heat to medium-low, and cook, stirring, for about 10 minutes, or until the pepper is soft and everything is shiny. Remove from the heat, stir in the black beans and scallions, and set aside.

2. Combine the dry ingredients in a medium bowl and make a well in the center.

3. Measure the buttermilk into a 2-cup liquid measure. Add the eggs and beat with a fork or a small whisk until smooth.

4. Add the buttermilk mixture and the sautéed vegetables, scraping the pan to include all the oil, into the well in the center of the dry ingredients. Using a spoon or a rubber spatula, stir from the bottom of the bowl until the dry ingredients are all moistened. Don't overmix; a few small lumps are OK.

5. Spray a skillet or griddle with nonstick spray and heat it over medium heat, then melt in a little butter and swirl to coat the pan. Heat for about 30 seconds (or until the pan is really hot). Use a ¼-cup measure to scoop as many cakes as will fit in a single layer into the pan and fry for 2 to 3 minutes on each side, or until golden. Continue to cook in batches (adding butter as needed) until all the batter has been used.

6. Serve hot or warm, with any of the Optional Enhancements.

OPTIONAL ENHANCEMENTS

Avocado-Grapefruit-Mango Saladita (page 378), Strawberry-Avocado Saladita (page 382), or Jicama–Pink Grapefruit Saladita (page 381) ❋ Torn cilantro leaves ❋ Chipotle Cream (page 371) ❋ Avocado "Mayo" (page 373) or guacamole ❋ Roasted Red Pepper Pesto (page 358) ❋ This goes beautifully with a simple green salad with Jalapeño-Cilantro-Lime Vinaigrette (page 367) and topped with toasted pumpkin seeds or Chili Pepitas (page 401). You can add the other half of the can of black beans to this or any other salad (or serve it with rice tomorrow).

Wild Rice Pancakes with Mushrooms and Goat Cheese

MAKES 4 OR 5 SERVINGS (2 OR 3 PANCAKES PER SERVING)

Savory and pungent, these are like small omelets filled with pockets of soft goat cheese and stripes of chewy mushrooms. The random little slants of wild rice add a wonderful taste-textural-visual presence that gives the pancakes (and you) a sense of groundedness. This is a lovely, understated opportunity to introduce more whole grains into your dinner (or brunch or lunch).

The recipe originally appeared in *Sunlight Café* as a breakfast dish. Having served it now many times for dinner, with Chili-Sesame Green Beans (page 345) on the side and guacamole on top, I want to give it an encore—this time, with more mushrooms.

❋ You can easily make these gluten-free by swapping in rice flour for the all-purpose flour.

❋ Put on the wild rice at least an hour ahead of time and get everything else ready while it cooks. Use ½ cup wild rice and cook it as you would pasta, in plenty of simmering water, until tender (40 or more minutes). Drain thoroughly and shake dry. You will have more than enough for this recipe.

❋ Mushroom it up further: Sauté a handful of thinly sliced (extra) shiitakes first in a little oil or butter, then spread them in a single layer and spoon the batter directly onto the mushrooms. This will create a delightful mushroom coating for what will become the top of the pancake after you flip it.

* The batter can be assembled well ahead of time. It keeps for up to 2 days in a tightly covered container in the refrigerator.

* To keep the pancakes warm, transfer them to a wire rack on a baking sheet in a 200°F oven until serving time. (The rack keeps them crisp.)

* Unlike most other pancakes, these are sturdy enough to reheat in a microwave or a toaster oven. They also taste good at room temperature, so try packing a few in your lunch bag for a late morning breakfast break or for lunch.

About 2 tablespoons olive oil

12 medium domestic mushrooms, wiped clean, stemmed if tough, and sliced

6 medium (2-inch cap) shiitake mushrooms, wiped clean, stemmed, and sliced thin

1 teaspoon salt

1 teaspoon minced or crushed garlic

2 teaspoons fresh lemon juice

4 large eggs

⅓ cup unbleached all-purpose flour or brown rice flour

4 scallions, minced

1 cup cooked wild rice (see note)

1 cup (about 5 ounces) crumbled, soft, fresh goat cheese

⅛ teaspoon black pepper

Nonstick cooking spray

Up to 3 tablespoons butter (optional)

1. Place a medium skillet over medium heat for about a minute, then add 1 tablespoon of the olive oil and swirl to coat the pan. Toss in the mushrooms and cook, stirring, over medium heat for 5 minutes. Sprinkle in ½ teaspoon of the salt and sauté for 5 minutes longer. Stir in the garlic and lemon juice and cook for 1 minute longer to soften the garlic before removing the pan from the heat.

2. Beat the eggs in a medium-large bowl. Whisk in the flour and the remaining ½ teaspoon salt. When this mixture is uniform, stir in the cooked mushrooms, including all their juices (there's no need to wash the pan). Add the scallions, wild rice, goat cheese, and black pepper and stir until well combined.

3. Wipe out the skillet and heat over medium heat for about a minute, then add about ½ tablespoon olive oil and swirl to coat the pan. Melt in about a teaspoon of butter, if desired, and tilt the pan to distribute the butter. When it's hot enough to instantly sizzle a crumb, use a nonstick-sprayed ¼-cup measure with a handle to scoop as many cakes as will fit in a single layer into the pan and fry for 2 to 3 minutes on each side, or until golden. Continue to cook in batches, using additional oil and/or butter as needed until all the batter has been used. Serve hot or warm.

OPTIONAL ENHANCEMENTS

* Top with sour cream, yogurt, or Chipotle Cream (page 371) * Thin rings of sliced scallion or baby leek on top * Torn fresh flat-leaf parsley on top * Fire-Roasted Bell Pepper Saladita (page 380) * Avocado "Mayo" (page 373) or guacamole * Serve with Chili-Sesame Green Beans (page 345) on the side

Zucchini-Ricotta Cloud Cakes

MAKES 4 SERVINGS (8 BIG, PUFFY PANCAKES)

"Zucchini! My favorite vegetable!" No one I know says that—until now, perhaps.

This is one of those privileged items that (like that Siamese cat of dishes, the soufflé) requires its eaters to be ready and waiting, and not the other way around. In addition, your guests must be willing to eat these cakes just as each cloud is at its peak of puffy splendor immediately off the griddle. The rest is one big sigh—pancakes and diners exhaling in blissful unison.

❋ You can use any kind of ricotta, but the higher quality the cheese, the more transcendent the result. So consider splurging on the best fresh cheese you can find—or possibly even make your own (page 413).

❋ Separate the eggs far enough ahead of time to allow them to get to room temperature. Place both yolks and whites in bowls large enough to accommodate additional ingredients and unabashed mixing, and cover them with a plate or plastic wrap while they stand.

❋ Consider making these in two large pans or on one large griddle, so more people will be able to enjoy the results at the same time.

❋ In the unlikely event that you are faced with leftover batter, you can relax in the knowledge that it will keep for about a day in a tightly covered container in the refrigerator. Second-day cloud cakes will still be delicious—just less inflated.

About 2 tablespoons olive oil

¾ cup finely minced onion

1 medium zucchini (about 7 ounces), sliced into very thin (⅛-inch-thick) quarter circles

1 teaspoon minced or crushed garlic

½ teaspoon salt

1 teaspoon white wine vinegar

Black pepper

3 large eggs, separated and at room temperature (see note)

1 cup ricotta (preferably whole milk)

⅓ cup unbleached all-purpose flour

3 tablespoons minced fresh mint leaves, or more to taste

A touch of butter (optional)

Nonstick cooking spray (optional)

1. Place a medium (8- to 9-inch) skillet over medium heat for about a minute, then add 1 tablespoon of the oil and swirl to coat the pan. Toss in the onion and cook, stirring often, for about 5 minutes, or until the onion becomes soft. Stir in the zucchini, garlic, and ¼ teaspoon of the salt and continue to cook, stirring occasionally, for about 5 minutes longer, or until the zucchini is wilted. Add the vinegar and some black pepper and set aside.

2. Use a handheld electric mixer to beat the egg whites until they form soft, firm peaks. Set aside, keeping the mixer handy (don't clean it yet).

3. Add the ricotta to the egg yolks and begin mixing with the electric mixer at medium speed. After a minute or two, lower the speed, and keep it going slowly as you sprinkle in the flour plus the remaining ¼ teaspoon salt. When the dry items are completely incorporated, use a rubber spatula to fold in the cooked vegetables and the mint.

4. Spoon the beaten egg whites on top, then fold them in gently but assertively with a few quick strokes of the rubber spatula, circling down to the bottom of the bowl and around the sides. It doesn't need to be uniform—just be sure the whites are reasonably distributed.

5. Place a large (10- to 12-inch) skillet over medium heat for about a minute, then add a scant ½ tablespoon olive oil and swirl to coat the pan. Melt in about a teaspoon of butter, if desired, and tilt the pan to distribute the butter. When it's hot enough to instantly sizzle a crumb, use a ⅓-cup measure (coated with nonstick spray, if you like) with a handle to scoop batter onto the hot pan and fry the cakes for about 2 to 3 minutes on each side, or until golden and puffy. Serve right away, fresh from the pan.

OPTIONAL ENHANCEMENTS

Serve accompanied by sliced, very sweet cherry tomatoes or Slow-Roasted Roma Tomatoes (page 393) ❋ Spoon some Romesco Sauce (page 359) on the side ❋ Pair with Radicchio Salad with Oranges and Pistachios (page 78)

VEGETABLES

✼ ✼ ✼

In vegetarian cooking, the vegetable is not just a "side." It is the soul—not an afterthought, but the thought itself.

When we put a green, orange, yellow, purple, or red plant at the center of the plate, everything shifts into new realms of possibility. Every rule goes out the window, and you can reinvent your dinner nightly—and lightly.

This chapter showcases freestanding vegetables—each with a twist: Brussels sprouts braised with cranberries; kale flash-fried in olive oil with garlic, almonds, and cheese; green beans, sesame-seared; small eggplants, halved, slapped onto a hot pan, then sauced royally. And if you prefer to keep things simple, you'll find guides for plainer approaches: roasting and twice-cooking, Italian-style—both of these very low on labor and high on reward.

Many of these dishes can be paired with one another, piled onto a mash, spooned onto (or sprinkled with) cooked grains, festooned with pasta, launched upon toast, or served solo as a small plate. They can also be frames for other dishes: topping or cradling a burger, a scoop of pilaf, or a triangle of polenta.

When does a vegetable cross over to main-dish territory? When you decide. Once again, the definition is up for grabs. The Optional Enhancements that follow the recipes will come in especially handy here, providing some maps to all the various upsides and chances for expansion.

Twice-Cooked Italian-Style Broccoli

MAKES 4 SERVINGS ❋ VEGAN

This is my favorite weeknight way to cook broccoli. First it's simmered briefly, then drained and dried, so it's ready for a delicious warm-up in gently heated, garlic-infused olive oil.

You can do the first phase up to 5 days ahead, which saves time at the last minute. Additional benefits to this approach: Cooked vegetables take up far less refrigerator space than raw ones, and the shelf life of a cooked vegetable is more than double that of an uncooked one. Once blanched, the vegetable becomes an instant side dish for that busy Tuesday when you come home from work.

❋ This method works well for many other vegetables. Try it with leafy greens, green beans, cauliflower, cabbage, Brussels sprouts, or potatoes.

2 pounds broccoli

2 tablespoons olive oil

1 teaspoon minced or crushed garlic

¼ teaspoon salt, or more to taste

Black pepper

Crushed red pepper

1. Put on a medium-large pot of water to boil over high heat.

2. Meanwhile, trim and discard the base from the stem ends of the broccoli and use a vegetable peeler to shave the tough outer skin from the stalks. (The intrior will be tender.) Cut the stem and florets into bite-sized pieces.

3. When the water boils, lower the heat to a simmer and add the broccoli. Cook for about 2 minutes if you like your broccoli tender-crisp, or for 3 minutes if you like it tender-tender.

4. Drain the broccoli in a colander, shaking it emphatically, and then patting it dry with paper towels or a kitchen towel. (*You can prepare the broccoli ahead of time up to this point and then keep it at room temperature for up to 2 hours or in the refrigerator in a resealable bag or tightly covered container for up to 5 days; let it come to room temperature or microwave it to warm it slightly before proceeding.*)

5. Place a large (10- to 12-inch) skillet over medium-low heat for about a minute, then add the olive oil and swirl to coat the pan. Toss in the broccoli and cook, turning it frequently with tongs, for 3 minutes. Add the garlic and continue to cook for 3 to 5 minutes, swishing the broccoli around so it can pick up the garlic flavor evenly. Stir in ¼ teaspoon salt, then taste to see if you'd like to add more, along with some black pepper and crushed red pepper. Serve hot or warm.

OPTIONAL ENHANCEMENTS

Drizzle with a small amount of a roasted nut or seed oil just before serving and garnish with the corresponding nut, chopped and toasted ❋ Squeeze fresh lemon juice over the broccoli just before serving

Smoky Brussels Sprouts and Onion

MAKES 3 OR 4 SERVINGS ❊ VEGAN

Brussels sprouts are simmered in water—but that is only the first step. From there they go on a smoke-infused oil odyssey. This is the good kind of smoke—flavor, not fumes—created by spiking the oil with smoked paprika or ground chipotle as it heats. The cooked sprouts then go gamely into the fray, hell-bent on some serious absorption, and emerge buttery soft with a spicy edge. The late-breaking onion provides a shiny, crisp, sweet contrast.

❊ Smoked paprika can vary in potency from one brand (or individual jar) to another. Try to find one with a predictable, pleasant smokiness that matches your palate. Also, go easy on your first use of ground chipotle, if this ingredient is new to you, so you can find the right degree of heat. You'll have an opportunity to adjust the amount upward later in the cooking process.

❊ If you are willing to spend a little extra time, you can divide the ingredients and make this in two batches (or in two simultaneous pans) for maximum pan exposure, color, and flavor. The first batch can wait on a plate while you cook the second one, and then you can add the two together at the end. There's no need to wash the pan in between.

2 pounds Brussels sprouts

2–3 tablespoons olive oil

½ teaspoon smoked paprika and/or ground chipotle, or more to taste

¼ teaspoon salt, or more to taste

1 cup minced onion

Black pepper

1. Put on a large pot of water to boil. Meanwhile, trim and halve or quarter the sprouts (unless they are tiny). Add them to the water when it boils, and simmer for 3 to 5 minutes, or until mostly tender. Drain them thoroughly in a colander, shaking them dry. (*The sprouts can be cooked up to several days ahead and refrigerated airtight or frozen in a heavy zip-style plastic bag. Defrost before proceeding.*)

2. Place a large (10- to 12-inch) skillet over medium heat for about a minute, then add 2 tablespoons of the oil and swirl to coat the pan. Sprinkle in the paprika and/or chipotle powder, spreading them into the oil to get the flavor distributed.

3. Add the drained Brussels sprouts, using tongs to arrange as many of the sprouts as your patience permits cut side down. Sprinkle in ¼ teaspoon of the salt and cook, moving and rearranging the sprouts occasionally and scraping the pan as necessary, for about 8 minutes, or until they are soft and shaggy. To check on their smokiness, pull out and taste a leaf. If you want a deeper flavor, sprinkle on more paprika and/or chipotle and gently mix it in.

4. Push some of the sprouts aside to make a little space, then add the onion, along with an additional drizzle of oil. Salt the onion lightly, sprinkle with pepper, and cook for another 5 to 10 minutes, stirring often, until the sprouts are deeply colored and the onion is shiny and sweet. Serve hot, warm, or at room temperature.

OPTIONAL ENHANCEMENTS

Accompany or top with fried eggs, either Olive Oil–Bread Crumb–Coated (page 408) or plain ❋ Add some extra olive oil to the empty pan, scraping some up of what might have stuck, and toast bread crumbs or thick slices of fresh bread ❋ Diced potatoes (up to ½ pound) can be cooked with the Brussels sprouts from the beginning ❋ Cabbage, cauliflower, and broccoli (any or all of them in bite-sized chunks) can swap in for all or some of the Brussels sprouts ❋ Throw in a few handfuls of baby spinach leaves when you add the onion ❋ Top the dish with diced in-season tomato or halved, very sweet cherry tomatoes ❋ Drizzle with a few drops of red or white wine vinegar or serve with lemon wedges ❋ Add up to 1 teaspoon minced or crushed garlic with the onion

Brussels Sprouts with Cranberries

MAKES 3 OR 4 SERVINGS ❋ VEGAN

I had been tempted to do this for years and finally made the leap: combining two classic Thanksgiving side dishes into one. Since these dishes usually end up on top of each other on the plate anyway, why not cook them together? While you're at it, you could serve this as a topping for baked sweet potatoes (make a slit down the center; stuff in some Brussels Sprouts with Cranberries, and let some tumble down).

Take this to the full-meal finish line by pairing it with Seitan Medallions in Good Gravy (page 306) and Wild Rice, Basmati, and Kidney Bean Salad (page 116). Maybe even add some mashed potatoes.

All of the above notwithstanding, this dish is very good on its own.

❋ With stovetop cooking (as opposed to oven-roasting; see page 336), Brussels sprouts are at their best if blanched first and then drained and finished in a skillet primed with flavor.

❋ For maximum pan exposure, color, and flavor, you can also divide the ingredients and make this in two batches (or in two simultaneous pans). If cooking in batches, set aside the first batch on a plate while you cook the second one and then reunite the two to finish cooking together in the pan. (There's no need to wash the pan in between.)

❋ This reheats very nicely on the stovetop over low heat or briefly in the microwave.

2 pounds Brussels sprouts

2 heaping cups cranberries (fresh or frozen)

¼ cup finely minced shallot

2 tablespoons olive oil

¼ cup balsamic or cider vinegar

2 tablespoons sugar

2 tablespoons pure maple syrup

½ teaspoon salt, or more to taste

Black pepper

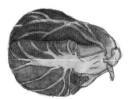

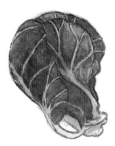

1. Put on a pot of water to boil. Meanwhile, trim and halve or quarter the sprouts (unless they are tiny). Add them to the water when it boils and simmer for 3 to 5 minutes, or until mostly tender. Drain them thoroughly in a colander, shaking them dry. (*The sprouts can be cooked up to several days ahead and refrigerated airtight or frozen in a heavy zip-style plastic bag. Defrost before proceeding.*)

2. Place the cranberries in a large (10- to 12-inch) skillet and cook over medium heat for 2 minutes, then stir in the shallot and olive oil. Cook, stirring occasionally, for another 5 minutes, or until the cranberries begin to pop.

3. Add the drained Brussels sprouts, plus the vinegar, sugar, maple syrup, and ½ teaspoon of salt and toss to combine. Reduce the heat to low and use tongs to arrange as many of the sprouts as your patience permits cut side down in the cranberry mixture, which will color them in addition to saturating them with flavor. Cover the pan and cook for another 10 minutes, or until done to your liking, stirring from time to time to rearrange the sprouts.

4. Adjust the salt, if desired, and add pepper to taste. Serve hot, warm, or at room temperature.

OPTIONAL ENHANCEMENTS

Toss in a handful of dried cranberries toward the end of the cooking ✻ Top with a few lightly toasted pecans ✻ Decorate with orange sections removed from their membranes ✻ Top it with Grilled Haloumi Cheese (page 406), cut into strips and crumbled; cut back on the salt if using this option ✻ Simple Buckwheat Pilaf (page 230) on top or underneath ✻ Top with strips of roasted yellow bell pepper for an intriguing color contrast

Green Beans, Edamame, and Peas

MAKES 4 SERVINGS ❋ VEGAN (IF MADE WITHOUT THE BUTTER)

If we get literal about green beans, we can include edamame (bright green soybeans) along with the more commonly expected varieties. This dish spells beautiful simplicity on its own, and is even better (and full-out Christmasy) in configuration with Cranberry Rice (page 198). It's also a perfect filling for scooped-out baked potatoes that have been sprinkled with grated cheddar and briefly broiled.

❋ Select the green beans carefully, one by one, to get an attractive set of matching size and smoothness. The dish will be all the lovelier for your effort.

❋ If serving this with the rice, make the rice in advance (it is a champ at reheating) and prepare the green beans right before serving. Do that anyway, as the vegetables are at their greenest best within about 10 minutes of being made.

❋ You can cook the green vegetables ahead of serving time and refresh them under cold water to arrest the cooking process. Then heat/coat them with the scallions and garlic just before they go to the table.

❋ To get 1 cup of fresh peas, you'll need to shell a pound of pods.

1 pound green beans, trimmed and cut into 1½-inch lengths

10 ounces frozen shelled edamame (green soybeans)

1 cup fresh or frozen green peas, or more to taste

1 tablespoon olive oil

A touch of butter (optional)

¾ cup minced scallion whites (from 4–6 scallions; mince the greens and save them for the top)

Up to 1 teaspoon minced or crushed garlic

¼ teaspoon salt, or more to taste

Black pepper

Chopped fresh mint (optional)

1. Put on a pot of water to boil. When the water boils, add the green beans and let them cook until slightly tender, 5 to 8 minutes, depending upon their thickness. When they are not quite done to your taste, add the edamame and let them cook together for another minute or so. At the very last moment, add the peas. When everything is still bright green and al dente, drain the whole potful into a colander. Refresh the vegetables under cold running water for a minute or so to stop the cooking. Leave them in the sink to drain completely.

2. Meanwhile, place a medium-large (9- to 10-inch) skillet over medium-low heat for about a minute, then add the oil, swirl to coat the pan, then melt in the butter, if desired, and swirl again. Toss in the scallion whites and the garlic, plus ¼ teaspoon salt, and cook for just a minute or two, until everything is coated with everything else and all is shiny and fragrant. (Don't allow the garlic to brown.)

3. Stir in the drained vegetables and heat everything together briefly, stirring to coat. It's very important that the vegetables retain their color and crunch. Add more salt, if desired, and some black pepper. Serve hot, warm, or at room temperature, topped with the scallion greens and the mint, if using.

Gingery Sweet-and-Sour Stir-Fry with Carrots, Pineapple, Pepper, and Walnuts

MAKES 4 MODEST MAIN-DISH SERVINGS ❧ VEGAN

Bright and quick (like some of my favorite people), with colors that could have come straight out of a box of Crayola markers, this shiny, surprisingly tart stir-fry will bring all-season brightness to your table. It can be a terrific first course or side dish on its own, and if you add tofu and serve it over rice, you'll have an easy complete meal.

❋ Ideally, the fresh pineapple should be cut at least an hour ahead of time, allowing it to give off a bit of juice as it stands. This can be the beginning of the cup of juice needed for the recipe, supplemented as needed with fresh orange juice or additional pineapple juice from a can.

❋ When cutting the pineapple, be sure to remove all the skin, so there will be nothing sharp remaining on the fruit. One medium pineapple will yield more than the amount you'll need for this recipe, so enjoy snacking on the extra. In a pinch, you could also use a 20-ounce can of pineapple chunks.

❋ Get everything ready ahead of time (including some rice, if you're planning to lay that as a foundation) and stir-fry at the very last minute. If your skillet or wok is large and hot, the actual cooking will take only about 6 minutes from start to finish.

❋ To roll-cut the carrots, slice on a shallow angle into ¼-inch-thick pieces, turning the carrots a quarter turn after each slice to create a diamond-like shape. This cut allows the carrots to cook evenly and still retain a nice crunch. You can also just slice the carrots into ⅛-inch-thick ovals.

❋ This reheats well in a microwave but is best freshly cooked.

1 cup pineapple juice or orange juice (see note)

1 teaspoon minced or crushed garlic

½ teaspoon *each* grated orange and lemon zest

1 teaspoon soy sauce

1 teaspoon cider vinegar

1 teaspoon agave nectar or brown sugar (optional)

1 teaspoon salt

1 tablespoon cornstarch

1 tablespoon grapeseed, canola, or peanut oil

1 medium red onion, cut into 1-inch squares (about 1½ cups)

1 tablespoon finely minced fresh ginger

1 pound carrots (4 medium), roll-cut or in ovals (see note)

1 medium red or yellow bell pepper, cut into 1-inch squares

2 cups ¾-inch fresh pineapple chunks, or more to taste, or one 20-ounce can juice-packed pineapple chunks, drained

Crushed red pepper

1 cup walnuts, toasted

1. Pour the juice into a 2-cup (or larger) liquid measuring cup with a spout. Add the garlic, zests, soy sauce, vinegar, agave or brown sugar (if using), and ½ teaspoon of the salt, and whisk to blend.

2. Place the cornstarch in a small bowl and pour in just enough of the juice mixture to cover. Whisk gently until the cornstarch is completely dissolved, then stir this slurry into the juice mixture. Set the cup near the stove, leaving in the whisk.

3. Place a large (10- to 12-inch) skillet or wok over medium heat for about a minute, then add the oil and swirl to coat the pan. Heat for another 30 seconds or so, then toss in the onion and ginger and turn up the heat to high. Stir-fry for about 30 seconds, until the onion glistens, then toss in the carrots and the remaining ½ teaspoon salt and stir-fry for about 2 minutes, or until the carrots just begin to soften. Add the bell pepper and stir-fry for another minute. Add the pineapple chunks and stir-fry for 30 seconds to heat through.

4. Whisk the juice mixture from the bottom to reincorporate the cornstarch, and pour it all into the pan. Keep stir-frying for another minute or so, until the sauce coats the vegetables and becomes thick and shiny. Serve right away, topped with a light sprinkling of crushed red pepper and the walnuts.

OPTIONAL ENHANCEMENTS

Strips or squares of tofu (plain or fried separately ahead of time) added with the sauce or Tofu "Noodles" (page 399) scattered on top ❋ Sliced water chestnuts added with the carrots ❋ Serve on a bed of freshly cooked brown basmati rice ❋ This looks especially beautiful garnished with bright green steamed broccoli florets

Cheese-Crusted Roasted Cauliflower

MAKES 4 SERVINGS

Cauliflower offers the broadest textural range of just about any vegetable. When spanking fresh, it's delightful raw: Its crunchy white puffballs make satisfying crudités. And at the other extreme, cauliflower is also brilliant when boiled to oblivion and mashed (page 172). In this recipe, the high-temperature roasting process allows the cauliflower to become simultaneously fork-tender and chewy, with delicately crisp surface points (helped along greatly by the cheese) surprising you at random.

❈ The roasted cauliflower will keep for up to 5 days in a tightly covered container in the refrigerator and will reheat beautifully.

❈ A version of this becomes the basis for Roasted Cauliflower Mac and Cheese (page 240) and Roasted Cauliflower Risotto (page 206).

1 tablespoon olive oil

1 medium head cauliflower (about 2 pounds), trimmed and broken or cut into ¾-inch pieces

2 cups minced onion (1 large)

¼ cup grated Italian fontina or sharp cheddar or shredded Parmesan, or more to taste

¼ teaspoon salt

Black pepper

1. Preheat the oven to 400°F, with a rack in the center position. Line a baking sheet with parchment paper or foil and slick it with the olive oil. (You can use a chunk of cauliflower to spread it around.)

2. Arrange the cauliflower pieces on the sheet and sprinkle them with the minced onion. Roast for 15 minutes, then shake the baking sheet and/or use tongs to loosen and redistribute the pieces—gently, so they won't pop off the baking sheet.

3. Roast for another 5 to 10 minutes, until the cauliflower is becoming uniformly golden, then push everything together in the center of the baking sheet, keeping it a single layer. Sprinkle evenly with the cheese.

4. Roast for 10 or so minutes longer, or until the cheese is thoroughly melted, forming an irresistible golden crust. Remove the baking sheet from the oven and season with the salt and pepper. Serve hot, warm, or at room temperature.

OPTIONAL ENHANCEMENTS

Roast a sliced carrot along with the cauliflower ❈ Try this same process using broccoli instead of, or in addition to, the cauliflower ❈ Sprinkle some toasted bread crumbs over the cauliflower after it comes out of the oven ❈ Serve topped with a pile of Egg "Noodles" (page 398) ❈ Garnish with Caramelized Onion and Lemon Marmalade (page 375) or Strawberry-Rhubarb Pickles (page 396)

A PRIMER ON ROASTING VEGETABLES

Roasting vegetables is one of the best ways to show-case their essence. The dry heat process draws out and evaporates the inner moisture, concentrating the flavor many times over. The result is a caramel-ized effect, delivering the vegetables' own natural sweetness in a slightly singed, delightfully textured package.

My standard vegetable-roasting temperature for most vegetables is 400°F. For sweeter items, such as winter squash, parsnips, and sweet potatoes, take it down to 375°F, so their high sugar content won't cause charring.

THE BEST VEGETABLES TO ROAST

Asparagus

Beets (see page 97)

Bell peppers (see page 358)

Bok choy

Broccoli

Brussels sprouts

Carrots

Cauliflower

Celery hearts

Eggplants

Fennel

Green beans

Onions

Parsnips

Potatoes

Sweet potatoes

Tomatoes (roast at 275°F; see page 393)

Winter squash (see page 351)

Zucchini and other summer squash

The most effective way to roast vegetables is to cut them into bite-sized chunks (with the exception of asparagus and green beans, which you can leave in long spears after trimming) and spread them out in a single layer on a foil- or parchment-lined bak-ing sheet slicked with olive oil. Swish the vegetables around in the oil, and roast in the center of the oven until fork-tender and/or done to your liking. This will take anywhere from 15 to 30 minutes, depending on the temperature, and on the vegetables and how you cut them, so pay attention as you go.

Check on the vegetables about every 10 minutes or so as they roast, and loosen and move them around, if necessary. The pieces may have stuck to the foil or parchment, even though you oiled it. The best way to loosen them is simply to lift the foil or parchment from all sides, patiently allowing the slightly stuck pieces to peel themselves off. Some gentle tong assistance can help things along. The vegetables are done when a fork slides in easily (or when you decide they're ready).

Salt the vegetables lightly while they are still hot and serve at any temperature, possibly with a small splash of fresh lemon or lime juice or vinegar.

For most vegetables you can increase the tem-perature to 425°F to get a more intensely flavored result. Just be sure to keep an eye on things.

Roast a larger amount of vegetables than you think you'll need for any one occasion. I guarantee you will love having leftovers around for all sorts of uses.

Lime-Drenched Sweet Corn and Pepper

MAKES 3 OR 4 SERVINGS ❊ VEGAN (WHEN MADE WITHOUT THE BUTTER)

Summertime, and the corn and bell peppers are crazy sweet. Lime juice knows exactly what to do here, as will be obvious when you take a bite.

❊ For easiest corn shucking, zap the ears for 4 to 6 minutes in a microwave, then wear oven mitts to carefully remove them. Slice off and discard about an inch from the tip, then shake/squeeze the cob from the husks and silk. It will slip out easily and miraculously clean.

❊ Save the ears after you shuck the corn. They are a terrific addition to homemade stock (see page 22).

1 tablespoon olive oil

1 teaspoon unsalted butter (optional)

½ cup finely minced onion

Salt

½ cup finely minced sweet bell pepper (any color)

3 cups corn kernels (from about 6 freshly shucked ears)

2 tablespoons fresh lime juice, or more to taste

Black pepper

1. Place a large (10- to 12-inch) skillet over medium heat for about a minute, then add the olive oil, melt in the butter, if using, and swirl to coat the pan. Add the onion and a pinch of salt and cook, stirring, for about 5 minutes, or until the onion begins to soften.

2. Toss in the bell pepper and another pinch of salt and cook, stirring often, for about 2 minutes, or until the bell pepper becomes very shiny and slightly tender.

3. Add the corn and stir to coat. Cook, stirring, for about a minute, then add the lime juice. Continue to cook, stirring, for another 5 minutes, then remove from the heat. Taste to possibly adjust the salt and lime juice, add some black pepper, and serve hot, warm, or at room temperature.

OPTIONAL ENHANCEMENTS

A touch of lime zest ❊ Salsa Verde (page 357) ❊ Tiny, very sweet cherry tomatoes ❊ Avocado "Mayo" (page 373) ❊ A tiny touch of minced jalapeño ❊ Crumbled feta ❊ Expand this into a sublime succotash by adding up to 2 cups cooked fava beans, lima beans, or shelled edamame ❊ Serve over Green Rice (page 194), accompanied by some Grilled Haloumi Cheese (page 406) and watermelon for a light summer dinner

Chard- or Collard-Wrapped Polenta-Chili Tamale Packages

MAKES 4 TO 6 SERVINGS (2 OR 3 PACKAGES PER SERVING)

A simple batch of chili-laced polenta is bundled into softened chard or collard leaves and wrapped up tightly. These little packages never fail to elicit surprise and delight. Serve them as a cocktail snack, a first course, or a light main—plain or sauced—and the moment will take on an aura of the low-key fantastic.

❋ This recipe only seems like a lot of work. It is, in fact, very straightforward. The only chopping required is the mincing of an onion and a chili. The chard and collard leaves stay whole, short of snipping off the stems after the initial boiling.

❋ The packages can be made up to 2 days ahead of the final sauté and serving. Store them on a tightly wrapped plate in the refrigerator.

2–3 tablespoons olive oil

1 cup finely minced onion

¼ teaspoon ground cumin

1 medium Anaheim or poblano chili, seeded if desired, finely minced (heaping ½ cup)

½ teaspoon salt

Black pepper

1 cup polenta (coarse cornmeal)

¼ (packed) cup grated Jack cheese (2 ounces)

1 dozen large, perfect chard or collard green leaves (8–10 inches long)

1. Put on a large pot of water to boil.

2. Meanwhile, place a medium saucepan over medium heat for about a minute, then add 1 tablespoon of the olive oil and swirl to coat the pan. Toss in the onion and cumin and cook, stirring, for about 5 minutes, until the onion softens. Add the chili, salt, and some pepper and sauté for another 5 minutes, or until the chili softens.

3. Add another tablespoon of oil, if desired, and sprinkle in the polenta, stirring to coat. Reduce the heat to medium-low and sauté the mixture for 5 minutes or so, or until the grains become lightly toasty.

4. When the water boils, add 3 cups, 1 cup at a time, to the polenta mixture, stirring it in, then covering the saucepan between additions so the polenta absorbs it (as if you were making risotto, but with less stirring). This should take about 10 minutes. (Leave the remaining water simmering in the pot on the stove.) When the 3 cups are incorporated and the mixture is tender, 6 to 8 minutes, remove it from the heat and immediately stir in the cheese. Set aside, covered.

5. Pick up each chard or collard leaf, one at a time, hold it by the stem, and immerse the entire leaf in the boiling water, down to the base, keeping it there until the spine becomes supple enough to bend without breaking, 20 to 30 seconds, depending on the size. Shake off any excess water and pile the blanched leaves on a plate as you go. Pat them dry with towels

and, using scissors, trim off the stems at the base of the leaves and discard.

6. To assemble the packages, place about ¼ cup of the filling (slightly more for larger leaves; less for smaller) near the bottom of each leaf and roll it up tightly, folding in the sides. Place all the filled leaves seam side down on a plate. If you have leftover filling, keep it handy.

7. Shortly before serving, place a large (10- to 12-inch) skillet over medium heat for about a minute, then add about ½ tablespoon olive oil and swirl to coat the pan. Add the packages and sauté on both sides for a total of 5 to 8 minutes, or until heated through. (You can also sauté any leftover filling or heat it in a microwave and serve it underneath or sprinkled on top.) Serve the packages hot or warm.

OPTIONAL ENHANCEMENTS

Add an ear's worth of freshly shucked sweet corn to the filling ✳ Serve over or under Mixed Mushroom Ragout (page 348), Romesco Sauce (page 359), or Roasted Red Pepper Pesto (page 358) ✳ Top with a dab of Fire-Roasted Bell Pepper Saladita (page 380) and a sprinkling of Chili Pepitas (page 401) ✳ Garnish with sliced avocado and lime wedges ✳ Serve on a warm puddle of Mushroom Gravy for Everyone (page 365) ✳ Serve as a small plate alongside Strawberry-Avocado Saladita (page 382) or Jicama–Pink Grapefruit Saladita (page 381)

Eggplant Slap-Down: A Trio

MAKES 2 SERVINGS

Mini eggplants can make wonderful, compact events in and of themselves, served as an appetizer or light lunch. They can also be a beautiful and very satisfying presence on a layered plate (see page 167), contributing to a more complete main dish. Somewhere in between these two, you can make them into a simple supper on top of freshly cooked brown basmati rice or couscous, possibly with a heap of something tasty alongside or piled on top.

Very little cutting is involved. Just slice small eggplants in half lengthwise, slap them cut side down into a hot pan, cook until tender, and pile on various combinations of flavor. Minutes later, they're ready to serve on a small plate with just a fork.

✻ Each of these preparations is at its best when freshly cooked, but can be reheated the next day and maybe even the next (but no longer).

CURRIED EGGPLANT SLAP-DOWN WITH YOGURT, ONION RELISH, AND POMEGRANATE

Curry powder is "fried" in oil, setting the stage for the eggplants to dive right in and gain an instant, transformative coating. Onions get their turn next—spiced into a quick relish in the same pan. Just 15 minutes, give or take, and it will taste like you slaved over it for half a day.

1 tablespoon grapeseed, canola, or peanut oil

Up to 1 teaspoon unsalted butter (optional)

½ teaspoon curry powder

2 4-ounce eggplants, trimmed and halved lengthwise

Salt

About 4 teaspoons plain Greek yogurt

½ teaspoon cumin seeds

⅛ teaspoon turmeric

½ cup minced onion

Pomegranate seeds and/or pomegranate molasses (see note, page 118)

1. Place a medium skillet over medium heat for about a minute, then add ½ tablespoon of the oil and swirl to coat the pan. Melt some butter into the oil, if desired, and sprinkle in the curry powder, which will sizzle upon contact.

2. Add the eggplant halves with their cut sides facing down, swishing them around (as though you're wiping the pan with them) to both distribute and acquire the curry. Reduce the heat to medium-low, cover the pan, and cook undisturbed for about 8 minutes, until each eggplant half becomes tender. (Peek underneath a few times to be sure the cut surfaces are not becoming too dark. If they are, lower the heat and/or turn the eggplants over.) The eggplants are cooked when the stem ends can easily be pierced with a fork.

3. Flip the eggplants onto their backs if you haven't already done so, sprinkle with ¼ teaspoon salt, and transfer to a plate. Spoon a little yogurt onto each cut surface, spreading it to cover; set aside while you prepare the onion relish.

4. To the same pan over medium-high heat, add the remaining ½ tablespoon oil, swirling to coat the pan. Sprinkle in the cumin seeds and turmeric (both should sizzle on contact) and mix them a little to pick up some of the flavor that may have adhered to the pan. Add the onion and a big pinch of salt, tossing to coat. Reduce the heat to medium and cook for about 5 minutes, or until tender-crisp, then remove the pan from the heat. Divide the onion relish evenly among the 4 eggplant halves, spooning it over the yogurt, scraping up and including any remaining tasty bits from the pan.

5. Top with pomegranate seeds and/or a drizzle of pomegranate molasses. Serve hot, warm, or at room temperature.

EGGPLANT SLAP-DOWN WITH GINGER-PLUM SAUCE

✿ VEGAN

So good! And so easy that you'll make this often. This is especially good served on freshly cooked rice.

✿ Instead of the very easy homemade plum sauce in the recipe, you can use Chinese plum sauce, straight from the jar, or Misoyaki Sauce (page 362) and skip to step 2. Make sure the sauce is at room temperature before you begin.

2 heaping tablespoons plum, peach, or apricot jam

1 tablespoon finely minced fresh ginger or minced pickled ginger with its juice

1 tablespoon cider vinegar or unseasoned rice vinegar

½ teaspoon minced or crushed garlic, or more to taste

2 teaspoons grapeseed or peanut oil

2 4-ounce eggplants, trimmed and halved lengthwise

Salt

¼ cup dry white wine or dry sherry

Crushed red pepper

1. In a small bowl, combine the jam, ginger, vinegar, and garlic and mix with a fork or small whisk to thoroughly combine. Set aside.

2. Place a medium skillet over medium heat for about a minute, then add the oil and swirl to coat the pan. Add the eggplant halves to the pan with their cut sides facing down. Turn the heat to medium-low, cover the pan, and cook undisturbed for about 8 minutes, until each eggplant half becomes tender. (Peek underneath a few times to be sure the cut surfaces are not becoming too dark. If they are, lower the heat and/or turn the eggplants over.) The eggplants are cooked when the stem ends can easily be pierced with a fork.

3. Flip the eggplants onto their backs if you haven't already done so, sprinkle them lightly with salt, and spoon a little plum sauce onto each cut surface, spreading it to cover. Reserve the remaining sauce. Flip the eggplants back onto their now-sauced cut sides and cook for a minute or less, just so the flavor can be cooked on. Loosen the eggplants with a thin-bladed spatula (including whatever might have stuck) and transfer them to a plate.

4. Reduce the heat to low and pour the wine or sherry into the pan. Scrape up any remaining specks and tidbits, mixing them in. Let the wine bubble and reduce for a minute or so, adding another touch of garlic, if you like, then spoon in a generous tablespoon of the plum sauce and stir to combine. Simmer for just a few seconds, then return the eggplants to the pan, skin side down, and let them bathe in the sauce for a minute or so. Serve hot, warm, or at room temperature, with the remaining sauce and a light scattering of crushed red pepper over the top.

OPTIONAL ENHANCEMENTS

Serve topped with Tofu "Noodles," Sesame Version (page 399) ✿ Scatter long, thin strips of scallion greens on top

EGGPLANT SLAP-DOWN WITH FIGS AND BLUE CHEESE

I modeled this after an eggplant appetizer I fell in love with at the venerable (and sadly, now defunct) Casablanca restaurant in Cambridge, Massachusetts. I knew (who doesn't?) that figs and blue cheese would go well together, but with eggplant? Skeptical, I thought I'd give it a try. And? A big surprise of the absolute best kind.

✳ Dried figs are even better than fresh for this dish, though it's a good use for harder fresh ones. If you do have some soft, ripe fresh figs, use them as a garnish.

✳ If blue cheese is too strong for your palate, you can go with a milder, crumbly white cheese, such as feta, manouri, or ricotta salata.

✳ Be sure to trim the stem ends from the dried figs. It's unpleasant to fish them out of your mouth while aspiring to elegance at the table.

1½ teaspoons olive oil

2 4-ounce eggplants, trimmed and halved lengthwise

¼ teaspoon salt

4–6 dried or firm fresh figs, stemmed and sliced

¼ cup crumbled blue cheese (any kind)

Balsamic vinegar

1. Place a medium skillet over medium heat for about a minute, then add the oil and swirl to coat the pan. Add the eggplant halves to the pan with their cut sides facing down. Turn the heat to medium-low, cover the pan, and cook undisturbed for about 8 minutes, until each eggplant half becomes tender. (Peek underneath a few times to be sure the cut surfaces are not becoming too dark. If they are, lower the heat and/or turn the eggplants over.) The eggplants are cooked when the stem ends can easily be pierced with a fork.

2. Flip the eggplants onto their backs if you haven't already done so, sprinkle with the salt, and arrange a layer of sliced figs all over each cut surface. Dot the figs with blue cheese, pressing the bits down gently. (You might want to turn off the heat while doing this.) Top each bedecked eggplant half with a few drops of balsamic vinegar, then cover and cook for about 2 minutes longer, until melty. Serve hot, warm, or at room temperature.

OPTIONAL ENHANCEMENTS

Baby arugula leaves—about a handful per serving—plain or tossed lightly with your favorite vinaigrette, scattered on top or as a bed underneath ✳ Top with pine nuts or chopped walnuts, lightly toasted

Chili-Sesame Green Beans

MAKES 4 SERVINGS ❦ VEGAN

Six ingredients, of which one is optional. And another is salt, so maybe we can call it four.

Green beans have the edge over most vegetables in their impressive aptitude for tenderness-within-crunch. Help them realize this potential by searing them in very hot oil over strong heat, and you'll have them at their vegetal best. This goes fast—just a few minutes over the flame, and spicy-crisp-juicy brilliance is served.

❂ Shop carefully for green beans; take your time selecting the freshest, brightest-green, smoothest-surfaced batch of uniform-sized specimens. Your effort will be well rewarded.

❂ Keep a little distance when you add anything chili-related to a pan on the stove to avoid inhaling the spicy steam.

2 tablespoons Chinese sesame oil, plus more to taste

1 pound green beans, trimmed

½ teaspoon salt

1 tablespoon minced or crushed garlic

Crushed red pepper

1–2 tablespoons sesame seeds (optional)

1. Place a large (10- to 12-inch) skillet or wok over medium heat for about 2 minutes, then add 2 tablespoons of the sesame oil and swirl to coat the pan. Heat for another 30 seconds or so, then toss in the green beans and ¼ teaspoon of the salt. Turn up the heat to medium-high and stir-fry for 2 minutes, shaking the pan and rearranging the beans with tongs or a wok spatula. Keep them moving, so they can all have contact with the hot oil. (If desired, you can drizzle a little extra oil down the sides of the pan as you go.)

2. Add the garlic, stirring to coat the beans, then do the same with a big pinch or two of crushed red pepper. Stir-fry for a minute or so longer, keeping the heat strong and the beans in motion. Taste to see if the beans are done to your liking. (If not, keep them going a little longer, still over strong heat.) Sprinkle in the remaining ¼ teaspoon salt and some sesame seeds, if desired, and serve right away.

Flash-Fried Kale with Garlic, Almonds, and Cheese

MAKES 2 SERVINGS

Kale goes into a hot pan and swishes around briefly with oil and garlic. Within minutes, it emerges tender, deep, and transformed—and ready to receive spots of almonds and cheese. A sprinkling of lemon juice takes it into spotlight terrain, so consider serving this as a solo course, before or after other courses.

❋ Any kind of kale works here. I tend to favor the lacinato (dino) variety, but in this case, I recommend you try purple-veined Russian kale or the more basic curly green type, just for variety. You can also combine them.

❋ Here is your chance to use some of the more fun kinds of almonds (roasted and salted, hickory-smoked, rosemary Marcona) you might normally pass up. You can also use blanched almonds that you have lightly toasted on a baking sheet for 15 to 20 minutes in a 275°F oven or toaster oven.

❋ The yield on this is low, so consider multiplying it and making serial batches. It goes very fast and tastes good warm or at room temperature.

❋ The kale keeps for several days, refrigerated in a tightly covered container (or frozen in a heavy zip-style plastic bag) and reheats beautifully on the stovetop or in the microwave. (If it's frozen, defrost before reheating.) Hold off on adding the almonds and cheese until just before serving.

¾ pound kale (1½ large or 3 small bunches)

1 tablespoon olive oil

Salt

2–3 tablespoons water (optional)

Up to 1 teaspoon minced or crushed garlic

Fresh lemon juice

½ cup diced fresh cheese (Mexican queso blanco, ricotta salata, manouri, feta)

¼ cup sliced or halved almonds (see note)

1. Slice off and discard the larger kale stems, make a uniform pile of the leaves, and cut into bite-sized pieces. (I like to make about 1½-inch squares.)

2. Place a large (10- to 12-inch) skillet over medium heat for about a minute, then add ½ tablespoon of the oil and swirl to coat the pan. Add the kale and a big pinch of salt and cook, stirring frequently, until the kale reduces to about half its original volume, 3 to 5 minutes. (If you prefer very tender leaves, you can splash in the water to steam them softer.)

3. When the kale is almost done to your liking, push it to the side of the pan, creating a small space. Pour the remaining ½ tablespoon oil onto that spot and reduce the heat to medium-low. Add the garlic and stir in increasingly wide circles, eventually including the kale in the motion to distribute the garlic into the leaves. (For more tenderness, you can turn off the heat and cover the pan after the garlic is stirred in, if desired.) This will take about 5 minutes.

4. When it's all combined, stir in a few drops of lemon juice. Use tongs to lift the kale onto individual plates and plunk down cubes of cheese over the top, letting them melt in ever so slightly. Serve hot, warm, or at room temperature, dotted with the almonds.

OPTIONAL ENHANCEMENTS

A few golden raisins scattered in (add at any time) ❋ Crushed red pepper ❋ Lemon wedges ❋ If you increase the oil and the garlic, you can add some cooked pasta to the pan and extend this dish into a main course ❋ You can also layer this with cooked rice for a main course

Mixed Mushroom Ragout

MAKES 4 OR 5 SERVINGS ❀ VEGAN (WHEN MADE WITHOUT BUTTER)

Mushrooms are brilliant multitaskers, doubling as both vegetable and seasoning. In this very satisfying example, with just a little backup from garlic, lemon, and white wine or sherry, the mushrooms pretty much season themselves.

In keeping with the versatility theme, this ragout offers multiple possibilities. It can be a side, or a main-dish stew—heaped upon Soft Polenta (page 184), accessorized with Crispy Polenta Triangles (page 185), or rounded out by the addition of a big hunk of grilled bread and a fried egg. It also highly achieves as a thick sauce for pasta, grains, or even other vegetables, plainly cooked.

❀ Feel free to augment this recipe with additional mushrooms of various types (whatever interesting ones you can find). The chewier wild varieties available these days can greatly diversify the texture.

❀ The porcini need to be soaked and prepped ahead of time. Allow 30 minutes or so.

❀ The reserved porcini-soaking water can be used to make polenta or added to risotto stock or pasta cooking water. You can also spill a little of it in here to make this ragout a bit richer tasting.

❀ Slicing the fresh mushrooms on the thick side will give you something to bite into. It also makes the preparation go a bit faster.

❀ This freezes so beautifully that no one will be able to tell it ever saw the inside of a freezer.

1 ounce dried porcini mushrooms

2 cups boiling water

2 tablespoons olive oil or a combination of olive oil and unsalted butter

1½ pounds mixed domestic and cremini mushrooms, wiped clean, stemmed as necessary, and thickly sliced

¾ teaspoon salt, or more to taste

8 medium (2-inch cap) shiitake mushrooms, wiped clean, stemmed, and sliced or chopped

2 teaspoons minced or crushed garlic

¼ cup dry white wine or dry sherry

1 tablespoon fresh lemon juice

Black pepper

1. Place the porcini in a medium-small bowl and pour in the boiling water. Cover with a plate and soak until tender, about 30 minutes. Drain over a second bowl, pressing out and saving all the soaking water. Mince the porcini and set aside.

2. Place a large (10- to 12-inch) skillet over medium heat for about a minute, then add the olive oil and butter, if using, and swirl to coat the pan. Toss in the domestic and cremini mushrooms, plus ½ teaspoon of the salt, and cook, stirring, for 5 minutes.

3. Add the minced porcini, shiitakes, garlic, and the remaining ¼ teaspoon salt. Sauté for another 3 minutes, then splash in the wine or sherry and lemon juice. (You can also add a tablespoon or two of the mushroom-soaking water.) Reduce the heat to medium-low and continue to sauté for another 5 minutes, or until everything has merged nicely.

4. Taste to adjust the salt, if necessary, and add black pepper to taste. Serve hot, warm, or at room temperature.

OPTIONAL ENHANCEMENTS

Top with a spoonful of Romesco Sauce (page 359) or Roasted Red Pepper Pesto (page 358) ✽ Lemon wedges ✽ Soft Polenta (page 184), possibly made with the porcini-soaking water, underneath or Crispy Polenta Triangles (page 185) served alongside ✽ Olive Oil Toasts (page 409) and fried eggs or Olive Oil–Bread Crumb–Coated Fried Eggs (page 408) on top ✽ You can use Mixed Mushroom Ragout as a sauce, backdrop, or plate partner for any other cooked vegetable. It's especially good served with Twice-Cooked Italian-Style Broccoli (page 325) and Slow-Roasted Roma Tomatoes (page 393).

PAN-GRILLED MUSHROOM SLICES AND MUSHROOM "BACON"

GRILLED MUSHROOMS are a compelling topping for savory dishes. Wipe them clean, stem them if necessary, slice them about ¼ inch thick, and lay them flat in a skillet that has been slicked with a little grapeseed, peanut, or canola oil and preheated for about a minute. Keep the heat on medium-high and cook for 3 to 4 minutes on each side, or until golden (it's OK to turn them more than once). Hold off on adding salt until they are done, so they will sweat minimally as they cook (this helps the edges brown and intensifies the flavor). When the mushrooms are done to your liking, remove them to a plate lined with paper towels, then sprinkle with salt. Snack on them and/or use them as a garnish.

FOR MUSHROOM "BACON," sprinkle some smoked paprika (up to 1 tablespoon per pound of mushrooms) into the oil and spread it around the oil before adding the mushrooms. Continue as for grilled mushrooms, salting generously when the mushrooms are done.

You can make and refrigerate the mushrooms ahead of time. Reheat them in a 300°F toaster oven on a foil-lined tray for 8 to 10 minutes, or in a lightly oiled skillet over medium-low heat until warmed through. They will acquire a nice additional chewiness through reheating.

Each pound of mushrooms will yield 3 or 4 servings.

VEGETABLE VESSELS: BORN TO BE STUFFED

MAKES 4 SERVINGS

Acorn squash, bell peppers, and portobello mushrooms are wonderful unadorned, no question—each delivering its unique flavor and soothing texture. Yet with their respective open-handed shapes, they seem to yearn for a filling. These vegetables are gracious hosts for a broad range of other dishes—just about any rice dish or mac and cheese will instantly relax into the savory embrace of a squash bowl, a mushroom cup, or a bell pepper boat. A grain dish or simple bean preparation, freshly made or left over, becomes a full meal when delivered to the table housed in an edible tureen.

The squash and portobellos need to be cooked on their own first, before they are filled. Bell peppers, halved and seeded, can be quickly blistered in a skillet slicked with olive oil over medium heat or filled raw.

Prepare the vessels well in advance, and then heat the stuffed vegetables in a 350°F oven.

TO PREPARE ACORN SQUASH FOR STUFFING

1 tablespoon olive oil

2 medium acorn squash (about 2 pounds each), halved and seeded

1. Preheat the oven to 400°F, with a rack in the center position. Line a baking sheet with foil and add 1 tablespoon of the olive oil. Place the squash halves cut side down on the oil, moving them around a little to spread the oil.

2. Roast the squash for 35 to 40 minutes, or until you can easily insert a fork or a sharp knife into the skin side. Remove from the oven and let the squash cool before turning over and stuffing.

TO PREPARE PORTOBELLO MUSHROOMS FOR STUFFING

4 medium (4-inch) firm portobello mushrooms

Up to 1 tablespoon olive oil

1. Remove the stems by laying each mushroom flat on its cap and slicing into the stem with a paring knife, cutting across, more than down. Twist the stem a little as you do this and it will come off fairly easily, leaving behind a protruding little stump. Wipe the caps clean with a damp paper towel.

2. Place a large (10- to 12-inch) skillet over medium heat for about a minute, then add the oil and swirl to coat the pan. Place the mushrooms cap side down in the hot oil and let them cook undisturbed for about 10 minutes. Turn them over and cook on the other side for 10 minutes, then flip them over one more time, to cook for 5 to 10 more minutes, until very firm and lightly browned. Remove from the heat and cool until comfortable to handle before stuffing.

TIPS ON ROASTING WINTER SQUASH

BUTTERNUT SQUASH

Golden roasted butternut squash is a welcome addition to just about any dinner plate. It is also great as an appetizer, laid out warm or at room temperature on a small plate and drizzled with vinaigrette.

To get the most out of a butternut squash, choose one that is mostly neck, with a minimal area of hollow, round base, where the seeds are. Use a sturdy peeler to remove the skin, being assertive about getting all of it off, so the flesh will be truly tender. After it's peeled, use a sharp knife to cut the squash into approximately ¾-inch cubes (they will not be uniform, which is part of the charm).

Line a baking sheet with foil and oil the foil. Place the squash cubes on the baking sheet and roast on the center rack of a preheated 375°F oven for 20 to 30 minutes (or possibly a touch longer), or until fork-tender. The squash will go through a steamed phase on its way to becoming beguilingly flavor-concentrated and chewy-crisp, so don't take it out of the oven too soon. (Check on it after about 10 minutes to loosen any morsels that may have stuck to the foil, even though you oiled it, lifting the foil from all sides, patiently allowing the slightly stuck pieces to detach. You can help this along with the gentle use of tongs.)

A 3- to 4-pound squash will yield 6 to 8 cups diced squash, which will cook down to 4 to 5 cups when roasted. Many squashes are larger than this, so if you can only get a huge one, you will have plenty of roasted squash on hand as a cherished ingredient to use spontaneously for many things. It also freezes well.

OTHER WINTER SQUASH

Delicata, acorn, and most of the other varieties are ridged, making effective peeling a pain, so I simply cut them into rings with the skin on, snip out the seeds with scissors, and roast them framed in their skin on a foil-lined, oiled baking sheet in the center of a 375°F oven, for anywhere from 10 to 20 minutes, or until they become fork-tender and their undersides are golden brown. (The timing will depend upon the kind of squash and the thickness of the slices.) People can eat unpeeled squash rings (or half circles) elegantly, with a knife and fork, cutting away the skin or including it as preferred. For optimal visual effect, invert the slices of squash after roasting them, since the undersides will have an inviting, golden-brown patina.

SPAGHETTI SQUASH

This kind has smooth skin, like butternut, but don't bother peeling it. Just bake it whole on a foil-lined baking sheet (no oiling needed) in the center of a 375°F oven until you can easily pierce the skin with a fork. A 4-pound spaghetti squash usually needs a full hour. After removing it from the oven, carefully cut a few slits to let steam escape, then let rest until it is a comfortable temperature to handle. Cut in half and then scoop the cooked flesh from the skin. It's fine to include the seeds, if you wish (or you can scoop them out).

SAUCES, VINAIGRETTES, TOPPINGS, and
Other Meaningful Touches

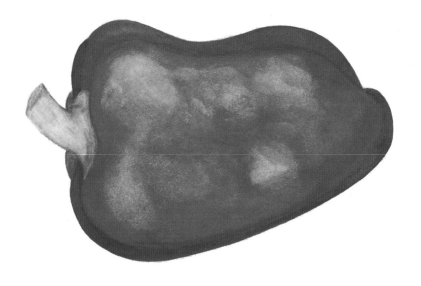

[continues]

✳ ✳ ✳

A drizzle of glaze, a dab of green herb paste, a dazzle of spiked seeds or nuts, a modest cluster of delicious crumbs, or a forkful of gaudy onion pickles are sometimes all it takes to transform a plain plate of beans, rice, and vegetables into a memorable meal. Whether it's the intrigue of color, the anticipation of contrasting flavor, or the potential of crunch, we are pulled in by these visual cues that welcome the eater to the plate.

Here you will find potent pastes made from various vegetables, oils, vinegars, and nuts; sweet-tart marmalades; and deeply marinated or pickled tidbits. Some are thick and can be spread underneath the rest of your menu. Others are of drizzling consistency and can be ladled or lashed on top or pooled on the side. Many can be the place where your planning begins. From them, ideas will hatch organically, and you will find sparks for improvisation.

The hidden greatness of these little concoctions is that they are, in and of themselves, nutritious—and they often deliver bona fide servings of fruits and vegetables. And in the Meaningful Touches department, batches of Egg "Noodles," Fried Lentils, Grilled Haloumi Cheese, Crunchy Chickpea Crumble, Tempeh Croutons, and others will raise the protein profile of your vegetarian meals, adding nutrition as well as novelty.

Knowing you have on hand something potently flavorful that can transform the plainest rice or vegetable or dish of pasta into something multidimensional and meal-worthy will greatly ease your menu planning. So consider devoting a little thought and time to these simple recipes on weekends and enjoy a certain tailwind on the nights that follow. This is eminently doable, as most of the recipes keep for at least several days without losing any of their brio. The biggest challenge may be remembering they are there, since smaller containers often get shoved to the back of the refrigerator. Make a list and post it somewhere visible to remind yourself. You will be glad you did.

Almond Faux Aioli

MAKES ABOUT 2 CUPS ❀ VEGAN

Ground almonds, sherry vinegar, lemon, olive oil, and garlic are the usual ingredients for a classic white gazpacho. In this recipe, we get off the texture train a few stops short of soup, arriving instead at a magnanimously rich, mayonnaise-like dip, topping, or spread. My favorite way to serve this is as an appetizer, tiled with a roof of grapes, surrounded by very crisp cucumber slices for dipping and some crisp white wine for sipping.

❀ Don't substitute another kind of vinegar—the sherry flavor is important. Also, use your highest-quality extra-virgin olive oil.

❀ You can swap in white grape juice for some of the water, if you like things less tart.

❀ Spread this on toast (topped with sliced grapes or peaches) or let it melt into the cavity of a freshly roasted acorn squash half.

❀ The aioli will keep for up to a week in a tightly covered container in the refrigerator.

1 cup blanched almonds, lightly toasted

½ teaspoon minced or crushed garlic

½ scant teaspoon salt

1 tablespoon fresh lemon juice

1 tablespoon sherry vinegar

½ cup extra-virgin olive oil

Up to ½ cup water, or ¼ cup water and ¼ cup white grape juice

Seedless red grapes, sliced in half, for topping (optional)

1. Combine the almonds, garlic, and salt in a blender or food processor and pulse until pulverized—a few degrees short of nut butter. Add the lemon juice and vinegar and buzz to combine.

2. Keep the machine going as you drizzle in the olive oil. It will emulsify as it goes in.

3. Transfer to a bowl and thin with water and/or white grape juice, stirring it in until the aioli reaches your desired consistency. Serve at room temperature or chilled, dotted all over with halved grapes, if desired.

Salsa Verde

MAKES ABOUT ¾ CUP ❧ VEGAN

Bright green fresh herbs are pulverized with garlic and a touch of vinegar, then bound with olive oil to make an emerald accent that lends both gravitas and shine to a broad variety of savory dishes. This is a sauce that you will find in my refrigerator at all times. I find myself dabbing it onto scrambled eggs, pasta (hot and cold), many soups, simple bean preparations, burgers, savory pancakes, plain cooked rice, and more.

As with pesto or chimichurri, this is a great way to store herbs—they will keep much longer as a paste and will take up a fraction of the refrigerator space.

❋ This will keep for up to a week in a tightly covered container in the refrigerator.

❋ If you are not a fan of cilantro, you can substitute an equal amount of fresh mint leaves.

½ (packed) cup *each* chopped fresh flat-leaf parsley, cilantro, and basil leaves

½ (packed) cup 1-inch pieces scallions (from about 4 large or 6 slim)

½ teaspoon minced or crushed garlic

Scant ¼ teaspoon salt, or more to taste

1 teaspoon white wine vinegar, fresh lemon juice, or fresh lime juice, or more to taste

6 tablespoons extra-virgin olive oil

1. Place the herbs, scallions, garlic, and salt in a food processor and pulverize with a few long pulses. You'll likely need to stop a couple of times to scrape down the sides.

2. Add the vinegar, lemon juice, or lime juice, buzz to blend, and then drizzle in the oil as you keep the machine running. When it's completely blended, taste for salt and possibly more vinegar, lemon juice, or lime juice.

OPTIONAL ENHANCEMENTS

Stir in lightly toasted pine nuts ❋ Add a pinch of grated lime zest ❋ Stir in 1 teaspoon Roasted Garlic Paste (page 173) ❋ Blend in a tablespoon or 2 of golden raisins or a couple of dried apricots ❋ Stir in a touch of Greek yogurt

Roasted Red Pepper Pesto

MAKES 1 CUP, ENOUGH FOR 4 TO 6 SERVINGS OF PASTA ❧ VEGAN

The sweet, complex flavor of roasted red bell peppers paradoxically makes this pesto both lighter and more substantial than the traditional Genovese version. It is also very pretty.

Serve it on pizza or pasta, on a baked potato, as a sandwich spread or dip for fresh vegetables, or as a topping for soups or stews or grains or anything else you might think of.

❋ You don't need to go to the trouble of roasting fresh peppers if you want this to be quick. Just open a jar of roasted peppers and drain the contents, keeping the juice to use, if needed, in pureeing the mixture in step 2.

❋ To roast red bell peppers: Preheat the oven to 400°F, with a rack in the center position. Line a baking sheet with foil and arrange the peppers on the sheet (there's no need for oil). Roast for up to 50 minutes, using tongs to rotate the peppers, in quarter turns, every 15 minutes or so. The peppers are done when the skins have wrinkled and largely blackened. Use tongs to transfer the roasted peppers to a bowl and cover it with foil or a plate for 30 minutes or longer to rest. They will give off delicious juices, which you should save for thinning the pesto, if needed, and for spooning onto grains or other vegetables. When they are cool enough to handle, use your hands to pull off and discard the skins, stems, and seeds. (*The peppers can be roasted up to 3 days in advance.*)

❋ The pesto will keep for up to 5 days in a tightly covered container in the refrigerator.

2 medium-large red bell peppers, roasted (see note), or one 12-ounce jar roasted red bell peppers, drained, liquid reserved

20–25 large fresh basil leaves

2 tablespoons pine nuts, lightly toasted

½ teaspoon minced or crushed garlic

½ teaspoon salt

1 teaspoon red wine vinegar

1–2 tablespoons extra-virgin olive oil and/or roasted walnut oil, plus more for storage

Pinch of sugar (optional)

Black pepper

Cayenne

1. Combine the peppers, basil, pine nuts, garlic, salt, and vinegar in a blender or a food processor and buzz until reasonably smooth.

2. With the motor running, drizzle in the oil. If the mixture seems too thick, you can add a little of the roasted pepper juices or packing liquid from the jar.

3. Transfer the pesto to a bowl and stir in a pinch of sugar, if desired, then add black pepper and cayenne to taste. Slick the top with a thin layer of oil, cover tightly, and refrigerate.

Romesco Sauce and a Cousin, Muhammara

MAKES ABOUT 1 CUP ❧ VEGAN

Roasted red peppers blended with nuts and seasonings come together quickly and extend themselves graciously into many contexts. Traditional versions of Romesco sometimes call for bread and tomatoes in addition to the traditional roasted peppers and almonds, but I like to keep it pared down to the essentials, so this version is probably the simplest one you'll see anywhere.

Muhammara (which means "reddened" in Arabic) is another version of the same idea: peppers and nuts—this time walnuts—plus touches of cumin, pomegranate, and lemon.

Uses? Blend it into freshly cooked pasta. Spoon it onto rice. Serve it with crackers and cheese. Spread it thickly on toast.

❀ Toast the almonds in a toaster oven at 250°F or in a small skillet over medium-low heat for 10 minutes, or until they have a moderate color and an immoderately wonderful aroma. Watch them carefully so they don't get overly dark or burn.

❀ This will keep for up to 5 days in a tightly covered container in the refrigerator.

½ cup blanched almonds, lightly toasted

½ teaspoon minced or crushed garlic

2 medium-large red bell peppers, roasted (see note, opposite page), or one 12-ounce jar roasted red bell peppers, drained

1½ teaspoons red wine vinegar, or more to taste

¼ teaspoon salt

Cayenne

Olive oil for storage

1. Place the almonds and garlic in a blender or a food processor and pulse a few times until the almonds are ground to a fine meal, just this side of the texture of polenta.

2. Add the roasted peppers and vinegar to the almonds and sprinkle in the salt and some cayenne. Process until very smooth, then taste to adjust the vinegar and/or cayenne. Transfer to a container with a tight-fitting lid, slick the top with a little olive oil, and refrigerate.

MUHAMMARA

Follow the instructions for Romesco (above), replacing the almonds with the same amount of lightly toasted walnuts and omitting the vinegar. Add ¼ teaspoon ground cumin, 1 teaspoon pomegranate molasses (see note, page 118), and ½ teaspoon (or a little more, to taste) fresh lemon juice to the other ingredients. If you have some Aleppo pepper on hand, a light sprinkling of it is good on top.

Tahini-Ginger-Pomegranate Sauce

MAKES A SCANT ½ CUP ✿ VEGAN

Tahini has been successfully blended with lemon, garlic, and salt forever, and that ancient combination might well be the most proven sauce of all time (see opposite page). Less well known is tahini's great affinity for ginger and pomegranate—such a natural trio that I now call this my sesame trifecta. Try it on broiled-until-tender eggplant, on plain cooked grains such as bulgur, and dabbed onto Spinach-Basmati Soup with Yogurt (page 45).

✿ The yield is low, but this is concentrated. You can easily multiply the recipe.

✿ Store in a tightly covered container in the refrigerator. It will keep for up to 2 weeks.

3 tablespoons tahini

2 teaspoons finely minced fresh ginger

½ teaspoon minced or crushed garlic

2 teaspoons pomegranate molasses (see note, page 118), or more to taste

1 teaspoon agave nectar or sugar

½ teaspoon salt, or more to taste

5–6 tablespoons hot water, or more as needed

1. Combine the tahini, ginger, garlic, pomegranate molasses, sweetener, and salt in a small bowl.

2. Add 5 tablespoons hot water, mashing it in and then stirring slowly to thoroughly combine. It may need another tablespoon or more of water. Also, taste to adjust the salt and molasses. You're aiming for a thick, drizzling consistency, something that takes its time exiting a spoon. Keep in mind that the sauce will thicken as it sits, and more hot water may be needed at serving time.

3. Serve right away or store tightly covered in the refrigerator and serve later. Bring to room temperature before serving.

OPTIONAL ENHANCEMENT

A generous scattering of pomegranate seeds blanketing the top is beautiful. If pomegranates are out of season, consider doing the same with another fruit (pitted, chopped dark cherries come to mind).

MINING A POMEGRANATE

Pomegranate seeds are juicy little jewels—bright red, tart, and crunchy. The problem is, they're encased in a hard, tight skin, which although lovely to look at, is difficult to break into. When you finally get the skin open, another challenge lies inside: The precious seeds are buried within a copious amount of pith. Here's how to coax out the precious cargo without splattering your kitchen with scarlet evidence.

Have ready a large bowl of water. Slice the pomegranate into quarters and immediately submerge the pieces. Pull the pieces apart underwater, pushing the pith out of the way as you dig, pull, or otherwise extract the seeds from the pith with your hands. The seeds will yield readily, sinking to the bottom of the bowl while the porous pith floats to the top. Skim the pith with a mesh utensil or slotted spoon, then drain the seeds, shaking them dry.

Basic Tahini-Lemon Sauce

MAKES ABOUT 1¼ CUPS ✿ VEGAN

Quick and easy—and with a refrigerator shelf life of a month, if tightly covered—this handy sauce can multitask, depending on how far you thin it down. At the supple end of the texture spectrum, it can be a salad dressing for a sturdy chopped salad of romaine, cucumbers, radishes, and tomatoes or a sauce for falafel. In thicker states, it can be a sauce for cooked vegetables, a dip for raw vegetables, a coating for grilled tofu, or a partner to combine in equal parts with mashed eggplant for a classic, cracker-loving appetizer.

6 tablespoons tahini

2½ tablespoons fresh lemon juice

½ teaspoon minced or crushed garlic, or more to taste

¼ teaspoon salt, or more to taste

Up to 1 cup hot water

Finely minced fresh parsley (optional)

Cayenne (optional)

1. Combine the tahini, lemon juice, garlic, and ¼ teaspoon salt in a small bowl.

2. Add ½ cup hot water, mashing it in and then stirring it slowly to thoroughly combine. If you like this consistency, simply adjust the salt to taste, and it's ready. You can also keep stirring in water until it's as thin as you desire, adjusting the salt as you go. If you prefer things on the garlicky side, add a touch more.

3. Serve immediately or store in the refrigerator, tightly covered, and serve later. Bring to room temperature and stir in a little minced parsley and cayenne to taste, if desired, before serving.

Miso-Almond Sauce

MAKES ABOUT ¾ CUP ✿ VEGAN

Three ingredients in as many minutes. This sauce keeps forever and is very delicious and good for you. Serve it on freshly cooked soba noodles, topped with steamed or grilled vegetables; spoon it onto sautéed greens or rice; or use it as a dip for cooked or raw vegetables.

✿ The sauce will keep for about 1 month, tightly covered and refrigerated.

3 tablespoons light (shiro) miso, or any variety you prefer

3 tablespoons almond butter

6 tablespoons warmed apple juice, or more to taste

1. Mash together the miso and almond butter in a small bowl.

2. Slowly add the warmed apple juice, mashing it in until the mixture becomes uniform.

3. Serve warm or at room temperature.

Misoyaki Sauce

MAKES ABOUT 1 CUP ✿ VEGAN

Miso is a soybean paste, often with a grain component, inoculated with a culture and fermented—hence the seemingly infinite shelf life. The many varieties of miso offer a range of tastes, from the sweetness of the lighter shades to the salty pungency of the deeper hues.

For this sauce, miso is softened with mirin and laced with garlic. That's the whole story. Thinning it with water is an option, but nothing further is needed. Serve over hot things, most notably onions (opposite page) or baste it over grilled or broiled eggplant, peppers, zucchini, summer squash, mushrooms (especially portobellos), or tofu.

❋ What kind of miso is best for this? Use what you can find. If you are lucky enough to live near a Japanese market, choose the lighter-colored, milder-tasting shiro miso. Feel free to experiment with other types as well, tailoring this recipe to your own preference.

❋ Important: When cooking with miso, keep the heat on medium or lower and check the bottom surface of your item frequently, as miso can burn if it gets too hot.

❋ This will keep for a month, tightly covered and refrigerated.

½ cup mirin (Japanese rice wine)

1 teaspoon minced or crushed garlic

½ cup light (shiro) miso, or any variety you prefer

Up to ½ cup water (optional)

1. Measure the mirin into a microwaveable liquid measuring cup and zap for about 1 minute, or until hot.

2. Add the garlic, letting the heat of the mirin cook it ever so slightly.

3. Put the miso in a small bowl and slowly pour in the garlic mirin, whisking gently until it is completely blended. You can also just add the miso directly to the measuring cup, until it reaches the 1 cup line. Add a little water, if you wish, to taste.

4. Serve immediately or store in the refrigerator, tightly covered, and serve later. Bring to room temperature before serving.

OPTIONAL ENHANCEMENT

Spoon the sauce (without added water) onto very firm tofu (cut into ½-inch-thick slabs) as you sauté it in a preheated, generously oiled pan over medium heat. Keep spooning on small amounts, and frequently loosen and turn the tofu after applying the glaze. It will turn a perfect shade of golden. Watch very carefully, because the glaze can burn easily.

MISOYAKI–SCRAMBLED ONION SAUCE

MAKES ABOUT 2 CUPS ❧ VEGAN

Try this quietly opulent sauce on eggplant, pasta, broccoli, noodles, toast, and potatoes. The amount of sauce may seem excessive when you add it to the onions in the pan, but it will all come together.

❋ This keeps for a week, covered and refrigerated.

1 recipe Misoyaki Sauce (with the optional ½ cup water; opposite page)

2–3 medium red onions (1–1½ pounds total), thickly sliced

1 tablespoon grapeseed, peanut, or canola oil

1. Combine the sauce and onions in a shallow pan, such as a 9-inch square baking pan or a pie pan, and marinate at room temperature for at least 1 hour and up to overnight (or refrigerate, if your kitchen is very hot).

2. Place a large (10- to 12-inch) skillet over medium heat for about a minute, then add the oil and swirl to coat the pan. Use tongs to lift the onions from the sauce, shaking most of the extra liquid back into the pan. Reserve the sauce.

3. Add the wet onions to the skillet (they will sizzle) and cook, stirring frequently, for 15 to 20 minutes, or until they become very soft.

4. Pour in all the Misoyaki Sauce from the pan (it will look like too much) and bring it to a boil. Turn the heat to low and keep cooking, stirring often (and eventually scraping the bottom of the pan), for about 15 minutes, or until the sauce is reduced by about half. Serve hot, warm, or at room temperature on just about anything.

Soy Caramel

MAKES ABOUT ¼ CUP ❧ VEGAN

Once you make this amazing syrup, I predict it will be summoned often. Compelling and thoroughly untemperamental, this little reduction delivers a fine touch of ambiguity, umami on the edge of salty and sweet. It will disappear into whatever you drizzle it on, so it's a nice way to provide a plateful of quiet surprise. You can also bring it to the table and let people enjoy drizzling it themselves onto plain cooked vegetables, grains, or Asian-style noodles.

❀ The yield may seem low, but this is very concentrated, so a little bit will go far. Also, you can easily multiply the recipe.

❀ Store the caramel, covered, at room temperature. It will keep for a month.

¼ cup agave nectar

¼ cup water

½ medium garlic clove

2 slices ginger (slightly larger and thicker than the size of quarters)

2 tablespoons soy sauce

1 tablespoon fresh lemon juice

1. Combine the agave and water in a small saucepan and whisk until uniform. Add the garlic and ginger and bring to a boil. Reduce the heat to a modest simmer and cook, uncovered, for about 5 minutes, or until reduced by about one third.

2. Add the soy sauce and let it bubble over low heat for another 5 minutes.

3. Remove from the heat, stir in the lemon juice, and let cool and infuse for at least 30 minutes before fishing out the garlic and ginger.

4. Store in a covered container at room temperature and serve as desired.

Mushroom Gravy for Everyone

MAKES 6 TO 8 SERVINGS ❈ VEGAN AND GLUTEN-FREE

Everyone needs gravy once in a while. But for people who eat neither meat nor wheat and also avoid dairy, it can be a gravy desert out there. Here, then, is a delicious dairy- and gluten-free recipe that I hope will tie together the loose ends of your dinner. Even meat, dairy, and wheat lovers will find this hits the spot.

❈ Use it on mashed potatoes, on or under other mashes, with Mini Buttermilk Rosemary-Walnut Biscuits (page 163) or Ginger-Pecan Mini Biscuits (page 142), or over plain steamed vegetables. For more ideas, check the menus on pages 12 to 17.

❈ This recipe stores well in a tightly covered container in the refrigerator for a week. It reheats easily, stirred over low heat.

2 tablespoons olive oil

1 medium onion, finely minced

¼ heaping teaspoon rubbed dried sage

¼ heaping teaspoon dried thyme

1 teaspoon minced or crushed garlic

10 medium-large mushrooms (a generous ½ pound), wiped clean, stemmed as necessary, and minced

1 teaspoon salt

¼ cup cornstarch

1 quart vegetable stock (page 22) or low-sodium store bought

Gluten-free soy sauce to taste (optional)

Black pepper

1. Place a medium saucepan over medium heat for about a minute, then add the oil and swirl to coat the pan. Toss in the onion and dried herbs and cook, stirring, for 5 minutes, or until the onion softens.

2. Stir in the garlic and cook, stirring often, for another minute or so, until the garlic becomes aromatic.

3. Stir in the mushrooms and salt, cover, and cook for 10 minutes, stirring once in a while, until the mushrooms cook down and release their juices.

4. Meanwhile, place the cornstarch in a bowl and slowly pour in about a cup of the stock, stirring with a small whisk until the mixture is completely smooth.

5. Pour the rest of the stock into the mushroom mixture and let it come to a boil uncovered over medium heat. When it boils, turn the heat to medium-low and drizzle in the cornstarch slurry, stirring constantly with a wooden spoon.

6. Keep cooking, stirring very often, for another 10 minutes, or until the gravy is glossy and gently thickened. Add soy sauce to taste, if you like, and season liberally with black pepper. Serve hot.

Basic Vinaigrette

MAKES A SCANT ⅔ CUP ✹ VEGAN

Every good home cook needs a basic vinaigrette. This one can be yours.

In addition to light-handedly coating your crisp salad greens with this vinaigrette, try it on any freshly cooked, still-warm vegetable and/or use it to marinate leftover cooked vegetables for tomorrow's salad or side dish. Pool it under steaming (or room-temperature) cooked potatoes, sweet potatoes, or beans. Venture into stone-fruit pairings or use it to lace cut-up apples and pears, studded with cheese and sprinkled with toasted nuts. Or put small bowls of vinaigrette on the table for dipping thick slices of crusty artisan bread.

✹ To get the sturdiest, most integrated emulsion, measure all the oil into a separate container first, so you can drizzle it gradually in one steady stream (rather than a tablespoon at a time) as you whisk it in.

✹ Vinaigrettes keep for at least 2 months in small, lidded jars in your refrigerator. (I have a whole section of them in mine.) Bring them to room temperature before using, so the oil will soften back into the original emulsion.

✹ Vinaigrettes can set sail in many directions. In addition to the variations on the following page, look through the salad chapter (pages 61 through 133) for more ideas. You can also invent your own.

1–2 tablespoons finely minced shallot

½ teaspoon salt

2 teaspoons agave nectar or sugar

2 tablespoons red wine vinegar

6 tablespoons extra-virgin olive oil

1. Combine the shallot, salt, sweetener, and vinegar in a small bowl or a jar with a lid, and whisk to thoroughly blend.

2. Drizzle in the olive oil, whisking as you go, until it is fully incorporated.

3. Store tightly covered in the refrigerator. Shake and/or stir from the bottom before using.

SWAPS

Garlic (about 1 teaspoon minced or crushed) instead of shallot ✹ Fresh lemon or lime juice swapped in for some of the vinegar ✹ Roasted nut oil (any kind) swapped in for some of the olive oil ✹ Light-colored honey or pure maple syrup swapped in for the agave nectar or sugar ✹ Experiment with various other vinegars

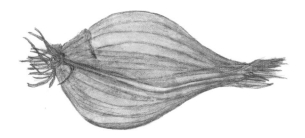

Favorite Vinaigrette Variations

ALL THESE YIELD A SCANT ⅔ CUP

ORANGE-SESAME VINAIGRETTE

🌱 VEGAN

In step 1, add ½ teaspoon grated orange zest and 1–2 tablespoons fresh orange juice in addition to the vinegar. In step 2, replace 1 tablespoon of the olive oil with Chinese sesame oil.

JALAPEÑO-CILANTRO-LIME VINAIGRETTE

🌱 VEGAN

In step 1, use fresh lime juice in place of the vinegar and add up to 1 tablespoon finely minced jalapeño, ¼ teaspoon cumin seeds, and 1–2 tablespoons finely minced cilantro.

POMEGRANATE VINAIGRETTE

🌱 VEGAN

In step 1, reduce the sweetener to 1 teaspoon and add 2–3 tablespoons pomegranate molasses (see note, page 118). In step 2, replace some of the olive oil with roasted walnut oil.

SHERRY-HONEY-TARRAGON-MUSTARD VINAIGRETTE

In step 1, use sherry vinegar and add up to 2 tablespoons Dijon or plain yellow mustard, a big pinch of dried tarragon or 1 tablespoon minced fresh, and use 1 tablespoon light-colored honey for the sweetener.

CREAMY BUTTERMILK VINAIGRETTE

In step 1, increase the sweetener to 1 tablespoon. In step 2, stir in ¼ cup buttermilk after the oil is incorporated.

Thick Cranberry-Orange Vinaigrette

MAKES 1¾ CUPS ❧ VEGAN

A mere dab of this potent, gaudy, sweet-tart sauce will transform any dish it graces. My favorite use for it is as a bright topping spooned onto a bowl of Sweet Potato–Pear Soup (page 33). It's also a main component of Spiced Carrots in Thick Cranberry-Orange Vinaigrette (page 102).

❋ This will keep for 3 months or longer, covered and refrigerated.

1 cup cranberries (fresh or frozen)

½ navel orange, coarsely chopped (peel included)

1 tablespoon chopped shallot

¼ teaspoon salt

3 tablespoons agave nectar or sugar

2 teaspoons cider vinegar

¼ cup extra-virgin olive oil

1. Combine the cranberries, orange pieces, shallot, and salt in a food processor and buzz until the fruit is pulverized into a thick, pulpy state.

2. Add the sweetener and vinegar and pulse a few times until it is blended.

3. With the machine running, add the olive oil, a tablespoon at a time. When it's all incorporated, it's ready.

Four Easy Sweet-Sour Glazes

BALSAMIC REDUCTION

MAKES ABOUT ½ CUP ❈ VEGAN

American versions of balsamic vinegar are fairly sweet, and if you enjoy their effect on savory dishes, you might well love this thickened version. You can drizzle this syrup over more foods than you might imagine—from roasted vegetables and grain dishes to mashes and grilled tempeh and tofu. It also works on pancakes, fruit, and sorbet.

❈ Store in a covered container at room temperature, where it will keep indefinitely. If it solidifies, zap it in a microwave for a few seconds or stir in a little boiling water, and it will soften right up again.

1 cup balsamic vinegar

1. Turn on the stovetop fan and/or open your kitchen windows—the fumes will be intense. Place the vinegar in a small nonaluminum saucepan (a shallow one, if possible) and heat to boiling.

2. Turn the heat down as low as possible and simmer uncovered for about 30 minutes, or until the vinegar is thick and reduced in volume by about half. Check it every 5 minutes or so, to be sure it isn't cooking down too quickly. You don't want it to reduce further than slightly more than half its original volume, nor do you want it to burn.

POMEGRANATE-LIME GLAZE

MAKES ABOUT ⅓ CUP ❈ VEGAN

Pomegranate molasses (see note, page 118) is available at Middle Eastern food shops or in the imported foods section of grocery stores. In this simple sauce, pomegranate molasses is mixed with some fresh lime juice for a stunning result. It's good on many hot or room-temperature vegetables, grains, tofu, cheese, burgers, fruit arrangements, and mashes. A little goes a long way.

❈ This keeps for 3 months in a covered container at room temperature.

¼ cup pomegranate molasses

1 tablespoon fresh lime juice, or more to taste

Combine the ingredients in a small bowl and mix until smooth, then adjust the lime juice to taste. Serve at room temperature.

SWEET-SOUR DIPPING-DRIZZLING SAUCE

MAKES A SCANT ½ CUP ❋ VEGAN (WHEN MADE WITH AGAVE NECTAR OR SUGAR)

Throw this very pretty glaze together in seconds. Drizzle it onto (or serve it next to) roasted or grilled vegetables or plain cooked grains or beans—also, Caramelized Onion–Brown Rice-Lentil Burgers (page 297), Wild Rice Pancakes with Mushrooms and Goat Cheese (page 318), Mashed Celery Root (page 174), or Golden Lentils with Soft, Sweet Onions (page 182), or dip pieces of Asparagus Puff Pastry Tart (page 282) into it.

❋ Wash your hands and equipment with soap and warm water after handling the chili.

❋ This will keep for 3 months in a covered container at room temperature.

¼ cup cider vinegar or unseasoned rice vinegar

2 tablespoons agave nectar, light-colored honey, or sugar

1–2 tablespoons chili paste (any kind)

¼ teaspoon salt

A few thin slices from 1 fresh, hot chili (optional)

A few tablespoons grated carrot (optional)

A few torn cilantro leaves (optional)

1. Combine the vinegar, sweetener, chili paste, and salt in a small bowl and mix to blend.

2. Add the chili, if desired. Add the carrot and/or cilantro, if using, shortly before serving. Serve at room temperature.

MAPLE-MUSTARD GLAZE

MAKES A SCANT 1 CUP ❋ VEGAN

Spoon this onto plain grilled tofu, portobellos, or eggplant slices. It's also a great condiment for the entire burger chapter (pages 289 to 321) and makes a good topping for just about any plain cooked vegetable, especially squash, sweet potatoes, and carrots.

❋ This glaze keeps for weeks in a tightly lidded jar or container in the refrigerator, although it might dry out a little, in which case you can refresh it with a few drops of water.

½ cup Dijon mustard

⅓ cup pure maple syrup

2 teaspoons Chinese sesame oil

2 teaspoons soy sauce

Combine all the ingredients in a small-medium bowl and whisk until blended. Serve at room temperature.

Two Quick Touches of Creaminess

When you long for a dab of creamy, flavorful richness with (or on) your food, here's how to whip up something fast and delicious with mostly ordinary ingredients. These two personal favorites can be assembled spontaneously and are best served freshly made.

CHIPOTLE CREAM

MAKES 1 CUP

Sour cream provides a cool counterpoint to the hot, smoky flavor of chipotle chilies, creating a perfect balance of edgy and smooth. Chipotle chilies (smoked jalapeños) are available canned in tomato sauce (called "adobo") in the imported foods section of many grocery stores and specialty shops. This two-ingredient recipe takes only a minute to throw together, and makes a great dip or topping for just about anything with Latin flavors. Spoon it on top of Soft Cuban-Style Black Beans (page 180) or Cumin-Scented Black Bean Burgers (page 292).

❋ Don't forget to wash the knife, cutting board, and your hands with soap and warm water after handling the chilies.

❋ Store the cream in a tightly covered container in the refrigerator, where it will keep for up to a week. The flavors continue to meld and develop as it sits.

1 cup sour cream

½ teaspoon minced canned chipotle chilies in adobo, or more to taste

1. Place the sour cream in a bowl, add ½ teaspoon minced chipotles, and whisk until smooth. Let the mixture sit for about 10 minutes, so the chipotle flavor can fully infuse the sour cream.

2. Add more chipotle if you prefer it stronger. Serve cold or at room temperature.

RAITA (INDIAN-STYLE YOGURT SAUCE)

MAKES 3 CUPS

Add a little Indian-style seasoning and some minced fresh vegetables to a bowlful of yogurt, and you have a raita—a general term, in Indian cooking, for the refreshing yogurt sauces that are served as a cooling contrast to spicy curries. It is also a fabulous dip to serve with crackers or breads.

❋ Make this as close to serving time as possible. It keeps for only 1 day in a tightly covered container in the refrigerator.

1 teaspoon cumin seeds

2 cups plain yogurt (low-fat or Greek are OK)

¼ teaspoon salt

⅛ teaspoon cayenne

1 small (6-inch) cucumber, peeled if the skin is bitter and minced

1. Lightly toast the cumin seeds in a small skillet over medium-low heat for 3 to 5 minutes, or until fragrant. Watch carefully so they don't burn.

2. Place the yogurt in a medium bowl and add the toasted cumin seeds, along with the salt, cayenne, and cucumber. Mix until thoroughly blended. Serve cold.

Five Easy Mayonnaise-Based Sauces

EACH MAKES 4 OR 5 DOLLOP-SIZED SERVINGS

Simple sauces that use mayonnaise as a base can augment your already delicious creations, giving them a satisfying, rich finish. Use a good brand of store-bought mayonnaise that contains neither sugar nor "low-fat" anything—just the plain, real thing, made with eggs, vinegar, and oil.

The instructions for all of these are the same: Combine everything in a small-medium bowl and stir to blend with a small whisk or a fork. Salt and pepper to taste are optional. Cover and let rest for at least 10 minutes in the refrigerator. Serve cold or at cool room temperature (full room temperature, if you're serving it dabbed onto something hot).

❋ All of these will keep for a week, tightly covered and refrigerated.

LEMON-TARRAGON MAYONNAISE

Serve this anywhere you would serve hollandaise: over asparagus, on top of poached or fried eggs, as a dip for artichokes, or on baked potatoes.

½ cup mayonnaise

1 tablespoon minced fresh tarragon or 1 teaspoon dried

1 tablespoon fresh lemon juice

Up to 1 teaspoon grated lemon zest (optional)

Salt and black pepper (optional)

WASABI MAYONNAISE

Use this lively mayo on sandwiches, burgers, potatoes, salads, and pretty much any other place you'd use regular mayonnaise.

❋ You can buy wasabi (spicy Japanese green horseradish) in powdered form or in a little tube of prepared paste. The powdered form is easily made into paste by stirring in some water per the package directions.

½ cup mayonnaise

2 teaspoons wasabi paste

2 teaspoons seasoned rice vinegar

Salt and black pepper (optional)

OPTIONAL ENHANCEMENTS

Minced shiso leaves (a Japanese herb, available in the produce sections of Asian grocery stores) ❋ A few drops of Chinese sesame oil ❋ Up to 1 tablespoon minced pickled ginger

GARLIC MAYONNAISE

Garlic mayo makes a tasty spread for burgers and sandwiches and goes brilliantly with vegetables. It's a natural with almost any kind of potatoes, from baked to fried. Be sure to keep this very cold and eat it within a couple of days.

½ cup mayonnaise

1–2 teaspoons finely minced or crushed garlic or 1 tablespoon Roasted Garlic Paste (page 173)

1 teaspoon cider vinegar or balsamic vinegar

Salt and black pepper (optional)

Avocado "Mayo"

❧ VEGAN

CUCUMBER MAYONNAISE

Think picnic: This is great on simple sandwiches or heaped onto grilled tofu, cold cooked potatoes, or vegetables.

½ cup mayonnaise

1 teaspoon fresh lemon juice

½ small (5–6 inch) cucumber, peeled, seeded, and finely minced (¼ cup)

Up to 1 tablespoon minced fresh dill and/or scallion (optional)

Salt and black pepper (optional)

CHILI-CILANTRO MAYONNAISE

If you love the flavor of cilantro, try this mayo on burritos, vegetables, sandwiches, and burgers.

½ cup mayonnaise

¼ cup finely minced cilantro

1 teaspoon chili powder

1 teaspoon fresh lime juice

Up to 3 tablespoons of your favorite tomato salsa (optional)

Salt and black pepper (optional)

Mash a peeled, pitted, perfectly ripe avocado on a plate with a fork. Add a few drops of fresh lemon or lime juice and salt and black pepper to taste. Use right away as a mayonnaise stand-in, or simply heaped onto a piece of excellent toast.

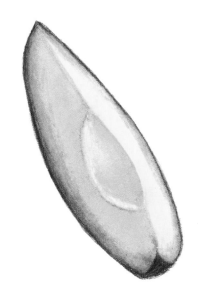

Beet, Orange, and Ginger Marmalade

MAKES A GENEROUS 2 CUPS ❀ VEGAN (WHEN MADE WITH AGAVE NECTAR)

When you need a spot of color and flavor on the dinner plate, here is your ticket. Just a spoonful of this potent condiment will punch up the meal, no matter how simple. Serve it with just about any burger, spooned onto cooked sweet potatoes or squash, or as a contrasting touch near or on a Cozy Mash.

❀ The beets need to be cooked well ahead of time and can be either roasted or boiled. Roasting instructions are on page 97. For boiling, simply simmer the unpeeled beets until fork-tender, then drain.

❀ Zest the orange before juicing it. For chopped zest, it's easiest to strip the peel (just the pigmented part—not the bitter, white pith layer immediately beneath) with a vegetable peeler, then chop it with a sharp knife. You'll likely need an extra orange or two to get the right amount of zest. Save the bald oranges for juice or for snacking.

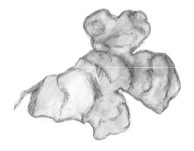

❀ Lightly spray the measuring spoon with nonstick spray before wrangling honey or agave. You'll see why.

❀ This keeps for up to 2 weeks in the refrigerator.

¾ pound cooked beets (about 3 medium)

½ teaspoon salt

2–3 tablespoons chopped orange zest (start with the lesser amount) from 2–3 large oranges

5 tablespoons fresh orange juice

1 tablespoon fresh lemon juice

⅓ cup minced crystallized ginger

2 tablespoons agave nectar or light-colored honey, or more to taste

1. Peel and coarsely grate or very finely mince the beets by hand or in a food processor with the large-hole grating attachment. Transfer to a medium bowl.

2. Add all the remaining ingredients, mix thoroughly, and taste to see if it needs more sweetener or orange zest.

3. Transfer to a jar with a tight-fitting lid. Cover and refrigerate for up to 2 weeks.

Caramelized Onion and Lemon Marmalade

MAKES ABOUT 2 CUPS ❧ VEGAN (WHEN MADE WITH AGAVE NECTAR OR SUGAR)

The interplay of onion and lemon steps up winningly, once again. Serve this marmalade with any savory dish or on toast, with cheese. It also goes beautifully with scrambled eggs, grilled tofu or tempeh, or plain cooked beans and/or grains.

❁ The best way to achieve chopped lemon zest is to shave the skin (just the yellow part, not the white) with a vegetable peeler, and then chop it with a sharp knife.

1 tablespoon grapeseed, canola, or peanut oil

4 cups minced yellow or red onions (2 large)

½ teaspoon salt

1 tablespoon balsamic vinegar

¼ cup fresh lemon juice, or more to taste (remove zest first)

1 tablespoon agave nectar, light-colored honey, or sugar

1 tablespoon chopped lemon zest

1. Place a large (10- to 12-inch) skillet over medium heat for about a minute, then add the oil and swirl to coat the pan. Toss in the onions and salt and cook, stirring, for 5 minutes.

2. Reduce the heat to low, cover, and cook, stirring occasionally, for 20 to 30 minutes, or until the onions are supersoft and deeply golden. (Splash in a little water to keep them from sticking, if they get dry.)

3. Stir in the vinegar, cover again, and cook for 5 minutes. Stir in the lemon juice and sweetener and cook, uncovered, for 5 minutes longer.

4. Remove the skillet from the heat and stir in the lemon zest. Cool to room temperature, then pack into a jar with a tight-fitting lid. Cover and refrigerate for up to 3 weeks.

Celery-Almond-Date Saladita

MAKES 4 OR 5 SERVINGS

Celery doesn't get top billing very often, which makes this dish even more of a standout and conversation piece than it already is. The olive oil, lemon, dates, blue cheese, and almonds are so at home here that it will seem as though they made this dish without you. "Meant to be," the meaning of the Yiddish word *beshert*, comes to mind.

Try this as part of a sampler of Little Salads (page 76). It's equally strong freestanding, as an appetizer, side dish, or after-dinner refresher. It's especially good with Butternut Risotto (page 204).

❋ Use a very sharp knife—or possibly even a mandoline—to slice the celery superthin.

❋ This is a good opportunity to buy and taste a small amount of a blue cheese you might have been curious about. If you add the cheese sooner, it blends into the dressing. Wait and sprinkle it on top at serving time, and it will be more distinct.

❋ The cheese provides more than enough salt for the recipe. People can add some at the table, if they want to, but that's unlikely.

2 teaspoons fresh lemon juice

1 teaspoon light-colored honey

1 tablespoon extra-virgin olive oil

3 large celery stalks, very thinly sliced

4–6 dates, pitted and chopped

1–2 ounces good blue cheese, crumbled

¼ cup almonds, chopped, or skinned slivered almonds, lightly toasted

Black pepper

1. Combine the lemon juice, honey, and olive oil in a medium bowl and whisk to blend.

2. Toss in the celery and dates and stir to coat. (You can stir in the blue cheese at this point, or wait until later.) Cover and chill for at least an hour; overnight is fine.

3. Serve cold or at cool room temperature, topped with blue cheese (if you didn't add it earlier), a sprinkling of almonds, and a delicate amount of black pepper.

SALADITAS

"Saladita" is my term for a colorful, slightly unusual medley of diced vegetables and/or fruit that is served cold or at cool room temperature as a side dish, relish, small salad, or topping, or anywhere you would use a salsa or a slaw. These combinations are quick, fresh, uncooked, and utterly accessible.

One of the many things I love about the saladita category is the immediacy of both the ingredients themselves and the preparation: Cut, toss, serve, and eat minutes later. Saladitas are also a wonderful opportunity to embrace simplicity—a small-scale expression of seasonal produce.

Avocado-Grapefruit-Mango Saladita

MAKES 4 OR 5 GENEROUS CONDIMENT SERVINGS ❋ VEGAN

Bright green avocado visits the other side of the color wheel to join purply-red onion, pink grapefruit, and sunny mango in this sparkling collaboration. Wonderful on its own—and a great brunch appetizer served in little bowls—this also goes well with any savory dish, especially cornmeal-based items, such as Fully Loaded Buttermilk Corn Cakes (page 316).

❋ Try to find a perfectly ripe avocado that is mostly firm but gives a little when you press it respectfully. You want one that is not too soft, so you can get clean little squares that stay distinct and won't mush into sauce.

❋ To remove the grapefruit sections from their membranes, first peel the fruit completely with a serrated knife. Then hold it over a bowl, sawing in and out of the membranes with the same knife to release the sections. (Push aside any seeds as you go.) Squeeze in the juice from the membranes and discard them. (Keep a few damp towels handy.) This method also works for oranges.

❋ Without the avocado, this will keep for up to a week in a tightly covered container in the refrigerator. Once the avocado is in, serve the dish within an hour.

⅓ cup minced red onion

2 pink grapefruits, peeled, sectioned, and sections removed from membranes (see note)

1–2 ripe mangoes or 1 cup diced frozen mango (see note, page 40)

A touch of salt (optional)

1 teaspoon agave nectar or sugar

1 perfectly ripe avocado

Cayenne

Torn cilantro leaves (optional)

1. Put on a kettle of water to boil. Place the onion in a strainer over a bowl in the sink. Pour the boiling water over the onion and let it drain for at least 5 minutes.

2. Put the grapefruit in a medium bowl. If using fresh mango, cut the mango off its pit, peel it, and cut the flesh into small pieces. (If using frozen mango, cut the undefrosted larger cubes into small dice.) Add the mango to the grapefruit, scraping in as much of the messy, delicious mango pulp as you can retrieve from the cutting board.

3. Stir in the onion, along with the salt (if using) and sweetener. Cover and refrigerate until shortly before serving.

4. Just before serving, pit, peel, and dice the avocado and gently stir it into the mixture. Adjust the salt, if desired, add a little cayenne to taste, and garnish with a few cilantro leaves, if desired. Serve cold.

Fire-Roasted Bell Pepper Saladita

MAKES ABOUT 6 SERVINGS AS AN ACCENT; 3 OR 4 SERVINGS AS AN APPETIZER OR MINI-SALAD ❋ VEGAN

Bell peppers acquire a subtle, smoky flavor when cooked in near-direct contact with very high heat. In this recipe, that high heat comes from a close-up encounter with a broiler, after which the peppers are peeled, minced, and marinated. The result is a bold relish that can be piled onto slices of fresh cheese (possibly on a cracker or piece of good toast) or served on a raft of sliced, cooked potato or thickly applied to a burger. Mix it into pasta or rice, spoon it into some cooked beans, or serve with Chard- or Collard-Wrapped Polenta-Chili Tamale Packages (page 338) or alongside Mushroom-Barley-Cashew Burgers (page 299). It can also be served freestanding as a first course, or on the side or top of a layered plate (see page 167).

❋ If you happen to have a charcoal grill heated to white-coal readiness, go ahead and cook the peppers there instead of under the broiler.

❋ This keeps for up to 2 weeks, tightly covered and refrigerated. It actually tastes best after it's had a chance to sit around for a day or so, allowing the flavors to develop and merge.

Olive oil for the baking sheet and for storage

4 large red, yellow, or orange bell peppers (about 2 pounds), or two 12-ounce jars roasted bell peppers, drained

1 teaspoon minced or crushed garlic

½ teaspoon salt, or more to taste

½ teaspoon ground cumin, or more to taste

2 teaspoons cider vinegar, or more to taste

1 tablespoon fresh lemon or lime juice, or more to taste

½ teaspoon agave nectar or sugar (optional)

Cayenne or crushed red pepper

1. If using fresh bell peppers, preheat the broiler and lightly brush a foil-lined baking sheet with olive oil.

2. Place the whole peppers on the baking sheet. Broil the peppers until they are blistered all over and covered with black patches, using tongs to carefully turn the peppers a few times while they are cooking. This will take up to 15 minutes, depending on your broiler.

3. Transfer the peppers to a bowl, cover with a plate, and cool for at least 45 minutes. They will give off a good amount of delicious juice while they cool.

4. Peel the peppers and remove and discard the seeds and stems. Mince the flesh, and return the minced peppers to the bowl. Stir in the garlic, salt, cumin, vinegar, and lime or lemon juice. Add as much of the saved juice from the peppers as you wish. (Save any extra juices for soup or just to spoon over rice or vegetables.) Stir to combine, then adjust the seasonings to taste, adding some sweetener if you like, and heating things up a touch with the cayenne or crushed red pepper.

5. Serve cold or at cool room temperature. If you are going to store the saladita in the refrigerator, coat the top with a slick of olive oil.

OPTIONAL ENHANCEMENTS

Make this into a salad by mixing in some minced cucumber ❋ Top with tiny dice of firm, ripe avocado ❋ Top with lightly toasted pine nuts or pumpkin seeds or with Chili Pepitas (page 401) ❋ Toss in some minced cilantro

Jicama–Pink Grapefruit Saladita

MAKES ABOUT 6 SERVINGS AS AN ACCENT; 3 OR 4 SERVINGS AS AN APPETIZER OR MINI-SALAD ✻ VEGAN

In Mexico, people are almost incapable of serving a fruit cup (or anything involving cut fruit) without including jicama. Vendors selling cups of fresh melon, cucumber, mango, papaya, and jicama sticks are ubiquitous on beaches in hot weather. In the United States, however, jicama is less familiar. Here's the lowdown: An unassuming, round root vegetable, jicama is light brown and somewhat heavy. It can be found in the produce section of enlightened grocery stores, often near the chilies and not far from the turnips and parsnips. Once peeled and cut open, the crunchy, refreshing interior can be described as a cross between a very crisp apple and a turnip. Jicama delivers the world's most refreshing snap when you take a bite.

Serve this cold as an appetizer, salad, or topping. It's especially good with Fully Loaded Buttermilk Corn Cakes (page 316), Chard- or Collard-Wrapped Polenta-Chili Tamale Packages (page 338), and Cumin-Scented Black Bean Burgers (page 292).

✻ To peel a jicama, find (or cut) a little tab of the skin to get a grip and then begin pulling it off. It will peel in strips, similar to a banana.

✻ You can make the saladita, short of adding the pumpkin seeds and cilantro, up to 2 days in advance. The jicama will stay crunchy and the grapefruit will continue to infuse the saladita.

✻ If you're unsure whether to serve this with a fork or a spoon, lay out both. Whichever you use, you're going to find yourself sipping the excellent juices from the bottom of the dish.

2 medium pink grapefruits, peeled, sectioned, and sections removed from membranes (see note, page 378)

½ medium jicama (½ pound), peeled and cut into ¼-inch-thick matchsticks

½ teaspoon chili powder

Dash or two of salt

2 tablespoons pumpkin seeds, or more to taste, lightly toasted

2 tablespoons minced cilantro, or more to taste

Cayenne (optional)

1. Put the grapefruit into a medium bowl, add the jicama sticks, and sprinkle in the chili powder and a little salt. Stir to thoroughly combine. (*At this point, you can cover and refrigerate it for up to 2 days.*)

2. Shortly before serving, stir in the pumpkin seeds and cilantro and taste to see if you might like to add some cayenne. Serve cold, as an appetizer, a salad, or a topping.

Strawberry-Avocado Saladita

MAKES ABOUT 6 SERVINGS AS AN ACCENT; 3 OR 4 SERVINGS AS AN APPETIZER OR MINI-SALAD ❧ VEGAN

Impress your dinner guests with an elegant cupful of diced strawberries and matching tiny cubes of avocado. Hidden within this pretty arrangement is minced crystallized ginger, which provides a small wave of heat, a hint of chewiness, and just the right amount of attitude to keep things perky.

This is delicious with Chard- or Collard-Wrapped Polenta-Chili Tamale Packages (page 338) and Fully Loaded Buttermilk Corn Cakes (page 316).

❀ Try to find a perfectly ripe avocado that is mostly firm, but gives a little when gently squeezed. You want one that is not too soft, so you can get clean little dice. Have the lime juice ready and waiting, so the avocado can be coated as soon as it's cut. The acid from the lime juice will help preserve the color.

❀ There are a couple of components you can prepare in advance: the optional jicama (for which I hope you will opt) and the crystallized ginger. If it's more than a few hours and your kitchen is hot, wrap the cut jicama in a little plastic bag or a wet paper towel and refrigerate until just before assembling. (For more on jicama, see page 381.)

❀ Dice and combine the strawberries and avocado at the very last minute, since these items seem to ripen within minutes of the first cut. Plan on serving the saladita soon after it is assembled.

10 perfect strawberries, wiped clean, hulled, and cut into ¼-inch dice

3–4 tablespoons minced crystallized ginger

½ cup peeled, diced (¼ inch) jicama (optional)

4 tablespoons fresh lime juice

1 medium firm, ripe avocado

A touch of salt (optional)

1. Place the strawberries in a medium bowl and sprinkle in the ginger, jicama, and 3 tablespoons of the lime juice. Toss to combine.

2. Pour the remaining 1 tablespoon lime juice onto a plate.

3. Halve, pit, and peel the avocado, then cut it into ¼-inch dice and immediately transfer to the plate. Gently move the diced avocado around to get it coated with juice, then slide the contents of the plate into the bowl of strawberries.

4. Mix very gently, add a bit of salt, if desired, and serve right away.

Sweet Corn and Blueberry Saladita

MAKES 4 OR 5 LITTLE SERVINGS ✿ VEGAN

This August-flavored salad seems unusual, but only at first glance. As soon as you taste it, you will say, "of course." And you will be saying that between some of the most mouth-pleasing, texturally playful bites imaginable. It's delicious with Marinated Grilled Zucchini with Corn and Tomatoes (page 109) (one can never have too much in-season corn) and Caramelized Onion–Brown Rice–Lentil Burgers (page 297).

✿ This tastes best within an hour or so of being assembled, although it will also be quite good the next day, if stored, tightly covered, in the refrigerator.

1–2 tablespoons extra-virgin olive oil, or more to taste

2–3 tablespoons fresh lime juice, or more to taste

A pinch of salt (optional)

2 cups corn kernels (from about 4 freshly shucked ears)

1 cup firm, fresh small blueberries (same size as the corn, if available)

Up to 1 cup chopped arugula (from small leaves)

1. Combine everything in a medium bowl and toss gently so you don't break the berries—just enough to combine.

2. Taste to adjust the oil, lime juice, and salt, if using. Serve cold or at a cool room temperature as a free-standing salad or appetizer, or as a delightful accompaniment to other things.

OPTIONAL ENHANCEMENTS

Minced sweet bell peppers ✿ Fresh mint, basil, or cilantro swapped in for the arugula ✿ A hint of finely minced poblano chili ✿ Minced jicama ✿ A few minced strawberries (firm, sweet ones) ✿ Top with a touch of minced firm, ripe avocado

Orange-Olive-Fig Saladita

MAKES UP TO 6 SERVINGS AS A CONDIMENT ❋ VEGAN

A salty-sweet relish, this beautiful saladita does wonders for a variety of savory dishes that might be a bit low-key on their own. Use this wherever the idea of orange tapenade sounds good.

Do consider augmenting it with any combination of the options listed below, some of which take this further into salad territory.

Serve with Quinoa-Couscous Pilaf with Carrot, Roasted Almond Oil, and Pickled Red Onions (page 220), Very Simple Lentil Stew (page 146), or Roasted Cauliflower Risotto (page 206).

❋ Olives can vary greatly. If you use a marinated variety, consider including some of the other items in the container (herbs, garlic slices). Picholine or lemon- and herb-marinated are my favorites, but you can also go with oil-cured black olives or kalamatas.

❋ Dried figs plump up just the right amount from contact with the orange juice. And if you have access to soft, sweet fresh figs, use those for a garnish on top.

❋ This doesn't keep well, so plan on serving it within a few hours of putting it together.

½ cup thinly sliced red onion

4 good-sized navel oranges

About 10 olives, pitted and cut into thin, lengthwise slices (½ cup)

About 10 dried figs (any kind), stemmed and sliced into rounds or slim wedges

Black pepper

1. Put on a kettle of water to boil and place the sliced onion in a colander in the sink. When the water boils, pour all of it over the onion. Let drain in the colander while you prepare the oranges.

2. Peel the oranges with a sharp serrated knife and release the sections from their membranes directly into a medium bowl (see page 128).

3. When they cool enough to comfortably handle, separate the onion slices and add them to the oranges. Toss in the olives and figs, add black pepper to taste, and it's ready.

OPTIONAL ENHANCEMENTS

Add up to 1 tablespoon very fruity extra-virgin olive oil (mixed in, or drizzled on top when you serve) ❋ Include a splash or 2 of lemon juice ❋ Sliced fresh figs for garnish ❋ Minced or julienned radicchio ❋ Shaved or minced fennel ❋ Thinly sliced radishes ❋ A tangle of baby arugula ❋ Thin strips of fresh mint ❋ Shaved hard cheese—or possibly some crumbled blue or goat cheese or a crumble of feta or ricotta salata

Seasonal Fruit–Herb Saladitas

✹ VEGAN

The simplest saladitas in my repertoire are the ones that pair a single fruit with just one fresh herb. These are as flexible as they are easy. Extra-virgin olive oil, fresh lemon or lime juice, and salt and pepper are all optional. A small pile of Pickled Red Onions (page 395) is always welcome on top. Make these shortly before serving.

SUMMER

NECTARINE-THYME SALADITA

Pit and slice a perfectly ripe nectarine, then cut the slices in half. Toss in about a tablespoon of fresh thyme leaves, stripped from the stems with your fingers. Serve right away—plain, or with a cruet of extra-virgin olive oil and a wedge of lime.

CANTALOUPE-BASIL SALADITA

Peel and seed a small, ripe cantaloupe. Cut the flesh into ½-inch dice or even smaller and place it in a bowl. Shortly before serving, add about a dozen minced fresh basil leaves and serve soon thereafter.

FALL

APPLE-PARSLEY SALADITA

Core and chop a crisp apple or two and toss with a small splash of fresh lemon juice or cider vinegar. Throw in a handful of minced fresh flat-leaf parsley. Drizzle with a little extra-virgin olive oil.

WINTER

POMEGRANATE-MINT SALADITA

Extract the seeds from a large pomegranate (see page 360) and place them in a bowl. Shortly before serving, toss with about 25 minced fresh mint leaves and serve pronto. I highly recommend Pickled Red Onions (page 395) as an accompaniment.

YEAR-ROUND

MANGO-CILANTRO SALADITA

Peel, pit, and cut 2 fresh mangoes (or 2 cups frozen mango chunks) into ¼-inch dice and splash with up to 2 tablespoons fresh lime juice. Just before serving, toss with a handful or two of cilantro, minced, and a sprinkling of crushed red pepper, if you like. Serve right away. It's great with Pickled Red Onions (page 395).

Crisp, Ethereal Onion Rings

MAKES ABOUT 2 CUPS, ENOUGH TO TOP 6 TO 8 SERVINGS ❧ VEGAN

Thin to the point of transparent, with a whispery coating that all but disappears into the ephemeral crunch, these onion echoes will melt quickly in your mouth. Serve them on top of Lemony Caramelized Onion Mac and Gorgonzola (page 236), Mashed Celery Root (page 174), and grain dishes like Bulgur and Spaghetti (page 222) and on or with many other things.

❈ For best results, use high-oleic safflower oil or regular grapeseed oil.

❈ The oil must be deep enough to cover the onion slices and instant-sizzle-hot before you add them.

❈ The rings take only a minute or so to cook per batch. Eat them immediately or let them sit at room temperature until needed. They also freeze incredibly well in heavy zip-style plastic bags.

❈ Equally delicious (and a great partner to the onions) are Crispy Fried Lemons (page 389), made the same way. If you add fresh fennel to the mix, you will have a bona fide *fritto misto* to serve as an appetizer to your very appreciative family and friends. See the instructions that follow this basic recipe.

[continues]

1 small (¼ pound) onion

½ cup unbleached all-purpose flour

1 teaspoon salt, or more to taste

5 or more tablespoons high-oleic safflower oil or grapeseed oil

1. Peel the onion and slice it superthin (think insect wings) on a mandoline or with a very sharp knife. Be very careful to keep your eyes on your hands while doing this.

2. Arrange the slices in a single layer on a double layer of paper towels or a kitchen towel. Pat and/or lightly squeeze them dry with the towels and let them sit and air dry while you get the other things ready. You can let them sit like this for a good hour or so.

3. Combine the flour and salt in a medium bowl, mixing until uniform.

4. Meanwhile, pour about 5 tablespoons oil into a large (10- to 12-inch) skillet and place it over medium-low heat. Situate a plate with a triple pile of fresh paper towels, plus tongs, by the stove.

5. Add the onion slices to the flour mixture, gently shaking and forking them around to get them completely coated. Transfer about half of the coated slices to a strainer (not too fine a mesh) and shake off as much of the flour mixture as you can back into the bowl. The coating should be barely perceptible.

6. When the oil is hot enough to instantly sizzle a fleck of the coating, use a fork or tongs to carefully lay in a batch of onion slices, arranging them more or less in a single layer. It's OK if they touch.

7. Increase the heat to medium as you fry this first batch until each piece stiffens and lightly browns. (The stiff part is more important than the color.) Use tongs to lift out the finished onion rings, transferring them immediately to the pile of paper towels on the plate. The entire frying process will likely take about a minute.

8. Repeat the process with the remaining onion slices. Augment the oil as needed, but make sure it is very hot before adding the onion slices. The second batch may take a little bit longer to fry. Also, don't worry about the sediment that may collect in the bottom of the pan as you fry successive batches.

9. Sprinkle the finished onion rings with a little additional salt, if you like, and serve.

CRISPY FRIED LEMONS

🌱 VEGAN

Lemon slices can be prepared in exactly the same way as onion rings. In fact, you can make them together in one expansive frying session, since the flavors of the two complement each other greatly, and they keep well.

Slice 2 small lemons (ideally a sweet kind, such as Meyer) on a mandoline or with a sharp knife, pressing hard with quick deliberate strokes. (Use caution around that blade!) Pick out any seeds, then transfer the slices to towels to mostly dry.

Dredge the lemons in the same flour mixture as with the onions and fry in the same way. If you are making batches of the onions and lemons together, you can store them together at room temperature.

OTHER CRISPY FRIED THINGS

Leeks, shallots, and fennel are also wonderful candidates for this process. Use a very sharp knife or a mandoline to make thin leek circles and shallot circles or slices and definitely use a mandoline to cut the fennel into feathery slices. (Dry the slices on paper towels, as with the onions.) Plan on a handful of slices per serving for a light snack or appetizer or as a topping for any savory dish.

VEGETABLES ON TOP

The small touch of one vegetable decorating a larger portion of another (or garnishing any savory dish) can be a fresh and easy way of adding depth and beauty to the plate. Think color (a spoonful of Beet Crush, page 169; a dab of Curried Mashed Carrots and Cashews, page 170) and volume (you are adding both heft and a sense of richness) as well as practicality (something nice to do with that less-than-a-full-serving of leftovers), and you will find yourself with a great new, frugal, creative habit.

Ideas for this abound throughout these pages. Here are a few of my favorite toppers.

Crisp, Ethereal Onion Rings/Crispy Fried Lemons/ Other Crispy Fried Things (page 387)

Browned Potatoes and Onion (page 391)

Crispy Sage Leaves (page 394)

Slow-Roasted Roma Tomatoes (page 393)

Grilled Mushroom Slices or Mushroom "Bacon" (see page 349)

Steamed edamame, fava beans, or peas

Steamed or grilled green vegetables (small spears of broccoli, for example)

Roasted butternut squash (page 351)

Roasted vegetables in general (see page 336)

And don't forget, you can pile little salads (page 76), slaws (page 66), or saladitas (page 377) on the tops of other dishes, too.

Browned Potatoes and Onion

MAKES 4 TO 6 SERVINGS AS A TOPPING ❈ VEGAN

At first glance, you could easily conclude that this is a recipe for home fries. And, in fact, it is. But these potatoes are headed for the top, rather than the base, of your plate—a tasty touch on the roof of your soup or stew or a simple little pile of savory beans.

1 pound potatoes (any kind)

2–3 tablespoons olive oil

1½ cups minced onion (1 medium)

¼ teaspoon salt, or more to taste

Black pepper

Cayenne

1. Scrub the potatoes and cut them into small (¼-inch) dice, then place them in a small saucepan with water to cover. Bring to a boil, lower the heat, and simmer until tender, about 8 minutes. Drain well.

2. Place a medium skillet over medium heat for about a minute, then add 1 tablespoon of the oil and swirl to coat the pan. Toss in the onion and cook, stirring, over medium heat for about 5 minutes, or until softened. Add the potatoes.

3. Sprinkle with ¼ teaspoon salt and sauté the onion and potatoes together over medium heat for 5 minutes.

4. Turn the heat down to medium-low and cook, stirring often and scraping the bottom of the pan, for up to 30 minutes, drizzling in extra oil as needed. Taste to see if you'd like it to have more salt, and add black pepper and cayenne to taste as well.

5. It's done when you decide it is—whenever it gets to your preferred shade of golden or brown (I like mine dark brown). Serve hot or warm as a topping on any savory dish.

OPTIONAL ENHANCEMENTS

Up to 1 teaspoon minced or crushed garlic, stirred in during step 4 ❈ A light sprinkling of savory dried herbs (thyme, marjoram, sage), added with the onion in step 3 ❈ Minced bell pepper, tomato, and/or zucchini, added with the potatoes in step 2 ❈ A little sour cream mixed in at the end, to give it a dreamy backdrop ❈ Finely minced fresh scallion, parsley, basil, or dill on top or stirred in at the end

Slow-Roasted Roma Tomatoes

MAKES 6 TO 8 SMALL SERVINGS (A FEW SLICES EACH) ❧ VEGAN

Welcome to what has become my official tomato sauce. After they're roasted, I simply mash these olive oil–laced tomatoes into a thick, textured pulp that is so delicious that no further seasoning (not even salt) is needed, and any thoughts of a traditional marinara fade away.

Actually, the mashing is optional. You can leave them whole and tuck them into the side, or plunk them on the top of a plateful of delicious dinner. Whatever your chosen format, be prepared for people to be amazed when they take a taste. I've heard, "Wow, how did you do this?" so consistently when serving these that I now wait for that response. And the true answer is, I didn't really do anything beyond turn on the oven, slick a baking sheet with olive oil, and cut up a bunch of tomatoes.

You don't need to wait for perfect late-summer specimens to get good results. Greenhouse-grown Roma tomatoes in any season, even if they start out hard as rocks, can taste wonderful after they are gradually rendered over several hours in a low oven—a process that shrinks them into chewy sweetness as their juices evaporate and their natural sugars caramelize. Call this a tomato rescue mission, if you like. Dressed lightly with olive oil, and with no need for any salt or other seasoning, these little pieces are as nutritious as they are sensuous and are a revelation piled high on your thin-crusted pizza, mashed into spaghetti sauce, or simply eaten as a surprisingly satisfying snack.

❀ These will keep for a week or longer in a covered container in the refrigerator. A small slick of olive oil on top will help preserve them.

1–2 tablespoons extra-virgin olive oil, plus more for storage

2 pounds medium Roma tomatoes

1. Preheat the oven to 275°F, with a rack in the center position. Line a baking sheet with foil or parchment paper, and coat it with 1 tablespoon of the olive oil.

2. Cut out and discard the little stem circles from the tops of the tomatoes. Halve the tomatoes lengthwise, then cut them in half again to make long quarters (unless they were small to begin with). Arrange the tomato wedges skin side down on the baking sheet; it's OK if they touch.

3. Roast for an hour or so. The tomatoes will have stuck slightly to the foil. Loosen them gently with a small spatula and/or by shaking the baking sheet. (The parts that tend to stick are the most delicious, so don't leave these stuck to the foil.)

4. Repeat this process of moving around and jostling every 10 minutes or so for another hour. Use tongs to turn the tomatoes over from time to time, so they won't stick.

5. After at least 2½ hours (and possibly longer) of total roasting time, the tomatoes will be done. The smaller slices will shrink and roast faster than larger ones, so you can remove those from the baking sheet with tongs as you go.

6. When the tomatoes are done to your liking, remove them from the oven and let them cool to room temperature on the foil. Transfer them to a storage container with a tight-fitting lid and drizzle the tops with a little extra olive oil. Refrigerate and use as desired.

Crispy Sage Leaves

MAKES 4 SERVINGS, WITH 4 OR 5 LEAVES APIECE ✿ VEGAN

I learned this trick in Tuscany, and it was worth the price of several plane tickets. Use these to garnish anything and everything—or just eat them as a snack. They keep beautifully in a jar at room temperature for a week or longer.

You must pay very close attention for just a few seconds. (If you try to do anything else at the same time, you'll burn the leaves.)

Try a trial run of cooking the first leaf or two separately until you see how fast they go. Different stoves and pans make this an imprecise art.

After success with sage leaves, try experimenting with other herbs. This works beautifully with cilantro, parsley, arugula, or basil as well.

1 tablespoon olive oil, or more as needed

16–20 large, fresh sage leaves, washed and carefully patted dry and flat

1. Line a plate with several layers of paper towels and set near the stove. Place a small skillet over medium heat. After about a minute, add 1 to 2 teaspoons olive oil—enough to generously coat the bottom of the pan.

2. Add 3 or 4 sage leaves, gently pressing them flat with a fork or the back of a spoon. Cook them for 5 to 7 seconds, then use tongs or the edge of a pancake turner to carefully flip them over.

3. Cook for about 5 seconds on the second side, or until they turn bright green with no hint of browning. Quickly transfer the leaves to the prepared plate to drain. They will crisp as they cool.

4. Repeat with the remaining leaves, adding more oil to the pan as needed. If the leaves begin to brown too quickly after your first or second batch, adjust your heat down to medium-low.

5. Serve at room temperature.

Pickled Red Onions

MAKES 1½ CUPS ❋ VEGAN (WHEN MADE WITH AGAVE NECTAR OR SUGAR)

This trick will alter and augment your cooking: Pour boiling water over sliced or diced red onions, then transfer them to a solution of vinegar, sweetener, and salt. The onions will brighten into a gaudy shade of purplish-pink and will keep indefinitely, mysteriously retaining their bright color and crisp texture.

You can vary the cut of the onions—and also the amounts of sweet and salt. Use as a dramatically colorful and refreshing tiara atop dinner plates, open-faced sandwiches, salads, cheeses, grilled tofu, or fish—anything savory. I use these often as an ingredient in cold soups and saladitas. (Mince, rather than slice, the onions, if they are headed for one of the cold soups.)

❋ Use a very sharp knife or a food processor with a thin slicing attachment to cut the onions most easily.

1 large red onion (¾ pound)

3 tablespoons vinegar (cider, red or white wine, or balsamic)

1–2 teaspoons agave nectar, light-colored honey, or sugar

¼ teaspoon salt

1. Put on a kettle of water to boil. Cut the onion into very thin slices or a mince and place it in a colander in the sink.

2. In a bowl large enough to comfortably fit all the onion, combine the vinegar, sweetener, and salt and whisk until blended.

3. Pour the boiling water over the onion and shake to drain. (It's fine if a little water still clings.)

4. Add the onion to the vinegar solution and stir to coat. Let it sit for at least an hour or up to several days, covered and refrigerated, occasionally stirring and/or shaking to allow maximum exposure to the liquid. Store in a jar with a tight-fitting lid in the refrigerator.

OPTIONAL ENHANCEMENTS

For beautiful, exotic pickled fruit, add fresh or frozen cherries, blueberries, or raspberries—or some small watermelon chunks—to the onion after the first hour of sitting time ❋ Add any of the following to the pickle mixture: Raw broccoli stems, peeled and cut into slender matchsticks ❋ Raw fennel, cut into thin slices ❋ Lightly steamed carrot slices ❋ Lightly steamed cauliflower, cut into 1-inch florets

Strawberry-Rhubarb Pickles

MAKES ABOUT 4 CUPS ❦ VEGAN (WHEN MADE WITH AGAVE NECTAR)

Here is a rare opportunity to experience rhubarb raw, in all its crisp and sour charm, minimally sweetened. Because rhubarb is so fibrous, it's important to slice it very thin for this recipe. White balsamic vinegar will allow the red color of the final product to be even brighter. Not essential, but it's a nice touch if you have some on hand.

These pickles are a great accompaniment to cheese platters or sandwiches (always a conversation starter) and also make a beautiful contribution when scattered into or onto a salad of sturdy greens, shaved hard cheese, and chopped sugar snap peas, laced with a fruity vinaigrette (pages 366 to 368). And you can sparkle up just about any plateful of savory food by simply forking a few of these onto the side of the plate and/or passing around a little bowlful from which people can help themselves.

½ cup balsamic vinegar (preferably white, but any kind is fine)

½ cup agave nectar or light-colored honey (or a combination)

2 large stalks rhubarb (½ pound), very thinly sliced (⅛ inch)

1 pound strawberries (a generous 1½ cups), wiped clean, hulled, and thickly sliced

1. Combine the vinegar and sweetener in a bowl or liquid measuring cup and whisk together until it becomes uniform.

2. Pack the rhubarb into a clean quart jar and pour in the vinegar mixture. Cover tightly and shake gently to distribute, then refrigerate for an hour or two. (It works best to give the rhubarb a head start and add the strawberries a little later.)

3. Add the strawberries, pushing them in to fit. Cover tightly and return to the refrigerator to continue pickling. (If you feel confident that the seal between the jar and its top is secure, go ahead and store it upside down for a couple of hours, so the liquid reaches all the fruit.)

4. The pickles will be ready about 4 hours after the strawberries are added, but will be more deeply flavorful if you wait at least a day before forking them out to use for this and that.

5. They will keep for a month or longer, refrigerated. The flavor will continue to develop, and the pickles will be increasingly delicious, but after the first day or two, their color will dull a bit. You can add up to another pint of strawberries after the pickles have had a chance to rest for a little while (3 or more hours), since extra liquid becomes available while they sit.

Egg "Noodles"

MAKES 4 SERVINGS AS A TOPPING

Canary yellow strips of cooked egg add intrigue (and protein) when presented on top of your dinner.

❊ You can cook the egg with nonstick spray and no added oil. Or you can use a little oil on its own, or in addition to the spray. Up to you. Whichever you choose, you will get the best results if you use an omelet pan and get it truly hot first, so the egg will separate easily from the cooking surface all in one piece.

❊ You can make the "noodles" up to an hour ahead of time; store and serve them at room temperature.

Nonstick cooking spray

Up to 2 teaspoons grapeseed or canola oil (optional)

2 large eggs, well beaten with a pinch of optional salt

1. Spray a 7- or 8-inch omelet pan with nonstick spray and heat the pan over medium heat for a minute or more. You want to err on the side of the pan being a touch too hot. Have a dinner plate ready by the stove.

2. Slick the pan with just a little oil (½ teaspoon), if desired, then add about one fourth of the beaten egg, lifting the pan and tilting it slowly to allow the egg to cover the entire bottom surface of the pan to make a very thin omelet (similar to a crepe).

3. Loosen the egg with a dinner knife, flip it, then turn it out assertively onto the waiting plate. Repeat until you've made four circles.

4. Let the circles cool, then roll them tightly and slice into thin "noodles." Serve at room temperature.

Tofu "Noodles"—Coconut or Sesame

MAKES 4 OR 5 SERVINGS ❧ VEGAN

If you can keep yourself from snacking away the entire batch, your vegetables, rice, soups, salads, and mashes are about to get a great new hat. These are guaranteed to torpedo any last vestiges of tofu prejudice among your less clued-in family and friends.

❋ Coconut oil comes in jars in natural food stores and is a solid at room temperature.

❋ In order to accommodate the range of current tofu packaging, this recipe calls for 12 to 16 ounces and is flexible. This will spare you from having an awkwardly small amount left over.

❋ If you simmer firm tofu ahead of time, it will firm up even further and will acquire more texture as it sautés. Simmering can be done up to several days ahead. Keep the precooked tofu covered and refrigerated (water storage is unnecessary after it's been simmered) until just before use.

❋ You can sauté the "noodles" in two batches or push them to the side of the pan and add more to the same pan, eventually stirring everything together.

COCONUT VERSION

12–16 ounces very firm tofu

1 tablespoon coconut oil

¼ heaping teaspoon salt

2 tablespoons shredded unsweetened coconut

1. If precooking the tofu, put on a medium pot of water to boil.

2. Use a sharp knife to cut the tofu into strips about 3 inches by ⅛ inch by ⅛ inch.

3. If precooking the tofu, add the strips to the boiling water and reduce the heat to a medium simmer. Cook for 10 minutes, then drain the tofu into a strainer or colander and transfer to paper towels in a single layer to dry for a few minutes.

4. Place a large (10- to 12-inch) skillet over medium heat for about a minute, then add the oil and swirl to coat the pan. Lay the tofu "noodles" into the hot pan and sprinkle with the salt. Try to spread them out in as thin a layer as you can, permitting maximum contact with the pan.

5. Keeping the heat at medium, stir gently and intermittently with a fork so as not to break the strands. Continue this process for about 15 minutes, or until the noodles shrink into chewiness and have turned a light golden color.

6. Sprinkle in the coconut and continue to cook, scraping the bottom of the pan with a small metal spatula to include all the flavor that might be adhering there.

7. It's your call as to when the noodles are done. My own total sautéing time tends to be about 20 minutes, but you can go longer if you prefer your batch to be darker and firmer. Serve hot, warm, or at room temperature.

SESAME VERSION

Follow the same recipe, substituting a blend of grapeseed and Chinese sesame oil (½ tablespoon each) for the coconut oil, and sesame seeds for the coconut.

Tofu "Bacon"

MAKES 4 OR 5 SERVINGS AS A TOPPING OR GARNISH ❀ VEGAN

Even if you are not a fan of vegetarian meat analogues, this tofu treatment will likely win you over. Just slice tofu very thin and fry it until crusty in smoke-infused oil, and then give it a good dose of salt. The chewy-crisp texture that ensues is close enough—and delicious enough—to hit that bacon-receptor many people retain regardless of their meat orientation or lack thereof.

❀ Plain firm tofu smoke-seasons very nicely here. And if you begin with smoked tofu, the flavor will be even more intense.

12–16 ounces firm tofu, plain or smoked

1 tablespoon grapeseed, canola, or peanut oil

1 teaspoon smoked paprika, or more to taste

Up to ½ teaspoon salt

1. Put on a pot of water to boil over medium heat.

2. Slice the tofu into thin rectangles, 3½ inches long, 1½ to 2 inches wide, and ¼ inch thick. Add them to the water when it boils, reduce the heat to low, and simmer slowly for 10 minutes.

3. Gently drain the tofu in a colander and lay the pieces flat on a towel to dry.

4. Meanwhile, place a large (10- to 12-inch) skillet over medium heat for about a minute, then add the oil and swirl to coat the pan. Sprinkle in the paprika and mix it around to distribute it into the oil. (If you like a strong smoky flavor, you can increase the paprika to 2 teaspoons.)

5. Lay the tofu strips flat in the hot oil and cook, stirring, over medium heat for 30 minutes, or possibly even longer, turning them every 5 minutes or so, allowing the strips to condense and eventually crispen. They will get increasingly sturdy as they fry. As the strips shrink, you can add more tofu, if you couldn't fit it all in at first.

6. When the "bacon" strips are done to your liking, transfer them to a paper towel–lined plate and season with salt. Serve right away, or store in the refrigerator for up to 3 days and reheat in a toaster over, hot skillet, or microwave. Reheated Tofu "Bacon" will be even chewier than freshly made.

Chili Pepitas

MAKES 1 CUP ❧ VEGAN

Heat, smoky flavor, and various kinds of crunch from large pumpkin seeds (pepitas) and tiny cumin seeds are delivered via a surprisingly simple preparation.

Sprinkle Chili Pepitas on any dish (beans, rice, soup, salad) that leans toward the south of the border. (And you absolutely must include this when making Goat Cheese–Stuffed Piquillo Peppers, page 85.)

❋ These will keep for a month in the refrigerator and for 3 months in the freezer, sealed in a heavy zip-style plastic bag.

1 tablespoon olive oil

1 cup hulled, raw pumpkin seeds (pepitas)

Up to 1 teaspoon cumin seeds

Crushed red pepper and/or 5–6 whole, small dried chilies

Salt

1. Place a small-medium (6- to 8-inch) skillet over medium heat for about a minute, then add the olive oil and swirl to coat the pan.

2. Toss in the pumpkin seeds, cumin seeds, and a dash (⅛ teaspoon or more) of crushed red pepper and/or the chilies.

3. Turn the heat to low and cook attentively, stirring often and shaking the pan, until the pumpkin seeds become lightly toasted and the cumin is noticeably fragrant. Remove from the heat and cool to a comfortable eating/handling temperature. Salt to taste before serving.

Pistachio Smash

MAKES 1 GENEROUS CUP ❧ VEGAN

Sometimes when you crush something, even though you've added very little to it, it ends up tasting like a different food from the one with which you began. Perhaps it's because extra flavor gets released in the process. Who knows? Whatever the physics (or metaphysics), this pistachio treatment is darned good. Sprinkle it on grains, salads, goat cheese toasts, and hither and yon, and especially on top of Beet Crush (page 169) in the Brilliant Beet Arrangement (page 168).

❀ This will keep for a month in the refrigerator—and 3 months in the freezer, sealed airtight in a heavy zip-style plastic bag.

1 heaping cup shelled pistachios, lightly toasted

¼ teaspoon salt (start with less if the nuts are salted)

1 tablespoon grapeseed or peanut oil

1. Combine the pistachios and salt in a blender or a small food processor and buzz until the pistachios become the size of bulgur.

2. Keep the machine going as you drizzle in the oil, then continue just long enough for all the nut pieces to become moistened.

3. Transfer the mixture to a bowl or container with a cover or a heavy zip-style plastic bag. Refrigerate or freeze.

Quinoa Crunch

MAKES 4 SERVINGS AS A TOPPING ❧ VEGAN

After soaking it briefly to rinse off some of the sometimes-bitter natural coating, you dry-toast quinoa on the stovetop, rather than cooking it in water. Tiny, delightful pinpoints of crunch are the result, giving you yet another option for bestowing an unexpected extra layer of interest to an assortment of dishes, either sprinkled on top or framing the plate around the sides.

This goes beautifully on top of cooked grains or surrounding a simple plate of Greek yogurt decorated with fruit (it's great for breakfast).

❀ You can soak and dry the quinoa well ahead of time. For that matter, go ahead and dry-roast the quinoa ahead of time, too. It will keep for a few hours, uncovered at room temperature, provided your kitchen isn't overly humid.

½ cup quinoa

¼ teaspoon salt

1 heaping teaspoon turbinado sugar or raw sugar

1. Place the quinoa in a small bowl and add water to cover. Let stand for 10 minutes, then drain it in a fine-mesh strainer and briefly pat it dry on a towel.

2. Transfer the soaked quinoa to a medium skillet over medium-low heat. Cook, stirring, for 8 to 10 minutes, or until the grains darken slightly and give off a toasty aroma. (Don't walk away; it can burn fast.)

3. Sprinkle with the salt and sugar and stir over the heat for another few seconds, or until the sugar melts. Serve warm or at room temperature.

Crunchy Chickpea Crumble

MAKES 4 TO 6 SERVINGS ❧ VEGAN

Dried chickpeas are first soaked, but then, instead of cooking them in water, you drain and dry them, grind them in a few bursts of the food processor, and then fry the resulting coarse mash in a modest amount of very hot oil. The finished product is crunchy and earthy.

Crunchy Chickpea Crumble is a great topping for many grain dishes (try it on Bulgur and Spaghetti, page 222) and can also be served under, next to, or on top of soups, pastas, or salads. It's especially in its element with grilled or broiled eggplant and Tahini-Ginger-Pomegranate Sauce (page 360). It is also the world's best bar snack, so keep it in mind for when you have people over for happy hour. A person can eat a lot of this.

❀ Preliminary: The chickpeas need a minimum of 4 hours of soaking time and can soak for as long 12 hours or so.

❀ Theoretically, this will keep for several days, tightly covered and refrigerated (or at room temperature, if your kitchen is not too hot). But I've never seen any left over.

1 cup dried chickpeas

2–3 tablespoons grapeseed oil, olive oil, or high-oleic safflower oil

½ teaspoon salt

Black pepper (optional)

1. Soak the chickpeas in water to cover for at least 4 hours or overnight. Drain and pat completely dry on a kitchen towel.

2. Run the chickpeas through a food processor for a few seconds, until they become coarse crumbs about the size of split peas. The crumbs will not be uniform.

3. Place a medium-large (9- or 10-inch) skillet over medium heat for about a minute, then add about ½ tablespoon of the oil and swirl to coat the pan. Let the oil continue to heat until it becomes hot enough to instantly sizzle a crumb, then add half the chickpeas, spreading them out.

4. Keep the heat to medium as you fry, stirring with a spatula with a thin metal blade, scraping frequently from the bottom of the pan, for about 2 minutes. Sprinkle with ¼ teaspoon of the salt and cook for another minute or so.

5. Drizzle in a little more oil (approximately ½ tablespoon) here and there, in spaces you make by pushing the mixture around. Keep moving the chickpea crumbs with the spatula to cook/crisp them evenly and to prevent them from sticking to the pan.

6. Cook for another 3 minutes or so, or until slightly golden (not too brown). There is no official "done" point, but for me the total cooking time is usually 5 to 6 minutes. You can keep them going a little longer if you want them darker and crunchier. Scrape this first batch from the pan onto a plate, and repeat with the second batch.

7. Serve hot, warm, or at room temperature, lightly sprinkled with black pepper, if you like.

OPTIONAL ENHANCEMENTS

A little cayenne or crushed red pepper ❀ A scattering of toasted cumin seeds ❀ Lemon or orange zest (in long strands) ❀ Slow-Roasted Roma Tomatoes (page 393) strewn within or arranged around as a frame ❀ Garnishes of olives and/or radishes

Fried Lentils

MAKES 1½ CUPS ❋ VEGAN

Revelation: You can fry soaked, uncooked lentils. Result: The coolest snack food/crunchy topping this side of Mumbai.

After making these in minutes, sprinkle them on many things: tossed salads, cooked grains (a great riff on beans and rice), or any kind of modular plate (see Brilliant Beet Arrangement, page 168). They are also a great snack.

❋ Use the smaller—red (aka orange), yellow, or black beluga—lentils for the crispest, most delicate results. If delicate results are not your goal, go ahead and try this with the larger, standard brown lentils—or even with yellow split peas. They will have a slightly chewy center, rather than becoming all-the-way crisp.

❋ You can soak and drain the lentils well ahead of time, and then leave them on the towel to dry for a few hours, or even overnight.

❋ These are at their best within an hour or so of being made, but will remain quite good for up to a day after that. Store uncovered at room temperature, if your kitchen is not overly humid. Also, they are easily freshened up in a 200°F toaster oven, spread out on foil in a thin layer. It will take anywhere from 5 to 10 minutes to take them back to crunchy.

1 cup lentils, any kind (see note)

3–4 tablespoons high-oleic safflower oil, olive oil, or grapeseed oil (possibly more)

Salt

1. Place the lentils in a bowl with water to cover. Soak for 1 hour.

2. Drain the lentils into a fine-mesh strainer, shaking out as much excess water as you can, then lay them out on absorbent towels in a single layer to dry. (You can help this along by gently shaking the lentils around a bit on the towel to air them out.)

3. Set a paper towel–lined plate and a slotted spoon by the stove. Pour 2 to 3 tablespoons oil (enough to generously cover the bottom) into a large (10- to 12-inch) skillet and place the pan over medium heat. When it's hot enough to sizzle a lentil on contact, carefully add about half the lentils, spreading them out into a single layer. Cook, stirring occasionally, for 5 to 6 minutes, or until they crisp and become ever-so-slightly translucent around the edges. (Red lentils will turn yellow.) You can keep them in the pan a little longer, if you like, until they reach a more dramatically crunchy state. Just be sure to extract them before they become overdone.

4. Lift out the lentils in batches with the slotted spoon, holding and slightly tilting each scoop over the pan to let the oil drain off, then transfer to the paper towels. Salt lightly.

5. Repeat with the remaining lentils, adding additional oil as needed, and being sure to wait until it is instant-sizzle hot before adding the lentils.

6. Serve warm or at room temperature.

Tempeh Croutons

MAKES 4 SERVINGS ❧ VEGAN

Tempeh is a firm, chewy, fermented "cake," made from partially cooked soybeans, sometimes with grains added. Even though it is available in most natural food stores (and pretty much anywhere tofu is sold), tempeh remains a bit obscure—probably due to its odd, chalky, waffley appearance and subtle, unusual flavor. Direct from the package, it is partly raw and needs further cooking in order to be edible.

Here, then, is an easy treatment to soften up tempeh's flavor while crunching up its texture. The one-two punch of first browning and then braising it in a flavorful liquid easily transforms it into something complex and delicious. The resulting pieces are small enough to sprinkle onto salads, vegetables, and grains—adding interest and terrific plant protein in collaboration with other dishes.

You can also serve the croutons as a little appetizer or lunch main course, on a plate with Romesco Sauce (page 359) or tossed or topped with Slow-Roasted Roma Tomatoes (page 393).

❀ Many different types of tempeh are available in natural food stores or the natural foods aisle of conventional groceries. Some are made with soy-plus-grains, others with straight soy. You can use any kind for this recipe.

❀ The croutons will keep in the refrigerator for a week or longer.

2 tablespoons grapeseed oil or olive oil

8 ounces tempeh, cut into ½-inch dice

1 cup minced onion

½ teaspoon salt

¼ cup apple juice

1. Place a medium skillet over medium heat for about a minute, then add 1 tablespoon of the oil and swirl to coat the pan. Toss in the tempeh and cook, stirring often, for 8 to 10 minutes, or until the pieces begin to brown. Use a sturdy spatula with a thin blade as needed to scrape the bottom of the pan if any of the pieces begin to stick slightly.

2. Drizzle in the remaining 1 tablespoon oil, swish (or swirl) it around, then toss in the onion and salt. Stir and brown for another 5 minutes or so, until the onion begins to soften.

3. Pour in the apple juice and turn the heat to low. Continue to cook, stirring and scraping, for another 10 to 15 minutes after the apple juice is absorbed, or until the tempeh is deep brown but not too dark.

4. Remove the tempeh from the heat. Serve hot, warm, at room temperature, or even cold.

Grilled Haloumi Cheese

MAKES 4 SERVINGS

Originally from Cyprus, Haloumi cheese has become widely available in the United States (some brands are actually made here)—usually shrink-wrapped or packed in a little tub of water. Haloumi slices cleanly and grills into beguiling softness with a delicately crisp coating. All from just one ingredient—no oil or seasoning necessary.

Wilt a leafy green salad with slices of just-grilled Haloumi, direct from the pan. Or put Haloumi in the center of the plate, surround it with your favorite vinaigrette-laced chopped vegetable, and call it an appetizer or even a salad. You can also serve it for lunch, surrounded by sweet in-season tomatoes and crisp cucumbers and topped with Strawberry-Rhubarb Pickles (page 396) or Pickled Red Onions (page 395). And here's my favorite way to serve Haloumi: hot and freshly grilled on chunks of ice-cold watermelon. Nothing else, except perhaps a drizzle of extra-virgin olive oil, a squeeze of fresh lime juice, and maybe some black pepper.

❋ If you aren't serving this fresh and hot from the pan, it will become a chewy, saltier topping (cut or broken into crumbs) for various things (great in salads). The salty taste does intensify, so it can be a twofer at the table, alleviating any need for a saltshaker. And if you prefer to cut the salty flavor, simply soak the cheese in fresh water for 15 to 20 minutes before grilling it.

❋ Grilled Haloumi will keep for a week if stored in an airtight container in the refrigerator. It will become chewier as it sits.

8–10 ounces Haloumi cheese

1. Drain and dry the cheese and slice it into rectangles about ¼ inch thick. (A little thicker is also fine.)

2. Place a ridged grill pan or a medium or large skillet over medium heat for about a minute. When the pan is warmed, arrange the cheese slices flat in a single layer. It's OK if they touch.

3. Grill over medium heat for 5 to 8 minutes on each side—or until a wonderful aroma wafts upward and a lacy, golden pattern forms all over the exposed surface areas. Use a sturdy spatula with a thin blade to loosen each slice and flip it over. If you end up turning it more than once in pursuit of deeper color and more crispness, that's fine. Take it to a deep golden, if you wish. This cheese can handle a lot of color, and it remains sturdy even as it becomes very soft.

4. Serve fresh from the pan (soft-within-crisp, oozy) or after it's cooled (tender-chewy, spunky, salty). This is delicious at any temperature.

Olive Oil–Bread Crumb–Coated Fried Eggs

MAKES 1 SERVING AND CAN BE DOUBLED

I love fried eggs, whether cooked sunny-side up or flipped and allover tender. Fried eggs can easily and inexpensively round out and enrich your meals—and can well become your universal crown for home-cooked comfort foods. And this is my absolute favorite version, coated all over with delicous fresh whole-wheat bread crumbs and fried in olive oil.

✿ To make fresh whole-wheat bread crumbs, lightly toast 4 average slices of your favorite whole-wheat bread. When they are crisp, buzz them to your desired consistency in a food processor or blender. This will yield (approximately) a generous cup of fine crumbs or 2 cups coarse crumbs (or anything in between). Store them in a heavy zip-style plastic bag in the freezer.

✿ Even though you toasted the bread before you made the crumbs, you'll be toasting the crumbs again in the pan for extra flavor.

¼ cup fresh whole-wheat bread crumbs

1½ teaspoons olive oil

2 large eggs

Salt

Black pepper

1. In a medium skillet, toast the bread crumbs over low heat, stirring pretty much constantly and keeping watch. They will brown quickly (5 minutes or less).

2. When the crumbs are toasted, add the olive oil, stirring it into the crumbs.

3. Push the oiled crumbs into 2 flat beds (not too thick—leave some crumbs on the side) and crack an egg onto each. Spoon any extra crumbs over the tops of the eggs and sprinkle very lightly with salt and pepper.

4. Cover the pan and cook very slowly over the lowest possible heat, so the crumbs don't get too dark. After several minutes, when the eggs have set, use a sturdy spatula with a thin blade to completely loosen them and carefully flip onto the second side, attempting to rearrange the bread crumbs for maximum coverage. (Don't fuss.)

5. Cover the pan again and cook until just set; the second side will go much more quickly than the first. Carefully but firmly loosen and lift the eggs out with the spatula onto a waiting plate and serve right away.

OLIVE OIL TOASTS ❧ VEGAN

Bread that has been brushed with olive oil and grilled in a skillet on the stovetop makes profoundly satisfying toasts that can tie together smaller dishes (a group of salads, perhaps, or a bowl of soup), lifting everything to meal status. This is a great way to give new life to day-old bread that would taste less fresh if toasted first and then buttered (or oiled) in a more traditional manner.

Shortly before serving, liberally brush medium-thick slices of ciabatta or another artisanal bread on both sides with olive oil and place them in a dry skillet over medium heat. Cook on each side until the toast reaches your preferred degree of crispness. Watch over the process attentively, so the toasts don't burn. Serve hot or warm.

ALMOND OIL TOASTS

Follow the above directions, but use a lighter touch with the olive oil. Brush the top side of each piece of toast with roasted almond oil when it comes out of the pan. (Almond oil is delicate and shouldn't be exposed to direct heat.)

DESSERTS

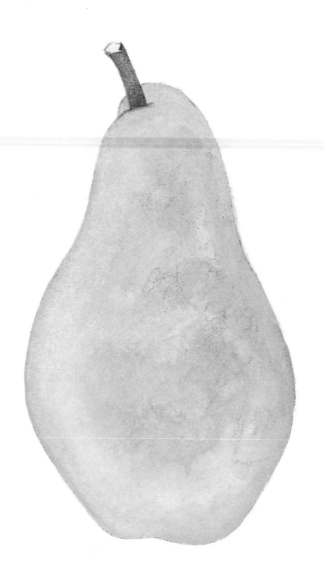

✻ ✻ ✻

It wasn't easy, but I have narrowed down the desserts in this book to a baker's dozen of my ultimate favorites. All these desserts, including those with idiosyncratic twists, are included not for the sake of novelty but because of their taste. My Baklava is made with all olive oil and no butter. So is the cornmeal crust housing the Pear Tart. The ridiculously good Chocolate Cream Pie is no more complicated than a standard chocolate pudding recipe and doesn't even require an oven, and Cranapple Walnut Cake is back by popular demand from my original, long-ago self-published Moosewood Cookbook.

Winter- and spring-specific fruit (persimmons and rhubarb, respectively) receive a moment in the spotlight, and the plain, clean taste of easy dairy treats (Buttermilk-Yogurt-Maple Sherbet and Homemade Ricotta) beckons artisan honey and/or in-season fruit. There's just one cookie recipe this time, and for me, at least, it's *the* one: Pecan Shortbread.

On days when you don't want to engage your oven or even your spoon, I cast my vote for the simplicity of ripe fresh fruit and a small sampler of carefully selected cheeses, with a scattering of toasted nuts. I am also enthusiastically in favor of dessert items for breakfast, high (or low) tea, coffee breaks, mood enhancement, seduction, idea generation, self-reward, holiday gifts, and rainy-day activity. Never miss a chance to make life sweet, even if just for a moment.

Homemade Ricotta

MAKES ABOUT 2 CUPS

Unlike the sampler platter we tend to expect when we think "after-dinner cheese," this is a singular richness—wondrous plain, and downright entrancing when anointed with a few drops of excellent honey or a touch of fruit. Once you try this recipe, you will officially have become a cheese maker—a bona fide artisan. Homemade ricotta is not only more soulful and delicious than anything you can buy, it's also more economical, producing approximately 1 pound of cheese for the price of a half gallon of milk and some yogurt.

❋ You will need cheesecloth, available at most supermarkets.

❋ Use a yogurt that is made with live, active cultures. This will be indicated on the label.

❋ You can determine the thickness of the cheese simply by keeping watch over the project and wrapping it up when the cheese achieves your preferred texture. The longer it stands, the firmer it becomes. Time and gravity are the textural determinants. You also get to decide on the salt content.

❋ The whey (liquid) that is drained off during the process is full of flavor and nutrients and can be used in place of water when you make yeasted dough.

❋ The cheese will keep, covered and refrigerated, for about 5 days.

½ gallon whole milk

1 cup plain whole-milk yogurt

½ cup fresh lemon juice

½ teaspoon salt, or to taste

1. Combine the milk and yogurt in a large saucepan and whisk until smooth. Warm over medium heat for about 15 minutes, or until tiny bubbles form along the sides. The top surface may bulge slightly and a little skin may develop. Watch carefully; it should not boil.

2. Remove the pan from the heat and pour in the lemon juice without mixing. Let stand at room temperature for 1 hour to curdle.

3. Prepare a net of four layers of cheesecloth, each 16 to 18 inches square. Lay this inside a medium-large fine-mesh strainer or colander balanced over a bowl, letting the cheesecloth drape down the sides. Pour the curdled cheese mixture into the net so the liquid drips into the bowl and the solids remain in the cheesecloth. Don't press it or try to hurry the process along in any way, or you'll lose some of the cheese. The whey needs to drip at its own pace.

4. After about an hour, lift the side flaps of cheesecloth and wrap them neatly around the cheese, tying them together without knotting them too tightly. Let the cheese stand, slowly dripping, for another 2 hours or even longer, if you like a firmer, drier cheese.

5. Salt the cheese to taste, transfer it to a tightly covered container, and refrigerate until serving time.

OPTIONAL ENHANCEMENTS

Toasted nuts ❋ Little cookies ❋ Let it double as an appetizer, with a drizzle of olive oil, some dried fruit, and an assortment of good crackers

Grapefruit-Lime Curd

MAKES ABOUT 1½ CUPS

Move over, lemons.

Is this a pudding to be eaten straight, with a spoon? Certainly. Surround it with a frame of matching or contrasting fruit, such as ruby grapefruit sections or lightly sugared blackberries or raspberries.

Can it be a topping? Most definitely, especially dabbed onto Pecan Shortbread Cookies (page 435) or spooned next to a slice of Fruit-Studded Madeleine Cake (page 422).

How about a tart or pie filling? Affirmative. Spread it into the vanilla cookie crust from Chocolate Cream Pie (page 424) or form the Pecan Shortbread dough into a crust, then bake and fill it. (The instructions are on page 436.)

❋ This is pucker-level tart. If you prefer things a little sweeter, you can increase the sugar by a few teaspoons, to taste.

❋ The curd will keep, tightly covered and refrigerated, for up to 2 weeks.

4 large egg yolks

½ cup sugar

3 tablespoons unbleached all-purpose flour

2 teaspoons grated grapefruit zest

2 teaspoons grated lime zest

⅔ cup fresh grapefruit juice

½ cup fresh lime juice

1 tablespoon unsalted butter, softened (optional)

1. Combine the egg yolks, sugar, flour, and zests in a medium, heavy saucepan and whisk to blend. Whisk in the juices and keep stirring until the mixture is smooth and uniform.

2. Bring to a boil over medium heat. Reduce the heat to low and simmer gently for 2 minutes, whisking frequently.

3. Remove from the heat and transfer to a bowl. (If you like, you can butter the top surface to help prevent a skin from forming.) Set aside to cool to room temperature. Cover tightly with plastic wrap and refrigerate until cold before serving.

Buttermilk-Yogurt-Maple Sherbet

MAKES ABOUT 1½ QUARTS

"My kids eat sherbet, and they pronounce it 'sherbert.' And they wish it was ice cream."
—Homer Simpson

I was never one to eat frozen desserts straight from the container, but this one ruined me. It's absurdly easy, if you have an ice cream machine. And if you don't have one yet, this might be your moment to acquire one. There are so many good ice cream recipes out there these days that I'm sure it will be well used.

2 cups cold buttermilk

2 cups plain whole-milk yogurt

½ cup pure maple syrup

1 teaspoon pure vanilla extract

1. Combine all the ingredients in a medium bowl and whisk until thoroughly blended.

2. Transfer to an ice cream machine and process according to the manufacturer's instructions.

3. Transfer to a lidded container, leaving a few inches of headspace so the sherbet can expand as it freezes. Cover tightly and freeze for at least 1 hour, or until firm. Let it soften for about 15 minutes, or longer, if necessary, in the refrigerator before serving.

OPTIONAL ENHANCEMENTS

Serve with any arrangement of fruit ✺ Drizzle with extra maple syrup or artisanal honey if you'd like it sweeter ✺ A cookie accompaniment is always welcome, and the Pecan Shortbread Cookies (page 435) are perfect for this

Brown Sugar–Roasted Rhubarb with Cinnamon-Toast Crumbs

MAKES ABOUT 8 SERVINGS

The art of working with rhubarb is finding the sweet spot—the perfect amount of sugar to bring it to life, while allowing it to maintain its edge. I was very happy with how this straightforward fruit crisp worked out, and am even happier to share it with you. A new signature dessert for spring is now all yours, to celebrate the fleetingness of rhubarb season (and of everything else, for that matter).

❋ The fleeting season notwithstanding, you can freeze cut rhubarb and enjoy it year-round. For this recipe, cut the rhubarb into ¼-inch slices, spreading it out on a tray for about 30 minutes to stay separate, then store in a heavy zip-style plastic bag for up to 3 months. No defrosting necesary.

❋ Bread crumb instructions, if you need them, are on page 235.

❋ You can put the topping together during the 20 minutes while the rhubarb bakes.

2 pounds rhubarb (about 8 jumbo stalks)

3 tablespoons unsalted butter

1 cup whole-wheat bread crumbs

1 teaspoon ground cinnamon

1 tablespoon granulated sugar

1 cup light or dark brown sugar

Pinch of salt

1 tablespoon grapeseed or canola oil

1. Preheat the oven to 400°F, with a rack in the center position.

2. Meanwhile, cut the rhubarb into ¼-inch-thick slices.

3. When the oven is hot, place 2 tablespoons of the butter in a 9-x-13-inch baking pan and set it in the oven for a few minutes so the butter can melt and the pan gets hot.

4. Carefully remove the pan and swirl to coat the entire inner surface with the butter. Scatter the chopped rhubarb in an even-ish layer and put the pan back in the oven for 20 minutes, shaking the pan once or twice to distribute the butter throughout the rhubarb.

5. Meanwhile, combine the bread crumbs with the cinnamon, granulated sugar, 1 tablespoon of the brown sugar, and the salt in a bowl. Melt the remaining 1 tablespoon of butter and add it to the crumbs, along with the oil. Toss with a fork until uniform.

6. After the rhubarb has baked for 20 minutes, remove it from the oven and sprinkle it all over with the remaining 7 tablespoons brown sugar, shaking or stirring to coat. Sprinkle the crumb mixture over the top and return the pan to the oven.

7. Bake for 10 to 12 minutes, or until the rhubarb bubbles with enthusiasm. Remove and let cool to desired eating temperature, 15 to 20 minutes. (The sugar gets *hot*.)

OPTIONAL ENHANCEMENTS

Serve with some excellent vanilla ice cream or Greek yogurt, or with a platter of superb cheeses and a little bowl of roasted walnuts

Brûléed Persimmon Pudding

MAKES 8 TO 12 SERVINGS

For years, a persimmon pudding recipe has circulated in the home-cooking community, having gone viral after being published in *Saveur* magazine. The proud creation of a retired elementary-school librarian in Mitchell, Indiana, it won the local persimmon pudding contest five years running. (The town's annual persimmon festival has been going strong since 1947.) So I knew I was inching out on a limb when I ventured to alter it. In the end, the lure of reduced sugar and butter and elimination of the heavy cream—bringing forward the flavors of the persimmons and buttermilk—won out, along with a final crystalline brûlée treatment on the top. Forgive me, good Hoosiers, for liking my version better.

❀ Quick persimmon primer: There are two types available in the United States, Hachiya (soft, oval, and good for baking) and Fuyu (crunchy, flat-bottomed, and good for salads or just eating raw). Use very ripe Hachiyas for this recipe.

❀ To make persimmon pulp: Working over a bowl, pierce the skins of the persimmons with a paring knife (or simply by poking them with a finger) and squeeze the pulp from the skins. (The process is a little messy, so roll up your sleeves.) Pluck out and discard any large black seeds, then use an immersion blender or a stand blender to briefly puree the fruit until smooth.

❀ You can freeze the pulp and enjoy this dessert when the brief persimmon season is over. Defrost it thoroughly before using. And if you have too few persimmons or none at all, unsweetened applesauce can supplement or even substitute.

2 cups persimmon pulp (from about 5 very ripe, soft Hachiya persimmons; 2½ pounds; see note)

½ cup sugar, plus 3–4 tablespoons more for the top

2 large eggs

1½ cups buttermilk, ideally at room temperature

1½ teaspoons pure vanilla extract

1½ cups unbleached all-purpose flour

¾ teaspoon ground cinnamon

¼ heaping teaspoon salt

3 tablespoons unsalted butter

1. Preheat the oven to 350°F, with a rack in the center position. Have ready a 9-x-9-inch square baking pan.

2. Beat the persimmon pulp and the ½ cup sugar in a medium-large bowl with a whisk until blended. Add the eggs, one at a time, beating well after each, then drizzle in the buttermilk, still whisking. Whisk in the vanilla.

3. Whisk the flour, cinnamon, and salt together in a second bowl. When they are thoroughly blended, gradually spoon the dry mixture into the wet, stirring with a spoon until completely combined.

4. Place the butter in the baking pan and put the pan in the oven for a minute or two until it melts. Carefully remove the pan from the oven and tilt it until it is thoroughly coated.

5. Pour in the batter and bake for 50 minutes, or until it pulls away from the sides of the pan and the top surface is springy to the touch. Remove from the oven.

6. Carefully adjust an oven rack to the top position and switch the oven to broil.

7. Use a serrated knife to carefully saw/slice the still-hot pudding into 8 to 12 squares or rectangles in the pan. Sprinkle the top as evenly as possible with 3 tablespoons sugar, adding 1 tablespoon more if needed to cover the entire surface. Return the sugared pudding to the oven and broil briefly, until the sugar appears shiny and spots of dark brown appear here and there. Watch carefully, as the sugar can burn quickly. You want it medium dark, not black/burnt. Remove from the oven and cool for at least 15 minutes before serving. (The cooked sugar will be very hot!)

OPTIONAL ENHANCEMENTS

Serve with yogurt, crème fraîche, whipped cream, or vanilla ice cream ✳ This is also nice garnished with sliced or diced fresh Fuyu persimmons (the crisp variety) and with a shower of pomegranate seeds decorating some whipped cream

Bittersweet Mocha Bundt Cake

MAKES 12 TO 14 SERVINGS

Dark, deep, mysterious, moist, and spot-hitting, this recipe celebrates the always exciting combination of coffee and chocolate. Serve it with cappuccino or chai to your grateful family and friends for brunch or tea as well as for dessert. It also makes a terrific birthday cake. Consider freezing it sliced, so you can pull out individual servings as desired.

❈ Unwrap the butter ahead of time and place it in the mixing bowl to soften.

❈ Brew some strong coffee ahead of time, so it has time to cool. Decaf is fine.

❈ This cake freezes well, if tightly wrapped.

Nonstick cooking spray

16 tablespoons (2 sticks) unsalted butter, softened

1¼ cups sugar

4 large eggs

1 tablespoon pure vanilla extract

2 cups unbleached all-purpose flour

⅓ cup unsweetened cocoa powder

1½ teaspoons baking powder

½ teaspoon salt

¾ cup strong brewed coffee, cooled at least to room temperature

¼ cup milk (low fat is OK)

1 cup semisweet chocolate chips

1. Preheat the oven to 350°F, with a rack in the center position. Lightly spray the bottom and center of a standard-sized Bundt or tube pan with nonstick spray.

2. Beat the butter for about 3 minutes in a large bowl with an electric mixer at high speed, until fluffy. Add the sugar and beat for 2 to 3 minutes longer, until completely incorporated and the mixture is very light. Add the eggs, one at a time, beating well after each addition, then beat in the vanilla.

3. In a second bowl, whisk together the flour, cocoa, baking powder, and salt. Combine the coffee and milk in a measuring cup with a spout.

4. Add the dry ingredients to the butter mixture in three installments, alternating with the coffee mixture, beginning and ending with the dry, using a spoon or rubber spatula to stir from the bottom of the bowl after each addition. Fold in the chocolate chips with the last addition of flour. Don't overmix.

5. Scrape the batter into the pan, spreading it evenly. Bake for 40 minutes, or until a sharp knife inserted all the way into the center comes out clean.

6. Cool in the pan on a wire rack for at least 30 minutes before removing the cake from the pan. If you used a Bundt pan, invert the cake onto a plate. If you used a tube pan, pull out the tube and gently lift the cake off and onto a plate, or if it is one piece, run a small knife around the sides of the pan and invert the cake onto a plate. Cool for another 10 to 15 minutes before slicing.

OPTIONAL ENHANCEMENTS

Sift confectioners' sugar over the top for a beautiful finish after it cools ❈ Serve with vanilla, coffee, or salted caramel ice cream

Fruit-Studded Madeleine Cake

MAKES 8 TO 10 SERVINGS

This highly buttery vanilla cake is the sunny circle on which you get to design a dreamy skyscape of berry stars and plum-slice half-moons. Fruit baked onto a cake: What could be better?

Using a tart pan with a removable rim will add to its quiet splendor (and birthday celebration worthiness).

❋ Unwrap the butter ahead of time and place it in the mixing bowl to soften.

❋ In the heart of the summer season, consider using a combination of variously colored plums: red, deep purple, yellow. Slice them lengthwise and place them all over the top in a random pattern of scattered half-moons.

❋ You can use fresh berries or frozen unsweetened ones, which can go directly onto the cake still frozen.

❋ If you have more fruit than will fit, make it into a fresh compote to serve on top or on the side.

Nonstick cooking spray

16 tablespoons (2 sticks) unsalted butter, softened

1 cup sugar

1½ teaspoons pure vanilla extract

3 large eggs

1½ cups unbleached all-purpose flour

½ teaspoon salt

½ teaspoon baking powder

¾ cup milk (low fat is OK)

4–5 firm, ripe plums, pitted and sliced

1 cup (or more) raspberries or blueberries, fresh or frozen

1. Preheat the oven to 350°F, with a rack in the center position. Lightly spray with nonstick spray the bottom of a 10- or 11-inch tart pan with a removable rim.

2. Beat the butter for about 3 minutes in a medium-large bowl with an electric mixer at high speed until fluffy. Add the sugar and vanilla and beat for 2 to 3 minutes longer, until completely incorporated and the mixture is very light. Add the eggs, one at a time, beating well after each.

3. In a second bowl, stir together the flour, salt, and baking powder.

4. Add the dry ingredients to the butter mixture in 2 installments, alternating with the milk. After each addition, mix from the bottom of the bowl with a spoon or a rubber spatula. Don't overmix.

5. Transfer the batter to the pan, spreading it evenly. Arrange the fruit on top of the batter. Bake for 20 to 25 minutes, or until the cake is golden on the edges, pulling away from the sides of the pan, and springy to the touch. Cool for at least 20 minutes before serving.

OPTIONAL ENHANCEMENTS

This is oh-so-good with a big spoonful of Grapefruit-Lime Curd (page 414) on the top or the side ✸ Try this with a scoop of Buttermilk-Yogurt-Maple Sherbet (page 415) ✸ Mango slices (fresh or frozen) or fresh peach or nectarine slices can substitute for some of the plums

Chocolate Cream Pie

MAKES 6 TO 8 SERVINGS ❧ VEGAN (IF PREPARED AS DIRECTED IN THE VARIATION)

Dark chocolate pudding relaxes into a vanilla cookie crust and gets a nimbus of whipped cream. Bonus: Your oven gets the day off.

❋ The best cookies to use for the crust are Leibniz Fine European Butter Biscuits, available in gourmet aisles and shops. You can also use graham crackers or any delicious-on-its-own plain vanilla cookie.

❋ Prepare and assemble the crust and filling and refrigerate the pie at least 4 hours—and up to a day—before you intend to serve the pie. It needs to chill. Whip the cream shortly before serving.

❋ The range of sugar in both the filling and the whipped cream topping is to accommodate taste preferences. Unless you have a die-hard sweet tooth, consider trying this at the lower end the first time you make it, and adjust it upward from there if desired.

CRUST

7–8 ounces plain vanilla cookies

8 tablespoons (1 stick) unsalted butter, melted

1. Place the cookies in a food processor and buzz to fine crumbs. You should have about 2 cups.

2. Transfer the crumbs to a medium bowl and pour in the melted butter. Mix to thoroughly combine. Transfer to a 9-inch pie pan.

3. Spread the crumbs out so that they cover the bottom completely and evenly and begin to climb up the sides of the pan. Pat them into place, gently at first and then firmly, turning the pan as you go and building up the sides until they are flush with the rim. Set aside while you make the filling.

FILLING

1 cup semisweet chocolate chips

2 cups whole milk

2–3 tablespoons granulated sugar or (packed) light brown sugar

1 teaspoon pure vanilla extract

3 tablespoons cornstarch

⅛ teaspoon salt

1. Combine the chocolate chips, milk, sugar, and vanilla in the top of a double boiler or in a metal bowl placed over a saucepan of quietly simmering water on medium-low heat. Cook until the chocolate is melted. This will take about 5 minutes; no stirring needed.

2. Place the cornstarch in a small bowl and stir in the salt. When the chocolate is melted and the mixture is warm, ladle a little into the cornstarch and beat with a small whisk until it is completely dissolved. Immediately return this slurry to the chocolate mixture, whisking it in.

3. Bring to a boil, stirring frequently, over medium heat, then cook, stirring with a wooden spoon as it thickens, for another 10 minutes or so, until the mixture becomes slow-moving and glossy. (The thickness will originate in the bottom; whisk it upward. When the mixture shows some resistance to being stirred, it's ready.)

4. Remove from the heat and pour the hot filling into the prepared crust. Let it cool to room temperature, about 40 minutes, then cover with plastic wrap and refrigerate until cold, at least 4 hours. Make and add the whipped cream shortly before serving.

WHIPPED CREAM

1 cup cold heavy cream

2–3 tablespoons confectioners' sugar

1 teaspoon pure vanilla extract

1. Combine all the ingredients in a large bowl and whisk or beat with a handheld electric mixer until the mixture forms soft peaks. (Be careful not to let it get too stiff.)

2. Use a rubber spatula to spread it evenly over the filling to the edge of the crust.

OPTIONAL ENHANCEMENTS

Chocolate sprinkles or a little finely chopped bittersweet chocolate or a dusting of unsweetened cocoa powder

VEGAN VARIATION

Use vegan cookies and swap in grapeseed or canola oil for the butter (you might end up using less). Use soy milk in the filling. Vegan Whipped Cream (recipe follows) tops it off beautifully.

VEGAN WHIPPED CREAM

MAKES ABOUT 1½ CUPS ✿ VEGAN

For a luxurious, dairy-free topping, hand-whip some coconut cream with touches of sugar, vanilla, and a pinch of salt. Coconut cream is available in Asian markets, the imported food sections of many grocery stores, and online. It comes in cans that look similar to coconut milk (and are often on the same shelf), so don't get them confused, since they are not identical. I use Chaokoh brand.

1 13½-ounce can coconut cream

2 tablespoons sugar

½ teaspoon pure vanilla extract

Heaping ⅛ teaspoon salt

Whisk everything together in a bowl for about 1 minute, or until uniform, then chill until serving time. (*This will last for about 2 days, covered and refrigerated, but is best after it's been chilled for about 2 hours.*)

Cranapple Walnut Cake

MAKES ABOUT 8 SERVINGS

Loaded with apple slices and popping with tart cranberries and crunchy walnuts, this easy winter treat is now back by popular demand—slightly updated from the original *Moosewood Cookbook*.

❋ You will likely want to serve this à la mode, with some excellent vanilla ice cream. If you do, you may want to reduce the brown sugar to 1½ cups.

❋ If you buy fresh whole cranberries in season and freeze some, you can enjoy them year-round. No defrosting necessary.

Nonstick cooking spray

1¾ (packed) cups light brown sugar

½ cup grapeseed or canola oil

1 teaspoon pure vanilla extract

2 large eggs

2 cups whole-wheat pastry flour or unbleached all-purpose flour

1 teaspoon baking powder

1 teaspoon ground cinnamon

½ teaspoon ground or freshly grated nutmeg

½ teaspoon salt

2 medium apples (about ½ pound), peeled, cored, and thinly sliced

½ pound whole cranberries (fresh or frozen)

½ cup coarsely chopped walnuts

1. Preheat the oven to 375°F, with a rack in the center position. Lightly spray a 9-x-13-inch pan with nonstick spray.

2. In a medium-large bowl, beat together the brown sugar, oil, and vanilla. Add the eggs, one at a time, beating well after each addition.

3. In a second bowl, whisk the flour with the other dry ingredients until thoroughly blended. Add the dry mixture to the wet, stirring until combined, folding in the fruit and nuts as you go. The batter will be very thick.

4. Spread the batter into the prepared pan (take your time spreading it into place) and bake for 40 to 45 minutes, or until the cake pulls away from the sides of the pan and the top surface is springy to the touch. Place the pan on a cooling rack for at least 15 minutes before serving.

Pear Tart with Olive Oil–Cornmeal–Pine Nut Crust

MAKES 10 TO 12 SERVINGS

Baking lemon-laced pears in a sturdy, slightly crunchy cornmeal–pine nut crust, crowned with a beautiful lattice top, might well become your new tradition. The loving care you invest in this preparation will reward you with a tart that will feed many and can freeze and defrost seamlessly— so you can feed many at a later time.

❋ This freezes well for up to 3 weeks, if wrapped very tightly. Defrost completely before serving.

PASTRY

¾ cup fine cornmeal

2¼ cups unbleached all-purpose flour, plus more for rolling

6 tablespoons sugar

1 teaspoon salt

½ cup olive oil

1 large egg, beaten

Up to ⅓ cup water

⅓ cup pine nuts

1. Combine the cornmeal, flour, sugar, and salt in a food processor and pulse for a few seconds to combine. Pour in the olive oil and run the machine in a few long pulses, until the oil is evenly distributed and the mixture resembles coarse meal. Add the beaten egg and pulse a few more times, just until incorporated, then buzz in enough water, 2 tablespoons at a time, to bring the dough together.

2. Remove the dough from the food processor and gather it together, kneading it briefly into a ball and folding/poking in the pine nuts as you go. Break the dough into 2 uneven pieces, one about twice as big as the other. Form each piece into a ball, then flatten each into a thick disk.

3. Lightly flour a work surface. Roll out the larger piece of dough into a 13-inch circle about ⅛ inch thick. Carefully lift the circle, and ease it into an ungreased 10- to 11-inch tart pan with a removable rim, gently guiding it into the corners and letting it climb the sides. Patch any breaks or holes by pressing the dough back together (with a touch of water if needed) and trim the edges flush with the top of the rim.

4. Scrape clean and lightly reflour the work surface, then roll out the smaller piece of dough into a smaller circle ⅛ inch thick. Cut it into strips about ½ inch wide.

5. Preheat the oven to 375°F, with a rack in the lower third position, while you make the filling.

FILLING

2½–3 pounds ripe pears, such as Bartlett, Comice, or Anjou (not Bosc or Asian, which are too grainy)

2 tablespoons fresh lemon juice

3 tablespoons pure maple syrup

2 tablespoons unbleached all-purpose flour

⅛ teaspoon salt

1. Peel and core the pears and cut them into thin slices. Transfer to a medium bowl and drizzle with the lemon juice and maple syrup.

2. Combine the flour and salt in a small bowl, then sprinkle this onto the pears and toss to coat.

3. Place the fruit in the crust, spreading it out as evenly as possible. Arrange the strips of dough on top in a crisscross pattern, then push the ends of the strips onto the edges of the bottom crust to hold them in place. (Use dabs of water, as needed, to make them stick.)

4. Place the filled tart on a baking sheet and bake for about 45 minutes, or until golden on the top and around the edges.

5. Cool for at least 15 minutes before removing the rim of the pan. Serve warm or at room temperature.

OPTIONAL ENHANCEMENTS

Vanilla and/or salted caramel ice cream ❋ Vanilla or fruit-infused frozen yogurt ❋ Buttermilk-Yogurt-Maple Sherbet (page 415) ❋ If you want to make this with walnuts instead of pine nuts, add ½ cup coarsely chopped walnuts to the cornmeal and flour in the food processor in step 1

Thai Tea Cheesecake with Chocolate Crumb Crust

MAKES 8 SERVINGS

Thai iced tea has a singular taste that has spawned legions of enthusiasts, yet remains hard to describe to the uninitiated. Those who already adore this milky, sweet, deep orange, vanilla-y beverage will not need to stretch their imagination to picture it expanded into dessert format. You know who you are, and this cheesecake is my valentine to you.

To those who are scratching your heads and wondering what I am talking about, try a glass of this elixir on your next visit to a Thai restaurant. If you love it, welcome to the club, and enjoy this recipe.

The filling will be bright orange (it will look like pumpkin) and the dark chocolate crust will frame it beautifully. None of this will betray how easy it is to make. No baking required—just a patted-into-place crumb crust and a stovetop filling. Cool to room temperature, then chill.

✽ Thai tea can be purchased in bulk in better spice shops where loose tea is sold, in Thai grocery stores, or online. It is inexpensive, keeps indefinitely, and is also delicious hot.

✽ Brew and strain the tea well ahead of time. To get the proper strength for this recipe, steep ½ cup Thai tea in 2½ cups boiling water for 10 minutes, then strain, pressing out as much of the water as you can. You will need 1½ cups for the filling and, optionally, 2 tablespoons for the topping.

CRUST

6–7 ounces graham crackers (10–11)

¼ cup unsweetened cocoa powder

1 tablespoon sugar

8 tablespoons (1 stick) unsalted butter, melted

1. Place the graham crackers in a food processor and buzz to fine crumbs. You should have about 2 cups.

2. Transfer the crumbs to a bowl, stir in the cocoa and sugar, and pour in the melted butter. Mix to thoroughly combine. Transfer to a 9-inch pie pan.

3. Spread the crumbs out so that they cover the bottom completely and evenly and begin to climb up the sides of the pan. Pat them into place, gently at first and then firmly, turning the pan as you go and building up the sides until they are flush with the rim. Set aside while you make the filling.

FILLING

½ cup sugar

3 tablespoons cornstarch

¼ teaspoon salt

2 large eggs, beaten

1½ cups strong brewed Thai tea, strained and cooled (see note)

1 teaspoon pure vanilla extract

8 ounces cream cheese, cut into pieces

1. In a medium saucepan, combine the sugar, cornstarch, and salt. Add the eggs and whisk until smooth. Stir in the tea and vanilla.

2. Bring to a boil over medium heat, whisking frequently. Cook, stirring, for 5 to 8 minutes, or until the custard thickens to the point where it starts to resist being stirred.

3. Remove from the heat and immediately add the cream cheese; it will melt in. Whisk until the cream cheese is completely incorporated and the mixture becomes uniform. This will take several minutes.

4. Pour the filling into the crust and let it cool to room temperature, about 40 minutes. Cover with plastic wrap and refrigerate until cold, at least 2 hours. Meanwhile, make the topping.

TOPPING

⅔ cup sour cream

2 tablespoons strong brewed Thai tea, strained and cooled (optional)

1 tablespoon sugar

½ teaspoon pure vanilla extract

Pinch of salt

1. Whisk together all the ingredients in a small bowl until smooth.

2. Spoon on top of the chilled pie, spreading it to the edges of the crust with a rubber spatula.

3. Carefully, so as not to disturb the top surface, cover with plastic wrap, then refrigerate until serving time. Serve cold.

Olive Oil–Walnut-Pomegranate Baklava

MAKES ENOUGH TO FEED A SMALL VILLAGE (MORE THAN 30 LITTLE DIAMONDS) ❧ VEGAN

Can baklava be made with all olive oil—and not even a speck of butter—and still be delicious? Come to find out it most definitely can.

When people first taste this, after the initial "Yum," they often ask, "Is there some kind of fruit in here?" That's followed by "Wow!" as someone says, reaching for seconds, "Pomegranate, of course."

What you're about to do: Make an easy filling of walnuts and cinnamon. Then you'll layer long sheets of filo dough on a big tray, brushing and/or spraying olive oil in between. The walnut mixture will be sprinkled very lightly on the layered pile at two points, and then more layers will form a roof. Score and slice the finished rectangle and bake it until crisp, while you simmer a syrup. When the pastry cools, pour on the syrup that has been infused with pomegranate—and possibly also rosemary—and let it soak in. And . . . baklava!

Give yourself some time, put on some music, and have a good time layering. The yield is huge—and the results keep beautifully for up to 3 weeks in a tightly covered container in the freezer or refrigerator.

❋ If the filo has been frozen, be sure it is thoroughly defrosted before you begin. The sealed package can sit in the refrigerator for weeks or even months before you open it. Once exposed to air, the leaves dry out quickly, so open the package right before you begin the assembly project and work uninterrupted.

❋ Each 1-pound package of filo contains about 20 sheets of the very thin pastry. Some may fold or crumble, but you can patch and improvise, and they will blend into the whole. If a few leaves go by the wayside, don't worry. This recipe factors that in.

❋ Pomegranate concentrate and pomegranate molasses are similar products, both reductions of pure pomegranate juice (with the molasses being thicker, having been more greatly reduced). They are somewhat interchangeable, if the volume is slightly adjusted. Find them at Middle Eastern groceries or online.

❋ You can make this entirely with olive oil, applied with a pastry brush. Or you can streamline preparations by using a combination of olive oil and olive oil spray. Don't use just the spray, though, since it does not deliver flavor.

1 1-pound package (20 leaves) filo dough, thoroughly defrosted, if frozen

4–6 cups walnuts

¾ teaspoon ground cinnamon

¼ heaping teaspoon salt

Up to 1 cup olive oil

Olive oil spray (optional)

2½ cups sugar

2 cups water

2–3 large sprigs fresh rosemary (optional)

1 cup pomegranate concentrate or ⅔ cup pomegranate molasses (see note)

A handful or two of pomegranate seeds (optional)

1. Preheat the oven to 350°F, with a rack in the center position. Have ready a large (approximately 12-x-17-inch) baking sheet, a small dish for the olive oil, and a pastry brush. Also have the filo near you.

[continues]

2. Combine the walnuts, cinnamon, and salt in a food processor and pulse a few times until the walnuts are ground to the size of small lentils. Stop short of walnut butter; you want the nuts dry, not oily.

3. Brush or spray the baking sheet lightly with olive oil, then carefully lift a sheet of filo and lay it flat on the baking sheet. If the filo exceeds the edges of the baking sheet, just allow the flaps to extend up the sides. (You'll be folding them down shortly.) Brush or spray the sheet with olive oil and add another sheet. Brush/spray and keep going until you have a pile of 6 or 7 oiled filo sheets. (Try to keep the leaves flat and whole, but if they buckle or break, that's OK.)

4. Sprinkle the top as evenly as possible with about half the walnut mixture. It will be thin. Keep layering and oiling, folding the edges down as you go, until you have another pile of 6 or so filo sheets. Sprinkle on the remaining walnut mixture. Continue to layer and oil until you come to the end of the filo dough. Do not oil the very top layer.

5. Use a very sharp serrated knife to first score the stack into 1½-inch diamonds. Using a sawing motion, cut the stack along the scored lines, holding the unoiled top layer steady with your free hand so it doesn't slide off the pile. Be patient—this will take a few minutes. After the baklava is completely sliced, oil the top layer. (The spray will be much easier than a brush for this one.)

6. Bake for 30 to 40 minutes, or until golden and very crisp. (Keep an eye on it, so it doesn't become too dark.) Remove from the oven and cool on a rack.

7. Meanwhile, combine the sugar and water in a medium saucepan over medium-high heat and whisk to dissolve. Add the rosemary sprigs, if using, and bring to a boil, then cook, uncovered, over medium heat for 10 minutes. Add the pomegranate concentrate or molasses, bring back to a boil, lower the heat to a simmer, and cook for another 20 to 30 minutes, until reduced by about one third and slightly thickened. Remove the sprigs if you used the rosemary.

8. When the baklava has cooled to room temperature (about 30 minutes), ladle the syrup over the top, letting it soak down between the diamonds. If desired, you can also cut tiny slits in the center of each piece and insert pomegranate seeds. Let stand at room temperature for at least 1 hour (overnight is ideal) before serving.

Pecan Shortbread Cookies

MAKES ABOUT 5 DOZEN COOKIES

Once I started adding ground nuts to shortbread dough, I was instantly hooked and haven't made it plain since. The nuts become thoroughly coated with butter and are toasted to perfection during the baking, and the cookies are infused with their flavor.

❋ Unwrap the butter ahead of time and place it in the mixing bowl to soften.

❋ This dough freezes beautifully for up to a month, if tightly wrapped. So do the finished cookies.

[continues]

1 heaping cup pecan halves

2 cups unbleached all-purpose flour, plus more for rolling

16 tablespoons (2 sticks) unsalted butter, softened

⅔ cup sugar

¼ heaping teaspoon salt

½ teaspoon baking powder

1. Preheat the oven to 375°F, with racks in the center and upper third positions.

2. Combine the pecans and 3 tablespoons of the flour in a food processor and pulse a few times until they acquire the texture of coarse meal.

3. Beat the butter in a medium bowl for 2 to 3 minutes with an electric mixer at high speed, until fluffy. Add the sugar and beat for about 3 minutes more, until completely incorporated and the mixture is very light.

4. In a second bowl, whisk the ground pecans, remaining flour, salt, and baking powder together. When they are thoroughly combined, add the dry ingredients to the butter mixture, using a spoon to mix the dough first, and then your hands, if necessary, mixing just until the dough holds together. (Don't overhandle it.)

5. Dust a work surface with flour and roll the dough to about ½ inch thick. Cut it into shapes with a knife or a cookie cutter and place the cookies close together on 2 ungreased baking sheets.

6. Bake for 10 to 12 minutes or until lightly browned on the bottoms and around the edges. Cool on the sheets for 5 minutes, then transfer the cookies to a cooling rack to crisp for at least another 10 minutes before eating.

PECAN SHORTBREAD TART CRUST

This recipe makes a tart crust perfect for filling with Grapefruit-Lime Curd (page 414) or any other tart fillings that might already be in your repertoire. It's more than enough to fit a 10- or 11-inch tart pan. Roll the dough between 2 sheets of plastic wrap into a 12- to 13-inch circle about ¼ inch thick. Remove the top sheet of plastic and use the other to flip the crust into the pan. Press down the dough, easing it gently into the corners, and letting it climb the sides. Patch any breaks or holes by simply pressing it back together (with a touch of water, if necessary) and trim the edges flush with the top of the rim. Prick it all over with a fork and bake it in the center of a 375°F oven for 20 to 25 minutes, or until deeply golden all over. Cool completely before filling.

ACKNOWLEDGMENTS
AND INDEX

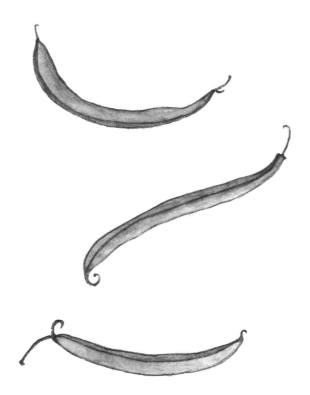

Acknowledgments

One of the best parts of writing a book is the opportunity it affords to appreciate people publicly.

To wit:

Rux Martin, dream editor, whose faith in me was as motivating as it was terrifying.

Nancy Austin, book designer extraordinaire, in whose hands I have felt so honored, understood, and well taken care of many blessed times over the years.

Jenny Wheeler, as dedicated, intelligent, and focused a recipe tester as one could hope for.

Melissa Lotfy, smoothing the path for functional beauty at every turn.

Steve Troha and Jeff Kleinman, agents and heartfelt personal cheerleaders.

Thanks to:

Bruce Nichols, for inviting me into this new publishing family.

Rebecca Springer, for overseeing countless details with great kindness and patience.

Laney Whitt, for your cheerful assistance at many turns.

Copy editor Jessica Sherman, for your eagle eyes and culinary heart.

Jacinta Monniere, for your patience as chunks of the book made their appearance, and not always in chronological (or logical) order.

Proofreaders Shelley Berg and Jane Tunks Demel, for catching bloopers, preventing bummers, and preserving (I hope!) reputations.

Carrie Bachman and Brad Thomas Parsons, for your enthusiasm and expertise in spreading the word.

Lisa Keating, for making it so much fun to have my picture taken.

Ten Speed Press, my original publisher—and specifically its founder, the late Phil Wood. I don't know where I'd be without your trust and vision. You will always feel like family to me.

Hyperion and Morrow, for past collaborations, and for gracious permission to repurpose some of the recipes from *Vegetable Heaven, Sunlight Café, Get Cooking,* and *The Vegetable Dishes I Can't Live Without*.

I am grateful to:

My father, Leon Katzen, ninety-four-and-a-half years old and still eating his blueberries and raising hell as of this writing. My children, Sam and Eve, who amaze me continuously by who and how they are, and everything they do. My brothers, Josh, Danny, and Ezra—and my lovely sisters-in-law, Amelia, Carol, and Karen, our many nieces and nephews, big and now small (*mmmwah*, guys!) and cousins—all of whom have been so supportive of me.

Thankful hugs to my dear long-term friends, many of whom provided helpful feedback and insights on various recipe tests and ideas: Hal Hershey, Patricia Cronin, Sarah Gowin, Sarah Sutro, Beth Shepard, Marissa Moss, Elisa Kleven, Peggy Stein, Doug Wheeler, Janis Plotkin, Deborah Kaufman, Alan Snitow, Gail Willett, Ruth Weiss, Will Schwalbe, Kathleen Caldwell, Denis Clifford, Daniele Spellman, Julie Kunstler, Ann Leda Shapiro, Ferron Salniker, Annie Black, Barbara Felsinger, Larry Teitelbaum, Tanya Starnes, Martina Reaves, Ruth Scovill, Elizabeth Fishel, Linda Williams, Janet Peoples, and Adrienne McDonnell.

These colleague-friends have been my teachers, perhaps unbeknownst to them. Thank you for the encouragement, wisdom, and inspiration-by-example: Greg Drescher, David Eisenberg, Martin Breslin, Preston Maring, Steve Siegelman, Lillian Cheung, Andy Weil, Karin Michels, Eric Rimm, Larry Kessel, and most of all, Walter Willett.

Big gratitude to Ted Mayer, Crista Martin, Patty Gregory, Laurie Torf, David Davidson, and the rest of the team with whom I had the privilege of co-creating the Heart of the Plate station at Sebastian's Café at the Harvard School of Public Health. To say it has been an honor and pleasure to work with you barely scratches the surface.

Chef MikeC., cofounder of Kitchen on Fire cooking school, thanks for the brulée on the Persimmon Pudding.

Grisecon Hillriegel, thank you for being my partner-in-website (seemingly) since such things were invented. You inspire me with your generous, artful heart.

David Lebovitz, *merci pour le* delicious book-slog commiseration—and for the pecorino-pear ice cream recipe, all of which kept me believing at the late stages of pulling this together.

Leela Punyarata-bandhu, your brilliant "She Simmers Thai Home Cooking" blog led me, among other things, to turn Thai iced tea into a dessert.

Nancy Harmon Jenkins, sharing a true Ribollita with you in Tuscany was a peak educational (and super fun) experience.

Paula Wolfert, thank you for the red pomegranate molasses, Muhamarra, and the greens. I have learned so much from your work.

Anna Thomas and Frances Moore Lappé, you paved the way, for which I (along with several million others) am grateful.

Kensington Farmers' Market, you have enriched our little community week after week, year-round, with your labor of local love. Thank you for bringing so much (and so many) together.

And a final note: Dear Natural Grocery Company, Monterey Market, Cheese Board Collective, and Meyer lemon tree outside my bedroom window, *muchas gracias* for making it the best kind of impossible for me to leave Berkeley.

Index

with grapes and pecans, 114–15

GREENS:

chard- or collard-wrapped polenta-chili tamale packages, 338–39

stems of, 68

see also kale; spinach

green salad, olive oil–buttermilk sherbet and strawberries on, 80–81

GRILLED:

bread and kale salad with red onions, walnuts, and figs, 71–72

Haloumi cheese, 406

marinated zucchini with corn and tomatoes, 109

ratatouille salad, 104–5

see also burgers; pancakes, savory

Gruyère cheese:

asparagus puff pastry tart, 282

Brussels sprout gratin with potatoes and spinach, 286

H

Haloumi cheese, grilled, 406

hazelnut–wilted frisée salad with sliced pear, 84

HERB(s):

seasonal fruit saladitas, 386

stems of, 68

tangle, 76

see also specific herbs

honey, 6–7

-sherry-tarragon-mustard vinaigrette, 367

hot-sweet-sour soup with tofu and pineapple, 42–43

I

immersion blenders, 8

INDIAN-STYLE COOKING AND FLAVORS:

onion pakoras, 139

tomato-coconut soup with Indian spices, 44

yellow split pea dal, 28–29

yogurt sauce (raita), 371

Indian summer lasagna stacks, 246–49

ITALIAN-STYLE COOKING AND FLAVORS:

caramelized onion frittata with artichoke hearts, zucchini, and goat cheese, 284–85

creamy Tuscan-style white bean soup, 26–27

farfalle and rapini in creamy walnut sauce, 260

farro and Tuscan white beans, 226–27

linguine and green beans in pesto Trapanese, 258–59

peach panzanella, 90–91

ravioli-kale salad, 125

ribollita, 144–45

twice-cooked broccoli, 325

vegetable pizza, 271–72

see also lasagna

J

jade rice, in green rice, 194–95

jalapeño(s):

-cilantro-lime vinaigrette, 367

fully loaded buttermilk corn cakes, 316–17

JAPANESE-STYLE COOKING AND FLAVORS:

misoyaki sauce, 362

misoyaki–scrambled onion sauce, 363

scattered sushi-style rice salad (*gomokuzushi*), 112–13

soba noodles with butternut squash, miso, smoked tofu, pumpkin seeds, and basil, 266–67

soba-seaweed salad, 132

jicama:

endive, and wild rice salad with blue cheese–yogurt dressing, 110–11

pink grapefruit saladita, 381

K

KALE:

angel hair tangle with orange-chili oil and toasted almonds, 128–29

Caesar, 68–69

flash-fried, with garlic, almonds, and cheese, 346–47

and grilled bread salad with red onions, walnuts, and figs, 71–72

ravioli salad, 125

ribollita, 144–45

stems of, 68

kasha, 230

varnishkes, 231

kibbeh balls, bulgur-walnut, 312–13

KIDNEY BEAN(s):

mac, chili, and cheese, 238–39

white, *see* cannellini beans

wild rice, and basmati salad, 116–17

kimchi stew, 158–59

knives, 7–8

L

lablabi (Tunisian chickpea soup), 30–31

LASAGNA, 234

autumn vegetable, 250–51

mushroom, 244–45

spring, 254–57

stacks, Indian summer, 246–49

winter, 252–53

LEEK(s):

potato soup, humble, 24–25

spring farro, 224–25

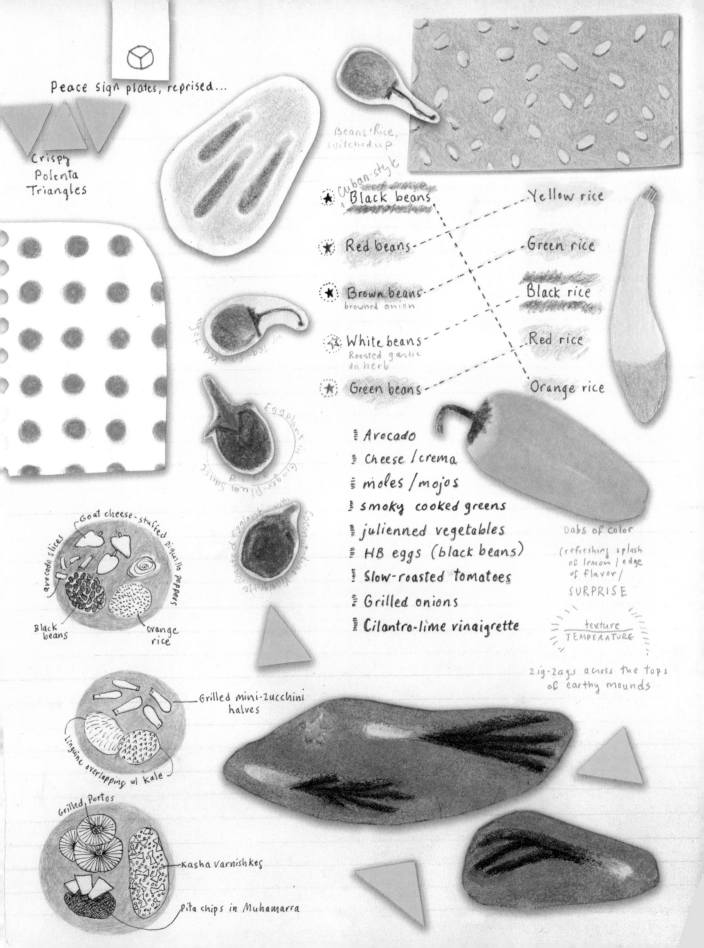

Peace sign plates, reprised...

Crispy Polenta Triangles

Beans+Rice, switched up

Cuban-style

★ Black beans ------- Yellow rice

★ Red beans - Green rice

★ Brown beans- Black rice
browned onion

⚝ White beans - Red rice
Roasted garlic
& herb

★ Green beans - Orange rice

Tea-smoked tofu

Eggplant in Ginger-Plum Sauce

Roasted Eggplant with Coconut-Lime Vinaigrette

⫶ Avocado
⫶ Cheese / crema
⫶ moles / mojos
⫶ smoky cooked greens
⫶ julienned vegetables
⫶ HB eggs (black beans)
⫶ Slow-roasted tomatoes
⫶ Grilled onions
⫶ Cilantro-lime vinaigrette

Dabs of Color

(refreshing splash
of lemon / edge
of flavor/
SURPRISE

texture
TEMPERATURE

Zig-zags across the tops
of earthy mounds

Goat cheese-stuffed Piquillo peppers

avocado slices

Black beans

orange rice

Grilled mini-zucchini halves

Linguine overlapping w/ kale

Grilled Portos

Kasha Varnishkes

Pita chips in Muhamarra

TASTY TOUCHES

(smaller hats)

- soil-packed dried tomatoes
- pickled red onions (w fruit)
- bread crumbs (good ones / well prepared)
- chewy grains (sprinkled as topping)
- criss-hatched cheese crust
- nut crust
- Dukkah / za'atar
- balsamic-rescued FIGS
- Just a few browned mushrooms (thickly sliced)

spicy
edible
blos
soms